JAVA
HOW-TO

THE DEFINITIVE JAVA PROBLEM-SOLVER

Waite Group Press™
A Division of
Sams Publishing
Corte Madera, CA

Madhu Siddalingaiah, Stephen D. Lockwood

Publisher: Mitchell Waite
Editor-in-Chief: Charles Drucker

Acquisitions Manger: Jill Pisoni
Acquisitions Editor: Joanne Miller

Editorial Director: John Crudo
Project Editor: Kurt Stephan
Copy Editor: Jan Jue

Production Director: Julianne Ososke
Production Manager: Cecile Kaufman
Production Editor: Mark Nigara
Cover Design: Sestina Quarequio
Design and Production: Mary Ann Abramson, Mona Brown, Bruce Clingaman, Karen Johnston,
                Louisa Klucznik, Sestina Quarequio, Laura A. Smith, Alyssa Yesh
Illustrations: Rogondino and Associates

Technical Review: Digital Connection™, New York, NY
                Joachim Kim, General Manager
Reviewers: Michael St. Hippolyte, Joachim Kim, Mark Nichols, R. Scott Schmitt

For more information regarding Digital Connection, see ad in back of book.

Printed in the United States of America
96 97 98 99 • 10 9 8 7 6 5 4 3 2

Library of Congress: 96-25836
ISBN: 1-57169-035-2

DEDICATION

To my grandparents, for shaping me in my formative years.
—Madhu Siddalingaiah

To Valerie, my wife and best friend, for all her support.
—Stephen Lockwood

Message from the
Publisher

WELCOME TO OUR NERVOUS SYSTEM

Some people say that the World Wide Web is a graphical extension of the information superhighway, just a network of humans and machines sending each other long lists of the equivalent of digital junk mail.

I think it is much more than that. To me, the Web is nothing less than the nervous system of the entire planet—not just a collection of computer brains connected together, but more like a billion silicon neurons entangled and recirculating electro-chemical signals of information and data, each contributing to the birth of another CPU and another Web site.

Think of each person's hard disk connected at once to every other hard disk on earth, driven by human navigators searching like Columbus for the New World. Seen this way the Web is more of a super entity, a growing, living thing, controlled by the universal human will to expand, to be more. Yet, unlike a purposeful business plan with rigid rules, the Web expands in a nonlinear, unpredictable, creative way that echoes natural evolution.

We created our Web site not just to extend the reach of our computer book products but to be part of this synaptic neural network, to experience, like a nerve in the body, the flow of ideas and then to pass those ideas up the food chain of the mind. Your mind. Even more, we wanted to pump some of our own creative juices into this rich wine of technology.

TASTE OUR DIGITAL WINE

And so we ask you to taste our wine by visiting the body of our business. Begin by understanding the metaphor we have created for our Web site—a universal learning center, situated in outer space in the form of a space station. A place where you can journey to study any topic from the convenience of your own screen. Right now we are focusing on computer topics, but the stars are the limit on the Web.

If you are interested in discussing this Web site or finding out more about the Waite Group, please send me e-mail with your comments, and I will be happy to respond. Being a programmer myself, I love to talk about technology and find out what our readers are looking for.

Sincerely,

Mitchell Waite

Mitchell Waite, C.E.O. and Publisher

200 Tamal Plaza
Corte Madera, CA 94925
415-924-2575
415-924-2576 fax

Website:
http://www.waite.com/waite

CREATING THE HIGHEST QUALITY COMPUTER BOOKS IN THE INDUSTRY

Waite Group Press
Waite Group New Media

Come Visit
WAITE.COM
Waite Group Press
World Wide Web Site

Now find all the latest information on Waite Group books at our new Web site, **http://www.waite.com/waite.** You'll find an online catalog where you can examine and order any title, review upcoming books, and send e-mail to our authors and editors. Our FTP site has all you need to update your book: the latest program listings, errata sheets, most recent versions of Fractint, POV Ray, Polyray, DMorph, and all the programs featured in our books. So download, talk to us, ask questions, on **http://www.waite.com/waite.**

The New Arrivals Room has all our new books listed by month. Just click for a description, Index, Table of Contents, and links to authors.

The Backlist Room has all our books listed alphabetically.

The People Room is where you'll interact with Waite Group employees.

Links to Cyberspace get you in touch with other computer book publishers and other interesting Web sites.

The FTP site contains all program listings, errata sheets, etc.

The Order Room is where you can order any of our books online.

The Subject Room contains typical book pages which show description, Index, Table of Contents, and links to authors.

Madhu Siddalingaiah received his B.S. in physics from the University of Maryland. Madhu has more than 10 years experience coding in C and assembly language, with strong emphasis on device drivers and performance-critical routines. Madhu was first exposed to the Internet in 1983; since then he has maintained interest in emerging technologies like the World Wide Web and Java. Madhu has worked with world leaders in the areas of hardware design, digital signal processing, research satellite instrumentation,  graphics accelerators, and communication receivers. In his spare time, Madhu can be found flying helicopters and attempting to play guitar; but not at the same time.

Stephen D. Lockwood received his B.S. (magna cum laude) in engineering physics from Embry Riddle Aeronautical University in Daytona Beach. Steve has over seven years experience in programming graphical user interfaces, scientific data analysis algorithms, and various other applications. Steve also served as development coordinator for several DoD operational software projects. Steve currently works as a consultant specializing in emerging technologies like Java. He lives along the Chesapeake Bay with his wife Valerie, and can be found on their Sea-Doo whenever the weather is nice.

TABLE OF CONTENTS

CONTENTS

A C K N O W L E D G M E N T S

There are a number of people who contributed toward this book and are deserving of our thanks. First, we would like to thank Mitch Waite, Kurt Stephan, Jill Pisoni, and Joanne Miller at Waite Group Press for being so patient and helpful throughout the writing process. The following individuals helped in checking the technical accuracy and content: W. Craig Trader, Tharakesh Siddalingaiah, Godmar Back, Paul Callahan, and Doug Gardner. In addition, we would like to thank Rob Levy, Vimala Siddalingaiah, Patrick Welsh, Virginia O'Conner, Thomas Drewry, Andrew C. Nicholas, and Donnie Vazquez for their contributions to the book. Also, we would like to thank Chris Ott and Kaizen Works, Inc., for supplying facilities and resources without which this book would not have been possible.

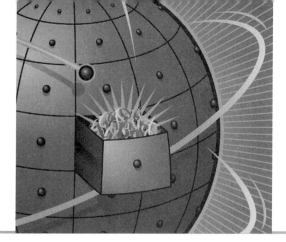

INTRODUCTION

In the next few years, Java could change the concept of what a computer should be. With Java the possibilities are endless. Java applets, included in HTML pages, allow for the use of real-time sound, graphics animation, and user interaction. Data and programs do not have to be stored on the local computer anymore. They can reside anywhere on the Internet and be downloaded only by those who need them, whenever they need them. With all these possibilities there is going to be a great deal of Java code written.

That is where *Java How-To* comes in—this book is designed to help you explore the uncharted areas of Java and discover solutions to many programming problems. Our aim is to give you easy access to useful Java techniques. By following a few simple steps, you can find answers to programming problems. *Java How-To* is packed with a wealth of useful tips and ready-to-use applets.

Question-and-Answer Format

Java How-To, like all books in the Waite Group's successful How-To series, emphasizes a step-by-step, problem-solving approach. How-Tos follow a consistent format that guides you through the technique and steps used to solve authentic problems. Each How-To describes a problem; develops a technique for solving the problem; presents a step-by-step solution; furnishes relevant tips, comments, and warnings; and presents alternative solutions where applicable. This book is designed to work well both as a tutorial and as a reference. It also includes a CD-ROM with the source code and byte code for every example.

Who This Book Is Written For

Java How-To is not a language specification or an introduction to the language; rather, it is a programmer-oriented, problem-solving guide that will teach and enhance Java programming skills. The book will be useful to a wide variety of people ranging from professional programmers to interested hobbyists who have read about Java in the daily newspaper. The problem/solution structure will teach programmers how to accomplish tasks by use of the Java language. Web page developers will also benefit from the book by implementing the many ready-to-use applets included on the CD-ROM. Hobbyists can use the book and examples on the CD-ROM as a teaching aid to learn how to program in Java, or just to see what all the excitement is about.

A programmer trying to master the Java language should have a few prerequisites to get the most out of the book. Basic knowledge of C programming and object-oriented (OO) techniques is a must. If you are not completely familiar with OO techniques, just concentrate on the easier How-Tos at first. This book makes no attempt to teach object-oriented techniques. Basic knowledge of the Java language and Java application programming interface (API) would also drastically speed up the learning process.

The topics in *Java How-To* are taken from real programming situations we encountered in writing various applications or from common questions asked on the Internet. The example code given does more than illustrate the topics. The examples use the topic in an actual application or problem that many programmers may encounter.

What You Need to Use This Book

To use this book, you will need a computer capable of running Windows 95 or Windows NT 3.51 (or higher). Other computers and operating systems may also be used, including Macintoshes (System 7.5) and Sun Sparcstations (Solaris 2.3 or higher). The Java Development Kit (JDK) is available free of charge for many platforms from Sun Microsystems. Please consult the Javasoft web site (www.java-soft.com) for the latest versions. The JDK includes a Java interpreter, which is required to run Java applications, and an Appletviewer, which can be used to view applets locally. There also exists serveral commercial Java development environments that may be purchased.

History of Java

Java originated as part of a research project to develop advanced software for writing control software for consumer electronics. The language was originally called *Oak*. The goal was to develop a small, reliable, portable, distributed, real-time operating environment. When the project started, C++ was the language of choice, but difficulties encountered with C++ led to creating an entirely new language. The design and architecture for Java is a combination of aspects from many languages such as Eiffel, SmallTalk, C, and Cedar/Mesa. This resulted in a language environment perfect for developing secure, distributed, network-based end-user applications in environments ranging from networked-embedded devices to the World Wide Web and the desktop.

Finding the Latest Java

Included on the CD-ROM bundled with *Java How-To* is the Java Development Kit (JDK) version 1.02 for several different platforms. The Java Home page contains the latest information and is located at *http://www.javasoft.com*.

What You'll Learn

To help you get the most out of the book, here is an overview of the topics covered. The book is divided into ten chapters and four appendixes.

Chapter 1—Java Explained introduces the language. The basic syntax, data types, and control statements are presented. In addition, stand-alone Java applications and applets are discussed.

Chapter 2—Getting Started deals with how to perform many basic operations by use of Java applications. You learn how to use data types and arrays, convert between strings and numbers, and take input from the keyboard and command line arguments. Printing text, file I/O, and math functions also are shown.

Chapter 3—Basic Graphics introduces the use of graphics in Java. Basic graphic topics such as drawing lines, shapes, using fonts, and using color are presented.

Chapter 4—Threads introduces the use of threads. Several examples are given to demonstrate aspects of threads, including: multiple threads, thread priority, synchonizing methods, and waiting for a thread.

Chapter 5—Events and Parameters concentrates on handling different events in Java. This chapter demonstrates how to handle many different events and the use of applet parameters.

Chapter 6—User Interface contains a series of examples that demonstrate different components of user interfaces including buttons, check boxes, list boxes, and many more.

Chapter 7—Advanced Graphics covers some of the more complicated graphic-manipulation techniques. In this chapter the use of images is discussed, and double buffering is explained.

Chapter 8—Multimedia introduces the use of sound in Java. Several examples demonstrate the playing of sounds.

Chapter 9—Networking demonstrates many of the networking capabilities contained in Java.

Chapter 10—Miscellaneous and Advanced Topics covers several interesting and more advanced topics. A few topics discussed are linking Java to other code, communicating between applets, and how to keep applets from being stolen.

Appendix A—The Java Class Hierarchy is a list of all classes in the Java API. This is included as a useful reference. It was used an uncountable number of times while writing this book.

Appendix B—Java Frequently Asked Questions (FAQ) is a list of some common questions concerning Java and their answers.

Appendix C—The Java Virtual Machine Specification is a summary of the operation of the Java virtual machine.

Appendix D—Java Applet Hall of Fame Gallery describes five cool third-part applets on the Web that demonstrate techniques used in this book.

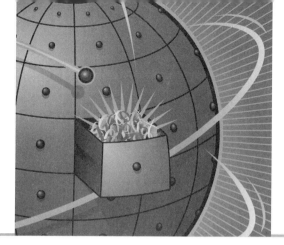

ABOUT THE CD-ROM

Please note this important information before using the CD included with *Java How-To*.

What's on the CD-ROM?

The CD-ROM bundled with Java How-To includes all sample Java code created in the book. All of these files are debugged, tested, and ready to run. Here's what you get:

- Complete Java source code and byte code for every How-To

- Image or sound files required where applicable

In addition, we've included the following bonus items:

- Java Development Kit (JDK) version 1.0.2 from Sun Microsystems—versions of the JDK are included for Solaris 2.3, 2.4, or 2.5, and Microsoft Windows 95/NT

- HotJava browser by Sun Microsystems

- Bonus third-party applets (see Appendix D, "Java Applet Hall of Fame Gallery," for details)

How the CD is Structured

The directory structure at the root of the *Java How-To* CD-ROM is as follows:
\APPLETS

\CHAP02

\CHAP03

\CHAP04

\CHAP05

\CHAP06

\CHAP07

\CHAP08

\CHAP09

\CHAP10

\HOTJAVA

\JDK

The CHAPXX directories contain all code and files for the How-Tos in the book, organized by chapter, with each individual How-To project contained in its own subdirectory within the appropriate chapter directory. The APPLETS directory includes bonus third-party applets. The HOTJAVA directory includes the HotJava browser, while the JDK directory contains the Java Developers Kit version 1.0.2 (all applicable platforms).

Installation

Please refer to the Read Me file at the root level of the CD-ROM for detailed instructions on installation of the included How-To files and bonus items.

CHAPTER 1

JAVA EXPLAINED

JAVA EXPLAINED

1.1   Java versus C/C++

Java has the familiar look of C and C++. Programmers with experience in C and C++ or related languages will experience a short learning curve. The flow control statements and operators function almost identically.

But Java, unlike C, is object-oriented. And Java gains simplicity from the systematic removal of dubious features from C and C++. This keeps Java relatively small and reduces much of the burden in programming robust applications.

Java eliminates much of the redundancy built into C and C++. C evolved over many years, developing many overlapping features. C++ added objects to C, but retained many inherent problems. One of the major problems with C and C++ is the preprocessor. The C/C++ preprocessor can be used to turn the language into something completely unintelligible. This results in a significant amount of time spent understanding preprocessor macros and directives. Header files containing type information aren't needed in Java, because class definitions are compiled into a binary form that retains type information. Java replaces # *defines* by using constants and replaces *typedef* by declaring classes.

In C++, structures and classes exhibit only subtle differences and are, for the most part, redundant. For this reason Java only supports classes. Unions are notoriously platform dependent and thus were not included in Java.

Object-oriented programming replaces functional and procedural styles. Anything that can be done with a function can be done by defining a class and creating methods for that class. For this reason functions outside of classes are unnecessary and are eliminated from Java.

C++ supports multiple inheritance, which can yield unpredictable results under pathological conditions. Java does not support multiple inheritance in the same manner as C++. A form of multiple inheritance is implemented by interfaces. An *interface* is a definition of a set of methods that one or more objects will implement. Interfaces declare only methods and constants, not variables. Interfaces strike a workable balance between full multiple inheritance and single inheritance only.

Although a powerful concept, operator overloading is not present in Java. Students of C++ find operator overloading difficult and cumbersome. In fact, many experienced C++ programmers do not exploit operator overloading effectively.

Although pointers are one of the greatest strengths of C, they are also one of its weaknesses. A misused pointer can yield unpredictable and catastrophic results. Even the most experienced programmer occasionally writes code that may run correctly for years and suddenly fails due to pointer misuse. Additionally, the Java runtime system checks all array indexing to ensure indices are within the bounds of an array.

1.2   Syntax

All programming languages are built with some concept in mind. C was built with the intent to be easy to compile, fast to run, and portable between systems. C++ was built with the intent to promote code reusability through the use of class libraries, but with as few basic differences from C as possible. Java was developed with the intent that it should be similar to C++, so that Java could be learned quickly, but safer than C++, so that Java programmers wouldn't have to spend so much time chasing memory errors.

The following chart lists the keywords defined in the Java language. Table 1-1 shows the Java operators listed in order of precedence.

JAVA KEYWORDS

abstract	boolean	break	byte	byvalue
case	cast	catch	char	class
const	continue	default	do	double
else	extends	final	finally	float
for	future	generic	goto	if

implements	import	inner	instanceof	int
interface	long	native	new	null
operator	outer	package	private	protected
public	rest	return	short	static
super	switch	synchronized	this	throw
throws	transient	try	var	void
volatile	while			

The keywords byvalue, cast, const, future, generic, goto, inner, operator, outer, rest, and var are reserved but not used in Java 1.0.

Note that *true* and *false* look like keywords but technically are Boolean literals.

PRECEDENCE	OPERATOR	TYPE(S)	OPERATION PERFORMED	
1	++		Arithmetic	Pre- or post increment
	—		Arithmetic	Pre- or post decrement
	+, -		Arithmetic	Unary plus, unary minus
	~		Integral	Bitwise complement
	!		Boolean	Logical complement
	(type)	Any	Cast	
2	*, /, %	Arithmetic	Multiplication, division, remainder	
3	+, -		Arithmetic	Addition, subtraction
	+		String	String concatenation
4	<<		Integral	Left shift
	>>		Integral	Arithmetic right shift
	>>>	Integral	Logical right shift	
5	<, <=	Arithmetic	Less than, less than or equal to	
	>, >=	Arithmetic	Greater than, greater than or equal to	
	instanceof	Object	Type comparison	
6	==		Primitive	Equal
	!=		Primitive	Not equal
	==		Object	Equal
	!=		Object	Not equal
7	&		Integral	Bitwise AND
	&		Boolean	Boolean AND
8	^		Integral	Bitwise XOR
	^		Boolean	Boolean XOR
9				Integral	Bitwise OR

continued on next page

continued from previous page

PRECEDENCE	OPERATOR	TYPE(S)		OPERATION PERFORMED
	|		Boolean	Boolean OR
10	&&		Boolean	Conditional AND
11	||		Boolean	Conditional OR
12	?:		Boolean, any, any	Conditional (ternary)
13	=, *=, /=, %=,	Variable, any Assignment with operator		
	+=, -=, <<=, >>=,			
	>>>=, &=, ^=, |=			

Table 1-1 Java operators

1.3   Data Types

Java supports all the primitive data types usually found in modern computer languages. For the most part, the Java language is similar to C and C++ with a few changes. The implementation of the data types has been more strictly defined to help simplify the language and allow for platform independence. The size and form of the data types are precisely defined. The primitive data types are summarized in Table 1-2.

Java does not allow casting between arbitrary types. Casting between numeric types and between sub- and superclasses of the same objects is allowed. When lossy casts are done (for example, *int* to *byte*), the conversion is done modulo the length of the smaller type.

Integer numeric types are 8-bit *byte,* 16-bit *short,* 32-bit *int,* and 64-bit *long.* An integer numeric type is a two's complement signed integer. There are no unsigned data types. The Java language adds the >>> operator to perform unsigned (logical) right shift.

Real numeric types are 32-bit *float* and 64-bit *double.* These types and their arithmetic operations are consistent with the IEEE 754 specification.

Character data is slightly different from that of C. Java uses the Unicode character set standard. The Unicode standard *char* is a 16-bit unsigned *char* rather than the 8-bit ASCII *char* used by C. *Chars* may not be cast into any other type, and no other type may be cast into *char.*

The *boolean* is a 1-bit data type that may take on the values True and False. In Java, a *boolean* is a distinct data type and may not be cast into any other type, and no other type may be cast into *boolean.*

Strings in Java are objects that differ from C or C++. In Java a string is not a null-terminated array of characters as it is in C. Instead it is an instance of the *java.lang.String* class.

Java arrays are objects and are single-dimensional. Multidimensional arrays are implemented as arrays of arrays. An array of length n has n components, and the components are referenced by use of integers from 0 to n-1.

TYPE	DESCRIPTION	SIZE	MIN VALUE MAX VALUE
boolean	True or false	1 bit	NA
			NA
char	Signed integer	16 bits	\u0000
			\uFFFF
byte	Signed integer	8 bits	-128
			127
short	Signed integer	16 bits	-32768
			32767
int	Signed integer	32 bits	-2147483648
			2147483647
long	Signed integer	64 bits	-9223372036854775808
			9223372036854775807
float	Signed integer	32 bits	+/-3.40282347E+38
			+/-1.40239846E-45
double	Signed integer	64 bits	+/-1.79769313486231570E+308
			+/-4.94065645841246544E-324

Table 1-2 Java primitive data types

1.4   Control Statements

Java contains *if, else, switch, for, while, do, break, continue,* and *try-catch* statements. These statements are very similar to those in C++. There are only two significant differences. The first is that the Java *boolean* type cannot be cast to other types. The other difference is that the values 0 and null are not the same as False, and nonzero and nonnull values are not the same as True.

1.5   Applets versus Applications

A Java application is composed of a Java class containing a *main( )* method declared public static void and accepting a string array argument, plus any other classes that are referenced by the class containing *main( )*. It derives its operating environment from the operating system on which it runs. An application can be as simple as a "Hello World" program, or as complicated as a modern word processor, or even a compiler (the javac compiler is itself a Java application). The full capabilities of the Java language and class libraries are available to Java applications.

A Java applet is composed of at least one public Java class that must be subclassed from java.awt.Applet (or subclassed from a class that subclasses java.awt.Applet). It derives its operating environment from a Java-enabled web browser, such as Netscape Navigator 2.0 or HotJava.

Applets are limited compared with applications, because they are intended to be used across unsecure networks, such as the Internet. Applets aren't allowed to read or write to the local file system, and typically are not allowed to open network connections to any system other than the host from which the applet was downloaded.

1.6   Platform Independence

A simple Java application can be written just by use of calls to *System.in.readln( )* for input and *System.out.println()* for output. It will resemble a simple command line program such as those typically found under UNIX or MS-DOS. For many applications, that is all that is necessary. On the other hand, most modern computers use a graphical user interface (GUI)—for example, Macintosh, Windows 95/NT, UNIX, and X Window. Application users expect to have windows, icons, and mouse control. GUI environments are completely different from one operating system to the next, so most programs are written for a specific GUI. The effort necessary to move a program between one environment and another is prohibitive. This is where Java truly shines: If Java code is written once, it can be used in any environment where the Java virtual machine has been ported. As of this writing, Java can run under Solaris, IRIX, Linux, Windows 95, Windows NT, and Macintosh. Ports are under way for OS/2, Windows 3.1, and even palm-top computers. This is the Holy Grail of truly portable code—write it once and it runs everywhere.

The key to this unprecedented portability is the Abstract Windowing Toolkit (AWT). The AWT is a set of Java classes that encapsulates the basic functionality that is available in all GUI environments, without being specific to any individual API. Each of these classes depends upon the Java virtual machine to translate this behavior to appropriate calls for the native GUI.

When a Java program is compiled, it is converted to an architecture-neutral byte-code format. This byte-code can then be run on any system, as long as that system implements the Java virtual machine. Since the Java program is compiled to byte code, and not native machine code, a Java interpreter is needed to execute the program. Therefore Java is an interpreted language and currently does not offer the performance of compiled C. The introduction of Just In Time compilers for Java will increase the speed to rival modern C and C++ compilers.

CHAPTER 2
GETTING STARTED

GETTING STARTED

How do I...

This chapter will cover how to perform many basic operations in Java. These operations include printing text, taking input from the keyboard, reading and writing files, using arrays, and manipulating strings and numeric types. The information contained in this chapter is very similar to C/C++ and should be very straightforward to understand for those with C experience.

Every example in this chapter will be an application and will not work as an applet. Some topics covered are specific to applications and would not work in applets. These include command line arguments (applets have applet parameters), and reading and writing to a file (applets may not read or write to the local hard drive). However, the fundamental operations, such as converting strings to/from numbers, concatenating strings and numbers, parsing strings, and using arrays and math methods, are applicable in applets and applications.

2.1   Print Text

This How-To shows how to print text. The sample illustrates printing of text and numeric values, but, unlike examples used in most computer books, it does not print "Hello World."

2.2   Accept Input from the Keyboard

This How-To demonstrates taking input from the keyboard. The example prompts the user to enter a string of characters, and then outputs the string and number of characters in the string.

2.3   Convert Strings to Numbers

The conversion of strings to numbers is very useful. In Java, input from the keyboard is returned as a string. If the input is needed as a number, the string must be converted to a numeric type. This example will demonstrate converting keyboard input to various numeric types.

2.4   Convert Numbers to Strings

This How-To demonstrates the conversion of numbers to strings. The example computes the current national debt. Since this number is so large, the application converts the debt to a string and inserts separating commas to make it easier to read. The Date constructor and *getTime* method are also discussed.

2.5   Access Command Line Arguments

Command line arguments are frequently used in programming. This How-To demonstrates the use of command line arguments in Java. The application takes the month and year as arguments, and outputs the calendar for that month. This example also uses methods contained in the *Date* class.

2.6   Read from a File

This application will demonstrate how to read a file in Java. The file name to be read is taken as a command line argument. The file is then displayed on the screen in a similar manner to the UNIX *more* utility.

2.7   Write to a File

Learning to read from a file would not be complete without learning how to write a file. This application will translate text files between DOS, UNIX, and Macintosh formats. The file will be read and the line terminators changed to the format specified in the command line argument.

2.8 Concatenate Strings and Numbers

The ability to concatenate strings and numbers is a very useful feature. It allows for easy printing of various values in one *print* statement. This How-To will concatenate a string with a date.

2.9 Use Arrays

The use of arrays is demonstrated in this How-To. The data from a file is read into an array and then sorted by using the quicksort algorithm.

2.10 Parse a String

This example demonstrates a very useful feature, the ability to parse a single string. The string is broken into substrings that are separated by arbitrary characters. The example searches a file of names and phone numbers for a name supplied as a command line argument.

2.11 Use Math Functions

Java contains many math functions that are required to perform various tasks. This How-To illustrates the use of several math functions by calculating the monthly payment for a loan.

COMPLEXITY
BEGINNING

2.1 How do I...
Print text?

Problem

I need to print some common conversion factors on the screen. I need to print both text and double-precision floating-point values. Strict formatting of the numbers is not necessary, but I want each of the factors on a different line. What is the easiest way to print text and numbers?

Technique

The Java runtime provides classes for printing strings and basic numeric types. The methods of interest for this example are *print* and *println*. These methods for printing to the screen (standard output) are contained in the *System.out* class.

Steps

1. Create the application source file. Create a new file called Convert.java and enter the following source:

```java
/*
 * Convert.class prints a short table of common conversion factors.
 */

class Convert {

/*
 * Note that the main method must be be defined as
 * public static void main (String []) to be called from
 * the Java interpreter.
 */

public static void main (String args[]) {

    double mi_to_km = 1.609;
    double gals_to_l = 3.79;
    double kg_to_lbs = 2.2;

    System.out.print ("1 Mile equals\t");      // No newline at end here
    System.out.print (mi_to_km);
    System.out.println ("\tKilometers");       // Print newline at end.

    System.out.print ("1 Gallon equals\t");
    System.out.print (gals_to_l);
    System.out.print ("\tLiters\n");           // \n works as newline also.

    System.out.print ("1 Kilogram equals\t");
    System.out.print (kg_to_lbs);
    System.out.println ("\tPounds");
}
}
```

2. Compile and test the application. Compile the source using javac or the makefile provided. Test the application by typing

```
java Convert
```

When the application is run, the conversion factors for miles to kilometers, gallons to liters, and pounds to kilograms should be printed on the screen. Figure 2-1 shows an example of the output.

How It Works

The Convert class contains only one method, *main*. This is analogous to the main function in C and C++. The Java interpreter begins execution of a stand-alone application by calling the *main* method.

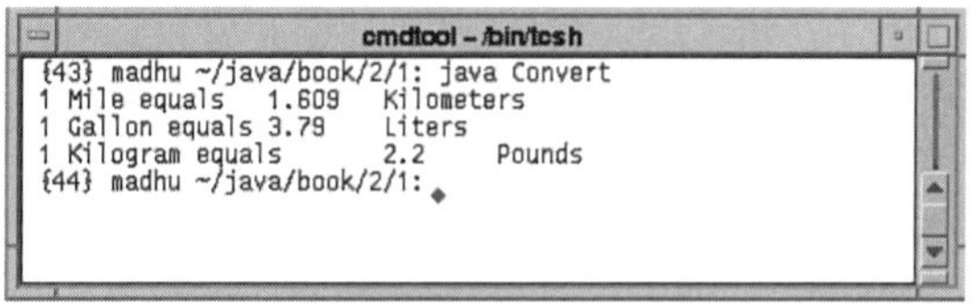

```
                    cmdtool – /bin/tcsh
{43} madhu ~/java/book/2/1: java Convert
1 Mile equals   1.609   Kilometers
1 Gallon equals 3.79    Liters
1 Kilogram equals    2.2    Pounds
{44} madhu ~/java/book/2/1:
```

Figure 2-1 Sample output from
Convert.java application

Three conversion factors are declared as type *double* and initialized to their respective values. Printing is done by calling the *System.out.print* or *System.out.println* methods. The latter forces a trailing newline, whereas the former does not. Several *print* and *println* methods exist, each accepting different types as arguments. This example uses the methods accepting String and *double*.

Many of the escape sequences familiar to the C/C++ programmer are available in Java. Table 2-1 lists the escape sequences and their functions. In this example \t is used for tabbing, and \n is used to force a newline.

ESCAPE SEQUENCE	UNICode Value	Function
\b	\u0008	Backspace BS
\t	\u0009	Horizontal tab HT
\n	\u000a	Line feed LF
\f	\u000c	Form feed FF
\r	\u000d	Carriage return CR
\"	\u0022	Double quote "
\'	\u0027	Single quote '
\\	\u005c	Backslash \
Octal Escape	\u0000 to \u00ff	Octal escape

Table 2-1 Java escape sequences

> **NOTE:**
>
> The *main* method must be defined as *i (String []). If it is not, the Java interpreter will not recognize it as the starting point for the application and will print an error message. Also note that the program source file name should agree with the name of the class containing *main*; for example, class myMainClass should be in file myMainClass.java.

Return from *main*, as in C/C++, terminates execution of the program. *main* cannot return values since it is of type *void*. A method analogous to the C function *exit()* provides a mechanism for returning application completion status. It will be demonstrated in later examples.

Comments

Java does not provide an equivalent of the C function *printf*. The C *printf* is capable of strict formatting of numeric values and accepts a variable argument list. The Java *print* methods are not as sophisticated; they do not allow the programmer to specify details of numeric formatting and, like all Java methods, accept only a fixed set of arguments and types.

Since the arguments to Java methods are always checked for type consistency, this precludes the possibility of variable arguments and types.

COMPLEXITY
BEGINNING

2.2   How do I...
Accept input from the keyboard?

Problem

I would like to take a string input from the keyboard and display the number of characters typed. How do I accept input from the keyboard?

Technique

The *readLine* method takes input from a DataInputStream and returns a String. This is the method needed to accept input from the keyboard. The length of the input string can be determined by use of the *length* method in the *String* class. The String and its length can be printed using *print* or *println*.

Steps

1. Create the application source file. Create a new file called Input.java and enter the following source:

```
import java.io.*;

/*
 * Input.class reads a line of text from standard input,
 * determines the length of the line, and prints it.
 */

class Input {
public static void main (String args[]) {
   String input = "";
```

```
   boolean error;

/*
 * DataInputStream contains the readLine method.
 * Create a new instance for standard input System.in
 */
   DataInputStream in = new DataInputStream(System.in);

/*
 * This loop is used to catch IO exceptions that may occur.
 */
   do {
      error = false;
      System.out.print ("Enter the string > ");

/*
 * We need to flush the output because there is no newline at the end.
 */
      System.out.flush ();

      try {
         input = in.readLine ();          // Read the input.
      } catch (IOException e) {
         System.out.println (e);          // Print exception
         System.out.println ("An input error was caught");
         error = true;
      }
   } while (error);

   System.out.print ("You entered \"");
   System.out.print (input);             // readLine does NOT keep the \n
                                         // or \r.
   System.out.println ("\"");
   System.out.print ("The length is ");
   System.out.println (input.length ()); // Print the length.
} // end of main ()
}
```

2. Compile and test the application. Compile the source using javac or the makefile provided. Test the application by typing

```
java Input
```

The application will prompt you to enter a string. Type the string and then press ⏎Enter. The string and the number of characters in the string will then be printed. Figure 2-2 shows sample output.

Figure 2-2 Output from Input.java application

How It Works

A new DataInputStream must be created for input from the keyboard. This is accomplished by calling the DataInputStream constructor with System.in (standard input) as the argument. *readLine* can throw an IOException, so a *do-while* loop containing a *try-catch* block is used to accommodate the exception. *readLine* returns a String that is assigned to the String variable input.

The String input is printed by using *print*. The length of input is determined by using the *length* method of the *String* class.

> **NOTE:**
> It is necessary to import classes in java.io, because that is where DataInputStream is located.

Strings that do not contain newlines at the end may not always be flushed on all systems. To ensure consistent results, *System.out* is flushed after the user prompt is printed.

It is not necessary to initialize *String input*. It was initialized here to suppress warnings from the compiler suggesting that input may take unknown values if an IOException is thrown.

Comments

It is unlikely an IOException will occur reading from the keyboard, but it is good programming practice to handle it anyway. The compiler will produce a warning if an exception is not caught.

readLine does not include a newline or carriage return at the end of the string it returns. This simplifies code in many cases.

COMPLEXITY
INTERMEDIATE

2.3 How do I...
Convert strings to numbers?

Problem

I need a program to calculate the tip for a bill. The user will enter the bill amount and the percent of tip in response to a prompt. To make the calculation, I need to convert the input strings to numbers. How do I convert strings to numbers?

Technique

The user will be prompted for the bill amount and tip percent by use of *print*. The input will be taken by use of *readLine*, as in the previous example. As seen in the previous example, *readLine* takes input from the keyboard and returns a string. The calculation requires the input string to be converted to numbers, *double* and *int,* in this case. The conversions are performed by using the *valueOf* method contained in both the *Double* and *Integer* classes.

Steps

1. Create the application source file. Create a new file called Tip.java and enter the following source:

```java
import java.io.*;

/*
 * Tip.class calculates the tip given the bill and tip percent.
 */

class Tip {
public static void main (String args[]) {
    String input = "";
    int tip_percent=0;
    double bill=0, tip=0;
    boolean error;

    DataInputStream in = new DataInputStream(System.in);

    do {
       error = false;
       System.out.print ("Enter the bill total > ");
       System.out.flush ();
       try {
           input = in.readLine ();
       } catch (IOException e) {
           System.out.println (e);
           System.exit (1);
       }

/*
 * Convert input string to double, catching NumberFormatException.
 */
       try {
           bill = Double.valueOf (input).doubleValue();
       } catch (NumberFormatException e) {
           System.out.println (e);
           System.out.println ("Please try again");
           error = true;
       }
    } while (error);

    do {
       error = false;
       System.out.print ("Enter the tip amount in percent > ");
```

continued on next page

continued from previous page

```
        System.out.flush ();
        try {
            input = in.readLine ();
        } catch (IOException e) {
            System.out.println (e);
            System.exit (1);
        }

/*
 * This time convert to Integer
 */
        try {
            tip_percent = Integer.valueOf (input).intValue();
        } catch (NumberFormatException e) {
            System.out.println (e);
            System.out.println ("Please try again");
            error = true;
        }
    } while (error);

    System.out.print ("The total is ");
    tip = bill * ((double) tip_percent)/100.0;
    System.out.println (bill + tip);
} // end of main ()
}
```

2. Compile and test the application. Compile the source using javac or the makefile provided. Test the application by typing

`java Tip`

This application will prompt the user for two values. The first will be the amount of the bill, the second, the percentage of tip you would like to leave. At each prompt type the value and press ⏎Enter. When both values are entered, the total amount of the bill plus tip will be printed. Please be kind to your servers. Figure 2-3 shows an example of output from Tip.java.

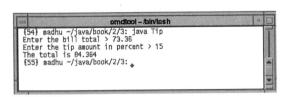

Figure 2-3 Output from Tip.java application

How It Works

A DataInputStream for System.in is created as in the previous example. The bill is converted to a *double* by use of *Double.valueOf (String).doubleValue ()*. The tip percentage is converted by use of a similar method to convert to an integer—*Integer.valueOf (input).intValue()*. The *valueOf* method can throw a NumberFormatException if the input string is improperly formatted, for example, if the user were to input *20..30*. This is handled gracefully, by asking the user to enter the value again.

The computation and printing of the bill total is straightforward.

Comments

In this example, an IOException caught during input causes the program to terminate with exit status 1. This is accomplished by calling System.exit with the exit status as an argument.

The calculation of the tip requires that the tip percent be cast to a *double*. Clearly, a simpler solution converts the tip percent to a *double* directly. The integer conversion was done for illustration.

COMPLEXITY
INTERMEDIATE

2.4   How do I...
Convert numbers to strings?

Problem

I have a first-order calculation of the national debt and the population. The problem is that the debt is such a large number, it is difficult to read the numbers without delimiting commas. I want to format the numbers with commas every three digits. The *print* method will not do this. What I need to do is convert the numbers to strings and print them with delimiting commas. How do I convert the numbers to strings?

Technique

The process of converting numbers to strings is similar to converting strings to numbers. The *valueOf* method contained in the *String* class performs exactly this function.

Once the numbers are converted to strings, separating commas can be printed by alternately printing three digits and a comma. The three digits are printed by use of the *substring* method in the *String* class.

Steps

1. Create the application source file. Create a new file called Debt.java and enter the following source:

```java
import java.util.Date;

/*
 * Debt.class calculates the approximate national debt,
 * population, and what each person owes.
 */
class Debt {

public static void main (String args[]) {
   Date now = new Date ();                  // The current date/time
   Date debtDate = new Date (92, 5, 29);  // June 29, 1992
   Date popDate = new Date (90, 6, 1);    // July 1, 1990
   long milliPerDay = 24*60*60*1000;      // Milliseconds per day

/*
 * now.getTime () units are milliseconds, convert to seconds for debt
 * and days for population
 */
   long debtSecs = (now.getTime () - debtDate.getTime ())/1000;
   long popDays = (now.getTime () - popDate.getTime ())/milliPerDay;

/*
 * Good thing longs are 64 bits! The debt growth rate on June 29, 1992, was
 * $14,132/second. The population growth rate on July 1, 1990, was
 * 6,170 persons/day. Use first-order approximations for simplicity.
 */
   long debt = 3965170506502L + (debtSecs * 14132);
   long pop = 250410000 + (popDays * 6170);

   print ("The national debt is $", debt);
   print ("The population is ", pop);
   print ("Each person owes $", debt/pop);
}

/*
 * print method converts a long to a string and prints it with commas
 * for easy reading. We need it with these big numbers!
 * String str     preceding label
 * long n      the long to format and print
 */
public static void print (String str,long n) {
   System.out.print (str);                // Print the label.
   String buf = String.valueOf (n);       // Integer to String

   int start, end, ncommas, i;
   int buflen = buf.length ();

/*
 * It's a crazy algorithm, but it does work. It works from left to right.
 */
```

```
    ncommas = buflen/3;
    if (ncommas * 3 == buflen) ncommas -= 1;
    start = 0;
    end = buflen-(3*ncommas);
    System.out.print (buf.substring (start, end));
    for (i=0; i<ncommas; i+=1) {
        start = end;
        end = start+3;
        System.out.print (",");
        System.out.print (buf.substring (start, end));
    }
    System.out.println ("");      // The final newline
}
}
```

2. Compile and test the application. Compile the source using javac or the makefile provided. Test the application by typing

`java Debt`

This application will print three lines containing the national debt, population, and each person's share of the debt. See Figure 2-4 for an example of the output. When you run this application, notice how much the debt has gone up since the figure was created.

How It Works

The current national debt and population are calculated to first order by multiplying the growth rates by the difference in time and adding values at known points in time. According to the literature, the national debt was $3,965,170,506,502 on June 29, 1992. The growth rate at that time was $14,132 per second. The population on July 1, 1990, was 250,410,000 with a growth rate of 6,170 persons per day.

The difference in seconds, for the debt calculation, must be calculated from the current time to June 29, 1990. The difference in days, for the population calculation, must be calculated from the current day to July 1, 1990. The Date constructor is called with year, month, and day of year as arguments; if no arguments are specified, the current date is used. The *getTime* method returns the number of milliseconds since the epoch. It is not necessary to know what the epoch is, since the milliseconds since the epoch of a specific date are subtracted from that of the

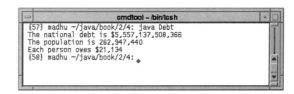

Figure 2-4 Output from Debt.java application

current date. This yields the milliseconds between the two dates, regardless of when the epoch is. The epoch is, however, 1970. This is divided by 1,000 to get the number of seconds, or divided by 24*60*60*1000 to get the number of days.

The time differences are multiplied by the growth rates and added to the initial values. This gives the current values of debt and population in 64-bit *long* integers. A *print* method is defined that prints a label and then formats and prints *long* integers with separating commas.

The *print* method takes a *long* integer and converts it to a string by using the *valueOf* method contained in the *String* class. The number of commas required is calculated. The first digits (up to three digits) are printed by extracting the substring. A *for* loop prints commas and the remaining three-digit groups in pairs.

Comments

String.valueOf, unlike *Long.valueOf*, does not throw any exceptions. Therefore, a *try-catch* block should not be used around the conversion.

Longs are 64-bit integers. The current national debt and the number of milliseconds since 1970 cannot be contained in a 32-bit integer.

The Date constructor can take the year, month, and day as arguments. The year is the number of years since 1900. The month is zero based, for example, 0=January, 1=February, 11=December. The day of the month is one based, that is, it takes on values from 1 to 31.

COMPLEXITY
BEGINNING

2.5   How do I...
Access command line arguments?

Problem

I want to write a calendar utility that will print a calendar for a given month and year. I want to provide the month and year as command line arguments to the utility. I know how to get the Date, but I need to access the command line arguments. How do I do that?

Technique

The command line arguments are passed to Java *main* methods as an array of strings. The argument count is determined by the *length* method. The arguments may be converted to numbers by using techniques discussed in previous sections of Chapter 2.

Steps

1. Create the application source file. Create a new file called Calendar.java and enter the following source:

```
import java.util.Date;

/* Calendar.class prints a calendar given the month and year
 * as command line arguments.
 */
class Calendar {

public static void main (String args[]) {

/*
 * Java, unlike C/C++, does not need argument count (argc).
 */
   if (args.length < 2) {
       System.out.println ("usage: java Calendar <month> <year>");
       System.exit (1);
   }

/*
 * Unlike C/C++ args[0] is the FIRST argument. The application
 * name is not available as an argument.
 */
   int month = Integer.valueOf (args[0]).intValue();
   int year = Integer.valueOf (args[1]).intValue();
   if (month < 1 || month > 12) {
       System.out.println ("Month must be between 1 and 12");
       System.exit (1);
   }
   if (year < 1970) {
       System.out.println ("Year must be greater than 1969");
       System.exit (1);
   }

/*
 * This version of Date needs year, month, and day.
 * Note the month is zero based (0-11), but day is 1 based (1-31).
 */
   Date date = new Date (year-1900, month-1, 1);
   System.out.println ("Sun\tMon\tTue\tWed\tThu\tFri\tSat");
   int i, day, ndays=0, lastday=28;

   switch (month) {
   case 1:  // January
   case 3:  // March
   case 5:  // May
   case 7:  // July
   case 8:  // August
   case 10: // October
```

continued on next page

continued from previous page

```
   case 12: // December
       lastday = 31;
       break;

/*
 * Special handling for leap year, it's more complicated than mod 4
 */
   case 2:  // February
       lastday = (year%4 == 0 && year%100 != 0) ||
           (year%400 == 0) ? 29 : 28;
       break;

   case 4:  // April
   case 6:  // June
   case 9:  // September
   case 11: // November
       lastday = 30;
       break;
   }

/*
 * First print spaces (tabs) to line up the days of the week.
 */
   for (i=0; i<date.getDay(); i+=1) {
       System.out.print ("\t");
       ndays += 1;
       if (ndays % 7 == 0) System.out.println ("");
   }

/*
 * Now print the days.
 */
   for (day=1; day<=lastday; day+=1) {
       System.out.print (day);
       System.out.print ("\t");
       ndays += 1;
       if (ndays % 7 == 0) System.out.println ("");
   }
   System.out.println ("");
}
}
```

2. Compile and test the application. Compile the source using javac or the makefile provided. Test the application by typing

```
java Calendar <month> <year>
```

A tabular calendar will be displayed. Try entering numbers out of range for the arguments (for example, a month equal to 15) or no arguments at all. Figure 2-5 contains sample output.

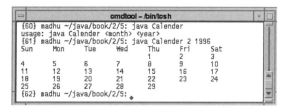

Figure 2-5 Output from Calendar.java
application

How It Works

Like all good utilities, Calendar first checks the number of arguments to make sure
that just the month and year have been entered. This is done by applying the *length*
method to the command line argument array args. If the number of arguments is
not correct, a proper-usage message is printed, and the program exits.

There are several differences between command line argument handling in Java
and C/C++:

 C/C++ explicitly passes the argument count to *main,* Java does not.

 C/C++ passes an array of characters, Java passes an array of Strings.

 The program name is the first argument, argv[0], in C/C++. In Java, the
program name is not available; the first argument is the first array ele-
ment, args[0].

The month and year are converted to integers by means of *Integer.valueOf* and checked
to be sure they are within limits. The Date constructor is called with the first day
of the month. The *getDay* method is called to determine the day of the week of the
first day of the month. Sunday is 0, Monday is 1, and Saturday is 6. See section 2.4
for additional information on the Date constructor.

The balance of the code is straightforward.

COMPLEXITY
BEGINNING

2.6   How do I...
Read from a file

Problem

I want to write a program similar to the UNIX *more* utility. I know how to print strings,
but I don't know how to read from a file. How do I open and read from a file?

Technique

Files are opened by creating a FileInputStream with the file name as an argument. FileInputStream throws an Exception if an error occurs. To read from the FileInputStream, a DataInputStream must be created from the FileInputStream. This is similar to the procedure outlined in previous examples for keyboard input.

Reading from the DataInputStream is accomplished by calling *readLine*. *readLine* returns null on end of file. A count of lines read/printed is maintained, and the user is prompted to see more when 23 lines are displayed.

Finally, the file is closed by applying the *close* method on the FileInputStream.

Steps

1. Create the application source file. Create a new file called More.java and enter the following source:

```
import java.io.*;

/*
 * More.class similar to UNIX more utility
 */
class More {

public static void main (String args[])
{
    String buf;
    FileInputStream fs=null;
    int nlines;

    if (args.length != 1) {
        System.out.println ("usage: java More <file>");
        System.exit (1);
    }

/*
 * Try to open the file name specified by args[0].
 */
    try {
        fs = new FileInputStream (args[0]);
    } catch (Exception e) {
        System.out.println (e);
        System.exit (1);
    }

/*
 * Create a DataInputStream associated with FileInputStream fs.
 */
    DataInputStream ds = new DataInputStream (fs);
    DataInputStream keyboard = new DataInputStream (System.in);
    nlines = 0;
    while (true) {
```

```
        try {
            buf = ds.readLine ();         // Read 1 line.
            if (buf == null) break;
        } catch (IOException e) {
            System.out.println (e);       // No newlines are in buf.
            break;
        }
        System.out.println (buf);
        nlines += 1;
        if (nlines % 23 == 0) {           // 23 lines/pages vt100
            System.out.print ("--More--");
            System.out.flush ();
            try {
                keyboard.readLine ();
            } catch (IOException e) {
            }
        }
    }
/*
 * close can throw an exception also, catch it for completeness.
 */
    try {
        fs.close ();
    } catch (IOException e) {
        System.out.println (e);
    }
}
}
```

2. Compile and test the application. Compile the source using javac or the makefile provided. Test the application by typing

```
java More <file>
```

The <file> specified will be displayed one screen at a time. The ⏎Enter key is used to advance to the next screen. An example of the output can be found in Figure 2-6.

How It Works

The name of the file to be viewed is available as the first command line argument, so this is used to create the FileInputStream, fs. An Exception will be thrown if the file does not exist, or if some other error occurs. The Exception is caught, printed, and causes immediate program termination.

Two DataInputStreams are opened. One is for the file, the other is for the keyboard. The program continues to read lines from the file until end of file is encountered. End of file results in a null return from *readLine*.

The file is closed when end of file is encountered. The *close* method throws an IOException that is caught and printed.

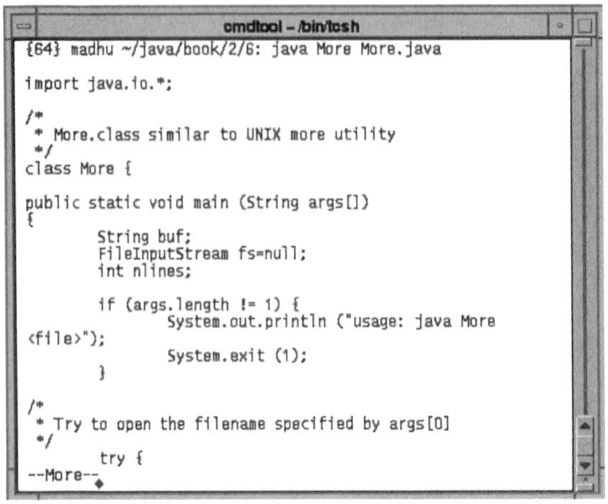

```
cmdtool - /bin/tcsh
{64} madhu ~/java/book/2/6: java More More.java

import java.io.*;

/*
 * More.class similar to UNIX more utility
 */
class More {

public static void main (String args[])
{
        String buf;
        FileInputStream fs=null;
        int nlines;

        if (args.length != 1) {
                System.out.println ("usage: java More
<file>");
                System.exit (1);
        }

/*
 * Try to open the filename specified by args[0]
 */
        try {
--More--
```

Figure 2-6 Output from More.java
application

Comments

Java does not differentiate between text files and binary files. This is immaterial on UNIX and Macintosh systems, but can be of some consequence on Windows machines. It is safe to assume that all files are treated as binary by the Java runtime.

Similar to keyboard input as shown in How-To 2.2, *readLine* from a file does not include the line terminator.

DataInputStream provides many *read* methods in addition to *readLine*. These allow reading of binary quantities like integers, floating-point values, and Unicode formats. Table 2-2 lists many of the methods available in DataInputStream.

METHOD	DESCRIPTION
DataInputStream(InputStream)	(Constructor) Creates a new DataInputStream
read(byte[])	Reads data into an array of *bytes*
read(byte[], int, int)	Reads data into an array of *bytes*
readBoolean()	Reads in a *boolean*
readByte()	Reads an 8-bit *byte*
readChar()	Reads a 16-bit *char*
readDouble()	Reads a 64-bit *double*
readFloat()	Reads a 32-bit *float*
readFully(byte[])	Reads *bytes*, blocking until all *bytes* are read
readFully(byte[], int, int)	Reads *bytes*, blocking until all *bytes* are read

METHOD	DESCRIPTION
readInt()	Reads a 32-bit *int*
readLine()	Reads in a line that has been terminated by a \n, \r, \r\n or EOF
readLong()	Reads a 64-bit *long*
readShort()	Reads 16-bit *short*
readUTF()	Reads a UTF format String
readUTF(DataInput)	Reads a UTF format String from the given input stream
readUnsignedByte()	Reads an unsigned 8-bit *byte*
readUnsignedShort()	Reads 16-bit *short*
skipBytes(int)	Skips *bytes*, blocking until all *bytes* are skipped

Table 2-2 DataInputStream class constructors and methods

COMPLEXITY
BEGINNING

2.7 How do I...
Write to a file?

Problem

Different systems use different line terminators for text files. DOS uses carriage return and line feed, Macintosh uses only carriage return, and UNIX uses only line feed. I use all these systems and occasionally need to translate text files from one machine to another. I would like to write a utility that could do this kind of translation.

I learned how to read files from the previous example, but now I need to write to files. How do I write to a file?

Technique

As with the previous example, a FileInputStream and a DataInputStream must be opened for reading a file. To write to a file, FileOutputStream and PrintStream are used.

The writing is done by applying the *print/println* methods to a PrintStream created from a valid FileOutputStream. Each line in the input file is read into a buffer and written to the output file. Depending on the type of format translation required, either a carriage return, line feed, or a carriage return–line feed is written.

When end of file is encountered, both files are closed, and the program terminates.

Steps

1. Create the application source file. Create a new file called Format.java and enter the following source:

```java
import java.io.*;

/*
 * Format.class translates a text file to either DOS, Mac, or UNIX
 * format. The differences are in  line termination.
 */
class Format {

static final int TO_DOS = 1;
static final int TO_MAC = 2;
static final int TO_UNIX = 3;
static final int TO_UNKNOWN = 0;

static void usage () {
    System.out.print ("usage: java Format -dmu <in-file> ");
    System.out.println ("<out-file>");
    System.out.println ("\t-d converts <in-file> to DOS");
    System.out.println ("\t-m converts <in-file> to MAC");
    System.out.println ("\t-u converts <in-file> to UNIX");
}

public static void main (String args[])
{
    int format=TO_UNKNOWN;
    String buf;
    FileInputStream fsIn = null;
    FileOutputStream fsOut = null;

    if (args.length != 3) {                   // You must specify format, in,
                                              // out
        usage ();
        System.exit (1);
    }

/*
 * args[0] is a String, so we can use the equals (String) method for
 * comparisons.
 */
    if (args[0].equals ("-d")) format = TO_DOS; else
    if (args[0].equals ("-m")) format = TO_MAC; else
    if (args[0].equals ("-u")) format = TO_UNIX; else {
        usage ();
        System.exit (1);
    }

    try {
        fsIn = new FileInputStream (args[1]);
    } catch (Exception e) {
        System.out.println (e);
        System.exit (1);
```

```
    }

/*
 * FileOutputStream is the complement of FileInputStream.
 */
    try {
        fsOut = new FileOutputStream (args[2]);
    } catch (Exception e) {
        System.out.println (e);
        System.exit (1);
    }
    DataInputStream dsIn = new DataInputStream (fsIn);
    PrintStream psOut = new PrintStream (fsOut);
    while (true) {
        try {
            buf = dsIn.readLine ();
            if (buf == null) break;          // Break on EOF
        } catch (IOException e) {
            System.out.println (e);
            break;
        }
        psOut.print (buf);
        switch (format) {
            case TO_DOS:
            psOut.print ("\r\n");
            break;

            case TO_MAC:
            psOut.print ("\r");
            break;

            case TO_UNIX:
            psOut.print ("\n");
            break;
        }
    }

/*
 * Not absolutely necessary to catch these individually
 * It keeps the compiler from issuing a warning about
 * IOException not caught.
 */
    try {
        fsIn.close ();
        fsOut.close ();
    } catch (IOException e) {
        System.out.println (e);
    }
}
}
```

2. Compile and test the application. Compile the source using javac or the makefile provided. Test the application by typing

```
java Format -dmu <input file> <output -file>
```

Use the -d option when conversion to DOS is required, -m option for Macintosh, and -u for UNIX. Figure 2-7 shows output from Format.java when no arguments are supplied and when arguments are supplied.

How It Works

Three command line arguments are expected: the conversion option, the input file name, and the output file name. If the arguments are not all present, a proper-usage message is printed and the program terminates immediately. The conversion option is tested for equality by using the *equals* method from the *String* class to determine which conversion is to be performed.

The input file is opened just like it was in previous examples. The output file is opened by calling the FileOutputStream constructor with the output file name as an argument. Like FileInputStream, FileOutputStream also throws an Exception if an error occurs.

A DataInputStream is created for the input file, and a *PrintStream* is created for the output file. Lines are read from the input file one at a time and written to the output file. A *switch* statement determines the type of line termination required and supplies it.

The files are closed when end of input file is encountered.

Comments

As a point of symmetry, you might ask why *PrintStream* was used for output instead of DataOutputStream. Many of the methods contained in DataInputStream have counterparts in DataOutputStream. Unfortunately, there is no counterpart to *readLine,* that is, there is no *writeLine.* Instead *print/println* perform the inverse function to *readLine* and are found in *PrintStream.* Also note that *print/println* do not throw any exceptions. Table 2-3 lists the methods available in *PrintStream,* while Table 2-4 lists the methods of DataOutputStream.

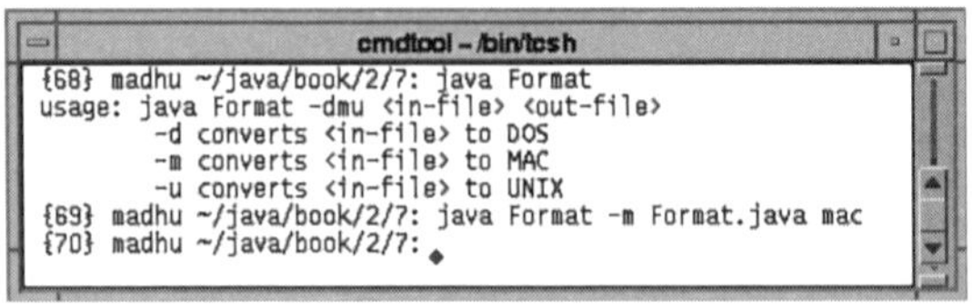

```
cmdtool – /bin/tcsh
{68} madhu ~/java/book/2/7: java Format
usage: java Format -dmu <in-file> <out-file>
        -d converts <in-file> to DOS
        -m converts <in-file> to MAC
        -u converts <in-file> to UNIX
{69} madhu ~/java/book/2/7: java Format -m Format.java mac
{70} madhu ~/java/book/2/7: ◆
```

Figure 2-7 Output from Format.java application

The final *try-catch* block containing the *close* methods could be done differently. Clearly, an error in the first *close* keeps the second from executing. In this case, there is little consequence, as the program immediately exits, and the operating system will close any open files.

METHOD	DESCRIPTION
PrintStream(OutputStream)	(constructor) Creates a new PrintStream
PrintStream(OutputStream,	Creates a new PrintStream, with auto
boolean)	(constructor) flushing
checkError()	Flushes the print stream and returns whether there was an error on the output stream
close()	Closes the stream
flush()	Flushes the stream
print(Object)	Prints an object
print(String)	Prints a String
print(char[])	Prints an array of characters
print(char)	Prints a character
print(int)	Prints an integer
print(long)	Prints a *long*
print(float)	Prints a *float*
print(double)	Prints a *double*
print(boolean)	Prints a *boolean*
println()	Prints a newline
println(Object)	Prints an object followed by a newline
println(String)	Prints a string followed by a newline
println(char[])	Prints an array of characters followed by a newline
println(char)	Prints a character followed by a newline
println(int)	Prints an integer followed by a newline
println(long)	Prints a long followed by a newline
println(float)	Prints a *float* followed by a newline
println(double)	Prints a *double* followed by a newline
println(boolean)	Prints a *boolean* followed by a newline
write(int)	Writes a *byte*
write(byte[], int, int)	Writes a subarray of bytes

Table 2-3 PrintStream Class constructors and methods

METHOD	FUNCTION
written()	The number of bytes written so far
DataOutputStream(OutputStream)	Creates a new DataOutputStream
flush()	Flushes the stream
size()	Returns the number of bytes written
write(int)	Writes a byte
write(byte[], int, int)	Writes a subarray of bytes
writeBoolean(boolean)	Writes a boolean
writeByte(int)	Writes an 8-bit byte
writeBytes(String)	Writes a String as a sequence of bytes
writeChar(int)	Writes a 16-bit char
writeChars(String)	Writes a String as a sequence of chars
writeDouble(double)	Writes a 64-bit double
writeFloat(float)	Writes a 32-bit float
writeInt(int)	Writes a 32-bit int
writeLong(long)	Writes a 64-bit long
writeShort(int)	Writes a 16-bit short
writeUTF(String)	Writes a String in UTF format

Table 2-4 DataOutputStream class constructors and methods

COMPLEXITY
INTERMEDIATE

2.8 How do I...
Concatenate strings and numbers?

Problem

I would like to print the date and the day of month along with some text. I know how to obtain the current date, and how to print strings and numbers. I would like to be able to print the text and date in a single *print* statement. How do I concatenate strings and numbers?

Technique

In Java the concatenation of strings and numbers is very straightforward. The strings and numbers are concatenated with the + character.

Steps

1. Create the application source file. Create a new file called Concat.java and enter the following source:

```java
import java.io.*;
import java.util.Date;

/*
 * Concat.class uses the Date class to print today's date.
 * The date and day of month are concatenated with a string
 * and printed using println.
 */
class Concat {

public static void main (String args[]) {
        Date date = new Date();
        String today = "";
        int monthday;

/* The string "Today is " and date are concatenated together and
 * assigned to the String today.
 */
        today = "Today is " + date;
        monthday = date.getDate();

/* The String today is printed with println.
 */
        System.out.println (today);

/* Here two text strings are concatenated with the integer
   monthday within the println method.
 */
        System.out.println ("Today is the " + monthday +
        " day of the month");

} // end of main ()
}
```

2. Compile and test the application. Compile the source using javac or the makefile provided. Test the application by typing

```
java Concat
```

Figure 2-8 shows output from Concat.java.

Figure 2-8 Output from Concat.java application

How It Works

This example is relatively straightforward. A date class for the current date is created. The concatenation of strings and numbers is illustrated in two ways. The first creates the string *today* and assigns it to the date concatenated with the string of characters "Today is" using the concatenation character +. The new string is then printed with *println*. The second example performs the concatenation sequence inside the *println* method.

Comments

It is also important to note that the second example could have been performed without creating the monthday integer. The *getDate()* method could have been placed inside the *println* method. This would look like:

```
System.out.println ("Today is the " + date.getDate() + " day of the
month");
```

COMPLEXITY
BEGINNING

2.9   How do I...
   # Use arrays?

Problem

I have a file of names that I would like to sort. I am told that quicksort is an efficient algorithm for sorting data, but the data must reside in an array of some type. I need to read the file into an array, sort it, and print it. How do I use arrays?

Technique

An array needs to be created to hold strings read from the input file. This is done by using the *new* keyword in the same way as is done with other data types. The data in the file is read into the array and sorted by using the quicksort algorithm. Quicksort is significantly faster than many other sorting methods such as bubble sort.

Steps

1. Create the application source file. Create a new file called Sort.java and enter the following source:

```
import java.io.*;

/*
```

```
 * Sort.class reads a text file specified by args[0] and
 * sorts each line for display.
 */
class Sort {

static final int NMaxLines = 128;        // An arbitrary limit

public static void main (String args[]) {
/*
 * Allocate new array of strings, this is where the file
 * is read in and sorted in place.
 */
   String sortArray[] = new String [NMaxLines];
   FileInputStream fs=null;
   int nlines;

   if (args.length != 1) {
       System.out.println ("usage: java Sort <file>");
       System.exit (1);
   }
   try {
       fs = new FileInputStream (args[0]);
   } catch (Exception e) {
       System.out.println ("Unable to open "+args[0]);
       System.exit (1);
   }
   DataInputStream ds = new DataInputStream (fs);
   DataInputStream keyboard = new DataInputStream (System.in);
   for (nlines=0; nlines<NMaxLines; nlines += 1) {
       try {
           sortArray[nlines] = ds.readLine ();
           if (sortArray[nlines] == null) break;
       } catch (IOException e) {
           System.out.println ("Exception caught during read.");
           break;
       }
   }
   try {
       fs.close ();
   } catch (IOException e) {
       System.out.println ("Exception caught closing file.");
   }

/*
 * Sort in place and print
 */
   QSort qsort = new QSort ();
   qsort.sort (sortArray, nlines);
   print (sortArray, nlines);
}

/*
 * print method prints an array of Strings of n elements.
```

continued on next page

continued from previous page

```
 * String a[]     array of strings to print
 * int n          number of elements
 */
private static void print (String a[], int n) {
    int i;

    for (i=0; i<n; i+=1) System.out.println (a[i]);
    System.out.println ("");
}
}


/*
 * QSort.class uses the standard quicksort algorithm.
 * Detailed explanations of the techniques are found in the literature.
 */
class QSort {

/*
 * This is used internally, so make it private.
 */
private void sort (String a[], int lo0, int hi0) {
    int lo = lo0;
    int hi = hi0;

    if (lo >= hi) return;
    String mid = a[(lo + hi) / 2];
    while (lo < hi) {
        while (lo<hi && a[lo].compareTo (mid) < 0) lo += 1;
        while (lo<hi && a[hi].compareTo (mid) > 0) hi -= 1;
        if (lo < hi) {
            String T = a[lo];
            a[lo] = a[hi];
            a[hi] = T;
        }
    }
    if (hi < lo) {
        int T = hi;
        hi = lo;
        lo = T;
    }
    sort(a, lo0, lo);       // Yes, it is recursive.
    sort(a, lo == lo0 ? lo+1 : lo, hi0);
}

/*
 * The method called to start the sort.
 * String a[]    an array of strings to be sorted in place
 * int n         the number of elements in the array
 */
```

```
public void sort (String a[], int n) {
    sort (a, 0, n-1);
}
}
```

2. Compile and test the application. Compile the source using javac or the makefile provided. Test the application by typing

```
java Sort <input file>
```

A test file is supplied on the CD-ROM, called PhoneBook.txt. Figure 2-9 shows the output from sorting the example file.

How It Works

An array of Strings is created by using the new String keywords along with array dimensions. In this example a fixed-size array of length 128 is used.

The input file is opened in the same way as previous examples. The data is read into the array, making sure that array bounds are not exceeded. The file is then closed.

The *QSort* class implements the standard quicksort algorithm, in this case comparing String variables. String comparison is done by using the *compareTo* method. This method returns an integer less than, equal to, or greater than 0, similar to the C function *strcmp*. The sorting is done in place, meaning no additional arrays are needed.

The sorted array is printed by a special function designed for printing arrays of strings.

Comments

Variable-length arrays cannot be allocated directly in Java. There are mechanisms to implement growable arrays, but this requires the use of the vector class, which is discussed in Chapter 8.

Figure 2-9 Output from Sort.java application

2.10 How do I...
Parse a string?

Problem

I have a file of telephone numbers. Each line in the file contains three fields separated by tabs or colons. The first field contains a name, the second field has a phone number, and the third field has an address.

I would like to write a program that will search for a record in the file that corresponds to a name given on the command line. I want the name, telephone number, and address printed on separate lines.

This requires some kind of string parsing. How do I parse a string?

Technique

A very useful class found in the util directory is StringTokenizer. StringTokenizer can take a string and return substrings which are separated by arbitrary characters. It is functionally similar to the *split* function found in Perl.

To use StringTokenizer, the constructor is called with the target string and an optional set of delimiting characters. Repeated calls to the *nextToken* method return strings delimited in the target string.

Steps

1. Create the application source file. Create a new file called Phone.java and enter the following source:

```java
import java.io.*;
import java.util.StringTokenizer;

/*
 * Phone.class implements a simple phone book with fuzzy
 * name lookup. The phone book file could be created with a
 * text editor or a spreadsheet saved as tab-delimited text.
 */
class Phone {

public static void main (String args[])
{
    String buf;
    FileInputStream fs=null;

    if (args.length != 1) {
        System.out.println ("usage: java Phone <name>");
        System.exit (1);
```

```
    }

/*
 * PhoneBook.txt is the name of the phone book file.
 */
    try {
        fs = new FileInputStream ("PhoneBook.txt");
    } catch (Exception e) {
        System.out.println ("Unable to open PhoneBook.txt");
        System.exit (1);
    }
    DataInputStream ds = new DataInputStream (fs);
    DataInputStream keyboard = new DataInputStream (System.in);
    while (true) {
        try {
            buf = ds.readLine ();
            if (buf == null) break;
        } catch (IOException e) {
            System.out.println ("Exception caught reading file.");
            break;
        }

/*
 * Create a new StringTokenizer for each new line read.
 * Explicitly specify the delimiters as both colons and tabs.
 */
        StringTokenizer st = new StringTokenizer (buf, ":\t");

        String name = st.nextToken ();
        if (contains (name, args[0])) {
            System.out.println (name);
            System.out.println (st.nextToken ());
            System.out.println (st.nextToken () + "\n");
        }
    }
    try {
        fs.close ();
    } catch (IOException e) {
        System.out.println ("Exception caught closing file.");
    }
}

/*
 * contains method is a fuzzy string compare that returns True
 * if either string is completely contained in the other one.
 * String s1, s2    two strings to compare
 */
static boolean contains (String s1, String s2) {

    int i;
    int l1 = s1.length ();
    int l2 = s2.length ();

    if (l1 < l2) {
```

continued on next page

continued from previous page

```
        for (i=0; i<=l2-l1; i+=1)
            if (s1.regionMatches (true, 0, s2, i, l1))
            return true;
    }
    for (i=0; i<=l1-l2; i+=1)
        if (s2.regionMatches (true, 0, s1, i, l2))
            return true;

    return false;
}
}
```

2. Compile and test the application. Compile the source using javac or the makefile provided. Test the application by typing

`java Phone <name>`

The program looks for a file called PhoneBook.txt in the current directory. The file must contain lines with three fields separated by tabs or colons. Such a file can be created with a text editor or a spreadsheet. A test file is supplied on the CD-ROM. Figure 2-10 shows output from Phone.java.

How It Works

The program opens the phone book file (PhoneBook.txt), reads each line and creates a StringTokenizer object, and compares the first field with the given name. A new StringTokenizer object must be created for each line read. So, a special string-compare function, *contains,* which ignores case and position, is used. The *contains* function returns True if either string contains the other.

If a match occurs, the name, phone number, and address are printed on separate lines. Multiple matches may occur.

Figure 2-10 Output from Phone.java application

Comments

StringTokenizer by default uses whitespace (space, tabs, newline, and carriage return) as delimiters. The constructor used in this example allows the set of delimiting characters to be specified explicitly. The delimiters may also be changed on a per-token basis. A summary of the constructors and methods available in the StringTokenizer class is presented in Table 2-5.

The *contains* method uses the *regionMatches* method, without case sensitivity, found in the String class. This provides a fuzzy matching mechanism that is more user friendly than the *equals* or *compareTo* methods.

METHOD	DESCRIPTION
StringTokenizer(String, String a boolean)	(Constructor) Constructs StringTokenizer on the specified String, using the specified delimiter set
StringTokenizer(String, String)	(Constructor) Constructs a StringTokenizer on the specified String, using the specified delimiter set
StringTokenizer(String)	(Constructor) Constructs a StringTokenizer on the specified String, using the default delimiter set (which is " \t\n\r")
countTokens()	Returns the next number of tokens in the String, using the current delimiter set
hasMoreElements()	Returns True if the Enumeration has more elements
hasMoreTokens()	Returns True if more tokens exist
nextElement()	Returns the next element in the Enumeration
nextToken()	Returns the next token of the String
nextToken(String)	Returns the next token, after switching to the new delimiter set

Table 2-5 StringTokenizer class constructors and methods

COMPLEXITY
BEGINNING

2.11 How do I...
Use math functions?

Problem

I want to write a program to calculate the monthly payment for a loan given the loan amount and annual interest rate. I have the equation for calculating the payment—it uses both the exponential function and the natural logarithm. How do I access these math functions?

Technique

Like all high-level languages, Java supports many of the math functions programmers require. Exponentiation and natural logarithm, along with many other functions, are contained in the *Math* class. These functions are declared static, so they may be accessed without creating an instance of the object.

Steps

1. Create the application source file. Create a new file called Amortize java and enter the following source:

```java
import java.io.*;

/*
 * Ammortize.class calculates monthly payment given
 * loan amount, interest, and the number of years of the loan.
 */
class Ammortize {
public static void main (String args[]) {
    double loanAmount=0, interest=0, years=0;

    DataInputStream in = new DataInputStream(System.in);

    loanAmount = inputDouble ("Enter the loan amount in dollars > ", in);

    interest = inputDouble ("Enter the interest rate in percent > ", in);

    years = inputDouble ("Enter the number of years > ", in);

    System.out.print ("The payment is $");
    System.out.println (payment (loanAmount, interest, years));
} // end of main ()

/*
 * inputDouble method prints a prompt and reads in a double
 * DataInputStream.
 */
static double inputDouble (String prompt, DataInputStream in) {
    boolean error;
    String input="";
    double value=0;

    do {
        error = false;
        System.out.print (prompt);
        System.out.flush ();
        try {
            input = in.readLine ();
        } catch (IOException e) {
            System.out.println ("An input error was caught");
```

```
        System.exit ;
    }
    try {
        value = Double.valueOf (input).doubleValue();
    } catch (NumberFormatException e) {
        System.out.println ("Please try again");
        error = true;
    }
} while (error);
return value;
} // end of inputDouble ()

/*
 * payment method does the magic calculation.
 * double A    loan amount
 * double I    interest rate in percent
 * double Y    number of years
 */
static double payment (double A, double I, double Y) {

/*
 * Call the exponentiation and natural log functions as
 * static methods in the Math class.
 */
    double top = A * I / 1200;
    double bot = 1 - Math.exp (Y*(-12) * Math.log (1 + I/1200));

    return top / bot;
} // end of payment ()
}
```

2. Compile and test the application. Compile the source using javac or the makefile provided. Test the application by typing

`java Ammortize`

The program prompts the user for the loan amount, interest rate, and length of the loan in years. The payment amount is then displayed. Figure 2-11 shows an example of calculating the loan payment for a typical new car. Run the Debt.java application and use each person's share of the national debt (see How-To 2.4) as the amortize amount. How long will it take you to pay your share?

Figure 2-11 Output from Ammortize.java application

How It Works

As was done in previous examples, the program creates a DataInputStream for taking input from the keyboard. An *inputDouble* method is defined to reduce the amount of code inside the body of *main*. After the values have been typed in, the *payment* method is called to calculate the monthly payment.

The *payment* method performs the standard equation for amortized payments. The derivation of the equation from first principles has been left as an exercise to the reader.

Java math functions are contained in the *Math* class. This example uses exponentiation and natural logarithm (log base e). These functions are declared static, so they may be accessed without creating an instance of the object. Table 2-6 lists the math functions available in the Math class.

FUNCTION	DESCRIPTION
E (constant)	The float representation of the value E
PI (constant)	The float representation of the value Pi
IEEEremainder(double, double)	Returns the remainder of f1 divided by f2 as defined by IEEE 754
abs(int a)	Returns the absolute integer value of a
abs(long a)	Returns the absolute long value of a
abs(float a)	Returns the absolute float value of a
abs(double a)	Returns the absolute double value of a
acos(double a)	Returns the arc cosine of a, in the range of 0.0 through Pi
asin(double a)	Returns the arc sine of a, in the range of -Pi/2 through Pi/2
atan(double a)	Returns the arc tangent of a, in the range of -Pi/2 through Pi/2
atan2(double a, double b)	Converts rectangular coordinates (a, b) to polar (r, theta)
ceil(double a)	Returns the "ceiling," or smallest whole number greater than or equal to a
cos(double)	Returns the trigonometric cosine of an angle
exp(double a)	Returns the exponential number e(2.718...) raised to the power of a
floor(double a)	Returns the "floor," or largest whole number less than or equal to a
log(double a)	Returns the natural logarithm (base e) of a
max(int a, int b)	Takes two *int* values, a and b, and returns the greater of the two
max(long a, long b)	Takes two *long* values, a and b, and returns the greater of the two
max(float a, float b)	Takes two *float* values, a and b, and returns the greater of the two
max(double a, double b)	Takes two *double* values, a and b, and returns the greater of the two
min(int a, int b)	Takes two *integer* values, a and b, and returns the smaller of the two
min(long a, long b)	Takes two *long* values, a and b, and returns the smaller of the two
min(float a, float b)	Takes two *float* values, a and b, and returns the smaller of the two

FUNCTION	DESCRIPTION
min(double a, double b)	Takes two *double* values, a and b, and returns the smaller of the two
pow(double a, double b)	Returns the number a raised to the power of b
random()	Generates a random number between 0.0 and 1.0
rint(double)	Converts a *double* value into an integral value in *double* format
round(float)	Rounds off a *float* value by first adding 0.5 to it and then returning the largest integer that is less than or equal to this new value
round(double)	Rounds off a *double* value by first adding 0.5 to it and then returning the largest integer that is less than or equal to this new value
sin(double)	Returns the trigonometric sine of an angle
sqrt(double)	Returns the square root of a
tan(double)	Returns the trigonometric tangent of an angle

Table 2-6 Math class methods

CHAPTER 3
BASIC GRAPHICS

BASIC GRAPHICS

How do I...

All of the examples in Chapter 2 were text-only applications. In this chapter, basic graphics will be demonstrated as applets and applications. Graphics make programs more aesthetically appealing and are almost a requirement in modern end-user software. *Applets* are small programs that can be downloaded to client machines via popular web browsers like Netscape Navigator. Applets are somewhat constrained with respect to access of the client system resources with the goal that they will not present a security risk. These constraints are modest and allow the programmer enough freedom to explore a variety of interactive ideas.

3.1   Draw a Line

The first step in creating graphics is drawing lines and points on the screen. In this example a sine curve is plotted on a graph with axes. It demonstrates the use of basic classes contained in the Abstract Windowing Toolkit (AWT) and the basic parts of an applet.

3.2   Add Color

The next step in creating attractive graphics is adding color. This example draws "flying" lines that continuously change color.

3.3   Draw Shapes

The Java API includes methods for drawing rectangles, ovals, arcs, and polygons. Variations of these basic shapes allow for other shapes such as circles, squares, and triangles. This example will read a file containing shape description records and draw them. This example can be used only as an application, because it must read files from a local disk.

3.4   Fill Shapes

Java supports drawing of filled shapes. This example shows how to fill several shapes by defining classes for plotting bar charts and pie charts. These classes could be used in other applets and applications.

3.5   Draw Text

Drawing text is fundamental to graphics toolkits. In this example, classes are defined to create scrolling text. This type of animation is used in many web pages published currently.

3.6   Use Fonts

Text in Java programs can be displayed in multiple fonts and styles. This How-To lists the available fonts and styles and demonstrates their use.

3.7   Handle Screen Updates

The screen updates in Java are handled by the *update()* method. If no *update()* method is declared, the default method is used. The default method will sometimes perform an operation that is not desired. This example will show how to create a custom *update()* method to avoid flickering.

3.8   Print Applet Status Messages

The status bar in the Appletviewer, Netscape browser, or other Java-enabled application can be accessed. A method exists in Java that allows for a message to be printed in the status bar. This example demonstrates how to print in the status bar.

3.1 How do I...
Draw a line?

Problem

I'd like to draw lines to the screen and be able to plot a mathematical function like the sine curve. I also want to plot both x and y axes. This can be done by drawing lines only. I know how to access math functions and generate values for plotting, but I don't know how to draw lines. How do I draw lines?

Technique

The Java graphics API, known as the Abstract Windowing Toolkit (AWT), supports many of the graphics primitives programmers expect, the simplest being *drawLine()*. The *drawLine()* method is contained in the **Graphics** class and takes four integers as arguments. These integers are the x and y values of the starting and the ending points of the line.

Steps

1. Create the applet source file. Create a new file called Sine.java and enter the following source:

```
import java.applet.Applet;
import java.awt.*;

/**
 * Sine curve applet/application
 * Draws one cycle of a sine curve
 */
public class Sine extends Applet {

/*
 * Width and height of the applet panel
 */
int width, height;

/*
 * init() is called when the applet is loaded.
 * Just get the width and height and save it.
 */
public void init () {

    Dimension d = size ();
```

continued on next page

continued from previous page

```
        width = d.width;
        height = d.height;
}

/**
 * paint() does the drawing of the axes and sine curve.
 * @param g - destination graphics object
 */
public void paint (Graphics g) {

    int x, x0;
    double y0, y, A, f, t, offset;

    A = (double) height / 4;
    f = 2;
    offset = (double) height / 2;
    x0 = 0;
    y0 = offset;

    g.drawLine (x0, (int) y0, width, (int) y0);
    g.drawLine (width/2, 0, width/2, height);
    for (x=0; x<width; x+=1) {
        t = (double) x / ((double) width);
        y = offset - A * Math.sin (2 * Math.PI * f * t);
        g.drawLine (x0, (int) y0, x, (int) y);
        x0 = x;
        y0 = y;
    }
}

/**
 * main() is the application entry point.
 * main() is unused when run as an applet.
 * Create a window frame and add the applet inside.
 * @param args[] - command line arguments
 */
public static void main (String args[]) {

    Frame f = new Frame ("Sine curve");
    Sine sine = new Sine ();

    f.resize (200, 200);
    f.add ("Center", sine);
    f.show ();
    sine.init ();
}
}
```

2. Create an HTML document that contains the applet. Create a new file called howto31.html as follows:

```
<html>
<head>
<title>Sine curve</title>
</head>
<applet code="Sine.class" width=200 height=200>
</applet>
<hr size=4>
</html>
```

3. Compile and test the applet. Compile the source using javac or the makefile provided. Test the applet using the Appletviewer by entering the following command:

```
APPLETVIEWER howto31.html
```

Sine.java may also be run as an application by typing

```
java Sine
```

When *Sine* is executed, a window will pop up with a sine curve drawn on a set of axes. Figure 3-1 shows an example of the running applet/application.

How It Works

The *Sine* class extends the *Applet* class so that it may be used as an applet. The Appletviewer, web browser, or other application that supports applets can load an applet class and execute it. Execution of an applet begins with the *init()* method. After return from *init()*, the applet *start()* method is called. One or both of these methods may be defined. The *init()* method is called when an applet is first loaded, typically this is used for initialization purposes. The *start()* method is called after the *init()* method and whenever the user returns to a previously visited page in a web browser. A *stop()* method, which is called when a user leaves a web browser page, may also be defined. This method is typically used to stop threads and perform cleanup actions.

If an applet is executed as a stand-alone application, like examples from Chapter 2, the Java interpreter will produce an error noting that a *main()* method was not found. To make an applet run as a stand-alone application, all that is needed is the

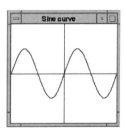

Figure 3-1 Sine applet

addition of a *main()* method, which creates a window for the applet and an instance of the applet. This is what the *main()* method does in the preceding example.

When the *main()* method is called, it creates a window frame by calling the *Frame()* constructor with the window title as an argument. An instance of the applet itself is created by the call to the *Sine()* constructor. The instance of *Sine()* is placed in the center of the window frame by the *add()* method. This can be done because *Applet()* is a subclass of *Panel()*. This will be discussed in greater detail in later chapters. The *main()* method then calls the *init()* method in the same manner as the Appletviewer or another Java-enabled application would.

The *init()* method gets the width and height of the bounding panel by invoking *size()* and stores it for later use. If the program is used as an applet, the size will be the dimensions specified by the width and height attributes of the <applet> tag in the associated html file. If the program is executed as a stand-alone application, the dimensions will come from the bounding window frame.

The *paint()* method is called asynchronously by the Java runtime. It is actually called from the *update()* method, which itself is called in response to update events like initialization and window expose events. Each time a Java window is created or exposed, all *update()* methods of all Panels within that window are called. In this case, a sine curve with axes is plotted.

The x and y axes are plotted first, each with a call to *drawLine()*. The arguments to *drawLine()* are the x and y coordinates of the starting and ending points of the line. The coordinate system follows the raster like most other windowing systems,

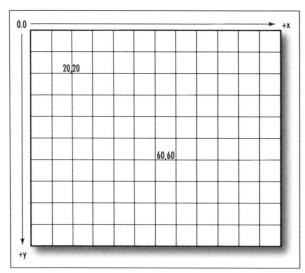

Figure 3-2 Java screen coordinate system

that is, 0,0 is the top left, with increasing values moving down and right. Figure 3-2 shows an example of the Java screen coordinate system. The axes are drawn in the center of the window by using the width and height to calculate the coordinates.

The sine curve is plotted by using the *sin()* method, from the *Math* class, and *drawLine()*. The *sin()* and *drawLine()* methods are called within a *for* loop that varies the value of *x* from 0 to the panel width. The *sin()* method computes the value of *y*. The *sin()* method returns a *double* between -1.0 and 1.0; this is scaled and translated appropriately to the window coordinates. The call to *drawLine()* in this case draws a line from the previous calculated value to the current calculated value. This in effect draws several small lines that look like a continuous sine curve.

Comments

In many cases, Applets may be used as applications by the mechanism described in this example. There are, of course, cases in which both execution environments cannot be supported. These will be explored in later examples.

The argument g to the *paint()* method is similar to a graphics or device context found in other windowing systems like X, MacOS, and Windows. It contains all the information you might expect, like foreground color and font.

The *main()* method could have been placed in a separate class and could have performed the same function. The downside is that the name of the class containing the *main()* method would have to be specified to the Java interpreter instead of the Applet class name.

Note that the Appletviewer provided in the Sun JDK is itself written in Java. Based on this example, you can speculate about how some of it works.

COMPLEXITY
BEGINNING

3.2   How do I...
Add color?

Problem

Whenever graphics are displayed or created, adding color is always important. In today's world of multimedia and high-impact documents, understanding how to use color is even more important. I want to demonstrate the use of color by drawing "flying" lines that continuously change color like many screen-saver programs that are in use today. I learned how to draw lines in the previous example. How do I add color?

Technique

The *Graphics* class passed to the *paint()* method controls the foreground and background color used when drawing to the screen. The foreground color is changed by calling the *setColor()* method from the *Graphics* class. The argument to *setColor()*

is a *Color* object. The *Color* class has several fixed colors defined, but it also contains methods to allocate arbitrary colors given red, green, and blue component values.

In this example, 24 different colors are allocated. These colors are used to set the foreground color of the flying lines.

Steps

1. Create the applet source file. Create a new file called Lines.java and enter the following source:

```
import java.applet.Applet;
import java.awt.*;

/**
 * class LineColors holds 24 color values.
 */
class LineColors {

/**
 * color[] array holds the colors to be used.
 */
Color color[];

/**
 * Class constructor
 * Initializes the color array using an arbitrary algorithm
 */
public LineColors () {

    color = new Color[24];
    int i, rgb;

    rgb = 0xff;
    for (i=0; i<24; i+=1) {
        color[i] = new Color (rgb);
        rgb <<= 1;
        if ((rgb & 0x1000000) != 0) {
            rgb |= 1;
            rgb &= 0xffffff;
        }
    }
}
}

/**
 * Class describing one line segment
 */
class Segment {

/*
 * x1, y1 - starting coordinates for this segment
 * x2, y2 - ending coordinates for this segment
 * dx1,...dy2 - velocities for the endpoints
```

```
 * whichcolor - the current index into color array
 * width, height - width and height of bounding panel
 * LC - instance of LineColors class
 */
double x1, y1, x2, y2;
double dx1, dy1, dx2, dy2;
int whichcolor, width, height;
LineColors LC;

/**
 * Class constructor
 * Initializes endpoints and velocities to random values
 * @param w - width of bounding panel
 * @param h - height of bounding panel
 * @param c - starting color index
 * @param lc - instance of LineColors class
 */
public Segment (int w, int h, int c, LineColors lc) {

    whichcolor = c;
    width = w;
    height = h;
    LC = lc;
    x1 = (double) w * Math.random ();
    y1 = (double) h * Math.random ();
    x2 = (double) w * Math.random ();
    y2 = (double) h * Math.random ();

    dx1 = 5 - 10 * Math.random ();
    dy1 = 5 - 10 * Math.random ();
    dx2 = 5 - 10 * Math.random ();
    dy2 = 5 - 10 * Math.random ();
}

/*
 * Increment color index.
 * Calculate the next endpoint position for this segment.
 */
void compute () {

    whichcolor += 1;
    whichcolor %= 24;

    x1 += dx1;
    y1 += dy1;
    x2 += dx2;
    y2 += dy2;

    if (x1 < 0 || x1 > width) dx1 = -dx1;
    if (y1 < 0 || y1 > height) dy1 = -dy1;
    if (x2 < 0 || x2 > width) dx2 = -dx2;
    if (y2 < 0 || y2 > height) dy2 = -dy2;
```

continued on next page

continued from previous page

```java
}

/**
 * Draw the line segment using the current color.
 * @param g - destination graphics object
 */
void paint (Graphics g) {

    g.setColor (LC.color [whichcolor]);
    g.drawLine ((int) x1, (int) y1, (int) x2, (int) y2);
}
}

/**
 * The applet/application proper
 */
public class Lines extends Applet {

/*
 * width, height - width and height of bounding panel
 * NLines - number of line segments to be displayed
 * lines - array of instances of Segment class
 * LC - instance of LineColors class
 */
int width, height;
final int NLines = 4;
Segment lines[] = new Segment[NLines];
LineColors LC = new LineColors ();

/**
 * init is called when the applet is loaded.
 * Save the width and height.
 * Create instances of Segment class.
 */
public void init () {

    Dimension d = size ();

    width = d.width;
    height = d.height;

    int i;
    for (i=0; i<NLines; i+=1)
        lines[i] = new Segment (width, height, (2*i) % 24, LC);
}

/**
 * Recompute the next endpoint coordinates for each line.
 * Invoke paint() method for each line.
 * Call repaint() to force painting 50ms later.
 * @param g - destination graphics object
 */
```

```
public void paint (Graphics g) {

    int i;
    for (i=0; i<NLines; i+=1) {
        lines[i].compute ();
        lines[i].paint (g);
    }
    repaint (50);
}

/**
 * Application entry point, unused when run as an applet
 * Create window frame and add applet inside.
 * @param args[] - command line arguments
 */
public static void main (String args[]) {

    Frame f = new Frame ("Colored lines");
    Lines lines = new Lines ();

    f.resize (200, 200);
    f.add ("Center", lines);
    f.show ();
    lines.init ();
}
}
```

2. Create an HTML document that contains the applet. Create a new file called howto32.html as follows:

```
<html>
<head>
<title>Flying Lines</title>
</head>
<applet code="Lines.class" width=200 height=200>
</applet>
<hr size=4>
</html>
```

3. Compile and test the applet. Compile the source using javac or the makefile provided. Test the applet using the Appletviewer by entering the following command:

```
APPLETVIEWER howto32.html
```

Lines.java may also be run as an application by typing

```
java Lines
```

When Lines is executed, a window will pop up with four lines that bounce around while continuously changing color. Figure 3-3 shows an example of the running applet.

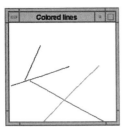

Figure 3-3 Lines
applet

How It Works

Two classes are defined in addition to the applet itself: *LineColors* and *Segment*. *LineColors* contains an array of 24 colors. The color values are initialized by the *LineColors* constructor, which uses the *Color()* constructor to allocate new colors. One of the *Color* constructors takes a single integer argument which specifies the red, green, and blue (RGB) color components in the lower 24 bits—the red component in bits 16–23, the green component in bits 8–15, and the blue component in bits 0–7 (least significant byte, see Table 3-2). The colors allocated in this example blend from blue to green to red in 24 steps. The algorithm rotates a full saturation bit pattern to generate the RGB values.

The *Segment* class describes a single line segment. It contains the endpoints of the segment, their velocities, an instance of *LineColors*, and an index to the current color of the segment. In addition to the constructor, a *compute()* method and a *paint()* method are defined. The constructor initializes the endpoints and velocities to random values using the *Math.random()* method. *Math.random()* returns a positive *double* between 0 and 1; this is scaled appropriately. The *compute()* method advances the color index and integrates the endpoints of the segment, implementing ideal reflection at the boundary. This gives the effect of bouncing. The *paint()* method sets the foreground color to the current color index using *setColor()* and draws the line.

The applet itself creates four line segments and stores them in an array. When the applet's *paint()* method is called in response to an update, it calls the *compute()* and *paint()* methods of the respective line segments in the array. In effect, it tells each line segment to compute and paint itself.

An applet can force an update by calling *repaint()*. This is what the example does to repeatedly draw the line segments in an animated fashion. *repaint()* queues update requests, which are later serviced by *update()*. Figure 3-4 shows the relationship between *repaint()*, *update()*, and *paint()*. The default *update()* method fills the applet panel with the current background color and calls *paint()*. *repaint()* can take an integer argument, which specifies the time in milliseconds when the next update should occur. In this example the value of 50 milliseconds is used. The final result is that the applet's *paint()* method is called approximately 20 times per second, producing the illusion of smooth motion.

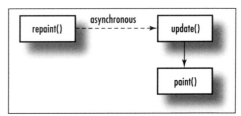

Figure 3-4 Relationship between
repaint(), update(), and *paint()*

Comments

The *Color* class contains several predefined colors. Their types are defined as static final new *Color()*, so they can be used without creating an instance of *Color*. For example, the following code fragment sets the foreground color to magenta:

```
void paint (Graphics g) {

    g.setColor (Color.magenta);
...
}
```

The predefined colors are listed in Table 3-1.

PREDEFINED COLOR RGB VALUES	
black	(0,0,0)
blue	(0,0,255)
cyan	(0,255,255)
darkGray	(64,64,64)
gray	(128,128,128)
green	(0,255,0)
lightGray	(192,192,192)
magenta	(255,0,255)
orange	(255,200,0)
pink	(255,175,175)
red	(255,0,0)
white	(255,255,255)
yellow	(255,255,0)

Table 3-1 Java predefined colors

The *Color* class contains several constructors which take color values in a variety of formats. In addition, useful utility methods are also included. Table 3-2 lists the constructors and methods contained in class *Color*.

METHOD	DESCRIPTION
Color(int, int, int)	(Constructor) Creates a color with the specified red, green, and blue values in the range (0–255)
Color(int)	(Constructor) Creates a color with the specified combined RGB value consisting of the red component in bits 16–23, the green component in bits 8–15, and the blue component in bits 0–7
Color(float, float, float)	(Constructor) Creates a color with the specified red, green, and blue values in the range (0.0–1.0)
HSBtoRGB(float, float, float)	Returns the RGB value, defined by the default RGB ColorModel, of the color corresponding to the given HSB color components
RGBtoHSB(int, int, int, float[])	Returns the HSB values corresponding to the color defined by the red, green, and blue components
brighter()	Returns a brighter version of this color
darker()	Returns a darker version of this color
equals(Object)	Compares this object against the specified object
getBlue()	Gets the blue component
getColor(String)	Gets the specified Color property
getColor(String, Color)	Gets the specified Color property of the specified Color
getColor(String, int)	Gets the specified Color property of the color value
GetGreen()	Gets the green component
GetHSBColor(float, float, float)	A static Color factory for generating a Color object from HSB values
getRGB()	Gets the RGB value representing the color in the default RGB ColorModel
getRed()	Gets the red component
HashCode()	Computes the hash code
toString()	Returns the String representation of this Color's values

Table 3-2 Color constructors and methods

Colors allocated in Java are not necessarily exact. The runtime attempts to find a color that is closest to the one requested. This, of course, is platform dependent.

The repeated calls to *paint*() and *repaint*() may appear to be recursive, but they are not. *repaint*() queues update requests and issues them asynchronously. In fact, there may not necessarily be a one-to-one correspondence between calls to *repaint*() and calls to *update*(). *update*() is called at the next convenient time.

3.3   How do I...
Draw shapes?

Problem

I want to write a simple interpreter capable of drawing standard shapes like rectangles, ovals, and polygons. I want the program to accept input from a text file and interpret the text to draw the objects specified. I know how to read lines from a file and break them up into tokens, but how do I draw shapes?

Technique

This example combines many aspects discussed in Chapter 2, such as reading files and string tokenizing, with an example of how to draw shapes. The Java AWT supports all of the graphic primitives mentioned earlier. Similar to *drawLine()*, from How-To 3.1, additional graphics primitives are contained in the *Graphics* class. They may be called from an application's *paint()* method like before.

The text file will contain one shape definition per line, with parameters separated by spaces. The grammar of a line of the text file is as follows:

```
<color>    <shape>
```

Where <color> is one of the following:

```
WHITE | LIGHTGRAY | GRAY | DARKGRAY | BLACK | RED | PINK | ORANGE | YELLOW
| GREEN| MAGENTA | CYAN | BLUE
```

and <shape> is one of the following shapes along with necessary parameters:

```
RECT top left width height
OVAL top left width height
ARC     top left width height startangle arcangle
POLY x1 y1 x2 y2 x3 y3 [ x4 y4 ...]
```

Each line in the input file is read and split into tokens by using *StringTokenizer()* as shown in Chapter 2. Each line is then checked to ensure it is valid and in proper format. A valid line is used to create a shape object described by the parameters in that line. An array of shape objects is maintained and painted in response to an update.

Applets cannot directly access disk files, so this example can be run only as an application.

Steps

1. Create the application source file. Create a new file called DrawApp.java
and enter the following source:

```java
import java.applet.Applet;
import java.awt.*;
import java.io.*;
import java.util.StringTokenizer;

/**
 * Class describing a shape
 */
class Shape {

/**
 * Constants for the shape type
 */
static final int rectType = 1;
static final int ovalType = 2;
static final int arcType = 3;
static final int polyType = 4;

/*
 * The shape type
 */
int type;

/*
 * Color for this shape
 */
Color color;
static final int MaxPoints = 10;

/*
 * Arrays of x and y points for this shape
 */
int xp[] = new int[MaxPoints];
int yp[] = new int[MaxPoints];

/*
 * The number of points in this shape
 */
int npoints;

/**
 * Shape constructor
 * Saves parameters
 * @param tp - shape type
 * @param n - number of points
 * @param pts[] - array of endpoints
 * @param c - color of the shape
 */
```

```java
public Shape (int tp, int n, int pts[], Color c) {

    int i;
    type = tp;
    color = c;
    npoints = n < MaxPoints ? n : MaxPoints;
    if (type == polyType) {
        npoints >>= 1;
        for (i=0; i<npoints; i+=1) {
            xp[i] = pts[i << 1];
            yp[i] = pts[(i << 1) +1];
        }
    } else {
        for (i=0; i<npoints; i+=1)
            xp[i] = pts[i];
    }
}

/**
 * Draw the shape.
 * @param g - destination graphics object
 */
void paint (Graphics g) {

    g.setColor (color);
    switch (type) {

    case rectType:
        g.drawRect (xp[0], xp[1], xp[2], xp[3]);
        break;

    case ovalType:
        g.drawOval (xp[0], xp[1], xp[2], xp[3]);
        break;

    case arcType:
        g.drawArc (xp[0], xp[1], xp[2], xp[3], xp[4], xp[5]);
        break;

    case polyType:
        g.drawPolygon (xp, yp, npoints);
        break;
    }
}
}

/**
 * Application class proper
 */
public class DrawApp extends Panel {

/*
 * The maximum number of shapes allowed
```

continued on next page

continued from previous page

```java
 */
static final int MaxShapes = 25;

/*
 * nshapes - the number of shapes read in
 * nlines - the line number in the input file
 */
static int nshapes, nlines = 0;

/*
 * Array of instances of class shape
 */
static Shape shapes[] = new Shape[MaxShapes];

/**
 * Invoke paint() method for each shape.
 * @param g - destination graphics object
 */
public void paint (Graphics g) {

    int i;
    for (i=0; i<nshapes; i+=1)
        shapes[i].paint (g);
}

/**
 * Application entry point
 * @param args - command line arguments
 */
public static void main (String args[]) {

    String buf;
    FileInputStream fs=null;
    int i, type = 0;

    if (args.length != 1) {
        System.out.println ("usage: java DrawApp <file>");
        System.exit (1);
    }

/*
 * Try to open the file name specified by args[0].
 */
    try {
        fs = new FileInputStream (args[0]);
    } catch (Exception e) {
        System.out.println (e);
        System.exit (1);
    }

/*
 * Create a DataInputStream associated with FileInputStream fs.
 */
    DataInputStream ds = new DataInputStream (fs);
```

```
    String token;
    Color color = Color.white;
    int pts[] = new int[2 * Shape.MaxPoints];

/*
 * Loop until end of file or error.
 * Read a line and parse it.
 */
    while (true) {
        try {
            buf = ds.readLine ();       // Read 1 line.
            if (buf == null) break;
        } catch (IOException e) {
            System.out.println (e);      // No newlines are in buf.
            break;
        }
        nlines += 1;
        StringTokenizer st = new StringTokenizer (buf);
        token = st.nextToken ();
        if (token.equals ("white")) {
            color = Color.white;
            token = st.nextToken ();
        } else if (token.equals ("lightgray")) {
            color = Color.white;
            token = st.nextToken ();
        } else if (token.equals ("gray")) {
            color = Color.gray;
            token = st.nextToken ();
        } else if (token.equals ("darkgray")) {
            color = Color.darkGray;
            token = st.nextToken ();
        } else if (token.equals ("black")) {
            color = Color.black;
            token = st.nextToken ();
        } else if (token.equals ("red")) {
            color = Color.red;
            token = st.nextToken ();
        } else if (token.equals ("pink")) {
            color = Color.pink;
            token = st.nextToken ();
        } else if (token.equals ("orange")) {
            color = Color.orange;
            token = st.nextToken ();
        } else if (token.equals ("yellow")) {
            color = Color.yellow;
            token = st.nextToken ();
        } else if (token.equals ("green")) {
            color = Color.green;
            token = st.nextToken ();
        } else if (token.equals ("magenta")) {
            color = Color.magenta;
            token = st.nextToken ();
        } else if (token.equals ("cyan")) {
            color = Color.cyan;
```

continued on next page

continued from previous page

```
                token = st.nextToken ();
        } else if (token.equals ("blue")) {
            color = Color.blue;
            token = st.nextToken ();
        } else {
            System.out.println ("Unknown color: "+token);
            System.out.println ("Line "+nlines);
            System.exit (1);
        }

        int npoints = 0;
        if (token.equals ("rect")) {
            npoints = getInt (st, pts, 4);
            type = Shape.rectType;
        } else if (token.equals ("oval")) {
            npoints = getInt (st, pts, 4);
            type = Shape.ovalType;
        } else if (token.equals ("arc")) {
            npoints = getInt (st, pts, 6);
            type = Shape.arcType;
        } else if (token.equals ("poly")) {
            npoints = getInt (st, pts, Shape.MaxPoints);
            type = Shape.polyType;
        } else {
            System.out.println ("Unknown shape: "+token);
            System.out.println ("Line "+nlines);
            System.exit (1);
        }
        shapes[nshapes++] = new Shape (type, npoints, pts, color);
    }
/*
 * close can throw an exception also, catch it for completeness
 */
    try {
        fs.close ();
    } catch (IOException e) {
        System.out.println (e);
    }

    Frame f = new Frame ("Drawing shapes");
    DrawApp drawApp = new DrawApp ();

    f.resize (410, 430);
    f.add ("Center", drawApp);
    f.show ();
}

/**
 * parse points
 * @param st - StringTokenizer for current line
 * @param pts[] - array of points to be returned
 * @param nmax - maximum number of points to accept
 */
```

```
static int getInt (StringTokenizer st, int pts[], int nmax) {

    int i;
    String token;

    for (i=0; i<nmax; i+=1) {
        if (st.hasMoreTokens () == false) break;
        token = st.nextToken ();
        try {
            pts[i] = Integer.valueOf (token).intValue ();
        } catch (NumberFormatException e) {
            System.out.println (e);
            System.out.println ("Line "+nlines);
            System.exit (1);
        }
    }
    return i;
}
}
```

2. Create the text file containing the shape definitions. Create a new file called testfile and enter the following text:

```
red rect 10 10 100 50
green oval 50 50 50 30
blue arc 75 75 60 70 45 90
cyan poly 100 100 200 200 300 100 100 100
```

3. Compile and test the application. Compile the application with javac or the makefile provided. DrawApp.java is an application and cannot be run as an applet. This is because it must open and read files from local disks. Test the application by typing

```
java DrawApp [file name]
```

When the application is started, a window will open and a red rectangle, green oval, blue arc, and cyan polygon will be drawn. Figure 3-5 shows an example of the output. Try editing testfile by changing colors, adding new shapes, or moving the shapes around. Then just run DrawApp again without recompiling. See if you can specify shapes in testfile that actually draw a picture.

How It Works

Unlike previous examples, class *DrawApp* extends class *Panel*. As discussed in How-To 3.1, *Applet* is a subclass of *Panel* and is only needed if a program is to be used as an applet. This example is used as an application exclusively; therefore, it is sufficient to create a subclass of *Panel*.

The class *Shape* contains all of the information necessary for a given shape. This includes the type of shape, its color, two integer arrays, and the number of points

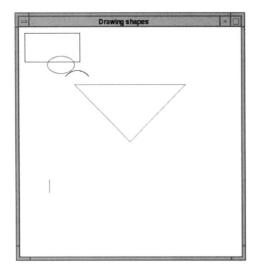

Figure 3-5 DrawApp application

in the arrays. The array *xp* is used to hold the coordinates, width, and height if the shape is a rectangle or oval. If the shape is an arc, two more parameters are used: the arc starting angle in degrees, and the number of degrees in the arc (relative to the starting angle). If the shape is a polygon, the *xp* array holds the x coordinates of the polygon vertices, and the *yp* array holds the y coordinates. The number of vertices in a polygon is stored in the variable *npoints*. The *yp* array and variable *npoints* are not used if the shape describes anything other than a polygon.

The *main()* method borrows some techniques from Chapter 2. It checks command line arguments for a file name and uses this to open the input file. Upon success, a *DataInputStream* is created in order to read from the input file. The file is read one line at a time. Each line is parsed using *StringTokenizer()* to split a line into tokens. The default delimiters for *StringTokenizer()* (spaces, tabs, and newlines) are sufficient, so they are not explicitly defined.

After a valid color is found, the program looks for one of the four possible shape names in the parameter and then reads the necessary number of points for the given shape. Rectangles and ovals require four points, whereas arcs require six. Polygons can take a variable number of points. All these cases are handled by the *getInt()* method. *getInt()* reads up to *nmax* points and returns the number of points actually found. After this is done, a new shape is created with the information parsed from the input line and then stored in an array of shapes.

The class *Shape* contains the *paint()* method in addition to its constructor. The *Shape.paint()* method is called from the *paint()* method in DrawApp, similar to previous examples. *Shape.paint()* sets the foreground color and draws the shape described in the class.

Comments

Rectangles are described by the top left corner, width, and height. It is best to use positive values for width and height in order to avoid anomalous behavior which may occur on some platforms. Ovals are described the same as rectangles; the oval is drawn inside the specified rectangle. Arcs are described by a bounding rectangle along with a starting angle in degrees and the number of degrees in the arc relative to the starting angle. Angles start from the positive x-axis (3 o'clock position) consistent with standard conventions. Positive arc angles indicate counterclockwise rotations; negative arc angles are drawn clockwise. Arcs are actually sections of ovals. The following code fragments draw the same shape:

```
drawOval (10, 10, 75, 90);
...

drawArc (10, 10, 75, 90, 0, 360);
...
```

Polygons are defined by an array of x points and y points. They can be drawn open, meaning the first and last vertices are not connected.

In addition to these four shapes, AWT supports several others. Table 3-3 lists the unfilled shape methods.

METHOD	DESCRIPTION
draw3DRect(int, int, int, int, boolean)	Draws a highlighted 3-D rectangle
drawArc(int, int, int, int, int, int)	Draws an arc bounded by the specified rectangle from startAngle to endAngle
drawOval(int, int, int, int)	Draws an oval inside the specified rectangle using the current color
drawPolygon(int[], int[], int)	Draws a polygon defined by an array of x points and y points
drawPolygon(Polygon)	Draws a polygon defined by the specified point
drawRect(int, int, int, int)	Draws the outline of the specified rectangle using the current color
drawRoundRect(int, int,	Draws an outlined rounded-int, int, int, int) corner rectangle using the current color

Table 3-3 Unfilled shape methods

DrawApp can be easily extended to support all of the shapes described earlier. In addition, filled shapes described in the following example can be added along with arbitrary color support. Other features like nonuniform rational B-splines (NURBS) could be implemented as line segments.

3.4   How do I...
Fill shapes?

Problem

I want to create classes that can draw bar and pie charts. The two types of charts share many similar features, so I want them to share a common superclass. I want to pass an array of values and colors along with coordinates and dimensions to a charts constructor.

I have a good idea of how to lay out the classes using unfilled shapes, but I want these charts to use filled shapes like the graphing utility in many spreadsheet programs. How do I fill shapes?

Technique

The class *Graphics* contains filled-shape counterparts to the unfilled shapes described in the previous example. They will be used to do the drawing.

Steps

1. Create the applet source file. Create a new file called ChartApp.java and enter the following source:

```
import java.applet.Applet;
import java.awt.*;

/**
 * Parent class
 */
class Chart {

/*
 * x and y positions of upper left of the chart
 * nvalues - number of values for this chart
 */
int xpos, ypos, nvalues;

/*
 * Width and height of this chart
 */
int width, height;

/*
 * Maximum number of values allowed
 */
```

```
final int MaxValues = 10;

/*
 * Data values for this chart
 */
double values[] = new double[MaxValues];

/*
 * Color associated with each value
 */
Color colors[] = new Color[MaxValues];

/*
 * Sum total of values, used for scaling purposes
 */
double total;

/**
 * Class constructor
 * Saves values and normalizes them so that the max. value is 1.0
 * @param x, y - top left coordinates
 * @param w, h - width and height
 * @param n - number of points
 * @param val[] - array of values
 * @param c[] - array of colors corresponding to values
 */
public Chart (int x, int y, int w, int h, int n, double val[], Color c[]) {

    int i;
    double extreme;

    xpos = x;
    ypos = y;
    width = w;
    height = h;
    nvalues = n;
    if (nvalues > MaxValues) nvalues = MaxValues;
    extreme = 0.0;
    for (i=0; i<nvalues; i+=1) {
        if (Math.abs (val[i]) > extreme)
            extreme = Math.abs (val[i]);
        colors[i] = c[i];
    }
    extreme = 1/extreme;
    total = 0;
    for (i=0; i<nvalues; i+=1) {
        values[i] = extreme * val[i];
        total += values[i];
    }
}
}

/**
```

continued on next page

continued from previous page

```
 * Class implements a bar chart.
 */
class BarChart extends Chart {

/**
 * Constructor just calls Chart constructor.
 * @param x, y - top left coordinates
 * @param w, h - width and height
 * @param n - number of points
 * @param val[] - array of values
 * @param c[] - array of colors corresponding to values
 */
public BarChart (int x, int y, int w, int h, int n, double val[], Color
➡ c[]) {

    super (x, y, w, h, n, val, c);
}

/**
 * Need to add a paint method
 * Draws the bar chart using fill3DRect
 * @param g - destination graphics object
 */
void paint (Graphics g) {

    int i;
    int barwidth = 3 * width / (4 * nvalues);
    int bardx = width / nvalues;
    int x, y, h;

    g.setColor (Color.black);
    g.fillRect (xpos, ypos-height, width, height);
    for (i=0; i<nvalues; i+=1) {
        g.setColor (colors[i]);
        x = xpos + bardx*i;
        h = (int) (values[i] * height);
        y = ypos - h;
        g.fill3DRect (x, y, barwidth, h, true);
    }
}
}

/**
 * Class implements a pie chart.
 */
class PieChart extends Chart {

/**
 * Class constructor just calls Chart constructor.
 * @param x, y - top left coordinates
 * @param w, h - width and height
 * @param n - number of points
 * @param val[] - array of values
```

```
 * @param c[] - array of colors corresponding to values
 */
public PieChart (int x, int y, int w, int h, int n, double val[], Color
➥c[]) {

    super (x, y, w, h, n, val, c);
}

/**
 * Need to add a paint method
 * Draws the pie chart using fillArc
 * @param g - destination graphics object
 */
void paint (Graphics g) {

    int i, y;
    int startAngle, arcAngle;

    startAngle = 0;
    y = ypos - height;
    for (i=0; i<nvalues; i+=1) {
        arcAngle = (int) (360.0 * values[i] / total);
        g.setColor (colors[i]);
        g.fillArc (xpos, y, width, height, startAngle, arcAngle);
        startAngle += arcAngle;
    }
}
}

/**
 * The applet/application proper
 */
public class ChartApp extends Applet {

/*
 * Width and height of the bounding panel
 */
int width, height;

/*
 * Instances of BarChart and PieChart
 */
BarChart bc1;
PieChart pc1;

/*
 * Called when applet is loaded
 * Generate random values and plot them.
 */
public void init () {

    int i;
    Dimension d = size ();
    double values[] = new double[5];
```

continued on next page

continued from previous page

```
    Color colors[] = new Color[5];

    width = d.width;
    height = d.height;
    colors[0] = Color.white;
    colors[1] = Color.orange;
    colors[2] = Color.yellow;
    colors[3] = Color.green;
    colors[4] = Color.magenta;

    for (i=0; i<5; i+=1) values[i] = Math.random () + 0.001;
    int w = (width-40)/2;
    int h = height-20;
    bc1 = new BarChart (10, height-10, w, h, 5, values, colors);
    pc1 = new PieChart (width/2, height-10, w, h, 5, values, colors);
}

/**
 * Invoke the chart paint methods.
 * @param g - destination graphics object
 */
public void paint (Graphics g) {

    bc1.paint (g);
    pc1.paint (g);
}

/**
 * Application entry point
 * Create a window frame and add the applet inside.
 * @param args[] - command line arguments
 */
public static void main (String args[]) {

    Frame f = new Frame ("Charts");
    ChartApp chart = new ChartApp ();

    f.resize (410, 230);
    f.add ("Center", chart);
    f.show ();
    chart.init ();
    chart.start ();
}
}
```

2. Create an HTML document that contains the applet. Create a new file called howto34.html as follows:

```
<html>
<head>
<title>Charts</title>
</head>
<applet code="ChartApp.class" width=400 height=200>
</applet>
```

```
<hr size=4>

</html>
```

3. Compile and test the applet. Compile the source using javac or the makefile provided. Test the applet using the Appletviewer by entering the following command:

```
APPLETVIEWER howto34.html
```

ChartApp.java may also be run as an application by typing

```
java ChartApp
```

When the applet is executed, a window with a bar chart and pie chart drawn inside it will open, as seen in Figure 3-6.

How It Works

The class *Chart* is the superclass for both bar and pie charts. Its constructor stores the array of values along with their corresponding colors. The values are normalized such that the largest value is 1.0. This makes the code more efficient, because the *paint()* method need only scale the values to the specified width and height. The total value is also computed, as it is needed for the pie chart.

The class *BarChart* extends class *Chart* so that it can inherit the variables and constructor. The constructor for *BarChart* simply passes its arguments to the *Chart* constructor by invoking its *super()* method. The *paint()* method is unique to each type of chart, so it must be defined in *BarChart.BarChart.paint()* scales the array of values to the specified height and draws the chart.

The class *PieChart* is similar. Its constructor also calls the *Chart* constructor by invoking *super()*. The *paint()* method draws the pie chart itself.

Comments

In addition to the filled shapes demonstrated, AWT supports several others. Table 3-4 lists the filled-shape methods.

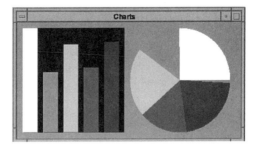

Figure 3-6 ChartApp applet

METHOD	DESCRIPTION
fill3DRect(int, int, int, int, boolean)	Paints a highlighted 3-D rectangle using the current color
fillArc(int, int, int, int, int, int)	Fills an arc using the current color
fillOval(int, int, int, int)	Fills an oval inside the specified rectangle using the current color
fillPolygon(int[], int[], int)	Fills a polygon with the current color using an even-odd fill rule (otherwise known as an alternating rule)
fillPolygon(Polygon)	Fills the specified polygon with the current color using an even-odd fill rule (otherwise known as an alternating rule)
fillRect(int, int, int, int)	Fills the specified rectangle with the current color
fillRoundRect(int, int, int, int, int, int)	Draws a rounded rectangle filled in with the current color

Table 3-4 Filled shape methods

COMPLEXITY
BEGINNING

3.5   How do I...
Draw text?

Problem

In Chapter 2, text was printed to the screen with *println()*. This method will not work to draw text in a graphic window. I would like to create a scrolling text marquee with the capability of moving the text in various directions. How do I draw text in a graphic window?

Technique

The *Graphics* class contains the method *drawString()*. This method is used to draw text in a graphics window. The *drawString()* method takes the string to be drawn and the position of the starting point of the baseline of the string as arguments.

Steps

1. Create the applet source file. Create a new file called ScrollApp.java and enter the following source:

```
import java.applet.Applet;
import java.awt.*;

/**
 * A class that handles scrolling text
 */
```

```
class Scroll {

/*
 * x and y coordinates of starting point
 */
int xstart, ystart;

/*
 * Width and height of bounding panel
 */
int width, height;

/*
 * The text to be scrolled
 */
String text;

/*
 * x and y velocities, respectively
 */
int deltaX, deltaY;

/*
 * The current x and y position of the text
 */
int xpos, ypos;

/*
 * The color of the text
 */
Color color;

/**
 * Class constructor just saves arguments.
 * @param x, y - starting coordinates
 * @param dx, dy - x and y velocities
 * @param w, h - width and height of bounding panel
 * @param t - the text string
 * @param c - color of the text
 */
public Scroll (int x, int y, int dx, int dy, int w, int h, String t, Color
➥c) {

    xstart = x;
    ystart = y;
    width = w;
    height = h;
    text = t;
    deltaX = dx;
    deltaY = dy;
    color = c;
    xpos = xstart;
    ypos = ystart;
```

continued on next page

continued from previous page

```
}

/*
 * Draw the text at the current position.
 * Advance the position and reinitialize  outside bounding panel.
 * @param g - destination graphics object
 */
void paint (Graphics g) {

    g.setColor (color);
    g.drawString (text, xpos, ypos);
    xpos += deltaX;
    ypos += deltaY;

    FontMetrics fm = g.getFontMetrics ();
    int textw = fm.stringWidth (text);
    int texth = fm.getHeight ();
    if (deltaX < 0 && xpos < -textw) xpos = xstart;
    if (deltaX > 0 && xpos > width) xpos = xstart;
    if (deltaY < 0 && ypos < 0) ypos = ystart;
    if (deltaY > 0 && ypos > height+texth) ypos = ystart;
}
}

/**
 * The applet/application proper
 */
public class ScrollApp extends Applet {

/*
 * Width and height of the bounding panel
 */
int width, height;

/*
 * Instances of Scroll for demonstration
 */
Scroll left, right, up, down, diag;

/*
 * Called when the applet is loaded
 * Create new instances of Scroll.
 */
public void init () {

    Dimension d = size ();

    width = d.width;
    height = d.height;

    left = new Scroll (400, 50, -5, 0, width, height,
        "Moving left", Color.red);
    right = new Scroll (0, 150, 5, 0, width, height,
        "Moving right", Color.green);
```

```
    up = new Scroll (100, 200, 0, -5, width, height,
        "Moving up", Color.blue);
    down = new Scroll (200, 0, 0, 5, width, height,
        "Moving down", Color.cyan);
    diag = new Scroll (0, 0, 7, 3, width, height,
        "Moving diagonally", Color.magenta);
}

/*
 * Invoke the paint method of each scrolling text instance.
 * Force a repaint 50ms later.
 */
public void paint (Graphics g) {

    left.paint (g);
    right.paint (g);
    up.paint (g);
    down.paint (g);
    diag.paint (g);
    repaint (50);
}

/*
 * Application entry point
 * @param args - command line arguments
 */
public static void main (String args[]) {

    Frame f = new Frame ("Scrolling text");
    ScrollApp scrollApp = new ScrollApp ();

    f.resize (410, 230);
    f.add ("Center", scrollApp);
    f.show ();
    scrollApp.init ();
}
}
```

2. Create an HTML document that contains the applet. Create a new file called howto35.html as follows:

```
<html>
<head>
<title>Scrolling Text</title>
</head>
<applet code="ScrollApp.class" width=400 height=200>
</applet>
<hr size=4>

</html>
```

3. Compile and test the applet. Compile the source using javac or the makefile provided. Test the applet using the Appletviewer by entering the following command:

```
APPLETVIEWER howto35.html
```

ScrollApp.java may also be run as an application by typing

`java ScrollApp`

When the applet is started, a window will open with five text strings scrolling in different directions. There will be one each string scrolling left, right, up, down, and diagonally. Figure 3-7 shows an example of the running applet.

How It Works

The class *Scroll* maintains all the information necessary to draw scrolling text. *xpos* and *ypos* are the initial positions of the text. When the text scrolls completely off the screen, it is moved back to the initial position. *deltaX* and *deltaY* are the velocities in the x and y directions, respectively. Positive and negative values are allowed, so that text can scroll in any direction. *width* and *height* are the width and height of the bounding panel; these are used to determine if the text has scrolled off the panel that contains the applet. *text* is the text to be scrolled, and *color* is the color of the text.

The *Scroll* constructor simply saves all of the parameters passed to it by the caller. Additional constructors could be defined that take fewer arguments and provide default actions. The constructor shown here is the most general.

The *paint()* method defined in class *Scroll* does all the work. It sets the foreground color to the color for this object and draws the text using *Graphics.drawString()*. *Graphics.drawString()* takes three arguments: the text to be scrolled, and its x and y positions. The x and y positions specify the bottom left corner of an imaginary rectangle enclosing the text. The current position is incremented by the velocity values as in previous examples.

The text in this example is drawn without specifying a font, therefore the default font is used. The discussion of using fonts in Java is left for How-To 3.6. However, it is necessary to explain a few concepts concerning fonts. The class *FontMetrics* is used to determine the width and height of the text. This is necessary because the width and height of text drawn graphically depends on the attributes of the font. *FontMetrics.stringWidth()* and *FontMetrics.getHeight()* perform exactly these functions. The text width and height are used to determine if the text has scrolled off the panel. If it has, it is moved back to the initial position.

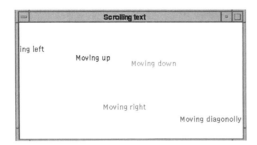

Figure 3-7 ScrollApp applet

The class *ScrollApp* is the applet itself. If the program is run as an application, the *main()* method will create a window frame and place an instance of the applet inside the frame. The applet entry point is the *init()* method. Five instances of class *Scroll* are created. Each instance has a different initial position, velocity, text, and color. *ScrollApp.paint()* simply invokes the *paint()* methods of each of the scrolling objects and forces a repaint 50 milliseconds later.

Comments

This example used *FontMetrics.stringWidth()* to determine the length of the string and *FontMetrics().getHeight()* to determine the height of the font. It is important to note that the *getHeight()* method returns the sum of *getLeading* + *getAscent* + *getDescent*. The *getLeading()* method returns the standard *leading,* or line spacing, of the font. This is the amount of space to be reserved between the descent of one line and the ascent of the next line. The *getAscent()* method returns the *font ascent,* which is the distance from the baseline to the top of the characters. The *getDescent()* method returns the distance from the baseline to the bottom of the characters, or the *font descent.* In this example, only ascent and descent are needed, but *getHeight()* was used to save time. The difference is not noticeable. The methods available from *FontMetrics* are summarized in Table 3-5.

METHODS	DESCRIPTION
FontMetrics(Font)	Creates a new FontMetrics object with the specified font
bytesWidth(byte[], int, int)	Returns the width of the specified array of bytes in this font
charWidth(int)	Returns the width of the specified character in this font
charWidth(char)	Returns the width of the specified character in this font
charsWidth(char[], int, int)	Returns the width of the specified character array in this font
getAscent()	Gets the font ascent
getDescent()	Gets the font descent
getFont()	Gets the font
getHeight()	Gets the total height of the font
getLeading()	Gets the standard leading, or line spacing, for the font
getMaxAdvance()	Gets the maximum advance width of any character in this font
getMaxAscent()	Gets the maximum ascent of all characters in this font
getMaxDescent ()	For backward compatibility only
getMaxDescent()	Gets the maximum descent of all characters
getWidths()	Gets the widths of the first 256 characters in the font
stringWidth(String)	Returns the width of the specified String in this font
toString()	Returns the String representation of this FontMetric's values

Table 3-5 FontMetrics methods

When this marquee is running, you may notice a considerable flickering of the text. The flickering can be eliminated with the use of double buffering. This will be discussed in Chapter 6.

COMPLEXITY
INTERMEDIATE

3.6 How do I...
Use fonts?

Problem

Programs are more visually interesting when different fonts and text styles are used. I want to write a utility that prints text in all the fonts available in normal, bold, and italic styles. I know how to draw text, but I need to change the font and text style. How do I find out what fonts and styles are available? How do I implement these fonts and styles?

Technique

When text is drawn in a given graphics context, the current font, style, and size are used. To draw text with a different font, the current font must be changed by using *Graphics.setFont()*. *Graphics.setFont()* takes a *Font* object as an argument. The style and size of the font are supplied as parameters to the *Font* constructor.

To determine which fonts are available, the method *getFontList()* is used. It returns an array of strings that are the names of available fonts. To create a font, the *Font* constructor is invoked with the name, style, and size as arguments.

Steps

1. Create the applet source file. Create a new file called Fonts.java and enter the following source:

```
import java.applet.Applet;
import java.awt.*;

/**
 * Class that determines which fonts are available
 */
public class Fonts extends Applet {

/*
 * Maximum number of fonts to display
 */
final int MaxFonts = 10;

/*
```

```
 * Width and height of bounding panel
 */
int width, height;

/*
 * Array of font names
 */
String fontName[];

/*
 * Array of fonts
 * Holds plain, italic, and bold for each font
 */
Font theFonts[] = new Font[3 * MaxFonts];

/*
 * The number of fonts found
 */
int nfonts = 0;

/*
 * Applet entry point
 */
public void init () {

    int i;
    Dimension d = size ();

    width = d.width;
    height = d.height;
    fontName = Toolkit.getDefaultToolkit().getFontList ();

    nfonts = fontName.length;
    if (nfonts > MaxFonts) nfonts = MaxFonts;
    for (i=0; i<nfonts; i+=1) {
        theFonts[3*i + 0] = new Font (fontName[i], Font.PLAIN, 12);
        theFonts[3*i + 1] = new Font (fontName[i], Font.BOLD, 12);
        theFonts[3*i + 2] = new Font (fontName[i], Font.ITALIC, 12);
    }
}

/*
 * Draw the font names.
 * @param g - destination graphics object
 */
public void paint (Graphics g) {

    int i;

    for (i=0; i<nfonts; i+=1) {
        g.setFont (theFonts[3*i + 0]);
        g.drawString (fontName[i], 10, 20*i+30);
        g.setFont (theFonts[3*i + 1]);
```

continued on next page

continued from previous page

```
        g.drawString ("Bold", 70, 20*i+30);
        g.setFont (theFonts[3*i + 2]);
        g.drawString ("Italic", 150, 20*i+30);
    }
}

/*
 * Application entry point
 * Creates a window frame and adds the applet inside
 * @param args[] - command line arguments
 */
public static void main (String args[]) {

    Frame f = new Frame ("Fonts");
    Fonts fonts = new Fonts ();

    f.resize (200, 200);
    f.add ("Center", fonts);
    f.show ();
    fonts.init ();
}
}
```

2. Create an HTML document that contains the applet. Create a new file called howto36.html as follows:

```
<html>
<head>
<title>Fonts</title>
</head>
<applet code="Fonts.class" width=200 height=200>
</applet>
<hr size=4>

</html>
```

3. Compile and test the applet. Compile the source using javac or the makefile provided. Test the applet using the Appletviewer by entering the following command:

```
APPLETVIEWER howto36.html
```

Fonts.java may also be run as an application by typing

```
java Fonts
```

When *Fonts* is executed, a window will pop up with the different font styles printed in plain, bold, and italic. Figure 3-8 shows an example of the running applet.

Figure 3-8 Fonts
applet

How It Works

The *init()* method gets the list of fonts by invoking *getFontList()*. This method is contained in the abstract class *Toolkit*. *getFontList()* is not defined as static, so it cannot be invoked via *Toolkit.getFontList()*. *Toolkit* is abstract, so an instance of it cannot be created. To call *getFontList()*, it needs to be invoked as *Toolkit.getDefaultToolkit().getFontList()*. This returns an array of strings, the length of which is the number of fonts available.

An array is created that will hold each of the fonts in plain, bold, and italic styles. The array is initialized using the *Font* constructor with the font name, style, and size as arguments. A fixed size of 12 was used in this example. The font styles are constants defined in class *Font*; they are summarized in Table 3-6. The style constants can be added to produce combined styles.

The method *paint()* simply goes through the array of fonts, sets the font using *Graphics.setFont()*, and draws the name of the font and the text "bold" and "italic" in their respective styles.

CONSTANT	DESCRIPTION
BOLD	The bold style constant
ITALIC	The italicized style constant
PLAIN	The plain style constant

Table 3-6 Font styles

Comments

Methods exist to obtain various properties of the font being used, such as width, height, and line spacing. These methods are contained in the *FontMetrics* class. The example in How-To 3.5 illustrated the use of the *FontMetrics* class.

The methods available in class *Font* are listed in Table 3-7.

METHOD	DESCRIPTION
Font(String, int, int)	(Constructor) Creates a new font with the specified name, style, and point size
equals(Object)	Compares this object to the specified object
getFamily()	Gets the platform-specific family name of the font
getFont(String)	Gets a font from the system properties list
getFont(String, Font)	Gets the specified font from the system properties list
getName()	Gets the logical name of the font
getSize()	Gets the point size of the font
getStyle()	Gets the style of the font
hashCode()	Returns a hash code for this font
isBold()	Returns True if the font is bold
isItalic()	Returns True if the font is italic
isPlain()	Returns True if the font is plain
toString()	Converts this object to a String representation

Table 3-7 Font methods

COMPLEXITY
INTERMEDIATE

3.7 How do I...
Handle screen updates?

Problem

I want to create an applet that draws text that jumps around in different colors without erasing the previously drawn text. The previous examples showed me how to do most of what I want, but they all erase the panel before drawing. I don't want to do that. I want to give the effect of the text growing on top of itself. How do I handle screen updates, or the lack thereof?

Technique

In all of the previous examples, the *paint()* method was used exclusively to do the drawing. The *paint()* method is called from the *update()* method. The default *update()* method fills the panel with the background color and then calls *paint()*. The result is that any previously drawn graphics are erased. To prevent previously drawn graphics from being erased, the default *update()* method must be overridden and replaced with a method that does not erase the panel.

The rest of the applet uses many of the techniques described previously.

Steps

1. Create the applet source file. Create a new file called CrazyText.java and enter the following source:

```java
import java.applet.Applet;
import java.awt.*;

/*
 * Application/applet class
 */
public class CrazyText extends Applet {

String text = "Java";    // String to be displayed
int delta = 5;           // "Craziness" factor: max pixel offset
String fontName = "TimesRoman";
int fontSize = 36;

char chars[];        // Individual chars in 'text'
int positions[];     // Base horizontal position for each char
FontMetrics fm;

/*
 * Called when the applet is loaded
 * Creates a font and initializes positions of characters
 */
public void init() {

    int fontStyle = Font.BOLD + Font.ITALIC;
    setFont(new Font(fontName, fontStyle, fontSize));
    fm = getFontMetrics(getFont());

    chars = new char[text.length()];
    text.getChars(0, text.length(), chars, 0);

    positions = new int[text.length()];
    for (int i = 0; i < text.length(); i++) {
        positions[i] = fm.charsWidth(chars, 0, i) + 20;
    }
}

/*
 * Draws the characters and forces a repaint 100ms later
 * @param g - destination graphics object
 */
public void paint (Graphics g) {

    int x, y;
    g.setColor (new Color((float) Math.random(),
            (float) Math.random(),
            (float) Math.random()));
    for (int i = 0; i < text.length(); i++) {
        x = (int)(Math.random() * delta * 2) + positions[i];
        y = (int)(Math.random() * delta * 2) + fm.getAscent() - 1;
```

continued on next page

continued from previous page

```
        g.drawChars (chars, i, 1, x, y);
    }
    repaint (100);
}

/*
 * Override default update() method to eliminate
 * erasing of the panel.
 */
public void update (Graphics g) {
    paint (g);
}

/*
 * Application entry point
 * Create a window frame and add the applet inside.
 * @param args[] - command line arguments
 */
public static void main (String args[]) {

    Frame f = new Frame ("Crazy");
    CrazyText crazy = new CrazyText ();

    f.resize (130, 80);
    f.add ("Center", crazy);
    f.show ();
    crazy.init ();
}
}
```

2. Create an HTML document that contains the applet. Create a new file called howto37.html as follows:

```
<html>
<head>
<title>Crazy Text</title>
</head>
<applet code="CrazyText" width=200 height=200>
</applet>
<hr size=2>
</html>
```

3. Compile and test the applet. Compile the source using javac or the makefile provided. Test the applet using the Appletviewer by entering the following command:

```
APPLETVIEWER howto37.html
```

CrazyText.java may also be run as an application by typing

```
java CrazyText
```

Figure 3-9
CrazyText
applet

When CrazyText is executed, a window will pop up with "Java" printed. As the applet is running, "Java" is repeatedly printed in different colors, and each character is moved slightly in a direction independent of the other characters. However, each time the characters are printed, the screen is not updated, and the previous printed characters are not erased. This produces an interesting effect. Figure 3-9 shows a snapshot of the running applet.

How It Works

The *init()* method creates a new 36-point, bold, italic Times Roman font. This is set as the default font for the panel. The characters for the text are extracted and put into an array of *char*s, so that they may be drawn individually. This is done by using the *String.getChars()* method. An array of positions is also maintained. This array holds the position offset from the left edge of each of the characters. The positions are calculated by using the *FontMetrics.charsWidth()* method, which determines the width of one character.

The method *paint()* sets the foreground color to a random value by using the *Math.random()* method. The characters are drawn, one at a time, with random variation in position by using the *Graphics.drawChars()* method. *Graphics.drawChars()* is similar to *Graphics.drawText()*, but takes an array of characters instead of a *String* as an argument.

The method *update()* overrides the default *update()* method. The default *update* method looks like this:

```
public void update (Graphics g) {
    g.setColor (getBackground ());
    g.fillRect (0, 0, width, height);
    g.setColor (getForeground ());
    paint (g);
}
```

The entire component is filled with the background color. The color is then set to the foreground color and method *paint()* is called. To prevent filling the component with the background color, the first three lines can be deleted, leaving only the call to *paint()*. The second call to *setColor()* is not needed because it would be redundant.

Comments

It appears that the code in the *paint()* method could be moved to the *update()* method and the *paint()* method eliminated entirely. This, however, will not work. The reason is that when an applet or application is first started, the *paint()* method, not *update()*, is called. If there is no *paint()* method defined, the default *paint()* method is used. The default *paint()* method does nothing, so no further calls to *update()* would be made, because *repaint()* was not called. The *update()* method must be called at least once to get the show started. Here is an example of an alternate solution:

```
public void update (Graphics g) {

    int x, y;
    g.setColor (new Color((float) Math.random(),
            (float) Math.random(),
            (float) Math.random()));
    for (int i = 0; i < text.length(); i++) {
        x = (int)(Math.random() * delta * 2) + positions[i];
        y = (int)(Math.random() * delta * 2) + fm.getAscent() - 1;
        g.drawChars (chars, i, 1, x, y);
    }
    repaint (100);
}

public void paint (Graphics g) {
    update (g);
}
```

In this code, when the applet is first started, *paint()* is called, which calls *update()*, and *update()* does the drawing. All subsequent calls from *repaint()* go directly to *update()*, and *paint()* is out of the loop. This solution is slightly more efficient than the code in the example.

COMPLEXITY
INTERMEDIATE

3.8   How do I...
Print applet status messages?

Problem

I liked the line-drawing applet that drew lines in shifting colors. What I want to do is add the necessary code to print the values of the red, green, and blue components of the foreground color as they change. I don't want to put this in the panel where the lines are bouncing. Rather, I want to print the color values in the status bar in the Netscape browser or in the Appletviewer. I know how to get the color component values, but how do I print applet status messages?

Technique

The status bar in the Appletviewer, Netscape browser, or other Java-enabled application can be accessed by the *Applet.showStatus()* method. This method takes a string as an argument that is the string to be printed in the status bar. In this example, the string will be comprised of hard-coded text concatenated with methods which return integer values. The current foreground red, green, and blue color components can be determined by calling the *Graphics.getColor().getRed()*, *Graphics.getColor().getGreen()*, and *Graphics.getColor().getBlue()* methods, respectively.

Steps

1. Create the applet source file. Create a new file called Status.java and enter the following source:

```java
import java.applet.Applet;
import java.awt.*;

/*
 * Class to hold color values
 */
class LineColors {

/*
 * An array of colors proper
 */
Color color[];

/*
 * The constructor initializes the color array using
 * an arbitrary algorithm.
 */
public LineColors () {

        color = new Color[24];
        int i, rgb;

        rgb = 0xff;
        for (i=0; i<24; i+=1) {
                color[i] = new Color (rgb);
                rgb <<= 1;
                if ((rgb & 0x1000000) != 0) {
                        rgb |= 1;
                        rgb &= 0xffffff;
                }
        }
}
}
} // class LineColors
```

continued on next page

continued from previous page

```
/*
 * Class to handle the drawing of one line segment
 */
class Segment {

/*
 * x1, y1 - x and y position of first endpoint
 * x2, y2 - x and y position of second endpoint
 */
double x1, y1, x2, y2;

/*
 * Velocities of the endpoints respectively
 */
double dx1, dy1, dx2, dy2;

/*
 * whichcolor - color index for this segment
 */
int whichcolor;

/*
 * Width and height of bounding panel
 */
int width, height;

/*
 * Instance of LineColors
 */
LineColors LC;

/*
 * Class constructor
 * Saves arguments and initializes position and velocities
 * to random values
 * @param w, h - width and height of bounding panel
 * @param c - starting color
 * @param lc - instance of LineColor
 */
public Segment (int w, int h, int c, LineColors lc) {

        whichcolor = c;
        width = w;
        height = h;
        LC = lc;
        x1 = (double) w * Math.random ();
        y1 = (double) h * Math.random ();
        x2 = (double) w * Math.random ();
        y2 = (double) h * Math.random ();

        dx1 = 5 - 10 * Math.random ();
        dy1 = 5 - 10 * Math.random ();
        dx2 = 5 - 10 * Math.random ();
```

```
        dy2 = 5 - 10 * Math.random ();
}

/*
 * Increments color index and calculates new endpoint positions
 */
void compute () {

        whichcolor += 1;
        whichcolor %= 24;

        x1 += dx1;
        y1 += dy1;
        x2 += dx2;
        y2 += dy2;

        if (x1 < 0 || x1 > width) dx1 = -dx1;
        if (y1 < 0 || y1 > height) dy1 = -dy1;
        if (x2 < 0 || x2 > width) dx2 = -dx2;
        if (y2 < 0 || y2 > height) dy2 = -dy2;
}

/**
 * Prints status message showing the values of the different colors
 * @param g - destination graphics object
 */
void paint (Graphics g) {

        g.setColor (LC.color [whichcolor]);
        g.drawLine ((int) x1, (int) y1, (int) x2, (int) y2);
}
} // class Segment

public class Status extends Applet {

/*
 * Width and height of bounding panel
 */
int width, height;

/*
 * The number of lines will be set to 1, because the color values
 * displayed will only be valid for one line.
 */
final int NLines = 1;

/*
 * Array of instances of Segment
 */
Segment lines[] = new Segment[NLines];

/*
 * Instance of LineColor
```

continued on next page

continued from previous page

```
 */
LineColors LC = new LineColors ();

/*
 * Called when applet is loaded
 * Save panel dimensions and create instance of Segment.
 */
public void init () {

        Dimension d = size ();

        width = d.width;
        height = d.height;

        int i;
        for (i=0; i<NLines; i+=1)
                lines[i] = new Segment (width, height, (2*i) % 24, LC);
}

/**
 * Draw the line and print status message.
 * @param g - destination graphics object
 */
public void paint (Graphics g) {

        int i;
        for (i=0; i<NLines; i+=1) {
                lines[i].compute ();
                lines[i].paint (g);
        }
        showStatus("red = "+g.getColor().getRed() + "  green = " +
                g.getColor().getGreen() + "   blue = " +
                g.getColor().getBlue());

        repaint (50);
}
}
```

2. Create an HTML document that contains the applet. Create a new file called howto38.html as follows:

```
<html>
<head>
<title>Applet Status</title>
</head>
<applet code="Status" width=200 height=200>
</applet>
<hr size=2>
</html>
```

3. Compile and test the applet. Compile the source using javac or the makefile provided. Test the applet using the Appletviewer by entering the following command:

Figure 3-10 Status applet

`APPLETVIEWER howto38.html`

Status.java may not be run as an application, because applications do not support the printing of status messages.

When Status is executed, a window will pop up with a "flying line" bouncing around while changing colors. This is identical to the example in How-To 3.2, except that only one line is used. One line is used because the multiple lines all had different colors; the color status being printed can only indicate the color of one line. Figure 3-10 shows a snapshot of the running applet. This illustrates the power and usefulness of the *showStatus()* method.

How It Works

Most of the code is identical to that of How-To 3.2. The difference is the addition of calls to *showStatus()* in *Status.paint()*. *ShowStatus()* takes a string as an argument and is straightforward.

CHAPTER 4
THREADS

4

THREADS

How do I...

All of the programs shown so far have been sequential programs. A *sequential program* has a beginning, an end, a sequence, and at any given time during the runtime there is a single point of execution. A *thread* is a single sequential flow of control within a process. A thread is very similar to a sequential program—it has a beginning, an end, a sequence, and at any given time the thread has a single point of execution. But a thread itself is not a program, and cannot run on its own.

One of Java's greatest strengths is the multithreading capability. *Multithreading* is the capability to have multiple independent threads that share data and run asynchronously.

4.1 Create a Thread

This example demonstrates how to create a single thread within an applet. An analog clock is displayed, and the thread is used to control the clock update.

4.2 Create Multiple Threads

This example demonstrates the use of multiple threads in one program by using the Lines applet/application of Chapter 3. Two independent threads are created and executed to graphically show independent activity.

4.3 Change a Thread's Priority

The Lines applet/application is used again. Several instances of the Lines class are defined and executed. The priority of each thread is assigned a different value. A graphical display showing differences in process time results.

4.4 Synchronize Methods

Synchronization mechanisms are necessary in any system that contains subsystems that are asynchronous with respect to each other. The classic problem of the "Dining Philosophers" is an example. In this section, synchronization is achieved by specifying the synchronized modifier to critical methods.

This example shows an animated first-in, first-out (FIFO) structure, often called a *queue*. This type of data structure is commonly used to accommodate variation in data transfer rates in asynchronous systems. Synchronized methods are used to avoid random access of shared data.

4.5 Synchronize Code Sections

Java provides mechanisms for specifying critical sections at the statement level in addition to the method level. This is generally not recommended, but is demonstrated here for completeness.

The animated FIFO of the previous example is modified to show how code sections can be synchronized.

4.6 Wait for a Thread

There are many instances where one thread must wait for some condition to occur in another thread. One way to do this is to regularly check for the condition. This is known as *polling*. Polling can be inconvenient and slow. Threads can wait for each other by using the built-in thread waiting. The FIFO example is again used to demonstrate this.

COMPLEXITY
BEGINNING

4.1   How do I...
Create a thread?

Problem

I want to write a clock applet. It should display a clock face with hands for hours, minutes, and seconds. I know I could continuously get the time, look for a change, and update the clock, but this is inefficient. What I want to do is create a separate thread that sleeps for a tenth of a second or so and then reads the time. I know how to get the current time and how to draw the graphics, but I don't know how to create a thread. How do I create a thread?

Technique

Java supports threads intrinsically. To create a thread, a class must implement the Runnable interface or extend the *Thread* class. The *Thread* class itself implements the Runnable interface. If a class extends *Thread*, it automatically implements Runnable. This example implements the Runnable interface to create a thread.

An instance of class *Thread* must be created with the class containing the thread as an argument. If the class containing the thread is creating the instance of thread, the self-reference can be used.

Classes containing a separate thread must also create a *run()* method that accepts no arguments and returns void. The *run()* method will be called when the thread is started. A thread is started by invoking the *Thread.start()* method. It can be stopped either by invoking the *Thread.stop()* method, or by returning from the *run()* method.

Steps

1. Create the applet source file. Create a new file called Clock.java and enter the following source:

```
import java.awt.*;
import java.applet.*;
import java.util.Date;

/*
 * Class for applet/application
 */
```

continued on next page

continued from previous page

```java
public class Clock extends Applet implements Runnable {

/*
 * The instance of Thread for checking the time periodically
 */
Thread thread = null;

/*
 * Saved values used to draw only when things have changed
 */
int lastxs=0;
int lastys=0;
int lastxm=0;
int lastym=0;
int lastxh=0;
int lastyh=0;

/**
 * Draws the clock face
 * @param g - destination graphics object
 */
public void paint (Graphics g) {

    int xh, yh, xm, ym, xs, ys, s, m, h, xcenter, ycenter;
    Date dat = new Date();
    Dimension dim = size();


    s = dat.getSeconds();
    m = dat.getMinutes();
    h = dat.getHours();

    xcenter=dim.width >> 1;
    ycenter=dim.height >> 1;

    xs = (int)(Math.cos(s * 3.14f/30 - 3.14f/2) * 45 + xcenter);
    ys = (int)(Math.sin(s * 3.14f/30 - 3.14f/2) * 45 + ycenter);
    xm = (int)(Math.cos(m * 3.14f/30 - 3.14f/2) * 40 + xcenter);
    ym = (int)(Math.sin(m * 3.14f/30 - 3.14f/2) * 40 + ycenter);
    xh = (int)(Math.cos((h*30 + m/2) * 3.14f/180 - 3.14f/2) * 30
        + xcenter);
    yh = (int)(Math.sin((h*30 + m/2) * 3.14f/180 - 3.14f/2) * 30
        + ycenter);

// Draw the circle and numbers.
    g.setFont(new Font("TimesRoman", Font.PLAIN, 14));
    g.setColor(Color.blue);
    g.drawOval (xcenter-50, ycenter-50, 100, 100);
    g.setColor(Color.darkGray);
    g.drawString("9",xcenter-45,ycenter+3);
    g.drawString("3",xcenter+40,ycenter+3);
    g.drawString("12",xcenter-5,ycenter-37);
```

```
        g.drawString("6",xcenter-3,ycenter+45);

// Erase if necessary, and redraw.
        g.setColor(Color.lightGray);
        if (xs != lastxs || ys != lastys) {
            g.drawLine(xcenter, ycenter, lastxs, lastys);
        }
        if (xm != lastxm || ym != lastym) {
            g.drawLine(xcenter, ycenter-1, lastxm, lastym);
            g.drawLine(xcenter-1, ycenter, lastxm, lastym);
        }
        if (xh != lastxh || yh != lastyh) {
            g.drawLine(xcenter, ycenter-1, lastxh, lastyh);
            g.drawLine(xcenter-1, ycenter, lastxh, lastyh);
        }

        g.setColor(Color.darkGray);
        g.drawLine(xcenter, ycenter, xs, ys);
        g.setColor(Color.red);
        g.drawLine(xcenter, ycenter-1, xm, ym);
        g.drawLine(xcenter-1, ycenter, xm, ym);
        g.drawLine(xcenter, ycenter-1, xh, yh);
        g.drawLine(xcenter-1, ycenter, xh, yh);
        lastxs=xs; lastys=ys;
        lastxm=xm; lastym=ym;
        lastxh=xh; lastyh=yh;
}

/*
 * Called when the applet is started
 * Create a new instance of Thread and start it.
 */
public void start() {

    if(thread == null) {
        thread = new Thread(this);
        thread.start();
    }
}

/*
 * Called when the applet is stopped
 * Stops the thread
 */
public void stop() {

    thread = null;
}

/*
 * The thread itself
 * Sleeps for 100ms and forces a repaint
 */
```

continued on next page

continued from previous page

```java
public void run() {

    while (thread != null) {
        try {
            Thread.sleep(100);
        } catch (InterruptedException e) { }
        repaint();
    }
    thread = null;
}

/**
 * Override the default update method to avoid
 * flickering caused by unnecessary erasing of the applet panel.
 * @param g - destination graphics object
 */
public void update(Graphics g) {
    paint(g);
}

/**
 * Application entry point
 * Not used when run as an applet
 * Create a new window frame and add the applet inside.
 * @param args[] - command line arguments
 */
public static void main (String args[]) {

    Frame f = new Frame ("Clock");
    Clock clock = new Clock ();

    f.resize (210, 230);
    f.add ("Center", clock);
    f.show ();
    clock.init ();
    clock.start ();
}
}
```

2. Create an HTML document that contains the applet. Create a new file called howto41.html as follows:

```html
<html>
<head>
<title>Clock</title>
</head>
<applet code="Clock.class" width=200 height=200>
</applet>
<hr size=4>

</html>
```

3. Compile and test the applet. Compile the source using javac or the makefile provided. Test the applet using the Appletviewer by entering the following command:

```
APPLETVIEWER howto41.html
```

Clock.java may also be run as an application by typing

```
java Clock
```

When Clock is executed, a window will open with an analog clock running in the center of it. Figure 4-1 shows an example of the running applet.

How It Works

The clock applet contains only one class, the applet itself. The class implements Runnable in order to create a separate thread. When the applet is started, the *start()* method is called. The *start()* method creates a new Thread instance and starts it by invoking *Thread.start()*. The *stop()* method kills the thread by setting it to null.

The *run()* method in the clock applet is called when the thread is started. The *run()* method immediately enters an infinite loop that forces painting by calling *repaint()*. The thread sleeps for 100 milliseconds by calling the *Thread.sleep()* method with the number of milliseconds to sleep as an argument. Figure 4-2 shows the flow of the thread. *Thread.sleep()* throws InterruptedException, which must be caught. No action is taken, in this example, if InterruptedException is encountered.

The *update()* method is called asynchronously after a *repaint()*. This method overrides the default *update()* method to avoid flickering caused by erasing in the default *update()*. The new *update()* method simply calls *paint()*.

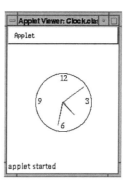

Figure 4-1 Clock applet

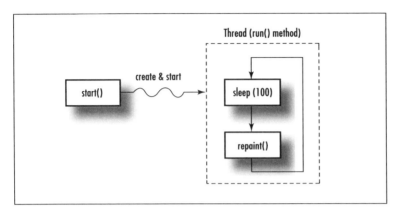

Figure 4-2 Clock applet thread

The *paint()* method does most of the work. It gets the current time by creating a new *Date()*. Simple trigonometry and line drawing are used to paint the clock hands. Drawing is done only once a second by testing the current second with the last second. The maximum error in the reading is 100 milliseconds, which is acceptable for most purposes.

Comments

The *Thread.sleep()* method only guarantees a minimum sleep time. The actual sleep time is dependent on system delays, priorities of other threads, and processes on the system.

COMPLEXITY
BEGINNING

4.2 How do I...
Create multiple threads?

Problem

I liked the *Lines* applet of Chapter 3. I want to create multiple panels with different *Lines* classes running in each. I could use a single thread to initiate drawing in each, but I would rather use multiple threads. I know how to create multiple instances of LineApp, but I don't know how to create multiple threads. How do I create multiple threads?

Technique

The *Lines* class is defined with an instance of Thread. Each instance of *Lines* creates a separate thread that can run independently. If multiple instances of Lines are created, multiple threads will execute.

The two instances of *Lines* are added to the main panel. This will display both threads running simultaneously.

Steps

1. Create the source file. Create a file called MultiThread.java and enter the following source:

```java
import java.applet.Applet;
import java.awt.*;

/**
 * Class LineColors holds 24 color values.
 */
class LineColors {

/**
 * color[] array holds the colors to be used.
 */
Color color[];

/**
 * Class constructor
 * Initializes the color array using an arbitrary algorithm
 */
public LineColors () {
    color = new Color[24];
    int i, rgb;

    rgb = 0xff;
    for (i=0; i<24; i+=1) {
        color[i] = new Color (rgb);
        rgb <<= 1;
        if ((rgb & 0x1000000) != 0) {
            rgb |= 1;
            rgb &= 0xffffff;
        }
    }
}
}

/**
 * Class describing one line segment
 */
class Segment {
```

continued on next page

continued from previous page

```
/*
 * x1, y1 - starting coordinates for this segment
 * x2, y2 - ending coordinates for this segment
 * dx1,...dy2 - velocities for the endpoints
 * whichcolor - the current index into color array
 * width, height - width and height of bounding panel
 * LC - instance of LineColors class
 */
double x1, y1, x2, y2;
double dx1, dy1, dx2, dy2;
int whichcolor, width, height;
LineColors LC;

/**
 * Class constructor
 * Initialize endpoints and velocities to random values
 * @param w - width of bounding panel
 * @param h - height of bounding panel
 * @param c - starting color index
 * @param lc - instance of LineColors class
 */
public Segment (int w, int h, int c, LineColors lc) {

    whichcolor = c;
    width = w;
    height = h;
    LC = lc;
    x1 = (double) w * Math.random ();
    y1 = (double) h * Math.random ();
    x2 = (double) w * Math.random ();
    y2 = (double) h * Math.random ();

    dx1 = 5 - 10 * Math.random ();
    dy1 = 5 - 10 * Math.random ();
    dx2 = 5 - 10 * Math.random ();
    dy2 = 5 - 10 * Math.random ();
}

/*
 * Increment color index.
 * Calculate the next endpoint position for this segment.
 */
void compute () {

    whichcolor += 1;
    whichcolor %= 24;

    x1 += dx1;
    y1 += dy1;
    x2 += dx2;
    y2 += dy2;

    if (x1 < 0 || x1 > width) dx1 = -dx1;
    if (y1 < 0 || y1 > height) dy1 = -dy1;
```

```
        if (x2 < 0 || x2 > width) dx2 = -dx2;
        if (y2 < 0 || y2 > height) dy2 = -dy2;
}

/**
 * Draw the line segment using the current color.
 * @param g - destination graphics object
 */
void paint (Graphics g) {

    g.setColor (LC.color [whichcolor]);
    g.drawLine ((int) x1, (int) y1, (int) x2, (int) y2);
}
}

/**
 * The applet/application proper
 */
class Lines extends Panel implements Runnable {

/*
 * width, height - width and height of bounding panel
 * NLines - number of line segments to be displayed
 * lines - array of instances of Segment class
 * LC - instance of LineColors class
 */
int width, height;
final int NLines = 4;
Segment lines[] = new Segment[NLines];
LineColors LC = new LineColors ();

/*
 * Instance of thread for this line
 */
Thread thread;

/**
 * init is called when the applet is loaded.
 * Save the width and height.
 * Create instances of Segment class.
 */
public void init () {

    Dimension d = size ();

    width = d.width;
    height = d.height;

    thread = new Thread (this);
    thread.start ();

    int i;
    for (i=0; i<NLines; i+=1)
```

continued on next page

continued from previous page

```
            lines[i] = new Segment (width, height, (2*i) % 24, LC);
}

/**
 * Recompute the next endpoint coordinates for each line.
 * Invoke paint() method for each line.
 * @param g - destination graphics object
 */
public void paint (Graphics g)
{

    int i;
    g.setColor (Color.black);
    g.drawRect (0, 0, width-1, height-1);
    for (i=0; i<NLines; i+=1) {
        lines[i].compute ();
        lines[i].paint (g);
    }
}

/*
 * The thread proper
 * Calls paint() every 50ms
 */
public void run()
{
    Graphics g = getGraphics();
    while (true) {
        paint (g);
        try {
            Thread.sleep (50);
        } catch(InterruptedException e) { }
    }
}
}

/*
 * The applet/application proper
 * Creates two instances of Lines and starts them
 * as separate threads
 */
public class MultiThread extends Applet {

/*
 * The instances of Lines
 */
Lines lines1;
Lines lines2;

/*
 * Called when the applet is loaded
 * Creates two instances of Lines and adds them to the
 * applet panel
```

```
    */
public void init () {

    setLayout (new GridLayout (2, 1, 0, 0));

    lines1 = new Lines ();
    lines2 = new Lines ();
    add (lines1);
    add (lines2);
    lines1.resize (200, 100);
    lines2.resize (200, 100);
    lines1.init ();
    lines2.init ();
}

/**
 * Application entry point, unused when run as an applet
 * Create window frame and add applet inside.
 * @param args[] - command line arguments
 */
public static void main (String args[]) {

    Frame f = new Frame ("Colored lines");
    f.setLayout (new GridLayout (2, 1, 0, 0));

    f.resize (200, 200);

    Lines lines1 = new Lines ();
    Lines lines2 = new Lines ();
    f.add (lines1);
    f.add (lines2);
    f.show ();
    lines1.init ();
    lines2.init ();
}
}
```

2. Create an HTML file that contains the applet. Create a file called howto42.html and enter the following text:

```
<html>
<head>
<title>Multi Thread</title>
</head>
<applet code="Multi Thread.class" width=200 height=200>
</applet>
<hr size=4>

</html>
```

3. Compile and test the applet/application. Compile the source using javac or use the makefile provided. Use the Appletviewer with the HTML file as an argument by typing

continued on next page

Figure 4-3
MultiThread
applet

```
appletviewer howto42.html
```

The program can be run as an application by typing

```
java MultiThread
```

When the program starts, a window should appear with two panels inside.
Each panel should display lines of changing color bouncing around inside.
Figure 4-3 shows an example of the running applet.

How It Works

The *Lines* class of Chapter 3 is modified slightly in order to handle multiple threads.
The *LineColors* and *Segment* classes are unchanged from the example in Chapter 3.

The *Lines* class extends Panel and implements Runnable. The Runnable interface
is necessary so that each instance of *Lines* can run as a separate thread. An instance
of Thread called *thread* is declared in the *Lines* class.

The *init()* method in the *Lines* class gets the width and height of its panel and saves
them for later use. A new instance is created by calling the *Thread()* constructor with
this as an argument. The thread is started by calling the *Thread.start()* method. Finally,
an array of *Lines* is created by calling the *Lines* constructor.

The *paint()* method in the *Lines* class is changed slightly from Chapter 3. It first
draws a black border around the panel so that each panel is more visible. It then computes and paints all of the lines for this instance by calling *Segment.compute()* and
Segment.paint().

The *run()* method is executed when the thread for this instance of *Lines* is started. The *run()* method enters an infinite loop that forces repainting and then sleeps
for 50 milliseconds. The cycle repeats forever.

The MultiThread class is the applet itself. If MultiThread is run as an applet, the *init()* method is called. If it is run as an application, the *main()* method is called. The *init()* method creates two instances of *Lines*, adds them to the applet panel, and starts them by calling their respective *init()* methods. The *main()* method is similar, but it must first create a window frame to contain the panels.

Comments

Creating multiple threads is no more difficult than creating single threads. An instance of Thread must be created for each class that contains an independent thread.

COMPLEXITY
INTERMEDIATE

4.3 How do I...
Change a thread's priority?

Problem

I want to experiment with multiple threads demonstrated in section 4.2. The different threads of example 4.2 appear to run at the same priority. I want to modify the program to work with differing priorities. I learned how to create multiple threads, but I don't know how to change a thread's priority. How do I change a thread's priority?

Technique

The *Thread* class contains methods to change a thread's priority. A method called *Thread.setPriority()* sets the priority of a thread. The method takes an integer argument between 0 and 10, 0 being the lowest priority and 10 being the highest. The default priority of a thread is 5.

Other methods exist to changed priority. They accomplish the same function as *Thread.setPriority()*. These methods are listed in Table 4-1.

METHOD	DESCRIPTION
MAX_PRIORITY	The maximum priority that a Thread can have
MIN_PRIORITY	The minimum priority that a Thread can have
NORM_PRIORITY	The default priority that is assigned to a Thread
Thread( )	Constructs a new Thread

continued on next page

continued from previous page

METHOD	DESCRIPTION
Thread(Runnable)	Constructs a new Thread which applies the *run( )* method of the specified target
Thread(ThreadGroup, Runnable)	Constructs a new Thread in the specified Thread group that applies the *run()* method of the specified target
Thread(String)	Constructs a new Thread with the specified name
Thread(ThreadGroup, String)	Constructs a new Thread in the specified Thread group with the specified name
Thread(Runnable, String)	Constructs a new Thread with the specified name and applies the *run()* method of the specified target
Thread(ThreadGroup, Runnable, String)	Constructs a new Thread in the specified Thread group with the specified name and applies the *run()* method of the specified target
activeCount()	Returns the current number of active Threads in this Thread group
checkAccess()	Checks whether the current Thread is allowed to modify this Thread
countStackFrames()	Returns the number of stack frames in this Thread
currentThread()	Returns a reference to the currently executing Thread object
destroy()	Destroys a thread, without any cleanup
dumpStack()	A debugging procedure that prints a stack trace for the current Thread
enumerate(Thread[])	Copies, into the specified array, references to every active Thread in this Thread's group
getName()	Gets and returns this Thread's name
getPriority()	Gets and returns the Thread's priority
getThreadGroup()	Gets and returns this Thread group
interrupt()	Sends an interrupt to a thread
interrupted()	Asks if you have been interrupted
isAlive()	Returns a boolean indicating if the Thread is active
isDaemon()	Returns the daemon flag of the Thread
isInterrupted()	Asks if another thread has been interrupted
join(long)	Waits for this Thread to die
join(long, int)	Waits for the Thread to die, with more precise time
join()	Waits forever for this Thread to die
resume()	Resumes this Thread execution
run()	Defines the actual body of this Thread. Subclasses of Thread should override this method
setDaemon(boolean)	Marks this Thread as a daemon Thread or a user Thread
setName(String)	Sets the Thread's name
setPriority(int)	Sets the Thread's priority
sleep(long)	Causes the currently executing Thread to sleep for the specified number of milliseconds

METHOD	DESCRIPTION
sleep(long, int)	Sleep for the specified number of milliseconds and nanoseconds
start()	Starts this Thread
stop()	Stops a Thread by tossing an object
stop(Throwable)	Stops a Thread by tossing an object
suspend()	Suspends this Thread's execution
toString()	Returns a String representation of the Thread, including the thread's name, priority, and thread group
yield()	Causes the currently executing Thread object to yield

Table 4-1 Thread methods

Steps

1. Create the source file. Create a file called MultiThread.java and enter the following source:

```java
import java.applet.Applet;
import java.awt.*;

/**
 * Class LineColors holds 24 color values.
 */
class LineColors {

/**
 * color[] array holds the colors to be used.
 */
Color color[];

/**
 * Class constructor
 * Initializes the color array using an arbitrary algorithm
 */
public LineColors () {
    color = new Color[24];
    int i, rgb;

    rgb = 0xff;
    for (i=0; i<24; i+=1) {
        color[i] = new Color (rgb);
        rgb <<= 1;
        if ((rgb & 0x1000000) != 0) {
            rgb |= 1;
            rgb &= 0xffffff;
        }
```

continued on next page

continued from previous page

```
      }
}
}

/**
 * Class describing one line segment
 */
class Segment {

/*
 * x1, y1 - starting coordinates for this segment
 * x2, y2 - ending coordinates for this segment
 * dx1,...dy2 - velocities for the endpoints
 * whichcolor - the current index into color array
 * width, height - width and height of bounding panel
 * LC - instance of LineColors class
 */
double x1, y1, x2, y2;
double dx1, dy1, dx2, dy2;
int whichcolor, width, height;
LineColors LC;

/**
 * Class constructor
 * Initializes endpoints and velocities to random values
 * @param w - width of bounding panel
 * @param h - height of bounding panel
 * @param c - starting color index
 * @param lc - instance of LineColors class
 */
public Segment (int w, int h, int c, LineColors lc) {

    whichcolor = c;
    width = w;
    height = h;
    LC = lc;
    x1 = (double) w * Math.random ();
    y1 = (double) h * Math.random ();
    x2 = (double) w * Math.random ();
    y2 = (double) h * Math.random ();

    dx1 = 5 - 10 * Math.random ();
    dy1 = 5 - 10 * Math.random ();
    dx2 = 5 - 10 * Math.random ();
    dy2 = 5 - 10 * Math.random ();
}

/*
 * Increment color index.
 * Calculate the next endpoint position for this segment.
 */
void compute () {
```

```
    whichcolor += 1;
    whichcolor %= 24;

    x1 += dx1;
    y1 += dy1;
    x2 += dx2;
    y2 += dy2;

    if (x1 < 0 || x1 > width) dx1 = -dx1;
    if (y1 < 0 || y1 > height) dy1 = -dy1;
    if (x2 < 0 || x2 > width) dx2 = -dx2;
    if (y2 < 0 || y2 > height) dy2 = -dy2;
}

/**
 * Draw the line segment using the current color.
 * @param g - destination graphics object
 */
void paint (Graphics g) {

    g.setColor (LC.color [whichcolor]);
    g.drawLine ((int) x1, (int) y1, (int) x2, (int) y2);
}
}

/**
 * The applet/application proper
 */
class Lines extends Panel implements Runnable {

/*
 * width, height - width and height of bounding panel
 * NLines - number of line segments to be displayed
 * lines - array of instances of Segment class
 * LC - instance of LineColors class
 */
int width, height;
final int NLines = 4;
Segment lines[] = new Segment[NLines];
LineColors LC = new LineColors ();

/*
 * Instance of thread for this line
 */
Thread thread;

/**
 * init is called when the applet is loaded.
 * Save the width and height.
 * Create instances of Segment class.
 */
public void init (int inPriority) {
```

continued on next page

continued from previous page

```java
    Dimension d = size ();

    width = d.width;
    height = d.height;

    thread = new Thread (this);
    thread.start ();
    thread.setPriority(inPriority);

    int i;
    for (i=0; i<NLines; i+=1)
        lines[i] = new Segment (width, height, (2*i) % 24, LC);
}

/**
 * Recompute the next endpoint coordinates for each line.
 * Invoke paint() method for each line.
 * @param g - destination graphics object
 */
public void paint (Graphics g)
{

    int i;
    g.setColor (Color.black);
    g.drawRect (0, 0, width-1, height-1);
    for (i=0; i<NLines; i+=1) {
        lines[i].compute ();
        lines[i].paint (g);
    }
}

/*
 * The thread proper
 * Calls paint() every 50ms
 */
public void run()
{

    Graphics g = getGraphics();
    int iterCount = 0;
    while (true) {
        paint(g);
        try {
            iterCount += 1;
            if (iterCount == 5) {
                Thread.sleep(10);
                iterCount = 0;
            }
        }
        catch (InterruptedException e) {
            System.out.println("Caught exception...");
        }
```

```
    }
}
}

/*
 * The applet/application proper
 * Creates two instances of Lines and starts them
 * as separate threads
 */
public class MultiThread extends Applet {

/*
 * The instances of Lines
 */
Lines lines[];

/*
 * The number of threads to be run
 */
public final static int NumThreads = 5;

/*
 * The priority of the first thread
 */
public final static int StartingPriority = Thread.NORM_PRIORITY;

/*
 * Called when the applet is loaded
 * Creates several instances of Lines and adds them to the
 * applet panel
 * Sets the priority of each thread to 1 less than the previous
 * one
 */
public void init () {

    setLayout (new GridLayout (MultiThread.NumThreads, 1, 0, 0));
    lines = new Lines[MultiThread.NumThreads];
    Dimension d = size ();

    for (int i = 0; i< MultiThread.NumThreads; i++) {
        lines[i] = new Lines ();
        add (lines[i]);
        lines[i].resize (d.width, d.height/MultiThread.NumThreads);
        lines[i].init (StartingPriority-i);
    }
}

/**
 * Application entry point, unused when run as an applet
 * Create window frame and add applet inside.
 * @param args[] - command line arguments
 */
public static void main (String args[]) {
```

continued on next page

continued from previous page

```
Frame f = new Frame ("Colored lines");
f.setLayout (new GridLayout (MultiThread.NumThreads, 1, 0, 0));

f.resize (500, 500);
Lines lines[] = new Lines[MultiThread.NumThreads];

for (int i = 0; i< MultiThread.NumThreads; i++) {
    lines[i] = new Lines ();
    f.add (lines[i]);
}

f.show ();

for (int i = 0; i< MultiThread.NumThreads; i++) {
    lines[i].init (StartingPriority-i);
}
}
}
```

2. Create an HTML file that contains the applet. Create a file called howto43.html and enter the following text:

```
<html>
<head>
<title>Multi Thread</title>
</head>
<applet code="MultiThread.class" width=200 height=200>
</applet>
<hr size=4>

</html>
```

3. Compile and test the applet/application. Compile the source using javac or use the makefile provided. Use the Appletviewer with the html file as an argument by typing

```
appletviewer howto43.html
```

The program can be run as an application by typing

```
java MultiThread
```

When the program starts, a window should appear with several panels inside. Each panel should display lines of changing color bouncing around inside at different speed. Figure 4-4 shows an example of the running applet.

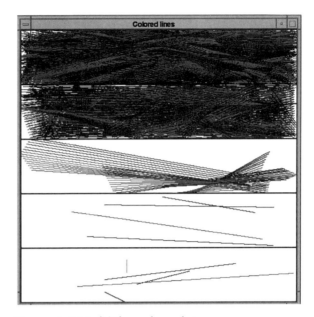

Figure 4-4 MultiThread applet

How It Works

The program is largely the same as that of How-To 4.2. The difference is the *init()* method in the Lines class and the initialization done in the *init()* and *main()* methods of the *MultiThread* class.

The *init()* method of the *Lines* class takes an integer argument. This argument is the priority to be assigned for this instance of *Lines*. The thread for this instance is created as before by calling the *Thread* constructor with this as an argument. The thread is started by calling *Thread.start()*. The priority is set by calling *Thread.set-Priority()* with the given priority as an argument.

The *init()* method of the *MultiThread* class creates several instances of *Lines*. Each instance of *Lines* is given slightly lower priority than its predecessor. A similar function is performed in the *main()* method. The result is a demonstration of multiple threads running at differing levels of priority.

Comments

The meticulous reader will notice the subtle change to the *run()* method of the *Lines* class. The difference is that five iterations of painting are done before *Thread.-*

sleep() is invoked. This was done purely for the purpose of producing a presentable demonstration. This addition to the code allows each thread more time before it is preempted. Without the little trick, the highest priority thread takes almost all of the time. This anomaly has to do more with the code in the example than with the Java runtime.

COMPLEXITY
INTERMEDIATE

4.4 How do I...
Synchronize methods?

Problem

I want to write an applet/application that graphically demonstrates a FIFO (first-in, first-out) or queue data structure. I want to create two threads that run asynchronously with respect to each other. The first thread writes data into the FIFO at a regular rate. The second thread waits for the FIFO to be half full and then reads out all the data until the FIFO is empty. There must be some synchronizing mechanism between the read and writing threads in order to avoid corruption of the data in the FIFO. I know how to create multiple threads and how to draw the graphics, but I don't know how to synchronize methods within the FIFO class. How do I synchronize methods?

Technique

All examples so far in this chapter have contained independent, asynchronous threads. Each thread contained all of the data and methods required for its execution, ran at its own pace, and didn't require any outside resources or methods. There are situations where separate simultaneously running threads share data and must consider the state of other threads.

Java supports the synchronization of methods with the use of monitors. A monitor is associated with a specific data item and functions as a lock on that data. When a thread holds the monitor for a data item, it creates a lock on the data such that other threads cannot manipulate that data.

The example in this section implements synchronization via the *synchronize* keyword in the method declaration. This will cause the methods to wait for a monitor before execution. When the method returns, the monitor is released.

Steps

1. Create the applet source file. Create a new file called SyncMethod.java and enter the following source:

```java
import java.awt.*;
import java.applet.Applet;

/*
 * A class for handling first-in, first-out data structure
 */
class FIFO {

/*
 * The maximum depth of the FIFO
 */
final int MaxDepth = 200;

/*
 * The real depth of this FIFO
 */
int depth;

/*
 * Write and read indexes into the data array.
 */
int writeIndex;
int readIndex;

/*
 * The number of data items currently in the FIFO
 */
int nItems;

/*
 * The data proper
 */
int data[] = new int[MaxDepth];

/*
 * Width and height of the FIFO graphical display
 */
int width;
int height;

/*
 * x and y position of the upper-left corner of the FIFO
 * graphical display
 */
int xpos;
int ypos;

/**
 * The constructor
 * @param d - depth of the FIFO
 */
public FIFO (int d) {
```

continued on next page

continued from previous page

```
        depth = d;
        writeIndex = 0;
        readIndex = 0;
        nItems = 0;

        width = depth + 4;
        height = 50;
        xpos = 50;
        ypos = 75;
}

/**
 * Write 1 integer value into the FIFO.
 * @param value - the value to write
 */
synchronized void write (int value) {

    if (nItems >= depth) return;

    data[writeIndex] = value;
    writeIndex += 1;
    writeIndex %= depth;
    nItems += 1;
}

/**
 * Read 1 integer value from the FIFO.
 */
synchronized int read (  ) {

    if (nItems < 1) return 0;

    int value = data[readIndex];
    readIndex += 1;
    readIndex %= depth;
    nItems -= 1;

    return value;
}

/**
 * Returns True if the FIFO is empty
 */
synchronized boolean empty () {

    return nItems > 0 ? false : true;
}

/**
 * Returns True if the FIFO is half full
 */
synchronized boolean halfFull () {
```

```
        return nItems > (depth >> 1) ? true : false;
}

/**
 * Returns True if the FIFO is full
 */
synchronized boolean full () {

        return nItems >= (depth) ? true : false;
}

/**
 * Draws the FIFO graphical display
 * @param g - destination graphics context
 */
synchronized void paint (Graphics g) {

        int x, y, w, h;

        g.setColor (Color.white);
        g.fillRect (xpos, ypos, width, height);
        g.setColor (Color.black);
        g.drawRect (xpos, ypos, width, height);

        x = writeIndex + xpos + 2;
        y = ypos - 22;
        g.drawLine (x, y, x, y + 20);
        g.drawString ("Write index "+writeIndex, x+2, y+10);

        x = readIndex + xpos + 2;
        y = ypos + height + 22;
        g.drawLine (x, y-20, x, y);
        g.drawString ("Read index "+readIndex, x+2, y);

        if (nItems < 1) return;

        if (nItems > (depth>>1)) g.setColor (Color.red);
        else g.setColor (Color.green);

        x = xpos + 2 + readIndex;
        y = ypos + 2;
        if (writeIndex > readIndex) w = nItems;
        else w = width - readIndex - 4;
        h = height - 4;
        g.fillRect (x, y, w, h);

        if (writeIndex > readIndex) return;

        x = xpos + 2;
        w = writeIndex;
        g.fillRect (x, y, w, h);
```

continued on next page

continued from previous page

```
}
}

/*
 * A class that generates data continuously
 */
class Source extends Thread {

/*
 * the FIFO to write into
 */
FIFO fifo;
int value;

/**
 * Constructor
 * Saves the FIFO instance and starts the thread
 * @param f - an instance of FIFO
 */
public Source (FIFO f) {

    fifo = f;
    value = 0;

    start ();
}

/*
 * The thread, which writes 1 word every 100 ms
 */
public void run () {

    while (true) {
        if (fifo.full() == false)
            fifo.write (value++);

        try {
            Thread.sleep (100);
        } catch (InterruptedException e) {
        }
    }
}
}

/*
 * A class that reads data from the FIFO
 */
class Sink extends Thread {

/*
 * The FIFO to read from
 */
FIFO fifo;
```

```
int value;

/**
 * Constructor
 * Saves the FIFO instance and starts the thread
 * @param f - an instance of FIFO
 */
public Sink (FIFO f) {

    fifo = f;

    start ();
}

/*
 * The thread that reads all data out after the FIFO is half
 * full
 */
public void run () {

    while (true) {
        if (fifo.halfFull()) {
            try {
                Thread.sleep (1000);
            } catch (InterruptedException e) {
            }
            while (fifo.empty() == false) {
                value = fifo.read ();
                try {
                    Thread.sleep (50);
                } catch (InterruptedException e) {
                }
            }
        }

        try {
            Thread.sleep (100);
        } catch (InterruptedException e) {
        }
    }
}
}

/*
 * The applet/application class
 */
public class SyncMethod extends Applet implements Runnable {

Source source;
Sink sink;
FIFO fifo;
Thread thread;

/*
```

continued on next page

continued from previous page

```
 * Called when the applet is loaded
 * Create instances of FIFO, Source, Sink, and Thread.
 */
public void init () {

    fifo = new FIFO (200);
    source = new Source (fifo);
    sink = new Sink (fifo);

    thread = new Thread (this);
}

/*
 * Start the graphics update thread.
 */
public void start () {

    thread.start ();
}

/*
 * Stop the graphics update thread.
 */
public void stop () {

    thread.stop ();
}

/*
 * The graphics update thread
 * Call repaint every 100 ms.
 */
public void run () {

    while (true) {
        repaint ();
        try {
            Thread.sleep (100);
        } catch (InterruptedException e) {
        }
    }
}

/**
 * Called from update() in response to repaint()
 * @param g - destination graphics context
 */
public void paint (Graphics g) {
```

```
    fifo.paint (g);
}

/**
 * main() is the application entry point.
 * main() is unused when run as an applet.
 * Create a window frame and add the applet inside.
 * @param args[] - command line arguments
 */
public static void main (String args[]) {

    Frame f = new Frame ("Synchronized methods example");

    SyncMethod syncMethod = new SyncMethod ();
    f.add ("Center", syncMethod);
    f.resize (400, 200);
    f.show ();

    syncMethod.init ();
    syncMethod.start ();
}
}
```

2. Create an HTML document that contains the applet. Create a new file called howto44.html as follows:

```
<html>
<head>
<title>Synchronize Code Methods</title>
</head>
<applet code="SyncMethod.class" width=410 height=230>
</applet>
<hr size=4>

</html>
```

3. Compile and test the applet. Compile the source using javac or the makefile provided. Test the applet using the Appletviewer by entering the following command:

```
APPLETVIEWER howto44.html
```

SyncMethod.java may also be run as an application by typing

```
java SyncMethod
```

When SyncMethod is executed, a window will open with a display illustrating the status of the FIFO. The reading and writing of the data is illustrated with markers that indicate the index of the data being read or written. The

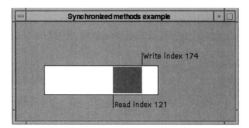

Figure 4-5 Synchronizing methods

space between the lines, which represents the data, is shown as a colored bar. The colored bar is green when the buffer is less than half full. When the buffer becomes half full, the bar becomes red and the data is read out until no data remains in the buffer. The cycle then repeats. Figure 4-5 shows an example of the running applet.

How It Works

Four classes are defined in the program—FIFO, *Source*, *Sink*, and *SyncMethod*. The FIFO class implements the first-in, first-out data structure. The Source class is a thread that writes data into the FIFO at a constant rate. The Sink class is a thread that reads the data out of the FIFO. The *SyncMethod* class is the applet class proper.

The FIFO class contains an array of integers for holding the data. The variables *writeIndex* and *readIndex,* are the write and read indices, respectively, for the data array. The variable *nItems* is the number of items in the data array.

Each of the methods in the FIFO class is declared synchronized so that data and indices cannot be examined or manipulated by more that one thread at a time. The *paint()* method draws a graphical representation of the FIFO in its current state. Markers showing the position of the write and read indices are drawn along with their values. Data within the FIFO is represented by a colored bar. The bar is green when the FIFO is less than half full, red when it is more than half full.

The *Source* method extends thread so that it may run as an independent thread. The constructor simply saves an instance of the FIFO and starts its thread by calling the *start()* method. An infinite loop is entered which writes arbitrary data into the FIFO as long as it is not full. A delay of 100 milliseconds is used to limit the rate of writing into the FIFO. The delay is accomplished by calling *Thread.sleep()* with 100 milliseconds as an argument.

The *Sink* method also runs as an independent thread by extending *Thread*. The constructor saves an instance of FIFO passed to it and starts its thread by calling *Thread.start()*. The *run()* method enters an infinite loop that waits for the FIFO to become half full before the data is read out. A delay of 1 second (1,000 milliseconds) is added so that the FIFO display will remain red for long enough for the observer to notice the change. The data is read out at twice the rate that it is written in. This guarantees that FIFO overflow will not occur. Data is read out until the FIFO is empty.

The *SyncMethod* class is the applet proper. The *init()* method creates a new instance of FIFO in addition to instances of *Source* and *Sink*. A thread for the applet is also created, which is used for regular updating of the graphical FIFO display. The *run()* method forces updating of the display by calling *repaint()*. The update rate is controlled by calling *Thread.sleep()* after each call to *repaint()*. The *paint()* method calls the *FIFO.paint()* method to update the display of the FIFO.

Comments

The *Source* and *Sink* methods do not implement the Runnable interface, because they extend the *Thread* class. The *Thread* class itself implements the Runnable interface, so another implement's Runnable would be redundant.

COMPLEXITY
INTERMEDIATE

4.5 How do I...
Synchronize code sections?

Problem

I liked the synchronize methods example in the previous section. This was very useful, but I would like to be able to synchronize code sections and not an entire method. I understand that Java supports a mechanism to synchronize code sections only. For the purposes of education, I want to implement the previous example by using synchronized code sections only. How do I synchronize code sections?

Technique

The previous example used monitors to synchronize methods. In object-oriented design, critical code sections are usually maintained in separate methods. However, it is possible to synchronize critical sections of code in a very similar manner.

Steps

1. Create the applet source file. Create a new file called SyncCode.java and enter the following source:

```
import java.awt.*;
import java.applet.Applet;
```

continued on next page

continued from previous page

```
/*
 * A class for handling first-in, first-out data structure
 */
class FIFO {

/*
 * The maximum depth of the FIFO
 */
final int MaxDepth = 200;

/*
 * The real depth of this FIFO
 */
int depth;

/*
 * Write and read indexes into the data array.
 */
int writeIndex;
int readIndex;

/*
 * The number of data items currently in the FIFO
 */
int nItems;

/*
 * The data proper
 */
int data[] = new int[MaxDepth];

/*
 * Width and height of the FIFO graphical display
 */
int width;
int height;

/*
 * x and y position of the upper-left corner of the FIFO
 * graphical display
 */
int xpos;
int ypos;

/**
 * The constructor
 * @param d - depth of the FIFO
 */
public FIFO (int d) {

    depth = d;
    writeIndex = 0;
```

```
        readIndex = 0;
        nItems = 0;

        width = depth + 4;
        height = 50;
        xpos = 50;
        ypos = 75;
    }

    /**
     * Write 1 integer value into the FIFO.
     * @param value - the value to write
     */
    void write (int value) {

        if (nItems >= depth) return;

        data[writeIndex] = value;
        writeIndex += 1;
        writeIndex %= depth;
        nItems += 1;
    }

    /**
     * Read 1 integer value from the FIFO.
     */
    int read () {

        if (nItems < 1) return 0;

        int value = data[readIndex];
        readIndex += 1;
        readIndex %= depth;
        nItems -= 1;

        return value;
    }

    /**
     * Returns True if the FIFO is empty
     */
    boolean empty () {

        return nItems > 0 ? false : true;
    }

    /**
     * Returns True if the FIFO is half full
     */
    boolean halfFull () {

        return nItems > (depth >> 1) ? true : false;
    }
```

continued on next page

continued from previous page

```
/**
 * Returns True if the FIFO is full
 */
boolean full () {

    return nItems >= (depth) ? true : false;
}
/**
 * Draws the FIFO graphical display
 * @param g - destination graphics context
 */
void paint (Graphics g) {

    int x, y, w, h;

    g.setColor (Color.white);
    g.fillRect (xpos, ypos, width, height);
    g.setColor (Color.black);
    g.drawRect (xpos, ypos, width, height);

    x = writeIndex + xpos + 2;
    y = ypos - 22;
    g.drawLine (x, y, x, y + 20);
    g.drawString ("Write index "+writeIndex, x+2, y+10);

    x = readIndex + xpos + 2;
    y = ypos + height + 22;
    g.drawLine (x, y-20, x, y);
    g.drawString ("Read index "+readIndex, x+2, y);

    if (nItems < 1) return;

    if (nItems > (depth>>1)) g.setColor (Color.red);
    else g.setColor (Color.green);

    x = xpos + 2 + readIndex;
    y = ypos + 2;
    if (writeIndex > readIndex) w = nItems;
    else w = width - readIndex - 4;
    h = height - 4;
    g.fillRect (x, y, w, h);

    if (writeIndex > readIndex) return;

    x = xpos + 2;
    w = writeIndex;
    g.fillRect (x, y, w, h);
}
}
```

```
/*
 * A class that generates data continuously
 */
class Source extends Thread {

/*
 * The FIFO to write into
 */
FIFO fifo;
int value;

/**
 * Constructor
 * Saves the FIFO instance and starts the thread
 * @param f - an instance of FIFO
 */
public Source (FIFO f) {

    fifo = f;
    value = 0;

    start ();
}

/*
 * The thread that writes 1 word every 100 ms
 */
public void run () {

    while (true) {
        synchronized (fifo) {
            if (fifo.full() == false)
                fifo.write (value++);
        }
        try {
            Thread.sleep (100);
        } catch (InterruptedException e) {
        }
    }
}
}

/*
 * A class that reads data from the FIFO
 */
class Sink extends Thread {

/*
 * The FIFO to read from
 */
FIFO fifo;
```

continued on next page

continued from previous page

```java
int value;

/**
 * Constructor
 * Saves the FIFO instance and starts the thread
 * @param f - an instance of FIFO
 */
public Sink (FIFO f) {

    fifo = f;

    start ();
}


/*
 * The thread that reads out all data after the FIFO is half
 * full
 */
public void run () {

    boolean empty;
    boolean halfFull;

    while (true) {
        synchronized (fifo) {
            halfFull = fifo.halfFull ();
        }
        if (halfFull) {
            try {
                Thread.sleep (1000);
            } catch (InterruptedException e) {
            }
            do {
                synchronized (fifo) {
                    value = fifo.read ();
                }
                try {
                    Thread.sleep (50);
                } catch (InterruptedException e) {
                }
                synchronized (fifo) {
                    empty = fifo.empty ();
                }
            } while (empty == false);
        }

        try {
            Thread.sleep (100);
        } catch (InterruptedException e) {
        }
    }
}
}
```

```
/*
 * The applet/application class
 */
public class SyncCode extends Applet implements Runnable {

Source source;
Sink sink;
FIFO fifo;
Thread thread;

/*
 * Called when the applet is loaded
 * Create instances of FIFO, Source, Sink, and Thread.
 */
public void init () {

    fifo = new FIFO (200);
    source = new Source (fifo);
    sink = new Sink (fifo);

    thread = new Thread (this);
}

/*
 * Start the graphics update thread.
 */
public void start () {

    thread.start ();
}

/*
 * Stop the graphics update thread.
 */
public void stop () {

    thread.stop ();
}

/*
 * The graphics update thread
 * Call repaint every 100 ms.
 */
public void run () {

    while (true) {
        repaint ();
        try {
            Thread.sleep (100);
        } catch (InterruptedException e) {
        }
```

continued on next page

continued from previous page

```
    }
}

/**
 * Called from update() in response to repaint()
 * @param g - destination graphics context
 */
public void paint (Graphics g) {

    synchronized (fifo) {
        fifo.paint (g);
    }
}

/**
 * main() is the application entry point.
 * main() is unused when run as an applet.
 * Create a window frame and add the applet inside.
 * @param args[] - command line arguments
 */
public static void main (String args[]) {

    Frame f = new Frame ("Synchronized code example");

    SyncCode syncCode = new SyncCode ();
    f.add ("Center", syncCode);
    f.resize (400, 200);
    f.show ();

    syncCode.init ();
    syncCode.start ();
}
}
```

2. Create an HTML document that contains the applet. Create a new file called howto45.html as follows:

```
<html>
<head>
<title>Synchronize Code Sections</title>
</head>
<applet code="SyncCode.class" width=410 height=230>
</applet>
<hr size=4>

</html>
```

3. Compile and test the applet. Compile the source using javac or the makefile provided. Test the applet using the Appletviewer by entering the following command:

```
APPLETVIEWER howto45.html
```

SyncCode.java may also be run as an application by typing

`java SyncCode`

When SyncCode is executed, a window will open with a display illustrating the status of the FIFO. The reading and writing of the data is illustrated with lines that indicate the index of the data being read or written. The space between the lines, which represents the data, is shown as a colored bar. The colored bar is green when the buffer is less than half full. When the buffer becomes half full, the bar becomes red and the data is read out until no data remains in the buffer. The cycle then repeats while the data is being written at a constant rate. Figure 4-6 shows an example of the running applet.

How It Works

Four classes are defined in the program—FIFO, *Source*, *Sink*, and *SyncMethod*. The FIFO class implements the first-in, first-out data structure. The *Source* class is a thread that writes data into the FIFO at a constant rate. The *Sink* class is a thread that reads the data out of the FIFO. The *SyncCode* class is the applet class proper.

This code is very similar to the previous example. The difference is that in the previous example the methods in the FIFO class were defined as synchronized. This example uses synchronizing on the code section of interest.

Comments

Synchronizing code sections is functionally adequate but technically violates strict object-oriented design. The technique of synchronizing methods is preferred.

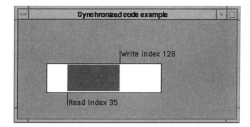

Figure 4-6 Synchronizing code sections

4.6   How do I...
Wait for a thread?

Problem

In the two previous examples, the *Sink.read()* method polled the FIFO every 100 milliseconds to determine if data was available. This seems inefficient. There must be a better way to wait for the FIFO to become occupied. How do I wait for a thread?

Technique

The *wait()* and *notify()* methods can be used to wait for a thread. When a method needs to wait for a condition, it may call *wait()*. Execution will be suspended until the *notify()* method is called from another thread.

There are two conditions that should cause a thread to block (wait). The first is during a read when no data is in the FIFO. The second is during a write when the FIFO is full.

In the first case, the *FIFO.read()* method should call *wait( )* if the number of data items in the FIFO is less than 1. The *notify()* method should be called after a data item has been written; this will release the thread waiting for a read.

The second case is analogous. *wait()* should be called in the *FIFO.write()* method when the number of items in the FIFO is equal to or greater than the FIFO size (depth). The *notify()* call for this case should be at the end of the *FIFO.read()* method, after an item has been read.

Steps

1. Create the applet source file. Create a new file called WaitDemo.java and enter the following source:

```
import java.awt.*;
import java.applet.Applet;

/*
 * A class for handling first-in, first-out data structure
 */
class FIFO {

/*
 * The maximum depth of the FIFO
 */
final int MaxDepth = 200;
```

```
/*
 * The real depth of this FIFO
 */
int depth;

/*
 * Write and read indexes into the data array.
 */
int writeIndex;
int readIndex;

/*
 * The number of data items currently in the FIFO
 */
int nItems;

/*
 * The data proper
 */
int data[] = new int[MaxDepth];

/*
 * Width and height of the FIFO graphical display
 */
int width;
int height;

/*
 * x and y position of the upper-left corner of the FIFO
 * graphical display
 */
int xpos;
int ypos;

/**
 * The constructor
 * @param d - depth of the FIFO
 */
public FIFO (int d) {

    depth = d;
    writeIndex = 0;
    readIndex = 0;
    nItems = 0;

    width = depth + 4;
    height = 50;
    xpos = 50;
    ypos = 75;
}

/**
 * Write 1 integer value into the FIFO.
```

continued on next page

continued from previous page

```
 * Invoke wait( ) if the FIFO is full.
 * @param value - the value to write
 */
synchronized void write (int value) {

    if (nItems >= depth) {
        try {
            wait ();
        } catch (InterruptedException e) {
        }
    }

    data[writeIndex] = value;
    writeIndex += 1;
    writeIndex %= depth;
    nItems += 1;
    notify ();
}

/**
 * Read 1 integer value from the FIFO.
 * Invoke wait() if the FIFO is empty.
 */
synchronized int read () {

    if (nItems < 1) {
        try {
            wait ();
        } catch (InterruptedException e) {
        }
    }

    int value = data[readIndex];
    readIndex += 1;
    readIndex %= depth;
    nItems -= 1;
    notify ();

    return value;
}

/**
 * Returns True if the FIFO is empty
 */
synchronized boolean empty () {

    return nItems > 0 ? false : true;
}

/**
 * Returns True if the FIFO is half full
 */
```

```
synchronized boolean halfFull () {

    return nItems > (depth >> 1) ? true : false;
}

/**
 * returns True if the FIFO is full
 */
synchronized boolean full () {

    return nItems >= (depth) ? true : false;
}

/**
 * Draws the FIFO graphical display
 * @param g - destination graphics context
 */
synchronized void paint (Graphics g) {

    int x, y, w, h;

    g.setColor (Color.white);
    g.fillRect (xpos, ypos, width, height);
    g.setColor (Color.black);
    g.drawRect (xpos, ypos, width, height);

    x = writeIndex + xpos + 2;
    y = ypos - 22;
    g.drawLine (x, y, x, y + 20);
    g.drawString ("Write index "+writeIndex, x+2, y+10);

    x = readIndex + xpos + 2;
    y = ypos + height + 22;
    g.drawLine (x, y-20, x, y);
    g.drawString ("Read index "+readIndex, x+2, y);

    if (nItems < 1) return;

    if (nItems > (depth>>1)) g.setColor (Color.red);
    else g.setColor (Color.green);

    x = xpos + 2 + readIndex;
    y = ypos + 2;
    if (writeIndex > readIndex) w = nItems;
    else w = width - readIndex - 4;
    h = height - 4;
    g.fillRect (x, y, w, h);

    if (writeIndex > readIndex) return;

    x = xpos + 2;
    w = writeIndex;
    g.fillRect (x, y, w, h);
}
}
```

continued on next page

continued from previous page

```
/*
 * A class that generates data continuously
 */
class Source extends Thread {

/*
 * The FIFO to write into
 */
FIFO fifo;
int value;

/**
 * Constructor
 * Saves the FIFO instance and starts the thread
 * @param f - an instance of FIFO
 */
public Source (FIFO f) {

    fifo = f;
    value = 0;

    start ();
}

/*
 * The thread that writes 1 word every 50 ms on average
 */
public void run () {

    while (true) {
        if (fifo.full() == false)
            fifo.write (value++);

        try {
            Thread.sleep ((int) (100 * Math.random ()));
        } catch (InterruptedException e) {
        }
    }
}
}

/*
 * A class that reads data from the FIFO
 */
class Sink extends Thread {

/*
 * The FIFO to read from
 */
FIFO fifo;
int value;

/**
```

```
 * Constructor
 * Saves the FIFO instance and starts the thread
 * @param f - an instance of FIFO
 */
public Sink (FIFO f) {

    fifo = f;

    start ();
}

/*
 * The thread that tries to read 1 word every 50 ms on average
 */
public void run () {

    while (true) {
        value = fifo.read ();

        try {
            Thread.sleep ((int) (100 * Math.random ()));
        } catch (InterruptedException e) {
        }
    }
}
}

/*
 * The applet/application class
 */
public class WaitDemo extends Applet implements Runnable {

Source source;
Sink sink;
FIFO fifo;
Thread thread;

/*
 * Called when the applet is loaded
 * Create instances of FIFO, Source, Sink, and Thread
 */
public void init () {

    fifo = new FIFO (200);
    source = new Source (fifo);
    sink = new Sink (fifo);

    thread = new Thread (this);
}

/*
 * Start the graphics update thread.
 */
```

continued on next page

continued from previous page

```java
public void start () {

    thread.start ();
}

/*
 * Stop the graphics update thread.
 */
public void stop () {

    thread.stop ();
}

/*
 * The graphics update thread
 * Call repaint every 100 ms.
 */
public void run () {

    while (true) {
        repaint ();
        try {
            Thread.sleep (100);
        } catch (InterruptedException e) {
        }
    }
}

/**
 * Called from update() in response to repaint()
 * @param g - destination graphics context
 */
public void paint (Graphics g) {

    fifo.paint (g);
}

/**
 * main() is the application entry point.
 * main() is unused when run as an applet.
 * Create a window frame and add the applet inside.
 * @param args[] - command line arguments
 */
public static void main (String args[]) {

    Frame f = new Frame ("FIFO Demo");

    WaitDemo waitDemo = new WaitDemo ();
    f.add ("Center", waitDemo);
    f.resize (400, 200);
    f.show ();

    waitDemo.init ();
```

```
    waitDemo.start ();
}
}
```

2. Create an HTML document that contains the applet. Create a new file called howto46.html as follows:

```
<html>
<head>
<title>Wait for a thread</title>
</head>
<applet code="WaitDemo.class" width=410 height=230>
</applet>
<hr size=4>

</html>
```

3. Compile and test the applet. Compile the source using javac or the makefile provided. Test the applet using the Appletviewer by entering the following command:

```
APPLETVIEWER howto46.html
```

WaitDemo.java may also be run as an application by typing

```
java WaitDemo
```

When WaitDemo is executed, a window will open showing the running applet/application. This example is slightly different in its behavior. The *Source* class thread writes data at a random rate, and the *Sink* class thread reads data at a random rate. The reading and writing rates are random, but their average rate is the same. This was done to avoid eventual filling of the FIFO and to show some variation in the number of items in the FIFO at a particular time. Figure 4-7 shows an example of the running applet.

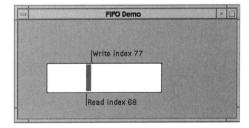

Figure 4-7 Wait for a thread applet

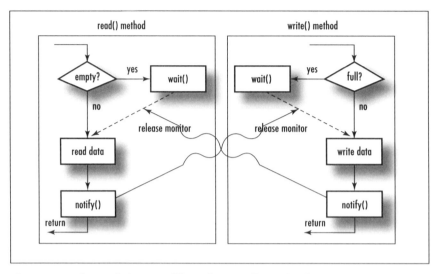

Figure 4-8 Flow of the *read()* and *write()* methods.

How It Works

As in the examples in How-To 4.4 and 4.5, four classes are defined: *FIFO*, *Source*, *Sink*, and *WaitDemo*. The *FIFO* class implements a first-in, first-out data structure with blocking (waiting) reads and writes. The *Source* class writes data into the *FIFO* at a random rate which averages to one item every 50 milliseconds. The *Sink* class reads data at a random rate which also averages to 50 milliseconds.

The FIFO constructor initializes the depth, write index, read index, and the number of items. It also initializes variables used for graphical display.

The *FIFO.write()* method first checks the number of items stored. If the number of items is equal to or greater than the depth, the calling thread is blocked by calling *wait()*. The calling thread will be released when *notify()* is called from the *FIFO.read()* method. This logic keeps the *FIFO* from overflowing, avoiding data loss. After the data is written, *notify()* must be called to release any threads that might be blocked by *FIFO.read()*. Figure 4-8 shows the flow of the *read()* and *write()* methods.

The *FIFO.read()* method checks to make sure that there is data in the *FIFO* to be read. If not, *wait()* is called, which blocks the calling thread. The calling thread will be released when *notify()* is called from the *FIFO.write()* method. After data has been read, *notify()* must be called to release any threads that might be blocked by *FIFO.write()*.

The remaining routines for determining the *FIFO* status are identical to those of How-To 4.4 and 4.5. The *FIFO.paint()* method draws the state of the *FIFO* graphically—this is also unchanged from How-To 4.4 and 4.5.

The *Source* and *Sink* classes appear simpler than in previous examples. This is because the testing and management for *FIFO* overflow and underflow is handled in the *FIFO* class. The *Source* class creates a thread which writes data into the *FIFO* at an average rate of one item every 50 milliseconds. The *Sink* class creates a thread which reads data at an average rate of one item every 50 milliseconds. These threads will block in order to avoid overflows and underflows.

The *WaitDemo* class is the *applet* class proper. It creates instances of *FIFO*, *Source*, and *Sink*. It also creates its own thread for paint updates. The WaitDemo thread forces a repaint every 100 milliseconds by calling *repaint()*. The *main()* method creates a window frame and adds an instance of WaitDemo in the event that the program is used as an application.

Comments

The use of *wait()* and *notify()* requires some consideration to avoid deadlock conditions which can result if a thread is blocked and cannot be released. This could occur in this example if the *FIFO* depth were 0, which is, of course, pathological.

Note that all of the methods (except for the constructor) are declared synchronized. This is still necessary to avoid data corruption. Synchronized code sections could have been used but would not be as clean.

EVENTS AND PARAMETERS

EVENTS AND PARAMETERS

How do I...

Event handling is an important part of programming. For a program to interact with the user, several types of events must be dealt with and controlled. An example of events commonly used would be those of an average word processor. The word processor can handle keyboard and mouse events.

This chapter will explain how to handle most of these events. These events are the basis for many of the more interesting and useful applications. By using the event handling covered in this chapter, you could create games, word processors, spreadsheets, and many other applications. Table 5-1 lists the variable indices contained in the *Event* class. The *Event* class contains indices for handling all types of events. The table is included here for simplicity and reference, since most examples in this chapter will use one or more variable indices from the *Event* class.

VARIABLE	DESCRIPTION
ACTION_EVENT	Action event
ALT_MASK	Alt modifier constant
CTRL_MASK	Control modifier constant
DOWN	DOWNARROW key
END	END key
F1	F1 key
F10	F10 key
F11	F11 key
F12	F12 key
F2	F2 key
F3	F3 key
F4	F4 key
F5	F5 key
F6	F6 key
F7	F7 key
F8	F8 key
F9	F9 key
GOT_FOCUS	Component gained the focus
HOME	HOME key
KEY_ACTION	Key action keyboard event
KEY_ACTION_RELEASE	Key action keyboard event
KEY_PRESS	Keypress keyboard event
KEY_RELEASE	Key release keyboard event
LEFT	LEFTARROW key
LIST_DESELECT	An item in a list has been deselected
LIST_SELECT	An item in a list has been selected
LOAD_FILE	File loading event
LOST_FOCUS	Component lost the focus
META_MASK	Meta modifier constant
MOUSE_DOWN	Mouse down event
MOUSE_DRAG	Mouse drag event
MOUSE_ENTER	Mouse enter event
MOUSE_EXIT	Mouse exit event
MOUSE_MOVE	Mouse move event
MOUSE_UP	Mouse up event
PGDN	PAGEDOWN key
PGUP	PAGEUP key

VARIABLE	DESCRIPTION
RIGHT	[RIGHTARROW] key
SAVE_FILE	File saving event
SCROLL_ABSOLUTE	Absolute scroll event
SCROLL_LINE_DOWN	Line-down scroll event
SCROLL_LINE_UP	Line-up scroll event
SCROLL_PAGE_DOWN	Page-down scroll event
SCROLL_PAGE_UP	Page-up scroll event
SHIFT_MASK	Shift modifier constant
UP	[UPARROW] key
WINDOW_DEICONIFY	De-iconify window event
WINDOW_DESTROY	Destroy window event
WINDOW_EXPOSE	Expose window event
WINDOW_ICONIFY	Iconify window event
WINDOW_MOVED	Move window event
arg	Arbitrary argument
clickCount	Number of consecutive clicks
evt	Next event
id	Type of this event
key	Key that was pressed in a keyboard event
modifiers	State of the modifier keys
target	Target component
when	Time stamp
x	x coordinate of the event
y	y coordinate of the event

Table 5-1 Event class constants and variables

5.1   Access Keyboard Events

The keyboard is the most important input device on the computer. Understanding the use of keyboard events allows the widest possible range of user input. This example creates a simple Tetris game. The keyboard will be used to control the game-piece movement and rotation.

5.2   Access Mouse Events

The mouse is an important part of any application that requires user interaction. All computer users have grown to expect programs to accept mouse input. This example shows how to access the mouse position and button presses by creating a simple drawing program that uses the mouse.

5.3   Access Other Events

Event handling is a very important aspect when creating graphical user interfaces of any kind. The first two examples of this chapter focus on certain keyboard and mouse events. This example shows a generalized *handleEvent( )* method that captures several events and prints them in a text area.

5.4   Access Applet Parameters

Java applets contain the capability to receive parameters from the html file that called the applet. This is very useful when creating robust applets that require input to determine the output or function. This How-To creates a scrolling text marquee similar to example 3.5 that accepts the text string as an applet parameter.

5.5   Parse Applet Parameters

The ability to parse applet parameters is useful when passing several parameters to the applet in a single parameter string. This example creates another text marquee that accepts the text itself, color, and direction as a single parameter. The applet can accept up to five different parameters, allowing all five to be scrolling at once.

COMPLEXITY
INTERMEDIATE

5.1   How do I...
Access keyboard events?

Problem

I would like to create a Tetris game that uses keystrokes to control the play. I would like to be able to move the game piece left, right, down, and be able to rotate the piece. How do I access keyboard events during the program operation?

Technique

Keyboard events are handled in Java by overriding the *keyDown( )* method. Whenever a keyboard event occurs within an applet's window, the runtime will call the *keyDown( )* method. The event object along with the key value itself is passed to *keyDown*. Which key was pressed is determined by comparing the value of the Event *key* variable with the character constants or the constants defined in the event class proper. Some of the constants include left, right, up, down, F1, F2, and so on. These correspond to the LEFTARROW, RIGHTARROW, UPARROW, and DOWN-ARROW keys, and function keys. A complete list of these key events is shown in Table 5-1.

Steps

1. Create the applet source file. Create a new file called Tetris.java and enter the following source:

```java
import java.applet.Applet;
import java.awt.*;

/**
 * Chapter 5, Example 1, Tetris.java
 *
 * The Square class handles an individual square that makes up
 * part of a specific falling piece.
 *
 * @see        java.applet.Applet
 * @version    1.0 24 Feb 1996
 */

class Square {

/**
 * The column that the square occupies
 */
int column;

/**
 * The row that the square occupies
 */
int row;

/**
 * The color of the square
 */
int color;

/**
 * Construct a square.
 *
 * @param column    The column that the square occupies
 * @param row       The row that the square occupies
 * @param color     The color of the square
 */
Square (int column, int row, int color) {

    this.column = column;
    this.row = row;
    this.color = color;
}

/**
 * Test to see if a square is within the boundaries of the board.
 *
 * @return          True if inbounds
 */
```

continued on next page

continued from previous page

```java
boolean InBounds () {

    return (column >= 0 && column < Tetris.cols &&
        row >= 0 && row < Tetris.rows+4);
}

/**
 * Test for equivalency between two squares (this and s).
 *
 * @param s    Square to test against this instance of a square
 * @return     True if both squares are equivalent.
 */
boolean IsEqual (Square s) {
    return column == s.column && row == s.row && color == s.color;
}
}

/**
 * The Tetris class actually implements the applet.
 *
 * @see java.applet.Applet
 * @see java.lang.Runnable
 */
public class Tetris extends Applet implements Runnable {

static          int     sqlength;          // length of tetris square
static final    int     xoffset = 200;     // distance from left
static          int     cols;          // columns
static          int     rows;          // rows

/**
 * field is a two-dimensional array that contains
 * color index values of squares. A value of zero
 * means that no square occupies that position.
 */
int         field[][];

/**
 * oldField is used to determine which pieces have changed.
 * Only the positions that have changed are drawn.
 */
int         oldField[][];

/**
 * curPiece is an array of squares describing the
 * piece currently in play.
 */
Square          curPiece[] = new Square[4];

/**
 * The variable gameInPlay is set to True if the game has
 * not been lost.
 */
boolean         gameInPlay;
```

```
/**
 * needNewPiece is set to True if a new piece must
 * be added to the play field from the top.
 */
boolean        needNewPiece;

/**
 * theThread is a thread-separate thread that causes the
 * pieces in the play field to fall normally.
 */
Thread         theThread = null;

/**
 * Color is an array that holds color values used in the
 * game.
 */
Color          colors[];
int            pieceValue, theScore=0;
int            playLevel;
int            totalPieces;
boolean        justupdating = false;

/**
 * Moves an array of squares the position "from" to
 * the position "to" if the position "to" is in bounds
 * and is not occupied by other squares
 *
 * @param from[]     Array of source Squares
 * @param to[]         Array of destination Squares
 */
boolean moveSquares (Square from[], Square to[]) {

     outerlabel:
    for (int i=0; i<to.length; i++) {
        if (to[i].InBounds () == false) return false;
        if (field[to[i].column][to[i].row] != 0) {
            for (int j=0; j<from.length; j++)
                if (to[i].IsEqual (from[j]))
                    continue outerlabel;
            return false;
        }
    }

/*
 * Getting here means that the squares can be moved,
 * so they are first erased from the field by setting
 * the color of the field at each square's location to
 * the blank color, which is indexed by zero.
 */
    for (int i=0; i<from.length; i++)
        if (from[i].InBounds ())
            field[from[i].column][from[i].row] = 0;

/*
 * The squares are made visible in the new position
```

continued on next page

continued from previous page

```
 * by setting the colors of the field in those positions
 * to nonblank colors.
 */
    for (int i=0; i<to.length; i++)
        field[to[i].column][to[i].row] = to[i].color;

    return true;
}

/**
 * Create a random new piece and place it at the top
 * of the play field. There are seven types of pieces,
 * all of different color and shape. They are each made
 * out of four squares.
 */
void newPiece () {

/*
 * The array old is used to determine if the game has been lost.
 */
    Square   old[] = new Square[4];
    old[0] = old[1] = old[2] = old[3] = new Square (-1, -1, 0);

    int middle = cols/2;
    int top = rows;

    switch ((int) (Math.random ()*7)) {
        case 0:
        // XXXX          red
        pieceValue = 100;
        curPiece[0] = new Square (middle-1, top-1, 1);
        curPiece[1] = new Square (middle-2, top-1, 1);
        curPiece[2] = new Square (middle,   top-1, 1);
        curPiece[3] = new Square (middle+1, top-1, 1);
        break;

        case 1:
        // X           orange
        // XXX
        pieceValue = 120;
        curPiece[0] = new Square (middle  , top-2, 5);
        curPiece[1] = new Square (middle  , top-1, 5);
        curPiece[2] = new Square (middle-1, top-2, 5);
        curPiece[3] = new Square (middle+1, top-2, 5);
        break;

        case 2:
        // XX          green
        //  XX
        pieceValue = 180;
        curPiece[0] = new Square (middle  , top-2, 2);
        curPiece[1] = new Square (middle-1, top-1, 2);
        curPiece[2] = new Square (middle  , top-1, 2);
```

```
            curPiece[3] = new Square (middle+1, top-2, 2);
            break;

            case 3:
            //  XX          blue
            //  XX
            pieceValue = 180;
            curPiece[0] = new Square (middle  , top-2, 7);
            curPiece[1] = new Square (middle+1, top-1, 7);
            curPiece[2] = new Square (middle  , top-1, 7);
            curPiece[3] = new Square (middle-1, top-2, 7);
            break;

            case 4:
            //  XX          light blue
            //  XX
            pieceValue = 100;
            curPiece[0] = new Square (middle-1, top-1, 3);
            curPiece[1] = new Square (middle  , top-1, 3);
            curPiece[2] = new Square (middle-1, top-2, 3);
            curPiece[3] = new Square (middle  , top-2, 3);
            break;

            case 5:
            //  XXX          purple
            //   X
            pieceValue = 120;
            curPiece[0] = new Square (middle  , top-1, 6);
            curPiece[1] = new Square (middle-1, top-1, 6);
            curPiece[2] = new Square (middle+1, top-1, 6);
            curPiece[3] = new Square (middle+1, top-2, 6);
            break;

            case 6:
            //  XXX          yellow
            //   X
            pieceValue = 120;
            curPiece[0] = new Square (middle  , top-1, 4);
            curPiece[1] = new Square (middle+1, top-1, 4);
            curPiece[2] = new Square (middle-1, top-1, 4);
            curPiece[3] = new Square (middle-1, top-2, 4);
            break;
        }
        gameInPlay = moveSquares (old, curPiece);
    }

    /**
     * Move the current piece by byx columns and byy rows.
     * The piece is rotated 90 degrees if rotate is set True.
     * Returns True if the piece is moved, False if it is not.
     */
    private synchronized boolean movecurPiece (int byx, int byy, boolean
    ⮕rotate) {
```

continued on next page

continued from previous page

```
    Square newpos[] = new Square[4];

    for (int i=0; i<4; i++) {
        if (rotate) {
            int dx = curPiece[i].column - curPiece[0].column;
            int dy = curPiece[i].row - curPiece[0].row;

            newpos[i] = new Square (curPiece[0].column - dy,
                        curPiece[0].row + dx,
                        curPiece[i].color);
        } else {
            newpos[i] = new Square (curPiece[i].column + byx,
                        curPiece[i].row + byy,
                        curPiece[i].color);
        }
    }
    if (moveSquares (curPiece, newpos) == false) return false;

    curPiece = newpos;
    return true;
}

/**
 * Finds rows completely filled with squares and deletes them
 */
void removelines () {

    outerlabel:
    for (int j=0; j<rows; j++) {
        for (int i=0; i<cols; i++)
            if (field[i][j] == 0)
                continue outerlabel;

/*
 * The jth row is completely filled with squares,
 * so move all other squares down one row.
 */
        for (int k=j; k<rows-1; k++)
            for (int i=0; i<cols; i++)
                field[i][k] = field[i][k+1];

// Recheck jth row
        j -= 1;
    }
}

/**
 * Applet entry point
 */
public void init () {

    sqlength = 20;
    cols = 10;
    rows = 20;
```

```
        field = new int[cols][rows+4];
        oldField = new int[cols][rows+4];

        resize (sqlength*cols+xoffset*2, sqlength* (rows+3));

    /*
     * Allocate colors used in the game.
     * Zeroth color is special, i.e., it means that no square
     * is occupied in a position with the zeroth color.
     */
        colors = new Color[8];
        colors[0] = new Color (40,40,40);       // off color
        colors[1] = new Color (255,0,0);        // red
        colors[2] = new Color (0,200,0);        // green
        colors[3] = new Color (0,200,255);      // light blue
        colors[4] = new Color (255,255,0);      // yellow
        colors[5] = new Color (255,150,0);      // orange
        colors[6] = new Color (210,0,240);      // purple
        colors[7] = new Color (40,0,240);       // dark blue
    }

    /**
     * Applet is started
     */
    public void start () {

        for (int i=0; i<cols; i++) {
            for (int j=0; j<rows+4; j++) {
                field[i][j] = 0;
                oldField[i][j] = -1;
            }
        }

        playLevel = 5;
        theScore = 0;
        totalPieces= 0;
        needNewPiece = true;
        gameInPlay = true;

        // Spawn gravity thread
        theThread = new Thread (this);
            theThread.start ();
        requestFocus ();
    }

    /**
     * Applet is stopped
     */
    public synchronized void stop () {

        if (theThread != null)
            theThread.stop ();
        theThread = null;
    }
```

continued on next page

continued from previous page

```
/**
 * Delay values in milliseconds.
 * Array index is the game playLevel.
 * higher levels => short delay => faster game
 */
static int delay_map[] = {
    600, 600, 600, 600, 500, 400, 300, 250, 200, 150, 100
};

/**
 * The main loop of the game
 */
public void run () {

    while (gameInPlay) {
        try {
            int t;
            if (playLevel > 10) t = 75;
            else t = delay_map[playLevel];
            Thread.sleep (t);
        } catch (InterruptedException e) {}
        if (needNewPiece) {
            if (pieceValue > 0) {
                theScore += pieceValue;
                totalPieces += 1;
                playLevel = 5 + totalPieces/30;
            }
            removeLines ();
            newPiece ();
            needNewPiece = false;
        } else {
            needNewPiece = !movecurPiece (0, -1, false);
            if (!needNewPiece) pieceValue -= 5;
        }
        repaint ();
    }
    theThread = null;
}

/**
 * Key is pressed
 */
public boolean keyDown (Event evt, int key)  {

    if (key != 's' && !gameInPlay)
        return true;

    switch (key) {
        case 's':
        stop ();          // Stop old game
        start ();         // Start new game
        break;

        case 'h':          // Left
```

```
              case Event.LEFT:
              pieceValue -= 5;
              movecurPiece (-1, 0, false);
              needNewPiece = false;
              repaint ();
              break;

              case 'k':          // Right
              case Event.RIGHT:
              pieceValue -= 5;
              movecurPiece (1, 0, false);
              needNewPiece = false;
              repaint ();
              break;

              case 'j':          // Rotate
              case Event.UP:
              pieceValue -= 5;
              movecurPiece (0, 0, true);
              repaint ();
              break;

              case ' ':          // Drop
              case Event.DOWN:
              while (movecurPiece (0, -1, false));
              repaint ();
              break;
        }
              return true;
}

/**
 * We need to override this method, otherwise repaint()
 * will erase the whole screen, causing tremendous flickering.
 */
public void update (Graphics g)  {

     justupdating = true;
     // Tell paint to draw only stuff that has changed.
     paint (g);
}

/**
 * Paint graphics on screen
 */
public synchronized void paint (Graphics g) {

     g.setFont (new Font ("Helvetica", 0, 18));
     int  gx = sqlength;
     int  gy = sqlength*rows/4;

     g.clearRect (gx, gy-25, xoffset-gx, 25);
     g.drawString ("Score: " + theScore, gx, gy);
```

continued on next page

continued from previous page

```
        gy += 30;
        g.clearRect (gx, gy-25, xoffset-gx, 25);
        g.drawString ("Level: " + playLevel, gx, gy);

        for (int i=0; i<cols; i++)
            for (int j=0; j<rows; j++) {
            if (!justupdating ||
                oldField[i][rows-1-j] == -1 ||
                oldField[i][rows-1-j] != field[i][rows-1-j]) {
                    g.setColor (colors[field[i][rows-1-j]]);
                    g.fill3DRect (
                    xoffset+sqlength*i,
                    sqlength+sqlength*j,
                        sqlength, sqlength, true);
            }
            oldField[i][rows-1-j] = field[i][rows-1-j];
            }
        justupdating = false;
}
} // end Tetris applet
```

2. Create an HTML document that contains the applet. Create a new file called howto51.html as follows:

```
<html>
<head>
<title>Tetris</title>
</head>
<applet code="Tetris.class" width=600 height=460>
</applet>
<hr size=4>

</html>
```

3. Compile and test the applet. Compile the source using javac or the makefile provided. Test the applet using the Appletviewer by entering the following command:

`APPLETVIEWER howto51.html`

When Tetris is executed, a window will open with the game board in the center. The game will start automatically with a game piece moving from the top to the bottom. To move the piece, the following keys are used—move left: H or LEFTARROW, move right: K or RIGHTARROW, rotate: J or UPARROW, and to drop the piece: SPACEBAR or DOWNARROW. Figure 5-1 shows an example of the running applet.

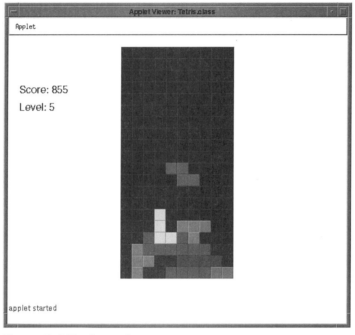

Figure 5-1 Tetris applet

How It Works

The Tetris application contains two classes: the *Square* class and the *Tetris* class, which is the applet itself.

A game piece in Tetris is made up of four squares combined to produce the shape of the game piece. The *Square* class is used to hold a position of a square and its color. It has three instance variables: *column x, row y,* and *color c*. The *column* is the square's column, the *row* is the square's row, and the *color* is the color of the square. The *square()* constructor takes these three variables and saves them. The *Square* class also has an *InBounds()* method, which compares the column and row of the square to the bounds of the play field and determines whether it is within the play field. A method called *IsEqual()* is also defined, and it determines whether the argument passed is equal to the current square.

The *Tetris* class extends Applet because it is an applet. It also implements Runnable because it will have a separate thread running within it. The play field of the game is implemented by defining a two-dimensional integer array called *field*. The values within *field* are actually indices to color values. A value of 0 within the array means that no square occupies that position. An additional array called *old-field* is also defined and is only used to determine the positions that are changed and which ones need to be drawn. A variable *curpiece* is an array of four squares describing the current piece in play. The variable *lost* is set to False if the game has not been lost. The method *movePiece* () moves an array of squares from one location to another location. It will only do this if the new location is not occupied by other squares and is within bounds. If the squares can be moved, they are moved and the method returns True. If they cannot be moved, the squares are not moved and the method returns False. The method *newPiece* () creates a new piece and adds it to the top row of the play field. There are seven possible pieces made up of four squares. The choice between these seven pieces is made at random. This is done by using the *Math.random*() method. Method *movecurPiece*() will move the current piece a specified number of rows or columns, or it will rotate the piece at 90 degrees. This method is called both in response to keyboard events, which can move a piece to the left, right, down, or rotate it, and in response to a running thread, which moves a piece down one row at a time. The method *removeLines*() searches for rows that are completely filled by squares, eliminates them, and moves the rest of the squares down one row.

The *init*() method initializes variables, allocates space for the arrays, and resizes the Applet panel to correspond to the number of rows and columns defined. Four extra rows are added at the top. These four rows are added because a new piece can occupy up to four rows. There are eight colors allocated and stored in an array of colors. The zero color is special. It is used for the off color and matches the play area color. The applet's *start*() method initializes the field to zero color. It also starts the thread that controls movement of the pieces autonomously. The *run*() method is the main loop of the game. It adds new pieces and removes lines when necessary. It also keeps track of the score, current play level, and the delay of the game. The delay is dependent on the play level and decreases with higher play level. The amount of delay is stored in the *delay_map* array. This causes the game to go faster and become more challenging at higher levels.

The *keyDown*() method is called in response to user key events. The value of *key* is compared with the character constants and also with constants defined in the *Event* Class. For example, if H is pressed or if the LEFTARROW key is pressed, the current piece is moved to the left one column. The *keyDown*() method, like many of the event-handling methods in Java, must return either True or False. It must return True if the event is handled by the applet, or it must return False if the event is not handled. In this example all the events that are passed to the *keyDown*() method are handled. For that reason *keyDown*() always returns True.

The *update*() method overrides the default *update*() method. The default *update*() method fills the frame with the background color, which is not necessary and creates excessive flickering. The *paint*() method simply draws the squares contained in the field array with the specific color using *fill3Drect*().

COMPLEXITY
INTERMEDIATE

5.2   How do I...
Access mouse events?

Problem

I would like to create a simple drawing program that uses the mouse. The mouse button should be held down to draw. It would also be nice to have a color bar and use the mouse to select the color to draw in. How do I access mouse events in Java?

Technique

One way to access mouse events using the AWT is to override the *mouseDown()* method. *mouseDown()* is defined in the *Component* class, so every subclass of component inherits *mouseDown()*. When the user presses the mouse button, *mouseDown()* will be called with the x and y position of mouse passed as arguments. Like all other event handler methods, *mouseDown()* should return True if this event has been handled, False if the event should be passed to the superclass.

Other methods exist for handling mouse drag and mouse up events. They are *mouseDrag()* and *mouseUp()* respectively.

Steps

1. Create the applet source file. Create a new file called Doodle.java and enter the following source:

```
import java.applet.Applet;
import java.awt.*;

/**
 * Chapter 5, Example 2
 *
 * The ColorBar class displays a color bar for fast color selection.
 */
class ColorBar {

int xpos, ypos;
int width, height;
int selectedColor = 3;
static Color colors[] = {
    Color.white, Color.gray, Color.red, Color.pink,
    Color.orange, Color.yellow, Color.green, Color.magenta,
    Color.cyan, Color.blue
};
```

continued on next page

continued from previous page

```
/**
 * Create the color bar.
 */
public ColorBar (int x, int y, int w, int h) {

    xpos = x;
    ypos = y;
    width = w;
    height = h;
}

/**
 * Paint the color bar.
 * @param g - destination graphics object
 */
void paint (Graphics g) {

    int x, y;     // Position of each color box
    int w, h;     // Size of each color box

    for (int i=0; i<colors.length; i+=1) {
        w = width;
        h = height/colors.length;
        x = xpos;
        y = ypos + (i * h);
        g.setColor (Color.black);
        g.fillRect (x, y, w, h);
        if (i == selectedColor) {
            x += 5;
            y += 5;
            w -= 10;
            h -= 10;
        } else {
            x += 1;
            y += 1;
            w -= 2;
            h -= 2;
        }
        g.setColor (colors[i]);
        g.fillRect (x, y, w, h);
    }
}

/**
 * Check to see if the mouse is inside a palette box.
 * If so, set selectedColor and return True,
 *         otherwise return False.
 * @param x, y - x and y position of mouse
 */
boolean inside (int x, int y) {

    int i, h;
```

```
        if (x < xpos || x > xpos+width) return false;
        if (y < ypos || y > ypos+height) return false;

        h = height/colors.length;
        for (i=0; i<colors.length; i+=1) {
            if (y < (i+1)*h+ypos) {
                selectedColor = i;
                return true;
            }
        }
        return false;
    }

}


/**
 * The Doodle applet implements a drawable surface
 * with a limited choice of colors to draw with.
 */
public class Doodle extends Applet {

static final int MaxPoints = 1000;
int xpoints[] = new int[MaxPoints];
int ypoints[] = new int[MaxPoints];
int color[] = new int[MaxPoints];
int lastx;
int lasty;
int npoints = 0;
ColorBar colorBar;
boolean inColorBar;

/**
 * Initialize the drawing space
 */
public void init () {

    setBackground(Color.white);
    colorBar = new ColorBar (10, 10, 30, 200);
}

/**
 * Redisplay the drawing space.
 * @param g - destination graphics object
 */
public void update (Graphics g) {

    int i;

    for (i=0; i<npoints; i+=1) {
        g.setColor (colorBar.colors[color[i]]);
        g.fillOval (xpoints[i]-5, ypoints[i]-5, 10, 10);
    }
    colorBar.paint (g);
}
```

continued on next page

continued from previous page

```java
/**
 * Repaint the drawing space when required.
 * @param g - destination graphics object
 */
public void paint (Graphics g) {

    update (g);
}


/**
 * Track mouse clicks and either choose a color from the
 * palette, or record a spot for painting later.
 */
public boolean mouseDown (Event evt, int x, int y) {

    if (colorBar.inside (x, y)) {
        inColorBar = true;
        repaint ();
        return true;
    }
    inColorBar = false;
    if (npoints < MaxPoints) {
        lastx = x;
        lasty = y;
        xpoints[npoints] = x;
        ypoints[npoints] = y;
        color[npoints] = colorBar.selectedColor;
        npoints += 1;
    }
    return true;
}


/**
 * Track mouse drags and record a spot for later painting.
 */
public boolean mouseDrag (Event evt, int x, int y) {

    if (inColorBar) return true;
    if ((x != lastx || y != lasty) && npoints < MaxPoints) {
        lastx = x;
        lasty = y;
        xpoints[npoints] = x;
        ypoints[npoints] = y;
        color[npoints] = colorBar.selectedColor;
        npoints += 1;
        repaint ();
    }
    return true;
```

```
}

/**
 * The main method allows this class to be run as an application,
 * in addition to being run as an applet.
 * @param args - command line arguments
 */
public static void main (String args[]) {

    Frame f = new Frame ("Doodle");
    Doodle doodle = new Doodle ();

    f.resize (410, 430);
    f.add ("Center", doodle);
    f.show ();
    doodle.init ();
}

}
```

2. Create an HTML document that contains the applet. Create a new file called howto52.html as follows:

```
<html>
<head>
<title>Doodle </title>
</head>
<applet code="Doodle.class" width=200 height=200>
</applet>
<hr size=4>

</html>
```

3. Compile and test the applet. Compile the source using javac or the makefile provided. Test the applet using the Appletviewer by entering the following command:

```
APPLETVIEWER howto52.html
```

Doodle.java may also be run as an application by typing:

```
java Doodle
```

When Doodle is executed, a window will open, containing a drawing area and a color palette on the left. The color palette contains ten colors. Use the mouse to select a color; then move to the right and hold down the mouse button, and use the mouse to draw. Try changing the color and draw something else. Figure 5-2 shows an example of the running applet.

Figure 5-2 Doodle applet

How It Works

The Doodle applet/application contains two classes: *Doodle* itself and *ColorBar*.

The *ColorBar* class draws a color toolbar containing a palette of ten colors that the user can use to doodle. The constructor for *ColorBar* saves the x and y position, width, and height for the toolbar in the variables *xpos, ypos, width,* and *height,* respectively.

The *paint()* method in *ColorBar* uses these variables to draw the color toolbar itself. The selected color (the color that the user selects with the mouse) is drawn as a slightly smaller filled rectangle.

The *inside()* method determines which color has been selected by comparing the mouse x and y values passed to it by the *mouseDown()* method in the *Doodle* class. *Inside()* returns True if the mouse x and y are inside the color toolbar; it also sets the *selectedColor* variable to the appropriate value.

If the *Doodle* class is run as an application, control is transferred to the *main()* method. The *main()* method creates a window frame to contain the applet, creates an instance of the *Doodle* class, and adds that instance to the *Frame*.

The *mouseDown()* method is called by the Java runtime whenever a mouse-down event occurs within the applet frame. The *mouseDown()* method receives the x and y mouse coordinates passed as parameters by the Java runtime. If the mouse-down position is inside the color toolbar, a repaint is forced by invoking the *repaint()* method; this repaints the toolbar with the selected color shown as selected. In this case, the *inColorBar* variable is set to True, so that the *mouseDrag()* method knows not to do any actual "painting" in the frame.

If the mouse coordinates are not within the color toolbar, the mouse coordinates are saved in two arrays, *xpoints* and *ypoints*. The color of the point is also saved in the array color. Since these arrays are static (dynamic arrays are covered in Chapter 8), the number of points actually saved (and therefore painted) is limited by the variable *MaxPoints*.

The *mouseDrag()* method is invoked whenever the user moves the mouse with the mouse button down. If the *inColorBar* variable is set to True, then no painting occurs; otherwise the current mouse position coordinates are added to their respective arrays.

The first time an applet is run, the *paint()* method is called directly. Every subsequent paint is achieved by calling *repaint()*. The *repaint()* method requests an update to occur as soon as it can. The default *update()* method erases the frame by filling the frame with the current background color and then calls *paint()*.

In this example, the *paint()* method calls the *update()* method. The *update()* method actually performs the painting. This *update()* method overrides the default *update()* method, since the default method continuously erases the frame, which is unnecessary and causes an annoying flicker. *update()* in turn calls the *filloval()* method to draw each point.

The idea of having *paint()* call *update()* may seem slightly illogical at first. If the flow of the applet is traced, it can be shown that this technique can actually be beneficial. In this example, the first time the applet is run, the *paint()* method is called, which calls *update()*. From that point on, every time a *repaint()* is requested, *update()* is called, which actually performs the painting. The *paint()* method is never called after the first time. The traditional flow has *update()* being called, which in turn calls *paint()* every time a *repaint()* was requested. The technique shown in this example reduces the number of methods being called. For example, if *repaint()* is requested 1,000 times, the default *update()* and *paint()* would each have to be called 1,000 times. By using the new technique, *update()* would be called 1,000 times, and *paint()* would be called only once.

Comments

Mouse events are passed to the preceding mouse-event methods (*mouseUp()*, *mouseDown()*, and *mouseDrag()*) by the *handleEvent()* method. If any of these mouse-event methods returns True, then *handleEvent()* infers that the mouse event has been "absorbed" and prevents that event from being passed to other mouse-event methods. This convention applies to all event-handling methods, as shown in Figure 5-3.

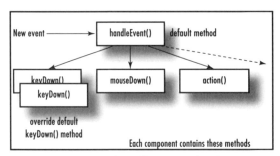

Figure 5-3 Event-handling method
conventions

COMPLEXITY
INTERMEDIATE

5.3 How do I...
Access other events?

Problem

I would like to be able to control various aspects that occur in response to an event.
I know how to handle basic keyboard and mouse events, but I would like to be able
to handle any event that occurs. How do I handle other events in Java?

Technique

Events are handled in Java by overriding the method of the event of interest.
Whenever a certain event occurs, such as a keypress or moving the mouse, the Java
runtime will call the appropriate method. This example will override the
handleEvent() method and illustrate how to handle several different events. The technique used here can be applied to any event. Table 5-1 lists the variable indices contained
in the event class.

Steps

1. Create the applet source file. Create a new file called EventApp.java and
enter the following source:

```
import java.awt.*;

/**
 * Application class
 * Lists events
 */
public class EventApp extends Frame {
```

```
/*
 * TextField used for demo only
 */
TextField location;

/*
 * The display area for event printing
 */
TextArea content;

/*
 * The constructor
 * Sets the app. window title and creates the user interface
 */
public EventApp () {

    int i;

    setTitle ("EventApp");
    setLayout(new BorderLayout());

    location = new TextField ("", 20);
    content = new TextArea ("", 24, 80);
    content.setEditable (false);

    Panel mypanel = new Panel ();
    mypanel.setLayout (new FlowLayout ());
    mypanel.add (location);
    mypanel.add (new Button ("Button"));
    mypanel.add (new Checkbox("Checkbox"));
    mypanel.add (new Checkbox("Checkbox"));

    add ("North", mypanel);
    add ("Center", content);

    resize (400, 300);
    show ();
}

/*
 * Called in response to events
 * Prints the type of event in the text area
 */
public boolean handleEvent(Event evt) {
    switch (evt.id) {

        case Event.KEY_ACTION:
                content.appendText("The key action keyboard event.\n");

            switch (evt.key) {
                    case Event.DOWN:
                    content.appendText("The down arrow key.\n");
                    return true;
            case Event.END:
```

continued on next page

continued from previous page

```
                        content.appendText("The end key.\n");
                return true;
        case Event.F1:
                        content.appendText("The F1 function key.\n");
                return true;
          case Event.F10:
                        content.appendText("The F10 function key.\n");
                return true;
          case Event.F11:
                        content.appendText("The F11 function key.\n");
                return true;
          case Event.F12:
                        content.appendText("The F12 function key.\n");
                return true;
          case Event.F2:
                        content.appendText("The F2 function key.\n");
                return true;
          case Event.F3:
                        content.appendText("The F3 function key.\n");
                return true;
          case Event.F4:
                        content.appendText("The F4 function key.\n");
                return true;
          case Event.F5:
                        content.appendText("The F5 function key.\n");
                return true;
          case Event.F6:
                        content.appendText("The F6 function key.\n");
                return true;
          case Event.F7:
                        content.appendText("The F7 function key.\n");
                return true;
          case Event.F8:
                        content.appendText("The F8 function key.\n");
                return true;
          case Event.F9:
                        content.appendText("The F9 function key.\n");
                return true;
          case Event.HOME:
                        content.appendText("The home key.\n");
                return true;
          case Event.LEFT:
                        content.appendText("The left arrow key.\n");
                return true;
          case Event.PGDN:
                        content.appendText("The page down key.\n");
                return true;
          case Event.PGUP:
                        content.appendText("The page up key.\n");
                return true;
          case Event.RIGHT:
                content.appendText("The right arrow key.\n");
                return true;
                        case Event.UP:
                content.appendText("The up arrow key.\n");
```

```
            return true;
    }

        return true;
    case Event.KEY_ACTION_RELEASE:
            content.appendText("The key action release keyboard
            ↩event.\n");

        switch (evt.key) {
            case Event.DOWN:
                    content.appendText("The down arrow key.\n");
                    return true;
            case Event.END:
                content.appendText("The end key.\n");
            return true;
            case Event.F1:
                    content.appendText("The F1 function key.\n");
            return true;
             case Event.F10:
                    content.appendText("The F10 function key.\n");
            return true;
             case Event.F11:
                    content.appendText("The F11 function key.\n");
            return true;
             case Event.F12:
                    content.appendText("The F12 function key.\n");
            return true;
             case Event.F2:
                    content.appendText("The F2 function key.\n");
            return true;
             case Event.F3:
                    content.appendText("The F3 function key.\n");
            return true;
             case Event.F4:
                    content.appendText("The F4 function key.\n");
            return true;
             case Event.F5:
                    content.appendText("The F5 function key.\n");
            return true;
             case Event.F6:
                    content.appendText("The F6 function key.\n");
            return true;
             case Event.F7:
                    content.appendText("The F7 function key.\n");
            return true;
             case Event.F8:
                    content.appendText("The F8 function key.\n");
            return true;
             case Event.F9:
                   content.appendText("The F9 function key.\n");
            return true;
               case Event.HOME:
                   content.appendText("The home key.\n");
            return true;
               case Event.LEFT:
```

continued on next page

continued from previous page

```
                    content.appendText("The left arrow key.\n");
              return true;
                case Event.PGDN:
                    content.appendText("The page down key.\n");
              return true;
                case Event.PGUP:
                    content.appendText("The page up key.\n");
              return true;
                    case Event.RIGHT:
              content.appendText("The right arrow key.\n");
              return true;
                    case Event.UP:
              content.appendText("The up arrow key.\n");
              return true;
        }
        return true;
    case Event.GOT_FOCUS:
            content.appendText("A component gained the focus.\n");
        return true;
    case Event.KEY_PRESS:
            content.appendText("The keypress keyboard event.\n");
        return true;
    case Event.KEY_RELEASE:
            content.appendText("The key release keyboard event.\n");
        return true;

    case Event.LIST_DESELECT:
            content.appendText("List Deselect.\n");
        return true;

    case Event.LOST_FOCUS:
            content.appendText("A component lost the focus.\n");
        return true;

    case Event.MOUSE_DOWN:
            content.appendText("The mouse down event. " +
            evt.x + ", " + evt.y + "\n");
        return true;
    case Event.MOUSE_DRAG:
            content.appendText("The mouse drag event. " +
            evt.x + ", " + evt.y + "\n");
        return true;
    case Event.MOUSE_ENTER:
            content.appendText("The mouse enter event. " +
            evt.x + ", " + evt.y + "\n");
        return true;
    case Event.MOUSE_EXIT:
            content.appendText("The mouse exit event. " +
            evt.x + ", " + evt.y + "\n");
        return true;
```

```
        case Event.MOUSE_MOVE:
              content.appendText("The mouse move event. " +
              evt.x + ", " + evt.y + "\n");
          return true;
        case Event.MOUSE_UP:
              content.appendText("The mouse up event. " +
              evt.x + ", " + evt.y + "\n");
          return true;
         case Event.WINDOW_DEICONIFY:
               content.appendText("The de-iconify window event.\n");
          return true;
         case Event.WINDOW_DESTROY:
              content.appendText("The destroy window event.\n");
          return true;
         case Event.WINDOW_EXPOSE:
               content.appendText("The expose window event.\n");
          return true;
         case Event.WINDOW_ICONIFY:
               content.appendText("The iconify window event.\n");
          return true;
         case Event.WINDOW_MOVED:
               content.appendText("The move window event.\n");
          return true;

    }
    return false;
}

/*
 * Application entry point
 * Create an instance of EventApp.
 */
public static void main (String args[]) {

    new EventApp ();
}
}
```

2. Compile and test the application. Compile the source using javac or the makefile provided. Test the application by typing:

`java EventApp`

When EventApp is executed, a window will open with a text field, a button, and a check box at the top, and a text area occupying the remaining area of the panel. Every time one of the events of interest occurs, a message will be printed in the text area stating the nature of the event. EventApp can only run as an application. It could be converted to run as an applet by extending the *Applet* class. Figure 5-4 shows an example of the running application.

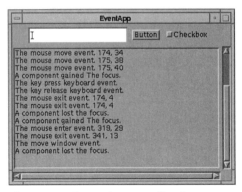

Figure 5-4 EventApp application

How It Works

The EventApp application contains only one class, the application itself. A TextField
called *location* and a TextArea called *content* are declared. The *EventApp()* constructor
sets the layout manager of the main container to BorderLayout. The TextField, *location,* is initialized to contain a blank string and be 20 columns wide. The TextArea,
content, is initialized to contain a blank string, have 24 rows and 80 columns, and
not be editable. A new panel, *mypanel,* is added to the top of the main panel, and
the TextField, a button, and a check box are added. The TextArea is added to the
center of the main panel.

The *handleEvent()* method is overridden for several different events. The type of
event that occurs is contained in the *Event.id* integer variable. The *Event* class
defines the ID of every event to be equal to a variable index, and these are shown
in Table 5-1. This makes catching the event very simple. A *switch* statement can be
used to switch off the *Event.id* value, and the event's index can be used to match the
ID value to the event. The method then prints the description of the event that occurred
and returns True. The text is printed to the TextArea by using the *appendText()* method.
This method takes a string input and appends it to the end of the TextArea.

There are several additional values associated with an event. These include *key,*
which is the key that was pressed in a keyboard event, and *x* and *y,* which are the
coordinates of the event. The list of event variables is also shown in Table 5-1. For
this example, the KEY_ACTION or KEY_ACTION_RELEASE events will also contain a *switch* statement to switch off the value of event.key. For example, if F12 is
pressed, the messages "The Key action Keyboard event." and "The F12 function key."
are added to the text area. Similarly, when the key is released, the messages "The Key
action release Keyboard event." and "The F12 function key." are added to the text
area.

If a mouse event occurs, a message stating which event along with the events coordinates is added to the text area. The coordinates of the event are stored in the *Event.x*
and *Event.y* variables.

COMPLEXITY
INTERMEDIATE

5.4 How do I...
Access applet parameters?

Problem

I liked the scrolling text marquee in example 3.5, except that it requires recompilation of the source every time the text is changed. I would like to run the marquee as an applet and be able to pass a parameter that contains the text to be scrolled. How do I access applet parameters?

Technique

This example will create a single scrolling text marquee. The text will scroll from left to right. The text that scrolls will be passed to the Java applet from the HTML file by using the <param> tag. Applet parameters are returned from the *Applet.getParameter()* method with the parameter name as an argument. *Applet.getParameter()* returns the value of the applet parameter as a String object.

Steps

1. Create the applet source file. Create a new file called ScrollApp.java and enter the following source:

```java
import java.applet.Applet;
import java.awt.*;

class Scroll {

int xstart, ystart;
int width, height;
String text;
int deltaX, deltaY;
int xpos, ypos;
Color color;

/**
 * Text scrolls in different directions.
 * @param xpos     initial x position
 * @param ypos     initial y position
 * @param deltax     velocity in x direction
 * @param deltay     velocity in y direction
 * @param width    bounding point for window panel width
 * @param height     bounding point for window panel height
 * @param text    text that is scrolled on the window
 * @param color     color of the text
```

continued on next page

continued from previous page

```
 */
public Scroll (int x, int y, int dx, int dy, int w, int h, String t, Color
➥c) {

    xstart = x;
    ystart = y;
    width = w;
    height = h;
    text = t;
    deltaX = dx;
    deltaY = dy;
    color = c;
    xpos = xstart;
    ypos = ystart;
}

/**
 * Called from update() in response to repaint()
 * @param g - destination graphics object
 */
void paint (Graphics g) {

    g.setColor (color);
    g.drawString (text, xpos, ypos);
    xpos += deltaX;
    ypos += deltaY;

    FontMetrics fm = g.getFontMetrics ();
    int textw = fm.stringWidth (text);
    int texth = fm.getHeight ();
    if (deltaX < 0 && xpos < -textw) xpos = xstart;
    if (deltaX > 0 && xpos > width) xpos = xstart;
    if (deltaY < 0 && ypos < 0) ypos = ystart;
    if (deltaY > 0 && ypos > height+texth) ypos = ystart;
}
} // Class Scroll


/*
 * The applet/application class
 */
public class ScrollApp extends Applet implements Runnable{

/*
 * Width and height of the bounding panel
 */
int width, height;

/*
 * Instance of a left-scrolling Scroll object
 */
Scroll left;
String input_text;
Font font = new Font("Helvetica",1,24);
Thread thread;
```

```java
/*
 * Called when the applet is loaded
 * Create instances of FIFO, Source, Sink, and Thread.
 */
public void init () {

    input_text=getParameter("text");
    Dimension d = size ();

    width = d.width;
    height = d.height;

    left = new Scroll (400, 50, -5, 0, width, height,
        input_text, Color.red);
} // init()

/*
 * Start the graphics update thread.
 */
public void start() {

    thread = new Thread(this);
    thread.start();
} // start()

/*
 * The graphics update thread
 * Call repaint every 100 ms.
 */
public void run() {

    while (true) {
        try {
            Thread.sleep(100);
        } catch (InterruptedException e) { }
        repaint();
    }
} // run()

/*
 * Stop the graphics update thread.
 */
public void stop() {

    thread.stop();
} // stop()

/**
 * Called from update() in response to repaint()
 * @param g - destination graphics object
 */
public void paint (Graphics g) {

    g.setFont(font);
    left.paint (g);
```

continued on next page

continued from previous page

```
} // paint()
} // class ScrollApp
```

2. Create an HTML document that contains the applet. Create a new file called howto54.html as follows:

```
<html>
<head>
<title>Marquee</title>
</head>
<applet code="ScrollApp.class" width=400 height=60>
<param name = "text" value = "The Java(tm) How-To">
</applet>
<hr size=4>

</html>
```

3. Compile and test the applet. Compile the source using javac or the makefile provided. Test the applet using the Appletviewer by entering the following command:

```
APPLETVIEWER howto54.html
```

ScrollApp may only be run as an applet because it requires applet parameters to be passed to it.

When ScrollApp is executed, a window will open with the words "The Java™ How-To" scrolling from the left to the right. Try changing the value of the "text" parameter in the howto54.html file and run the applet again. The text will change to whatever is specified in the html file. ScrollApp does not have to be recompiled to effect the change. Figure 5-5 shows an example of the running applet.

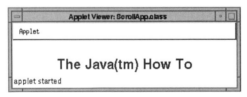

Figure 5-5 Accessing applet parameters

How It Works

The ScrollApp applet contains two classes, *ScrollApp* and *Scroll*. *ScrollApp* is the applet itself, and *Scroll* contains the methods for computing and drawing the moving text.

ScrollApp extends Applet since it is the applet, and implements Runnable because it will have a separate thread running within it. An instance of the *Scroll* class, called left; a String, called input_text; and a Thread, called thread, are created. The font is set to 24-point, bold, helvetica.

The *init()* method uses the *getParameter()* method to retrieve the parameter from the html file. The *getParameter()* method takes a string value as a parameter. This string value is the name the parameter is given in the html file. The parameter is defined in the html file using the <param> tag. An example of defining a parameter with a name of "myparameter" and a value of "This is what I want to send" in an html file is

```
<param name = "myparameter" value = "This is what I want to send" >
```

This must all be within the <applet> </applet> section of the html file. In the next step, the *width* and *height* are set to the width and height of the panel. A new scroll is created with an initial starting location of 400,50; a horizontal velocity of -5; a vertical velocity of 0; a width and height equal to the panel size; a text value to scroll; and the color red.

The *start()* and *run()* methods are used to create a thread that will sleep for a 100 milliseconds and then redraw the marquee.

The *Scroll* class is identical to that used in section 3.5.

Comments

This applet draws the text to be scrolled directly to the screen. This method may cause the text to flicker slightly. To eliminate this flickering, a method known as "double buffering" should be used. This will be covered in Chapter 7.

COMPLEXITY
INTERMEDIATE

5.5   How do I...
Parse applet parameters?

Problem

I liked the text marquee in example 3.5 with the text moving in all different directions. I would like to be able to control the direction of the moving text and the text itself without recompiling the source every time. I want to pass the applet the text to be scrolled, the color, and the direction in a single parameter from the html file. I know how to access applet parameters, but how do I parse applet parameters?

Technique

The text that will scroll, its color, and the direction will be passed to the Java applet from the html file by using the <param> tag. The parameter will be parsed in the Java applet by using the *StringTokenizer()* method.

Steps

1. Create the applet source file. Create a new file called ScrollApp.java and
enter the following source:

```java
import java.applet.Applet;
import java.awt.*;
import java.util.*;

class Scroll {

int xstart, ystart;
int width, height;
String text;
int deltaX, deltaY;
int xpos, ypos;
Color color;

/**
 * Text scrolls in different directions.
 * @param xpos   initial x position
 * @param ypos   initial y position
 * @param deltax         velocity in x direction
 * @param deltay         velocity in y direction
 * @param width bounding point for window panel width
 * @param height         bounding point for window panel height
 * @param text  text that is scrolled on the window
 * @param color color of the text
 */
public Scroll (int x, int y, int dx, int dy, int w, int h, String t, Color
➡c) {

    xstart = x;
    ystart = y;
    width = w;
    height = h;
    text = t;
    deltaX = dx;
    deltaY = dy;
    color = c;
    xpos = xstart;
    ypos = ystart;
}

/**
 * Called from update() in response to repaint()
 * @param g - destination graphics object
 */
void paint (Graphics g) {

    g.setColor (color);
    g.drawString (text, xpos, ypos);
    xpos += deltaX;
    ypos += deltaY;
```

```
      FontMetrics fm = g.getFontMetrics ();
      int textw = fm.stringWidth (text);
      int texth = fm.getHeight ();
      if (deltaX < 0 && xpos < -textw) xpos = xstart;
      if (deltaX > 0 && xpos > width) xpos = xstart;
      if (deltaY < 0 && ypos < 0) ypos = ystart;
      if (deltaY > 0 && ypos > height+texth) ypos = ystart;
}
} // Class Scroll

/*
 * The applet class
 */
public class ScrollApp extends Applet implements Runnable {

/*
 * Width and height of the bounding panel
 */
int width, height;

/*
 * The number of scrolling objects
 */
int nscroll = 0;

/*
 * Array of scrolling objects
 */
Scroll scr[] = new Scroll[5];
Font font = new Font("Helvetica",1,24);
Thread thread;

/*
 * Called when the applet is loaded
 * Parses applet parameters
 */
public void init () {

    String scr_text[] = {"test1","test2","test3","test4","test5"};
    int scr_xvel[] =   {-5,5,0,0,7};
    int scr_yvel[] =   {0,0,-5,5,3};
    int scr_xpos[] =   {400,0,100,200,0};
    int scr_ypos[] =   {50,150,200,0,0};
    int scr_red[] =    {255,0,0,100,200};
    int scr_green[] = {0,255,0,200,100};
    int scr_blue[] =   {0,0,255,50,50};
    Color scr_color[] = new Color[5];
    int i;
    Dimension d = size ();

    width = d.width;
    height = d.height;
    for (i=1; i<=5; i+=1) {
        String param, token;
        int j = 0;
```

continued on next page

continued from previous page

```
param = getParameter ("Scroll"+i);
if (param == null) break;

StringTokenizer st = new StringTokenizer (param, ",");
token = st.nextToken ();
scr_text[nscroll] = token;

token = st.nextToken ();
try {
    j = Integer.valueOf (token).intValue();
} catch (NumberFormatException e){
}

switch (j) {
    case 0: //Scroll left.
        scr_xvel[nscroll] = -5;
        scr_yvel[nscroll] = 0;
        scr_xpos[nscroll] = 400;
        scr_ypos[nscroll] = 50;
        break;

    case 1: //Scroll right.
        scr_xvel[nscroll] = 5;
        scr_yvel[nscroll] = 0;
        scr_xpos[nscroll] = 0;
        scr_ypos[nscroll] = 150;
        break;

    case 2: //Scroll up.
        scr_xvel[nscroll] = 0;
        scr_yvel[nscroll] = -5;
        scr_xpos[nscroll] = 100;
        scr_ypos[nscroll] = 200;
        break;

    case 3: //Scroll down.
        scr_xvel[nscroll] = 0;
        scr_yvel[nscroll] = 5;
        scr_xpos[nscroll] = 200;
        scr_ypos[nscroll] = 0;
        break;

    case 4: //Scroll diagonally.
        scr_xvel[nscroll] = 7;
        scr_yvel[nscroll] = 3;
        scr_xpos[nscroll] = 0;
        scr_ypos[nscroll] = 0;
        break;
}

token = st.nextToken ();
try {
    scr_red[nscroll] = Integer.valueOf (token).intValue();
} catch (NumberFormatException e) {
}
```

```
        token = st.nextToken ();
        try {
            scr_green[nscroll] = Integer.valueOf (token).intValue();
        } catch (NumberFormatException e) {
        }

        token = st.nextToken ();
        try {
            scr_blue[nscroll] = Integer.valueOf (token).intValue();
        } catch (NumberFormatException e) {
        }

        scr_color[nscroll] = new Color(scr_red[nscroll],
            scr_green[nscroll], scr_blue[nscroll]);
        nscroll +=1;
    }
    for (i=0; i<nscroll; i+=1) {
        scr[i] = new Scroll (scr_xpos[i], scr_ypos[i],
            scr_xvel[i], scr_yvel[i], width, height,
            scr_text[i], scr_color[i]);
    }
} // init()

/*
 * Start the graphics update thread.
 */
public void start() {

    thread = new Thread(this);
    thread.start ();
} // start()

/*
 * The graphics update thread
 * Call repaint every 100 ms.
 */
public void run() {

    while (true) {
        try {
            Thread.sleep(100);
        } catch (InterruptedException e) { }
        repaint();
    }
} // run()

/*
 * Stop the graphics update thread.
 */
public void stop() {

    thread.stop();
} // stop();

/**
```

continued on next page

continued from previous page

```
 * Called from update() in response to repaint()
 * @param g - destination graphics object
 */
public void paint (Graphics g) {

    int i;

    g.setFont(font);
    for (i=0; i<nscroll; i+=1) {
        scr[i].paint (g);
    }
} // paint()
} // Class ScrollApp
```

2. Create an HTML document that contains the applet. Create a new file called howto55.html as follows:

```
<html>
<head>
<title>Scrolling Marquee</title>
</head>
<applet code="ScrollApp.class" width=400 height=200>
<param name = "Scroll1" value = "The Java(tm),0,255,0,0">
<param name = "Scroll2" value = "How To,4,0,255,255">
</applet>
<hr size=4>

</html>
```

3. Compile and test the applet. Compile the source using javac or the makefile provided. Test the applet using the Appletviewer by entering the following command:

```
APPLETVIEWER howto55.html
```

ScrollApp.java can only be run as an applet because it requires applet parameters.

When ScrollApp is executed, a window will open with two different marquees scrolling in different directions. The words "The Java(tm)" will be scrolling from left to right and are red. The words "How-To" will scroll diagonally and are cyan. The text, color, and direction can all be changed from the html file. The parameters passed from the html file need to have the following format:

text value to scroll, direction, red comp, green comp, blue comp

The direction is an integer that is 0 for left, 1 for right, 2 for up, 3 for down, and 4 for diagonal. The red, green, and blue comps are the RGB components of the desired color from 0 to 255. Each value must be separated by a comma. There can be up to five different parameters in the html file, but they must be called "Scroll1," Scroll2," and so on. The parameters must be named sequentially starting from Scroll1; numbers cannot be skipped. Figure 5-6 shows an example of the running applet.

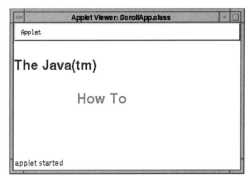

Figure 5-6 Parsing applet parameters

How It Works

The applet is very similar to the example in section 5.4. ScrollApp contains two classes, *ScrollApp* and *Scroll*.

The *ScrollApp* class creates an array of Scroll with five elements. The font is set to 24-point, bold, helvetica. A String array, scr_text, is initialized to contain five elements with values of "test1" to "test5." Arrays are also created for the *x* and *y* velocity and starting position, and the red, green, and blue color components. Each element of each array is initialized to a default value. These values are arbitrary and were used to ensure a value was set. A *for* loop is used to obtain the parameters from the html file. If the parameter returned is equal to null, it is assumed the end of the parameters has been reached, and the loop is stopped with *break*. *StringTokenizer()* is used to parse the parameter at the commas. The first token is stored in the scr_text array. The next token represents the direction and should be from 0 to 4. The value is converted to an integer, and a *switch* statement is used to set the *x* and *y* starting positions and velocities for the various directions. The last three tokens represent the color values. They are converted to integers and stored in the appropiate array. The *nscroll* variable keeps track of the number of tokens retrieved. A *for* loop is then used to create the scrolling marquees for the number of parameters retrieved.

The remainder of the code is identical to example 5.4.

Comments

This example uses hard-wired velocities and initial positions for the five different directions. To make the applet more versatile, the exact positions and velocities could be included in the applet parameter.

CHAPTER 6
USER INTERFACE

6

USER INTERFACE

How do I...

Graphical user interfaces are an important part of programming. For your program to be able to interact with users, you need to understand several types of components or *widgets*. An example of widgets commonly used would be those of an average word processor. The word processor contains buttons, choice lists, sliders, check boxes, and menus.

This chapter will explain how to create many widgets. These are the basis for many of the more interesting and useful applications. With the use of the event handling covered in Chapter 5 and the widgets here, you could create games, word processors, spreadsheets, and many other applications.

6.1   Create Buttons

This example shows how to create buttons for a simple mathematical calculator. The mouse is used to press the buttons of the calculator keypad.

6.2   Create Check Boxes

Check boxes can be implemented in two ways: an individual check box, or grouped check boxes that are usually referred to as *radio buttons*. A digital/analog clock demonstrates the use of both kinds of check boxes.

6.3   Create Menus

Menus allow the user to perform a task from a predefined set. This How-To modifies the drawing program from section 5.2 and adds a menu bar.

6.4   Use Choice Lists

Choice lists allow the user to select a choice from a list. Choice lists are commonly used in forms or questionnaires in HTML documents. This How-To creates a conversion tool that allows for conversion between various English and metric units of length.

6.5   Create Text Fields and Text Areas

Text fields and text areas allow for the user to enter information. This example creates a spreadsheet that implements the four basic mathematical functions: addition, subtraction, multiplication, and division.

6.6   Use Sliders

In Java, sliders are implemented with the *Scrollbar* class. Sliders allow the user to select a value within a predetermined range. This example demonstrates the use of sliders with a simple RGB color selection tool.

6.7   List Boxes

List boxes are another important user interface. This example implements a simple phone book that uses list boxes to present a list of names. When the user selects a name in the list box, the phone number and e-mail address are displayed.

6.8   Layout Managers

In Java, every container has an associated layout manager. This How-To describes each layout manager the Java AWT provides.

6.9   Absolute Positioning

Occasionally, one of the provided layout managers may not fit the application needed. Instead, you can position a component at a specified location, as this example shows.

6.10 Create Windows

Windows can be created in Java by using the *Frame* class. These windows are useful if you want window independence from the browser. This example creates a window and uses it to output debugging information.

6.11 Create Dialogs

Modal and Modeless dialog boxes are another important user interface component. These are typically used to interact with the user by displaying error messages or information. In this example we will use modal dialogs for reporting error messages in a spread sheet.

6.12 File Dialogs

Java's *FileDialogs* class creates file-selection widgets. This example creates a simple notepad program that implements *FileDialogs* to open and save files.

COMPLEXITY
INTERMEDIATE

6.1 How do I...
Create buttons?

Problem

I want to create a simple calculator applet that implements the four basic mathematical functions: addition, subtraction, multiplication, and division. The calculator should draw the buttons on the screen, and the mouse should be used to press the buttons. I know how to use math functions and access mouse events, but how do I create buttons?

Technique

The calculator will use the *Button* class to create the buttons of a calculator.

Steps

1. Create the applet source file. Create a new file called Calc.java and enter the following source:

```
import java.util.*;
import java.awt.*;
import java.applet.*;

/**
 * A simple calculator
 */
```

continued on next page

continued from previous page

```
public class Calc extends Applet {

    Display  display = new Display();

/**
 *   Initialize the Calc applet.
 */
    public void init () {

        setLayout(new BorderLayout());
        Keypad    keypad = new Keypad();

        add ("North", display);
        add ("Center", keypad);
    }

/**
 * Handle the calculator functions.
 */
    public boolean action (Event ev, Object arg) {

        if (ev.target instanceof Button) {

            String label = (String)arg;
            if (label.equals("C")) {
              display.Clear ();
              return true;
            }
            else if (label.equals(".")) {
                display.Dot ();
                return true;
            }
            else if (label.equals("+")) {
                display.Plus ();
                return true;
            }
            else if (label.equals("-")) {
                display.Minus ();
                return true;
            }
            else if (label.equals("x")) {
                display.Mul ();
                return true;
            }
            else if (label.equals("/")) {
                display.Div ();
                return true;
            }
            else if (label.equals("+/-")) {
                display.Chs ();
                return true;
            }
            else if (label.equals("=")) {
```

```
                    display.Equals ();
                    return true;
                }
                else {
                    display.Digit (label);
                    return true;
                }
            }
            return false;
        }


/**
 * This allows the class to be used either as an applet
 * or as a stand-alone application.
 */
public static void main (String args[]) {

    Frame f = new Frame ("Calculator");
    Calc calc = new Calc ();

    calc.init ();

    f.resize (210, 200);
    f.add ("Center", calc);
    f.show ();
}
}


/* -------------------------------------------------- */

/**
 * The Keypad handles the input for the calculator
 * and writes to the display.
 */
class Keypad extends Panel {

/**
 * Initialize the keypad, add buttons, set colors, etc.
 */
    Keypad (){

        Button  b = new Button();
        Font    font = new Font ("Times", Font.BOLD, 14);
        Color   functionColor = new Color (255, 255, 0);
        Color   numberColor = new Color (0, 255, 255);
        Color   equalsColor = new Color (0, 255, 0);
        setFont (font);
        b.setForeground (Color.black);

        add (b = new Button ("7"));
        b.setBackground (numberColor);
        add (b = new Button ("8"));
```

continued on next page

continued from previous page

```
            b.setBackground (numberColor);
            add (b = new Button ("9"));
            b.setBackground (numberColor);
            add (b = new Button ("/"));
            b.setBackground (functionColor);

            add (b = new Button ("4"));
            b.setBackground (numberColor);
            add (b = new Button ("5"));
            b.setBackground (numberColor);
            add (b = new Button ("6"));
            b.setBackground (numberColor);
            add (b = new Button ("x"));
            b.setBackground (functionColor);

            add (b = new Button ("1"));
            b.setBackground (numberColor);
            add (b = new Button ("2"));
            b.setBackground (numberColor);
            add (b = new Button ("3"));
            b.setBackground (numberColor);
            add (b = new Button ("-"));
            b.setBackground (functionColor);

            add (b = new Button ("."));
            b.setBackground (functionColor);
            add (b = new Button ("0"));
            b.setBackground (numberColor);
            add (b = new Button ("+/-"));
            b.setBackground (functionColor);
            add (b = new Button ("+"));
            b.setBackground (functionColor);

            add (b = new Button ("C"));
            b.setBackground (functionColor);
            add (new Label (""));
            add (new Label (""));
            add (b = new Button ("="));
            b.setBackground (equalsColor);

            setLayout (new GridLayout (5, 4, 4, 4));
        }

}


/* ------------------------------------------------- */

/**
 * The Display class manages displaying the calculated result,
 * as well as implementing the calculator function keys.
 */
class Display extends Panel{
```

```
    double        last = 0;
    int           op = 0;
    boolean       equals = false;
    int           maxlen = 10;
    String        s;
    Label         readout = new Label("");

/**
 * Initialize the display.
 */
    Display () {

    setLayout(new BorderLayout());
    setBackground (Color.red);
        setFont (new Font ("Courier", Font.BOLD + Font.ITALIC, 30));
        readout.setAlignment(1);
        add ("Center",readout);
    repaint();
        Clear ();
    }

/**
 * Handle pressing a digit.
 */
    void Digit (String digit) {
        checkEquals ();

        /*
         *      Strip leading zeros.
         */
        if (s.length () == 1 && s.charAt (0) == '0' && digit.charAt (0)
        ➥!= '.')
            s = s.substring (1);

        if (s.length () < maxlen)
            s = s + digit;
        showacc ();
    }

/**
 * Handle a decimal point.
 */
    void Dot () {
        checkEquals ();

        /*
         *      Already have '.'
         */
        if (s.indexOf ('.') != -1)
            return;

        if (s.length () < maxlen)
            s = s + ".";
```

continued on next page

continued from previous page

```
            showacc ();
    }

/**
 * If the user presses equal without pressing an operator
 * key first (+,-,x,/), zero the display.
 */
    private void checkEquals () {
            if (equals == true) {
                            equals = false;
                s = "0";
            }
    }

/**
 * Stack the addition operator for later use.
 */
    void Plus () {
            op = 1;
            operation ();
    }

/**
 * Stack the subtraction operator for later use.
 */
    void Minus () {
            op = 2;
            operation ();
    }

/**
 * Stack the multiplication operator for later use.
 */
    void Mul () {
            op = 3;
            operation ();
    }

/**
 * Stack the division operator for later use.
 */
    void Div () {
            op = 4;
            operation ();
    }

/**
 * Interpret the display value as a double, and store it
 * for later use (by Equals).
 */
    private void operation () {
            if (s.length () == 0) return;
```

```
            Double xyz = Double.valueOf (s);
            last = xyz.doubleValue ();

            equals = false;
            s = "0";
        }
/**
 * Negate the current value & redisplay.
 */
    void Chs () {
            if (s.length () == 0) return;

            if (s.charAt (0) == '-') s = s.substring (1);
            else s = "-" + s;

            showacc ();
        }

/**
 * Finish the last calculation & display the result.
 */
    void Equals () {
            double acc;

            if (s.length () == 0)   return;
            Double xyz = Double.valueOf (s);
            switch (op)  {
                case 1:
                acc = last + xyz.doubleValue ();
                break;

                case 2:
                acc = last - xyz.doubleValue ();
                break;

                case 3:
                acc = last * xyz.doubleValue ();
                break;

                case 4:
                acc = last / xyz.doubleValue ();
                break;

                default:
                acc = 0;
                break;
            }

            s = new Double (acc).toString ();
            showacc ();
            equals = true;
            last = 0;
            op = 0;
```

continued on next page

continued from previous page

```
    }

/**
 * Clear the display and the internal last value.
 */
    void Clear () {
            last = 0;
            op = 0;
            s = "0";
            equals = false;
            showacc ();
    }

/**
 * Demand that the display be repainted.
 */
    private void showacc () {
            readout.setText(s);
            repaint ();
    }

}
```

2. Create an HTML document that contains the applet. Create a new file called howto61.html as follows:

```
<html>
<head>
<title>Calculator</title>
</head>
<applet code="Calc.class" width=200 height=200>
</applet>
<hr size=4>

</html>
```

3. Compile and test the applet. Compile the source using javac or the makefile provided. Test the applet using the Appletviewer by entering the following command:

```
APPLETVIEWER howto61.html
```

Calc.java may also be run as an application by typing

```
java Calc
```

When Calc is executed, a window will open containing 18 buttons (numeric from 0 to 9, +, -, *, /, =, +/-, ., and C) with a display bar above the buttons. Use the mouse to press the buttons. The Calc applet is a fully functional mathematical calculator. Figure 6-1 shows the applet in action.

Figure 6-1
Calculator applet

How It Works

The Calc.java applet/application contains three classes: *Calc*, *Keypad*, and *Display*. The *Calc* class extends Applet and is the applet itself. The *Keypad* and *Display* classes extend *Panel* and are used to hold the calculator keypad and display area, respectively.

The *Calc* class creates a new *Keypad* and *Display*, and adds the display to the top (North) of the main panel and the keypad to the center (Center) of the display panel. The event handler is used to catch all action events that are an instance of a button press. If the label of the button that was pressed is equal to any of the operator buttons (C, ., +, _, x, /, +/-, =), the appropriate method in the *Display* class is called. If the button press was not any of the operator buttons, that is, it was a number button, the *Digit* method in the *Display* class is called, with the button label (number) as a parameter.

The *Keypad* class initializes the keypad and adds the buttons. The buttons are added by using the constructor for the *Button* class, with a string as a parameter. This string is the label that will be written on the button when it is created. The text color of the button is set to black with the *setForeground* method in the component class. The button background button is set to various colors with the *setBackground* method, also in the component class. The number buttons are set to blue, the function buttons are set to yellow, and the equal button to green. The button text is set to 14-point, bold, Times font.

The *Display* class contains methods for handling all the button presses. If a number button is pressed, the *Digit* method is called with the button Label as the argument. There are similar methods for each operator button.

The *Button* class contains several constructors and methods. Table 6-1 contains a list of the constructors and methods for the *Button* class.

METHOD	DESCRIPTION
Button()	Constructs a Button with no label
Button(String)	Constructs a Button with a string label
addNotify()	Creates the peer of the button
getLabel()	Gets the label of the button
paramString()	Returns the parameter String of this button
setLabel(String)	Sets the button with the specified label

Table 6-1 Button class constructors and methods

COMPLEXITY
INTERMEDIATE

6.2 How do I...
Create check boxes?

Problem

I would like to write a clock applet that allows the user to toggle back and forth from a digital clock to an analog clock. I know how to create buttons, but it is nice to have a check box that shows the current state of the choice. I also want to have grouped check boxes that allow for only one to be selected at a time. How do I create check boxes?

Technique

This example demonstrates the use of individual and grouped check boxes. Two check boxes will be grouped that allow you to toggle a clock from digital to analog. Only one of the grouped check boxes can be selected at a time. Grouped check boxes are commonly called *radio buttons*. An individual check box will be used to toggle between displaying the date or not.

Steps

1. Create the applet source file. Create a new file called Clock.java and enter the following source:

```java
import java.awt.*;
import java.applet.*;
import java.util.Date;

/**
 * The applet class
 */
```

```
public class Clock extends Applet implements Runnable {

/*
 * Flags for determining what is displayed
 */
boolean analog = false;
boolean digital = false;
boolean date = false;

/*
 * A thread used to check the time periodically
 */
Thread thread = null;

/*
 * The saved time used so that painting is
 * only done when the time changes
 */
int lastxs=0;
int lastys=0;
int lastxm=0;
int lastym=0;
int lastxh=0;
int lastyh=0;
int lasts = 0;
int lastm = 0;
int lasth = 0;
int lastmon = 0;
int lastd = 0;
int lasty = 0;
int type = 1;
int lasttype = 0;
String lasttimestring = " ";
String lastdatestring = " ";
String months[] = {"January","February","March","April","May","June","July",
                   "August", "September", "October", "November",
                   ➥"December"};

/*
 * Called from update() in response to repaint()
 * This will typically be called every 100ms.
 * @param g - destination graphics object
 */
public void paint(Graphics g) {

    Dimension dim = size();

    if ( type == 0 ) {
        digital = true;
        analog = false;
    }
    if ( type == 1 ) {
        digital = false;
        analog = true;
```

continued on next page

CHAPTER 6
USER INTERFACE

continued from previous page

```
    }

    if ( type != lasttype) {
        g.setColor(getBackground());
        g.fillRect(0, 0, dim.width , dim.height);
        lasttype = type;
    }

    if (analog) {

        int xh, yh, xm, ym, xs, ys, s, m, h, xcenter, ycenter;
        Date dat = new Date();

        s = dat.getSeconds();
        m = dat.getMinutes();
        h = dat.getHours();
        xcenter=dim.width>>1;
        ycenter=dim.height>>1;

// a= s* pi/2 - pi/2 (to switch 0,0 from 3:00 to 12:00)
// x = r(cos a) + xcenter, y = r(sin a) + ycenter
        xs = (int)(Math.cos(s * 3.14f/30 - 3.14f/2) * 45 + xcenter);
        ys = (int)(Math.sin(s * 3.14f/30 - 3.14f/2) * 45 + ycenter);
        xm = (int)(Math.cos(m * 3.14f/30 - 3.14f/2) * 40 + xcenter);
        ym = (int)(Math.sin(m * 3.14f/30 - 3.14f/2) * 40 + ycenter);
        xh = (int)(Math.cos((h*30 + m/2) * 3.14f/180 - 3.14f/2) * 30
             + xcenter);
        yh = (int)(Math.sin((h*30 + m/2) * 3.14f/180 - 3.14f/2) * 30
             + ycenter);

// Draw the circle and numbers.

        g.setFont(new Font("TimesRoman", Font.PLAIN, 14));
        g.setColor(Color.blue);
        g.drawOval (xcenter-50, ycenter-50, 100, 100);
        g.setColor(Color.darkGray);
        g.drawString("9",xcenter-45,ycenter+3);
        g.drawString("3",xcenter+40,ycenter+3);
        g.drawString("12",xcenter-5,ycenter-37);
        g.drawString("6",xcenter-3,ycenter+45);

// Erase if necessary, and redraw.

        g.setColor(Color.lightGray);
        if (xs != lastxs || ys != lastys) {
            g.drawLine(xcenter, ycenter, lastxs, lastys);
        }

        if (xm != lastxm || ym != lastym) {
            g.drawLine(xcenter, ycenter-1, lastxm, lastym);
            g.drawLine(xcenter-1, ycenter, lastxm, lastym);
        }
        if (xh != lastxh || yh != lastyh) {
```

```
            g.drawLine(xcenter, ycenter-1, lastxh, lastyh);
            g.drawLine(xcenter-1, ycenter, lastxh, lastyh);
        }
        g.setColor(Color.darkGray);
        g.drawLine(xcenter, ycenter, xs, ys);
        g.setColor(Color.red);
        g.drawLine(xcenter, ycenter-1, xm, ym);
        g.drawLine(xcenter-1, ycenter, xm, ym);
        g.drawLine(xcenter, ycenter-1, xh, yh);
        g.drawLine(xcenter-1, ycenter, xh, yh);
        lastxs=xs; lastys=ys;
        lastxm=xm; lastym=ym;
        lastxh=xh; lastyh=yh;
    } // end analog


    if (digital) {
        int s, m, h;

        String secstring = "";
        String minstring = "";
        Date today = new Date();
        Font font = new Font("Helvetica",1,30);
        g.setFont(font);
        s = today.getSeconds();
        m = today.getMinutes();
        h = today.getHours();
        if ( m < 10) minstring = "0" + m;
        else minstring += m;
        if ( s < 10) secstring = "0" + s;
        else secstring += s;
        String timestring = h + ":" + minstring + ":" + secstring ;
        FontMetrics fm = g.getFontMetrics();
        if (s != lasts || m != lastm || h != lasth) {
            int textwidth = fm.stringWidth(lasttimestring);
            g.setColor(Color.lightGray);
            g.drawString(lasttimestring,
                ((dim.width>>1) - (textwidth>>1)),
                dim.height>>1);
        }

        g.setColor(Color.blue);
        int textwidth = fm.stringWidth(timestring);
        g.drawString(timestring, ((dim.width>>1) - (textwidth>>1)),
            dim.height>>1);
        lasts = s; lastm = m; lasth = h;
        lasttimestring = timestring;
    } //end digital

    if (!date) {
        Font font = new Font("Helvetica",1,18);
        g.setFont(font);
        g.setColor(Color.lightGray);
```

continued on next page

continued from previous page

```
            FontMetrics fm = g.getFontMetrics();
            int textwidth = fm.stringWidth(lastdatestring);
            g.drawString(lastdatestring, ((dim.width>>1) - (textwidth>>1)),
                dim.height - 20);
        }

    if (date) {
        int m, d, y;
        Date today = new Date();
        Font font = new Font("Helvetica",1,18);
        g.setFont(font);
        m = today.getMonth();
        d = today.getDate();
        y = today.getYear();
        String datestring = months[m] + " " + d + ", " + y ;
        FontMetrics fm = g.getFontMetrics();

        if (m != lastmon || d != lastd || y != lasty) {
            int textwidth = fm.stringWidth(lastdatestring);
            g.setColor(Color.lightGray);
            g.drawString(lastdatestring,
                ((dim.width>>1) - (textwidth>>1)), dim.height - 20);
        }
        int textwidth = fm.stringWidth(datestring);
        g.setColor(Color.blue);
        g.drawString(datestring, ((dim.width>>1) - (textwidth>>1)),
            dim.height - 20);
        lastmon = m; lastd = d; lasty = y;
        lastdatestring = datestring;
    } // end date
}

/*
 * Called when the applet is started
 * Create the thread and start it.
 */
public void start() {

    if(thread == null) {
        thread = new Thread(this);
        thread.start();
    }
}

/*
 * Called when the applet is stopped
 */
public void stop() {

    thread.stop ();
}

/*
```

```
 * The thread proper
 * Calls repaint every 100ms
 */
public void run() {

    while (thread != null) {
        try {
            Thread.sleep(100);
        } catch (InterruptedException e) { }
        repaint();
    }
    thread = null;
}

/*
 * Override the default update method to avoid flickering.
 * @param g - destination graphics object
 */
public void update (Graphics g) {

    paint(g);
}
}
```

2. Create the applet source file. Create a new file called CheckBoxApp.java and enter the following source:

```
import java.awt.*;
import java.applet.Applet;

/*
 * Applet/application that demonstrates
 * the use of check boxes by creating a
 * clock
 */
public class CheckBoxApp extends Applet {

/*
 * A panel to hold the controls
 */
Panel controls = new Panel();

/*
 * An instance of Clock
 */
Clock clock = new Clock();

/*
 * Used to group some of the check boxes
 * such that they are mutually exclusive
 */
CheckboxGroup group = new CheckboxGroup();

/*
```

continued on next page

continued from previous page

```
 * The checkbox instances
 */
Checkbox digitalcb = new Checkbox("Digital", group, false);
Checkbox analogcb = new Checkbox("Analog", group, true);
Checkbox datecb = new Checkbox("Date");

/*
 * Flags used to determine if the check box
 * states have changed
 */
boolean previousdstate = false;
boolean previousastate = true;
boolean previousdtstate = false;

/*
 * Called when the applet is loaded
 * Add the controls and start the clock.
 */
public void init() {

    this.setLayout(new BorderLayout());
    controls.setLayout(new FlowLayout());
    add("North", controls);

    controls.add(digitalcb);
    controls.add(analogcb);
    controls.add(datecb);
    clock.type = 1;
    add("Center", clock);
    clock.start();
    repaint();
}

/**
 * Handle check box events.
 * @param evt - event object
 * @param arg - object receiving the event
 */
public boolean action(Event evt, Object arg) {

    boolean astate = analogcb.getState();
    boolean dstate = digitalcb.getState();
    boolean dtstate = datecb.getState();

    if (evt.target instanceof Checkbox) {
        if (astate & (astate != previousastate)) {
            clock.type = 1;
        }

        if (dstate & (dstate != previousdstate)) {
            clock.type = 0;
        }
    }
```

```
    if (evt.target == datecb) {
        if (dtstate) clock.date = true;
        else clock.date = false;
    }

    previousastate = astate;
    previousdstate = dstate;

    return true;
}

/**
 * Called in response to an update
 * Forces painting of all objects
 * @param g - destination graphics object
 */
public void update (Graphics g) {

    paintAll(g);
}

/**
 * Application entry point
 * Create a window frame to contain the applet.
 * @param args - command line arguments
 */
public static void main(String args[]) {

    Frame f = new Frame("CheckBox App ");
    CheckBoxApp check = new CheckBoxApp();
    f.add("Center", check);
    f.resize(300, 300);
    f.show();
    check.init();
    check.start();
}
}
```

3. Create an HTML document that contains the applet. Create a new file called howto62.html as follows:

```
<html>
<head>
<title>Digital/Analog Clock</title>
</head>
<applet code="CheckBoxApp.class" width=300 height=300>
</applet>
<hr size=4>

</html>
```

4. Compile and test the applet. Compile the source using javac or the makefile provided. Test the applet using the Appletviewer by entering the following command:

```
APPLETVIEWER howto62.html
```

Figure 6-2
CheckBoxApp applet

CheckBoxApp.java may also be run as an application by typing

`java CheckBoxApp`

When CheckBoxApp is executed, a window will open with an analog clock running in the center of the panel and three check boxes on the top. The Digital and Analog check boxes are grouped so only one can be selected at a time. Grouped check boxes in Java are basically equivalent to radio buttons. Select the Digital button and the clock will change to a digital clock. The Date check box is an individual check box and toggles the date to be displayed or not. Figure 6-2 shows an example of the running applet.

How It Works

The CheckBoxApp applet/application contains two classes: the *Clock* class and the *CheckBoxApp* class. The *Clock* class is a separate file, and it defines the clocks and date. The CheckBoxApp is the applet itself.

CheckBoxApp creates an instance of *Clock*, three check boxes, and a panel to hold the check boxes. The first check box, digitalcb, is created with a label of "Digital," a group of group, and a state of False. The second one, analogcb, has the same group, but the label is "Analog" and the state is True. The datecb check box is created with a label of "Date" and is not given a group. Table 6-2 contains the constructors and methods contained in the *Checkbox* class. The layout of the main panel is set to BorderLayout. The controls panel layout is set to FlowLayout and is added to the top (North) of the main panel. The three check boxes are added to controls from the left to right.

The *Checkbox* action events are captured by using the *action* method. Three *boolean* variables are set to the current check box states by using the *getState( )* method. If the Event.target was an instance of a check box, the state of the check boxes is then evaluated, and the *clock.type* variable is changed if the state of the grouped check boxes changed. If the Event target was the Date check box, the *clock.date boolean* variable is set to the value of the Date check box.

The *Clock* class is very similar to How-To 4.1. The class extends Panel and implements Runnable because it has a separate thread running. The analog portion is almost identical to How-To 4.1. The difference is the addition of the digital portion, the date portion, and the logic to decide which clock to display.

The default *paint()* method is overridden to display the clocks and the date. The integer type is used to decide which clock is displayed. If type = 0, the digital clock is displayed; if type = 1, the analog clock is displayed. The *boolean* date is used to decide if the date should be displayed. If date = True, the date will be displayed; if it is False, it will not be displayed. The analog portion is identical to the example in 4.1 and will not be explained here.

The digital portion works similarly to the analog portion. A new Date is created and *s* is set to seconds with *getSeconds()*, *m* is set to minutes with *getMinutes()*, and *h* is set to hours with *getHours()*. If the minutes or seconds are less than 10, a leading zero is added to maintain the standard two-digit display. The String *timestring* is created by appending the hours, minutes, and seconds with colons between each. If any of the hours, minutes, or seconds are not equal to the previous values, then the color is set to the background color and the previous time is drawn on top of the old one. Otherwise, the color is set to blue and the current time is drawn. FontMetrics is used to get the string length to center the text in the panel.

There are two sections for the date display. The first section is run if the *date* variable is set to False. This section just draws the previous date in the background color. The other section runs if the *date* variable is True. This section works similarly to the digital clock portion. A new Date is created and *m* is set to the months with *getMonth()*, *d* is set to the day of month with *getDate()*, and *y* is set to the year with *getYear()*. A string array, months, is defined that contains the names of the months. The string *datestring* is created by appending the months element, day of month, and year with appropriate spaces and commas. FontMetrics is used to get the string length to center the text in the panel.

The default *update()* method is overridden, because the default method fills the entire panel with the background color every time it is called. This produces an undesirable flicker.

METHOD	DESCRIPTION
Checkbox()	Constructs a Checkbox with no label, no Checkbox group, and initialized to a false state
Checkbox(String)	Constructs a Checkbox with the specified label, no Checkbox group, and initialized to a false state

continued on next page

continued from previous page

METHOD	DESCRIPTION
Checkbox(String,	Constructs a Checkbox with the specified label,
CheckboxGroup, boolean)	specified Checkbox group, and specified Boolean state
addNotify()	Creates the peer of the Checkbox
getCheckboxGroup()	Returns the Checkbox group
getLabel()	Gets the label of the button
getState()	Returns the Boolean state of the Checkbox
paramString()	Returns the parameter String of this Checkbox
setCheckboxGroup	Sets the CheckboxGroup to the specified group
(CheckboxGroup)	
setLabel(String)	Sets the button with the specified label
setState(boolean)	Sets the Checkbox to the specified Boolean state

Table 6-2 Checkbox constructors and methods

COMPLEXITY
INTERMEDIATE

6.3 How do I...
Create menus?

Problem

I would like to learn how to add menu bars to applications. I would like to modify the Doodle example from section 5.2 to include a menu. How do I create menus?

Technique

Pull-down menus can only exist for a frame and not a panel. Therefore, any program that uses pull-down menus must be run as an application. A menu bar is created by invoking the MenuBar constructor.

Steps

1. Create the applet source file. Create a new file called Doodle.java and enter the following source:

```
import java.applet.Applet;
import java.awt.*;

/**
 * The ColorBar class displays a color bar for color selection.
```

```
  */
class ColorBar {

/*
 * The top left coordinate of the color bar
 */
int xpos, ypos;

/*
 * The width and height of the color bar
 */
int width, height;

/*
 * The current color selection index into the colors array
 */
int selectedColor = 3;

/*
 * The array of colors available for selection
 */
static Color colors[] = {
    Color.white, Color.gray, Color.red, Color.pink,
    Color.orange, Color.yellow, Color.green, Color.magenta,
    Color.cyan, Color.blue
};

/**
 * Create the color bar.
 */
public ColorBar (int x, int y, int w, int h) {

    xpos = x;
    ypos = y;
    width = w;
    height = h;
}

/**
 * Paint the color bar.
 * @param g - destination graphics object
 */
void paint (Graphics g) {

    int x, y, i;
    int w, h;

    for (i=0; i<colors.length; i+=1) {
        w = width;
        h = height/colors.length;
        x = xpos;
        y = ypos + (i * h);
        g.setColor (Color.black);
```

continued on next page

continued from previous page

```
            g.fillRect (x, y, w, h);
            if (i == selectedColor) {
                x += 5;
                y += 5;
                w -= 10;
                h -= 10;
            } else {
                x += 1;
                y += 1;
                w -= 2;
                h -= 2;
            }
            g.setColor (colors[i]);
            g.fillRect (x, y, w, h);
        }
    }

    /**
     * Check to see if the mouse is inside a palette box.
     * If so, set selectedColor and return True,
     *        otherwise return False.
     * @param x, y - x and y position of mouse
     */
    boolean inside (int x, int y) {

        int i, h;

        if (x < xpos || x > xpos+width) return false;
        if (y < ypos || y > ypos+height) return false;

        h = height/colors.length;
        for (i=0; i<colors.length; i+=1) {
            if (y < ((i+1)*h+ypos)) {
                selectedColor = i;
                return true;
            }
        }
        return false;
    }
}

/**
 * The Doodle applet implements a drawable surface
 * with a limited choice of colors to draw with.
 */
public class Doodle extends Frame {

    /*
     * The maximum number of points that can be
     * saved in the xpoints, ypoints, and color arrays
     */
    static final int MaxPoints = 1000;
```

```
/*
 * Arrays to hold the points where the user draws
 */
int xpoints[] = new int[MaxPoints];
int ypoints[] = new int[MaxPoints];

/*
 * The color of each point
 */
int color[] = new int[MaxPoints];

/*
 * Used to keep track of the previous mouse
 * click to avoid filling arrays with the
 * same point
 */
int lastx;
int lasty;

/*
 * The number of points in the arrays
 */
int npoints = 0;
ColorBar colorBar;
boolean inColorBar;

/**
 * Set the window title and create the menus
 * Create an instance of ColorBar.
 */
public Doodle () {

    setTitle ("Doodle");

    setBackground(Color.white);

    MenuBar menuBar = new MenuBar();
    Menu fileMenu = new Menu("File");
    fileMenu.add(new MenuItem("Open")).disable();
    fileMenu.add(new MenuItem("New"));
    fileMenu.add(new MenuItem("Close"));
    fileMenu.add(new MenuItem("-")).disable();
    fileMenu.add(new MenuItem("Quit"));
    menuBar.add (fileMenu);

    Menu editMenu = new Menu("Edit");
    editMenu.add(new MenuItem("Undo")).disable();
    editMenu.add(new MenuItem("Cut")).disable();
    editMenu.add(new MenuItem("Copy")).disable();
    editMenu.add(new MenuItem("Paste")).disable();
    editMenu.add(new MenuItem("-")).disable();
    editMenu.add(new MenuItem("Clear"));
    menuBar.add (editMenu);
    setMenuBar (menuBar);
```

continued on next page

continued from previous page

```
    colorBar = new ColorBar (10, 75, 30, 200);

    resize (410, 430);
    show ();
}

/**
 * Track mouse clicks and either choose a color from the
 * palette, or record a spot for painting later.
 */
public boolean handleEvent(Event evt) {

    int x, y;

    x = evt.x;
    y = evt.y;
    switch (evt.id) {
        case Event.WINDOW_DESTROY:
        System.exit (0);
        return true;

        case Event.ACTION_EVENT:
        if ("Quit".equals(evt.arg)) {
            System.exit (0);
            return true;
        }
        if ("New".equals(evt.arg)) {
            Doodle doodle = new Doodle ();
            return true;
        }
        if ("Clear".equals(evt.arg)) {
            npoints = 0;
            getGraphics().clearRect (0, 0, size().width,
                size().height);
            repaint ();
            return true;
        }
        break;

        case Event.MOUSE_DOWN:
        if (colorBar.inside (x, y)) {
            inColorBar = true;
            repaint ();
            return true;
        }
        inColorBar = false;
        if (npoints < MaxPoints) {
            lastx = x;
            lasty = y;
            xpoints[npoints] = x;
            ypoints[npoints] = y;
            color[npoints] = colorBar.selectedColor;
            npoints += 1;
```

```
            }
            npoints = 0;
            return true;

            case Event.MOUSE_DRAG:
            if (inColorBar) return true;
            if ((x != lastx || y != lasty) && npoints < MaxPoints) {
                lastx = x;
                lasty = y;
                xpoints[npoints] = x;
                ypoints[npoints] = y;
                color[npoints] = colorBar.selectedColor;
                npoints += 1;
                repaint ();
            }
            return true;
        }
        return false;
    }

    /**
     * Redisplay the drawing space.
     * @param g - destination graphics object
     */
    public void update (Graphics g) {

        int i;

        for (i=0; i<npoints; i+=1) {
            g.setColor (colorBar.colors[color[i]]);
            g.fillOval (xpoints[i]-5, ypoints[i]-5, 10, 10);
        }
        colorBar.paint (g);
    }

    /**
     * Repaint the drawing space when required.
     * @param g - destination graphics object
     */
    public void paint (Graphics g) {

        update (g);
    }

    /**
     * The main method allows this class to be run as an application.
     * @param args - command line arguments
     */
    public static void main (String args[]) {

        Doodle doodle = new Doodle ();
    }
}
```

2. Compile and test the applet. Compile the source using javac or the makefile provided. Test the application by typing

`java Doodle`

Doodle can only be run as an application. When Doodle is executed, a window will open containing a drawing area, color palette, and a menu bar. Figure 6-3 shows an example of the running application.

How It Works

This version of the Doodle application includes pull-down menus. Like the version of Doodle described in How-To 5.2, this one contains a *ColorBar* class and a *Doodle* class. The *ColorBar* class is identical to that described in How-To 5.2. The *Doodle* class is different from that described in How-To 5.2 in two ways. First, this *Doodle* class extends Frame instead of extending Applet, since pull-down menus can only exist for a frame and not a panel (as you'll recall, Applet is a subclass of Panel). Second, the *main* method simply creates an instance of *Doodle*, and does not explicitly create a frame (the default *Frame* method takes care of that).

The Doodle constructor sets the title of the frame by invoking the *setTitle()* method, then sets the background color to white by invoking *setBackground()*. It then creates a menu bar by invoking the MenuBar constructor, and creates a new file menu by invoking the Menu constructor with the name of the menu ("file") as an argument. Next, menu items are added to the file menu by invoking the *add()* method

Figure 6-3 Doodle application with menu bar

with a MenuItem constructor as an argument, which in turn is passed the name of that menu item (for example, "Open"). A menu is added to the menu bar by invoking the *add* method of the menuBar instance. The Edit menu is created in the same way. Finally, the menu bar is displayed by invoking the *setMenuBar* method with menuBar as an argument.

An instance of ColorBar is created as in How-To 5.2. Instead of using *mouseDown()* and *mouseDrag()* methods, a *handleEvent()* method is created that overrides the default *handleEvent()* method.

Actual events are specified by the contents of the evt event record (which is of type Event). The event record specifies the x and y mouse coordinates in the evt.x and evt.y arguments. The event record also contains evt.id, which specifies the type of event that occurred. If a WINDOW_DESTROY event occurs (meaning that the user has clicked in the window's Close box), then the program exits by invoking System.exit.

If an ACTION_EVENT occurs, evt.arg is compared with the menu item names to determine which menu item has been selected. The Quit menu item simply exits the program. The New item creates a new instance of Doodle (including a new frame and color toolbar). The Clear menu item erases the window and deletes all of the painted points in the point arrays.

The MOUSE_DOWN and MOUSE_DRAG events perform the same functions as the *mouseDown()* and *mouseDrag()* methods used in How-To 5.2.

In all other respects, this version of Doodle is a duplicate of that used in How-To 5.2.

Comments

If the MOUSE_DOWN and MOUSE_DRAG events are handled by the *handleEvent()* method as in this example, the *mouseDown()* and *mouseDrag()* methods are not called.

COMPLEXITY
INTERMEDIATE

6.4 How do I...
Use choice lists?

Problem

I would like to add choice lists to applications. I want to create a converter application that has dimensions listed in choice lists and that gives the conversion factor between the two selected dimensions. How do I create choice lists?

Technique

This example will create two choice lists. Each one will contain the following choices: Centimeters, Meters, Kilometers, Inches, Feet, and Miles. The first choice list is used to select the dimension to convert from. The second list is the dimension to convert to. A text field will be used to display the conversion factor.

Steps

1. Create the applet source file. Create a new file called Converter.java and enter the following source:

```java
import java.awt.*;
import java.applet.Applet;

/*
 * The applet class
 */
public class Converter extends Applet {

/*
 * The "from" unit index
 */
int fromindex = 0;

/*
 * The "to" unit index
 */
int toindex = 0;

/*
 * A place to print the conversion factor
 */
TextField textfield = new TextField(12);

/*
 * Where the choice lists are displayed
 */
Panel listpanel = new Panel();

/*
 * Where the text field is displayed
 */
Panel textpanel = new Panel();
Choice unit1 = new Choice();
Choice unit2 = new Choice();

/*
 * An array of conversion factors
 */
String values[][] = {
    {"1.000", "1.000 E-2", "1.000 E-5", "3.397 E-1", "3.937 E-2", "6.214 E-
    ➥6"},
```

```
        {"1.000 E+2", "1.000", "1.000 E-3", "39.37", "3.28", "6.214 E-4"},
        {"1.000 E+5", "1.000 E+3", "1.000", "3.937 E+4", "3.281 E+3", "6.214
        ➥1"},
        {"2.54", "0.0254", "2.54 E-5", "1.000", "12.0", "1.578 E-5"},
        {"30.48", "0.3048", "3.048 E-4", "12.0", "1.000", "1.894 E-4"},
        {"1.609 E+5", "1.609 E+3", "1609", "6.336 E+4", "5280", "1.000"}
};

/*
 * Called when the applet is loaded
 * Create the user interface.
 */
public void init() {

        textfield.setText(values[fromindex][toindex]);
        textfield.setEditable (false);

        this.setLayout(new BorderLayout());
        listpanel.setLayout(new FlowLayout());
        add("North", listpanel);
        add("South", textpanel);

        Label fromlabel = new Label ("To Convert From  ",1);
        listpanel.add(fromlabel);
        unit1.addItem("Centimeters");
            unit1.addItem("Meters");
            unit1.addItem("Kilometers");
            unit1.addItem("Inches");
            unit1.addItem("Feet");
            unit1.addItem("Miles");
            listpanel.add(unit1);

            Label tolabel = new Label (" to    ",1);
        listpanel.add(tolabel);
        unit2.addItem("Centimeters");
        unit2.addItem("Meters");
        unit2.addItem("Kilometers");
        unit2.addItem("Inches");
        unit2.addItem("Feet");
        unit2.addItem("Miles");
        listpanel.add(unit2);

        Label multlabel = new Label ("Multiply by  ",1);
        textpanel.add(multlabel);
        textpanel.add(textfield);
}

/**
 * Called when an action event occurs
 * @param evt - the event object
 * @param arg - the target object
 */
public boolean action(Event evt, Object arg) {
```

continued on next page

continued from previous page

```
    if (evt.target.equals (unit1)) {
        fromindex = unit1.getSelectedIndex();
        textfield.setText(values[fromindex][toindex]);
        repaint();
    } else if (evt.target.equals (unit2)) {
        toindex = unit2.getSelectedIndex();
        textfield.setText(values[fromindex][toindex]);
        repaint();
    }
    return true;
}

/**
 * Application entry point
 * @param args - command line arguments
 */
public static void main(String args[]) {

        Frame f = new Frame("Converter ");
        Converter converter = new Converter();
        converter.init();
        converter.start();
        f.add("Center", converter);
        f.resize(500, 100);
    f.show();
}
}
```

2. Create an HTML document that contains the applet. Create a new file called howto64.html as follows:

```
<html>
<head>
<title>Converter</title>
</head>
<applet code="Converter.class" width=500 height=100>
</applet>
<hr size=4>

</html>
```

3. Compile and test the applet. Compile the source using javac or the makefile provided. Test the applet using the Appletviewer by entering the following command:

```
APPLETVIEWER howto64.html
```

Converter.java may also be run as an application by typing

```
java Converter
```

When Converter is executed, a window will open with two choice lists and a text field. The first choice list is the convert-from dimension, and the second choice list is the convert-to dimension. The text field displays the conversion factor. Figure 6-4 shows an example of the running applet.

How It Works

The converter applet/application contains only a single class, the applet itself. The string value is a two-dimensional array that holds the conversion factor for the specified dimensions in the choice lists. The fromindex and toindex values are used to obtain the conversion factor from the values array and are initialized to zero. A text field, textfield, is created with 12 columns and will be used to display the conversion factor. Two panels, listpanel and textpanel, are created to hold the choice lists and text field, respectively. Two choice lists, unit1 and unit2, are created and will be the selection tool for the dimensions.

The *init()* method sets the text field value to the initialized value of the array and sets the text field as uneditable. The layout for the main panel is set to BorderLayout and listpanel is set to FlowLayout. The listpanel is added to the top (North) of the main panel, and the textpanel is added to the bottom (South) of the main panel. The selections for the choice lists are added by using the *addItem* method, and the choice lists are then added to the listpanel. A Label is added before the unit1 choice lists that says "To Convert From" and a Label is added before the unit2 choice list that says "to." A Label "Multiply by" and the text field are added to the textpanel.

The choice list events are captured by using the *action* method. If the Event.target is equal to unit1, then the fromindex is set to the index of the choice list using the *getSelectedIndex()* method. The *getSelectedIndex()* method is contained in the *Choice* class and returns the index of the selected value in the choice list. This value can be in the range of zero to the number of elements - 1. This is then used to obtain the correct element of the values array. If unit2 is selected, the same things occurs, except that toindex is set to the index selected in unit2. Table 6-3 shows the constructors and methods contained in the *Choice* class.

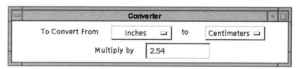

Figure 6-4 Converter applet

METHOD	DESCRIPTION
Choice()	Constructs a new Choice
addItem(String)	Adds an item to this Choice
addNotify()	Creates the Choice's peer
countItems()	Returns the number of items in this Choice
getItem(int)	Returns the String at the specified index in the Choice
getSelectedIndex()	Returns the index of the currently selected item
getSelectedItem()	Returns a String representation of the current Choice
paramString()	Returns the parameter String of this Choice
select(int)	Selects the item with the specified position
select(String)	Selects the item with the specified String

Table 6-3 Choice class constructor and methods

COMPLEXITY
INTERMEDIATE

6.5   How do I...
Create text fields and text areas?

Problem

I would like to create a simple spreadsheet program. I know how to access keyboard and mouse events, but how do I create text fields and text areas?

Technique

TextFields and TextAreas both can be edited and enable selections with the mouse. TextFields are limited in size and don't scroll, and therefore are good for text entry. TextAreas can be any given height and width and have scrollbars. TextAreas are good for displaying larger amounts of data.

Steps

1. Create the source file. Create a new file called SpreadSheet.java and enter the following source:

```
import java.awt.*;
import java.applet.*;

/*
 * The applet class
 */
```

```java
public class SpreadSheet extends Applet {

/*
 * The text entry field
 */
TextField textField;

/*
 * Instance of the sheet panel
 */
Sheet sheet;

/*
 * Initialize the applet.
 */
public void init () {

    setLayout(new BorderLayout());

    textField = new TextField ("", 80);
    sheet = new Sheet (10, 5, 400, 200, textField);
    add ("North", textField);
    add ("Center", sheet);
}

/*
 * Check for return keypresses.
 */
public boolean handleEvent(Event e) {

    if ((e.target instanceof TextField)
        && (e.id == Event.ACTION_EVENT)) {

        sheet.enter (textField.getText ());
        return true;
    }
    return false;
}

/*
 * Application entry point
 * Not used when run as an applet
 * @param args - command line arguments
 */
public static void main (String args[]) {

    Frame f = new Frame ("SpreadSheet");
    SpreadSheet spreadSheet = new SpreadSheet ();

    spreadSheet.init ();

    f.resize (440, 330);
    f.add ("Center", spreadSheet);
    f.show ();
}
}
```

2. Create the source file. Create a new file called Sheet.java and enter the following source:

```java
import java.awt.*;

/*
 * The panel that holds the cells
 */
public class Sheet extends Panel {

/*
 * The number of rows and columns in the spreadsheet
 */
int rows;
int cols;

/*
 * Width and height of the panel
 */
int width;
int height;

/*
 * The array of cells
 */
Cell cells[][];

/*
 * Offsets into the panel where the cells are displayed
 */
int xoffset;
int yoffset;

/*
 * The row and column selected by a mouse click
 */
int selectedRow = 0;
int selectedCol = 0;

/*
 * The text entry field
 */
TextField textField;

/*
 * Constructor
 * Create all the cells and init them.
 * @param r - number of rows
 * @param c - number of columns
 * @param w - width of the panel
 * @param h - height of the panel
 * @param t - instance of text entry field
 */
public Sheet (int r, int c, int w, int h, TextField t) {
```

```
    int i, j;

    rows = r;
    cols = c;
    width = w;
    height = h;
    xoffset = 30;
    yoffset = 30;
    textField = t;

    cells = new Cell[rows][cols];
    for (i=0; i<rows; i+=1) {
        for (j=0; j<cols; j+=1) {
            cells[i][j] = new Cell (cells, rows, cols);
        }
    }
}

/*
 * A mapping array for converting column indexes to characters
 */
static String charMap[] = {
    "a", "b", "c", "d", "e", "f", "g", "h", "i", "j",
    "k", "l", "m", "n", "o", "p", "q", "r", "s", "t",
    "u", "v", "w", "x", "y", "z"
};

/*
 * Paint each cell.
 * @param g - destination graphics object
 */
public void paint (Graphics g) {

    int i, j;
    int x, y;
    int w, h;
    double val;
    String s;

    w = width / cols;
    h = height / rows;

    x = 0;
    g.setColor (Color.black);
    for (i=0; i<rows; i+=1) {
        y = (i * height / rows) + yoffset;
        g.drawString (String.valueOf (i+1), x, y+h);
    }
    y = yoffset-2;
    for (j=0; j<cols; j+=1) {
        x = (j * width / cols) + xoffset+(w/2);
        g.drawString (charMap[j], x, y);
    }
    for (i=0; i<rows; i+=1) {
```

continued on next page

continued from previous page

```
        for (j=0; j<cols; j+=1) {
            s = cells[i][j].evalToString ();
            x = (j * width / cols) + xoffset + 2;
            y = (i * height / rows) + yoffset - 2;
            if (i == selectedRow && j == selectedCol) {
                g.setColor (Color.yellow);
                g.fillRect (x, y, w-1, h-1);
            } else {
                g.setColor (Color.white);
                g.fillRect (x, y, w-1, h-1);
            }
            g.setColor (Color.black);
            g.drawString (s, x, y+h);
        }
    }
}

/*
 * Called to recalculate the entire spreadsheet
 */
void recalculate () {

    int i, j;

    for (i=0; i<rows; i+=1) {
        for (j=0; j<cols; j+=1) {
            cells[i][j].evaluate ();
        }
    }
}

/*
 * Handle mouse down events.
 * @param evt - event object
 * @param x - mouse x position
 * @param y - mouse y position
 */
public boolean mouseDown (Event evt, int x, int y) {

    int w = width / cols;
    int h = height / rows;

    int sr = (y-yoffset)/h;
    int sc = (x-xoffset)/w;

    if (sr < 0 || sr >= rows || sc < 0 || sc > cols) return true;

    selectedRow = sr;
    selectedCol = sc;
    repaint ();
    textField.setText (cells[selectedRow][selectedCol].text);
    return true;
}
```

```
/*
 * Called to enter a text into a selected cell
 * @param s - the string to enter
 */
void enter (String s) {

    cells[selectedRow][selectedCol].enter (s);
    recalculate ();
    repaint ();
}
}
```

3. Create the source file. Create a new file called Cell.java and enter the following source:

```
import java.awt.*;

/*
 * Defines an individual cell
 */
public class Cell {

/*
 * Token types returned by Lex()
 */
static final int NUMBER = 1;
static final int EQUALS = 2;
static final int PLUS = 3;
static final int MINUS = 4;
static final int STAR = 5;
static final int SLASH = 6;
static final int TEXT = 7;
static final int EOT = 8;
static final int LEFT = 9;
static final int RIGHT = 10;
static final int UNKN = 11;
static final int FORMULA = 12;
static final int REFERENCE = 13;

/*
 * What is in this cell
 */
int type;

/*
 * The numeric value, if this cell is numeric
 */
double value;

/*
 * Numeric value for this token
 */
double lexValue;

/*
```

continued on next page

continued from previous page

```
 * Index into input string (used for parsing)
 */
int lexIndex;

/*
 * Token value returned from Lex()
 */
int token;

/*
 * The text contents of this cell
 */
String text;
int textLength;
int textIndex;

/*
 * Reference to all cells in spreadsheet
 */
Cell cells[][];

/*
 * Error flag, set if parse error detected
 */
boolean error;

/*
 * Used to force rereading of tokens
 */
boolean lexFlag;

/*
 * Number of rows and columns in the spreadsheet
 * Used for bounds checking
 */
int cols;
int rows;

public Cell (Cell cs[][], int r, int c) {

    cells = cs;
    rows = r;
    cols = c;
    text = "";
    lexFlag = true;
    type = UNKN;
}

/*
 * Called to get the numeric value of this cell
 */
double evaluate () {
```

```
        resetLex ();
        error = false;
        switch (type) {
            case FORMULA:
            Lex ();
            value = Level1 ();
            if (error) return 0;
            return value;

            case NUMBER:
            value = lexValue;
            return value;

            case UNKN:
            return 0;
        }
        error = true;
        return 0;
}

/*
 * Returns the string representation of the value
 */
String evalToString () {

    String s;

    if (type == TEXT || type == UNKN) return text;
    s = String.valueOf (value);
    if (error) return "Error";
    else return s;
}

/*
 * Called to enter a string into this cell
 */
void enter (String s) {

    text = s;
    textLength = text.length ();
    resetLex ();
    error = false;
    switch (Lex ()) {
        case EQUALS:
        type = FORMULA;
        break;

        case NUMBER:
        type = NUMBER;
        value = lexValue;
        break;
```

continued on next page

continued from previous page

```
            default:
            type = TEXT;
            break;
    }
}

/*
 * Top level of the recursive descent parser
 * Handle plus and minus.
 */
double Level1 () {

    boolean ok;
    double x1, x2;

    x1 = Level2 ();
    if (error) return 0;

    ok = true;
    while (ok) switch (Lex ()) {
        case PLUS:
        x2 = Level2 ();
        if (error) return 0;
        x1 += x2;
        break;

        case MINUS:
        x2 = Level2 ();
        if (error) return 0;
        x1 -= x2;
        break;

        default:
        Unlex ();
        ok = false;
        break;
    }
    return x1;
}

/*
 * Handle multiply and divide.
 */
double Level2 () {

    boolean ok;
    double x1, x2;

    x1 = Level3 ();
    if (error) return 0;

    ok = true;
    while (ok) switch (Lex ()) {
```

```
            case STAR:
            x2 = Level3 ();
            if (error) return 0;
            x1 *= x2;
            break;

            case SLASH:
            x2 = Level3 ();
            if (error) return 0;
            x1 /= x2;
            break;

            default:
            Unlex ();
            ok = false;
            break;
        }
        return x1;
}

/*
 * Handle unary minus, parenthesis, constants, and cell references.
 */
double Level3 () {

    double x1, x2;

    switch (Lex ()) {
        case MINUS:
        x2 = Level1 ();
        if (error) return 0;
        return -x2;

        case LEFT:
        x2 = Level1 ();
        if (error) return 0;
        if (Lex () != RIGHT) {
            error = true;
            return 0;
        }
        return x2;

        case NUMBER:
        case REFERENCE:
        return lexValue;
    }
    error = true;
    return 0;
}

/*
 * Reset the lexical analyzer.
 */
void resetLex () {
```

continued on next page

continued from previous page

```
    lexIndex = 0;
    lexFlag = true;
}

/*
 * Push a token back for rereading.
 */
void Unlex () {

    lexFlag = false;
}

/*
 * Returns the next token
 */
int Lex () {

    if (lexFlag) {
        token = lowlevelLex ();
    }
    lexFlag = true;
    return token;
}

/*
 * Returns the next token in the text string
 */
int lowlevelLex () {

    char c;
    String s;

    do {
        if (lexIndex >= textLength) return EOT;
        c = text.charAt (lexIndex++);
    } while (c == ' ');
    switch (c) {
        case '=':
        return EQUALS;

        case '+':
        return PLUS;

        case '-':
        return MINUS;

        case '*':
        return STAR;

        case '/':
        return SLASH;

        case '(':
        return LEFT;
```

```
            case ')':
                return RIGHT;
        }

        if (c >= '0' && c <= '9') {
            s = "";
            while ((c >= '0' && c <= '9') || c == '.' ||
                   c == '-' || c == 'e' || c == 'E') {
                s += c;
                if (lexIndex >= textLength) break;
                c = text.charAt (lexIndex++);
            }
            lexIndex -= 1;
            try {
                lexValue = Double.valueOf (s).doubleValue();
            } catch (NumberFormatException e) {
                System.out.println (e);
                error = true;
                return UNKN;
            }
            return NUMBER;
        }
        if (c >= 'a' && c <= 'z') {
            int col = c - 'a';
            int row;
            s = "";
            if (lexIndex >= textLength) {
                error = true;
                return UNKN;
            }
            c = text.charAt (lexIndex++);
            while (c >= '0' && c <= '9') {
                s += c;
                if (lexIndex >= textLength) break;
                c = text.charAt (lexIndex++);
            }
            lexIndex -= 1;
            try {
                row = Integer.valueOf (s).intValue() - 1;
            } catch (NumberFormatException e) {
                error = true;
                return UNKN;
            }
            if (row >= rows || col >= cols) {
                error = true;
                return REFERENCE;
            }
            lexValue = cells[row][col].evaluate();
            if (cells[row][col].error) error = true;
            return REFERENCE;
        }
        return TEXT;
    }
}
```

4. Create an HTML document that contains the applet. Create a new file called howto65.html as follows:

```
<html>
<head>
<title>SpreadSheet</title>
</head>
<applet code="SpreadSheet.class" width=430 height=300>
</applet>
<hr size=4>

</html>
```

5. Compile and test the applet. Compile the source using javac or the makefile provided. SpreadSheet actually has three source files that must be compiled: SpreadSheet.java, Sheet.java, and Cell.java. Test the applet using the Appletviewer by entering the following command:

```
APPLETVIEWER howto65.html
```

SpreadSheet.java may also be run as an application by typing

```
java SpreadSheet
```

When SpreadSheet is executed, a window will open and a text area will be displayed above a sheet. The sheet contains five columns labeled "a" to "e," and ten rows labeled "1" to "10." A cell is activated by clicking inside it with the mouse. To enter a value in an active cell, click on the text area, type the desired value, and press (ENTER). The spreadsheet implements the four basic mathematical functions: addition, subtraction, multiplication, and division.

To evaluate a mathematical expression, an equal sign is entered as the first character in the text area. For example, to add cell a1 and cell b1, select the cell to hold the evaluation and enter the following text in the text area:

```
= a1 + b1
```

If the values in a1 or b1 are changed, the cell containing the expression will change automatically. Figure 6-5 shows an example of the running applet.

How It Works

The SpreadSheet applet/application contains three classes: the *Cell* class, which defines variables and methods for an individual cell; the *Sheet* class, which holds a two-dimensional array of cells and the methods necessary for displaying a cell; and the SpreadSheet class, which is the applet itself.

SpreadSheet creates a text field at the top of the frame, and also creates an instance of *Sheet*, which it places in the center of the frame. The TextField constructor takes the initial string and the number of characters as arguments. The text field is passed as an argument to the *Sheet* constructor for convenience.

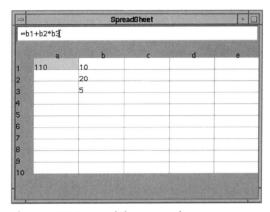

Figure 6-5 SpreadSheet applet

The Sheet constructor takes the number of rows, number of columns, width, height, and the instance of TextField as arguments. The *SpreadSheet* class handles text field events (for example, the Return key) by sending the entered text to the *enter* method of the *Sheet* class (the *enter* method is described below). The Sheet constructor simply saves its arguments and creates a two-dimensional array of cells for the given number of columns and rows.

The *paint()* method in the *Sheet* class evaluates each cell and prints its contents in the appropriate frame location. It also highlights a cell that has been selected by a previous mouse click. The *recalculate()* method invokes each cell's *evaluate()* method to affect recalculation. The *mouseDown()* method computes the selected row and selected column from the mouse x and y coordinates and also displays the contents of the selected cell in the text field. This is done by using the *setText()* method of the *TextField* class.

The *enter()* method is invoked when the user presses the ENTER or RETURN key (you'll recall this was invoked from handleEvent in the *SpreadSheet* class). The *enter()* method invokes the *enter()* method of the selected cell, passing the text string as an argument. It then forces a recalculation by invoking *recalculate()* and forces a repaint by invoking *repaint()*, which then displays all of the recalculated values.

The Cell constructor saves its arguments and initializes values. The String text holds the text for this cell. When text is entered in a cell via the *enter()* method, it is copied into the text variable, and its length is saved for convenience. Next the *enter()* method determines whether the text is a formula, a numeric constant, or just text, and it sets the type variable accordingly. Text starting with an = is considered a formula; if it starts with a digit, it is assumed to be a numeric constant; otherwise it is treated as text. This text parsing is handled by the *Lex()* method. Next, the *recalculate()* method invokes *evaluate()*, which uses the cell type to determine if it is a formula, and if so, to evaluate the formula. If the cell is a numeric constant or a string, then *evaluate()* simply returns the cell's contents.

If the cell contains a formula, then the expression is parsed by mutually recursive methods *Level1( ), Level2( ),* and *Level3( )*. *Level1( )* handles addition and subtraction. *Level2( )* handles multiplication and division. *Level3( )* handles unary minus, parenthetical expressions, and numeric constants and cell references.

The low-level lexical analysis is handled by the method *lowlevelLex( )*. It uses brute-force techniques to extort tokens from the text.

Comments

This spreadsheet can easily be extended to include math functions, more operators, and more key events (such as arrow keys for navigating cells).

Another design for a Java spreadsheet (and perhaps the most purely object-oriented) is to treat the contents of each cell as Java byte codes to be interpreted by the Java virtual machine. In effect, each cell would be its own applet. This exercise is left to the ambitious reader.

COMPLEXITY
INTERMEDIATE

6.6 How do I...
Use sliders?

Problem

I would like to make a color selection tool. The tool should have a slider bar for the red, green, and blue components. The color defined by the RGB values should be displayed. How do I use slider bars?

Technique

Java contains a *Scrollbar* class that is used to create scrollbars and sliders. Each color component (red, green, blue) will have a separate scrollbar and text field to display the scrollbar value. The *Color* class will then be used to get the color defined by the three color components. This color will then be displayed as a panel background color.

Steps

1. Create the applet source file. Create a new file called ColorPicker.java and enter the following source:

```
import java.applet.Applet;
import java.awt.*;
```

```
/*
```

```
 * The Applet class
 */
public class ColorPicker extends Applet {

/*
 * The panel that holds the sliders that
 * control the RGB values
 */
Panel controls = new Panel();

/*
 *The panel that holds the sample color
 */
Panel sample = new Panel();

/*
 *The red scrollbar
 */
Scrollbar sbRed;

/*
 * The green scrollbar
 */
Scrollbar sbGreen;

/*
 * The blue scrollbar
 */
Scrollbar sbBlue;

/*
 * The red component TextField
 */
TextField tfRed;

/*
 * The green component TextField
 */
TextField tfGreen;

/*
 * The blue component TextField
 */
TextField tfBlue;
int min = 0;
int max = 255;

/*
 * Initializes the applet
 */
public void init () {

    this.setLayout(new BorderLayout());
    controls.setLayout (new GridLayout(3,3,5,5));
```

continued on next page

continued from previous page

```
    this.add ("South",controls);
    this.add ("Center",sample);

    tfRed = new TextField (5);
    tfGreen = new TextField (5);
    tfBlue = new TextField (5);
    controls.add (new Label ("Red",1));
    controls.add (new Label ("Green",1));
    controls.add (new Label ("Blue",1));
    controls.add (tfRed);
    controls.add (tfGreen);
    controls.add (tfBlue);

    sbRed = new Scrollbar (Scrollbar.HORIZONTAL, 0, 1, min, max);
    //Set the values for the scrollbar
    // value, page size, min, max.
    controls.add (sbRed);

    sbGreen = new Scrollbar (Scrollbar.HORIZONTAL, 0, 1, min, max);
    //Set the values for the scrollbar
    // value, page size, min, max.
    controls.add (sbGreen);

    sbBlue = new Scrollbar (Scrollbar.HORIZONTAL, 0, 1, min, max);
    //Set the values for the scrollbar
    // value, page size, min, max.
    controls.add (sbBlue);

    // sets the text fields to the slider value
    tfRed.setText(String.valueOf(sbRed.getValue()));
    tfGreen.setText(String.valueOf(sbGreen.getValue()));
    tfBlue.setText(String.valueOf(sbBlue.getValue()));

    changecolor();
}

/* Gets the current value in the text field.
 * That's guaranteed to be the same as the value
 * in the scroller (subject to rounding, of course).
 * @param textField - the textField
 */
double getValue(TextField textField) {

    double f;
    try {
        f = Double.valueOf(textField.getText()).doubleValue();
    } catch (java.lang.NumberFormatException e) {
        f = 0.0;
    }
    return f;
}

/*
 * Respond to user actions.
```

```
    * @param evt - the event object
    */
public boolean handleEvent(Event evt) {

    if (evt.target.equals (sbRed)) {
        tfRed.setText(String.valueOf(sbRed.getValue()));
        changecolor();
    } else if (evt.target.equals (sbGreen)) {
        tfGreen.setText(String.valueOf(sbGreen.getValue()));
        changecolor();
    } else if (evt.target.equals (sbBlue)) {
        tfBlue.setText(String.valueOf(sbBlue.getValue()));
        changecolor();
    } else if ((evt.target.equals (tfRed))
        && (evt.id == Event.ACTION_EVENT)) {
        setSliderValue(sbRed, getValue(tfRed));
        tfRed.setText(String.valueOf(sbRed.getValue()));
        changecolor();
    } else if ((evt.target.equals (tfGreen))
        && (evt.id == Event.ACTION_EVENT)) {
        setSliderValue(sbGreen, getValue(tfGreen));
        tfGreen.setText(String.valueOf(sbGreen.getValue()));
        changecolor();
    } else if ((evt.target.equals (tfBlue))
        && (evt.id == Event.ACTION_EVENT)) {
        setSliderValue(sbBlue, getValue(tfBlue));
        tfBlue.setText(String.valueOf(sbBlue.getValue()));
        changecolor();
    }
    return false;
}

/*
 * Sets the slider value
 * @param slider - the scrollbar instance
 * @param f - the value to set the slider
 */
void setSliderValue(Scrollbar slider, double f) {

    int sliderValue = (int)f;

    if (sliderValue > max)
        sliderValue = max;
    if (sliderValue < min)
        sliderValue = min;
    slider.setValue(sliderValue);
}

/*
 * Changes the color of the sample to the
 * color defined by the RGB values set by
 * the user
 */
public void changecolor () {
```

continued on next page

continued from previous page

```
    int i;

    sample.setBackground(new Color((int)getValue(tfRed),
        (int)getValue(tfGreen), (int)getValue(tfBlue)));
    repaint();
}

public void update (Graphics g) {

    paintAll(g);
}

/*
 * Application entry point
 * Not used when run as an applet
 * @param args - command line arguments
 */
public static void main (String args[]) {

    Frame f = new Frame ("ColorPicker");
    ColorPicker colorPicker = new ColorPicker ();

    colorPicker.init ();
        f.resize (300, 200);
        f.add ("Center", colorPicker);
    f.show ();
}
}
```

2. Create an HTML document that contains the applet. Create a new file called howto66.html as follows:

```
<html>
<head>
<title>Color Picker</title>
</head>
<applet code="ColorPicker.class" width=200 height=200>
</applet>
<hr size=4>

</html>
```

3. Compile and test the applet. Compile the source using javac or the makefile provided. Test the applet using the Appletviewer by entering the following command:

```
APPLETVIEWER howto66.html
```

ColorPicker.java may also be run as an application by typing

```
java ColorPicker
```

When ColorPicker is executed, a window will open with a colored panel at the top (set to black on startup) and three scrollbars near the bottom. Each

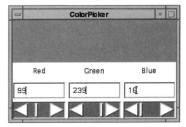

Figure 6-6 ColorPicker applet

scrollbar has a corresponding label and text field. The scrollbar can be moved, and the text field value and the color of the top panel will be updated automatically. A value can also be entered in the text field, and the scrollbar will be moved to the correct position and the color updated. Figure 6-6 shows an example of the running applet.

How It Works

The ColorPicker applet/application contains only one class, the applet itself. Two panels are created, controls, which will hold the scrollbars and sample, which will be an empty panel that is used to display the defined color. Three Scrollbars (sbRed, sbGreen, and sbBlue) and three TextFields (tfRed, tfGreen, and tfBlue) are created for the selection tool.

The *init()* method sets the layout for the main panel to BorderLayout. The layout for controls is set to GridLayout with three rows, three columns, and a row and column spacing each of five. This will allow us to add three Scrollbars, three TextFields, and three labels. Using GridLayout will align all components in a grid, and each grid cell will be of equal size. Section 6.8 will discuss layout managers in more detail. The controls panel is added to the bottom (South), and sample is added to the center (Center) of the main panel. The three TextFields are constructed each with five columns. The Scrollbars are constructed by using a Scrollbar constructor that takes five integer parameters. The first parameter is orientation, which is either Scrollbar.HORIZONTAL or Scrollbar.VERTICAL. The other four parameters, in order, are the initial value of the scrollbar, the size of the visible portion of the scrollbar, the minimum value, and the maximum value. The size of the visible portion is sometimes referred to as the *finger size* or the *step increment* of the slider. Table 6-4 lists all the constructors and methods contained in the *Scrollbar* class. The Scrollbars are then added to the controls panel with the *add* method. The textFields are set to display the value of the corresponding scrollbar by calling the *getValue()* method for each scrollbar. The value returned from *getValue()* is converted to a String and set to the TextField's displayed string by using the *setText()* method. The method *changeColor()* is called, which sets the background of panel sample to the selected color.

The *changeColor()* method changes the background color of panel sample to the color defined by the Scrollbar values. The call to *setBackground()* uses a new Color constructor with the *getValue()* method for each TextField as the arguments. The *getValue()* method returns the current value of the TextField as a *double*. The value must then be cast to an integer for the color constructor. *repaint()* is then called to update the color.

The *handleEvent()* method is overridden to capture the scrollbar and textfield events. If the Event.target is equal to one of the scrollbars, the TextField value is set to the scrollbar value with the *setText()* method, and the *changecolor()* method is called. If the event was one of the TextFields, then the corresponding slider value is set to the entered value with the *setSliderValue()* method. The TextField is then set to the slider value using the *setText()* method. It may sound unnecessary to set the scrollbar value from the textfield and then set the textfield from the scrollbar. This is in case the value entered in the textfield was out of the range of the scrollbar. The *setSliderValue()* method verifies that the value entered is not greater than the max value or less than the min value. If it is, then the slider is set to either the max or min. The scrollbar is then set by using the *setValue* method contained in the *Scrollbar* class. The textfield then must be updated to match the scrollbar position.

METHOD	DESCRIPTION
Scrollbar()	Constructs a new vertical Scrollbar
Scrollbar(int)	Constructs a new Scrollbar with the specified orientation
Scrollbar(int, int, int, int, int)	Constructs a new Scrollbar with the specified orientation,
	value, page size, and minimum and maximum values
addNotify()	Creates the Scrollbar's peer
getLineIncrement()	Gets the line increment for this scrollbar
getMaximum()	Returns the maximum value of this Scrollbar
getMinimum()	Returns the minimum value of this Scrollbar
getOrientation()	Returns the orientation for this Scrollbar
getPageIncrement()	Gets the page increment for this scrollbar
getValue()	Returns the current value of this Scrollbar
getVisible()	Returns the visible amount of the Scrollbar
paramString()	Returns the String parameters for this Scrollbar
setLineIncrement(int)	Sets the line increment for this scrollbar
setPageIncrement(int)	Sets the page increment for this scrollbar
setValue(int)	Sets the value of this Scrollbar to the specified value
setValues(int, int, int, int)	Sets the values for this Scrollbar
HORIZONTAL	The horizontal Scrollbar variable
VERTICAL	The vertical Scrollbar variable

Table 6-4 Scrollbar class constructors and methods

Comments

It would be useful to create a new class called *Slider*. This class should extend *Scrollbar* and contain the capability of displaying the scrollbar and a text field. This would be useful if sliders needed to be used often.

COMPLEXITY
ADVANCED

6.7   How do I...
Use list boxes?

Problem

I want to write a phone book application. It should have three text entry fields: one for name, one for phone number, and one for e-mail address. It should have four buttons: Find Name, Add, Delete, and Save. I want to use a list box to display the names. When the user selects a name from the list box, the name, phone number, and e-mail address should appear in the appropriate text fields. I know how to use text fields and buttons, but I don't know how to use list boxes. How do I use list boxes?

Technique

The Java AWT supports list boxes, similar to other GUI APIs. The class *List* contains methods to create, add, delete, select, and deselect items among numerous other utility methods. The methods in the List class are listed in Table 6-5.

List box events are delivered to Java programs as an action event with the target set to the list box. The method *List getSelectedIndex()* can be used to determine which item in the list was selected.

METHOD	DESCRIPTION
List()	Creates a new scrolling list initialized with no visible lines or multiple selections
List(int, boolean)	Creates a new scrolling list initialized with the specified number of visible lines and
	a *boolean* stating whether multiple selections are allowed
addItem(String)	Adds the specified item to the end of scrolling list
addItem(String, int)	Adds the specified item to the end of scrolling list
addNotify()	Creates the peer for the list
allowsMultipleSelections()	Returns True if this list allows multiple selections
clear()	Clears the list

continued on next page

continued from previous page

METHOD	DESCRIPTION
countItems()	Returns the number of items in the list
delItem(int)	Deletes an item from the list
delItems(int, int)	Deletes multiple items from the list
deselect(int)	Deselects the item at the specified index
getItem(int)	Gets the item associated with the specified index
getRows()	Returns the number of visible lines in this list
getSelectedIndex()	Gets the selected item on the list or -1 if no item is selected
getSelectedIndexes()	Returns the selected indexes on the list
getSelectedItem()	Returns the selected item on the list or null if no item is selected
getSelectedItems()	Returns the selected items on the list
getVisibleIndex()	Gets the index of the item that was last made visible by the method makeVisible
isSelected(int)	Returns True if the item at the specified index has been selected; False otherwise
makeVisible(int)	Forces the item at the specified index to be visible
minimumSize(int)	Returns the minimum dimensions needed for the number of rows in the list
minimumSize()	Returns the minimum dimensions needed for the list
paramString()	Returns the parameter String of this list
preferredSize(int)	Returns the preferred dimensions needed for the list with the specified number of rows
preferredSize()	Returns the preferred dimensions needed for the list
removeNotify()	Removes the peer for this list
replaceItem(String, int)	Replaces the item at the given index
select(int)	Selects the item at the specified index
setMultipleSelections (boolean)	Sets whether this list should allow multiple selections

Table 6-5 List class constructors and methods

Steps

1. Create the source file. Create a file PhoneBook.java and enter the following
code:

```java
import java.applet.Applet;
import java.awt.*;
import java.io.*;
import java.util.StringTokenizer;

/**
 * Phone book application class
 * Demonstrates the use of list boxes
 * Cannot be run as an applet because
 * local file reading is necessary
```

```
 */
public class PhoneBook extends Frame {

/*
 * The maximum number of phone numbers
 */
final int MaxNumbers = 25;

/*
 * An instance of list box
 */
List phoneList;

/*
 * The button instances
 */
Button addButton;
Button deleteButton;
Button findButton;
Button saveButton;

/*
 * The text field instances
 */
TextField nameField;
TextField phoneField;
TextField emailField;

/*
 * An array of strings that holds all of the
 * phone numbers
 */
String data[] = new String[MaxNumbers];
int NNumbers = 15;

/*
 * Constructor
 * Add all user interface components
 * and read in the data file.
 * Display names in the list box.
 */
public PhoneBook () {

    int i;

    setTitle ("Phone book");
    setLayout (new BorderLayout ());

    Panel buttonPanel = new Panel ();
    buttonPanel.setLayout (new FlowLayout ());
    buttonPanel.add (findButton = new Button ("Find name"));
    buttonPanel.add (addButton = new Button ("Add"));
    buttonPanel.add (deleteButton = new Button ("Delete"));
    buttonPanel.add (saveButton = new Button ("Save"));
```

continued on next page

continued from previous page

```
    Panel fieldPanel = new Panel ();
    fieldPanel.setLayout (new GridLayout (6, 1, 5, 5));
    fieldPanel.add (new Label ("Name"));
    fieldPanel.add (nameField = new TextField ("", 32));
    fieldPanel.add (new Label ("Phone number"));
    fieldPanel.add (phoneField = new TextField ("", 32));
    fieldPanel.add (new Label ("Email address"));
    fieldPanel.add (emailField = new TextField ("", 32));

    phoneList = new List (5, false);

    FileInputStream fs = null;

        try {
                fs = new FileInputStream ("PhoneBook.txt");
        } catch (Exception e) {
                System.out.println ("Unable to open PhoneBook.txt");
                System.exit (1);
        }
        DataInputStream ds = new DataInputStream (fs);

    NNumbers = 0;
    for (i=0; i<MaxNumbers; i+=1) {
                try {
                        data[i] = ds.readLine ();
                        if (data[i] == null) break;
            NNumbers += 1;
                } catch (IOException e) {
                        System.out.println ("Exception caught reading
                        ➡file.");
                        break;
                }
        StringTokenizer st = new StringTokenizer (data[i], ":\t");
        phoneList.addItem (st.nextToken ());
    }
        try {
                fs.close ();
        } catch (IOException e) {
                System.out.println ("Exception caught closing file.");
        }

    add ("North", buttonPanel);
    add ("South", fieldPanel);
    add ("Center", phoneList);

    resize (300, 400);
    show ();
}

/*
 * Handle button presses and list box select events.
 */
public boolean action (Event evt, Object arg) {
```

```
int i;
StringTokenizer st;
String dname;
String tname;

tname = nameField.getText ();
if (evt.target == findButton || evt.target == nameField) {
    for (i=0; i<NNumbers; i+=1) {
        st = new StringTokenizer (data[i], ":\t");
        dname = st.nextToken ();
        if (contains (tname, dname)) {
            phoneList.select (i);
            nameField.setText (dname);
            phoneField.setText (st.nextToken ());
            emailField.setText (st.nextToken ());
            break;
        }
    }
    return true;
}

if (evt.target == addButton) {
    if (NNumbers < MaxNumbers) {
        tname = nameField.getText ();
        dname = tname + ":" + phoneField.getText() +
            ":" + emailField.getText();
        data[NNumbers] = dname;
        NNumbers += 1;
        phoneList.addItem (tname);
    }
    return true;
}

if (evt.target == deleteButton) {
    i = phoneList.getSelectedIndex ();
    phoneList.delItem (i);
    for (; i<NNumbers-1; i+=1) data[i] = data[i+1];
    NNumbers -= 1;
    nameField.setText ("");
    phoneField.setText ("");
    emailField.setText ("");
    return true;
}

if (evt.target == saveButton) {
    FileOutputStream fs = null;

        try {
        fs = new FileOutputStream ("PhoneBook.txt");
    } catch (Exception e) {
        System.out.println ("Unable to open PhoneBook.txt");
        System.exit (1);
    }
    PrintStream ps = new PrintStream (fs);
```

continued on next page

continued from previous page

```
        for (i=0; i<NNumbers; i+=1) {
            ps.println (data[i]);
                }
        return true;
    }

    if (evt.target == phoneList) {
        i = phoneList.getSelectedIndex ();
        st = new StringTokenizer (data[i], ":\t");
        nameField.setText (st.nextToken ());
        phoneField.setText (st.nextToken ());
        emailField.setText (st.nextToken ());
        return true;
    }

    return false;
}

/*
 * contains method is a fuzzy string compare that returns True
 * if either string is completely contained in the other one.
 *       String s1, s2    two strings to compare
 */
boolean contains (String s1, String s2) {

        int i;
        int l1 = s1.length ();
        int l2 = s2.length ();

        if (l1 < l2) {
                for (i=0; i<=l2-l1; i+=1)
                        if (s1.regionMatches (true, 0, s2, i, l1))
                                return true;
        }
        for (i=0; i<=l1-l2; i+=1)
                if (s2.regionMatches (true, 0, s1, i, l2))
                        return true;

        return false;
}

/**
 * Application entry point
 * @param args - command line arguments
 */
public static void main (String args[]) {

    new PhoneBook ();
}
}
```

2. Compile and test the application. Compile the source by invoking the java
compiler or use the makefile provided. Run the application by typing

```
java PhoneBook
```

Figure 6-7 PhoneBook
application

PhoneBook.java can only be run as an application, since it must read the PhoneBook.txt file. A sample phone book file called PhoneBook.txt is included on the CD-ROM. When PhoneBook is executed, a window will open with four buttons on top: Find Name, Add, Delete, and Save. Below the buttons is a list box that lists the names in the PhoneBook.txt file. Below the list box are three text fields: Name, Phone Number, and Email Address. Click on one of the listed names to display the phone number and e-mail address of that name. The name can also be typed into the text field and the Find Name button pressed to locate that name. The Add and Delete buttons can be used to add or delete entries from the phone book. Figure 6-7 shows an example of the application.

How It Works

The program can only be written as an application because it reads and writes files on the local hard disk. For that reason, the class PhoneBook extends Frame so that a window frame is created for the application.

The PhoneBook constructor sets the window title and sets the layout for the window frame to BorderLayout. Two panels are created, buttonPanel and fieldPanel. buttonPanel contains all the buttons and is added to the top (north) of the window frame. fieldPanel contains all the text edit fields and labels for each field. It uses GridLayout to evenly space the label and input fields. fieldPanel is added to the bottom (south) of the window frame. A list box is created by using the List box constructor. The constructor used in this example takes two arguments: the number of visible lines, and a flag that specifies whether multiple selections are allowed.

The phone book file is opened, and all lines are read into an array of strings called data. The format of the file is the same as that of the phone application in How-To 2.10. The fields are split by using *StringTokenizer*. The first field, name, is added into the list box by using the *List.addItem()* method. After all lines are added, the file is closed.

The *action()* method overrides the default *action()* called by *handleEvent()*. If a findButton event or a nameField event are encountered, the data array is searched by using a fuzzy compare function, *contains()*, introduced in How-To 2.10. *contains()* returns True if there is a match between the text in the name text field and the name field in the data array. If a match is found, the *List.select()* method is used to highlight the corresponding item in the list box.

If the Add button is pressed, a new string is created by using the strings entered in the text fields. This new string is added to the end of the list box by using the *List.addItem()* method. Duplicate names are not checked, so redundancy could occur.

If the Delete button is pressed, the index of the selected item in the list box is retrieved by using the *List.getSelectedIndex()* method. This method returns -1 if no item was selected. The item is removed from the list box by using the *List.delItem()* method. The entry is removed from the data array, and the text fields are cleared.

The Save button causes the program to save the data array into the phone book file PhoneBook.txt.

If a list box item is selected by the user, the index is retrieved by using *List.getSelectedIndex()*, and the fields are displayed in the appropriate text fields. This is similar to the code in the inner *if* statement of the findButton event.

The *contains()* method is taken from How-To 2.10. It is a case-insensitive fuzzy compare method that returns True if one string is contained within the other. The *main()* method simply creates an instance of PhoneBook.

Comments

List boxes in Java are straightforward and easily mastered. Some implementation dependencies exist, like single-click versus double-click to deliver an event.

COMPLEXITY
ADVANCED

6.8 How do I...
Use layout managers?

Problem

I understand how to create various components such as buttons, text areas, and choice lists. I would like to be able to position the components inside a container in various ways. Java contains several layout managers in the AWT. How do I use layout managers?

Technique

This How-To will focus on the layout managers available for containers in Java. To maintain a complete and comprehensive discussion, every layout manager will be demonstrated. However, to discuss each manager in detail, it will not be feasible to illustrate all layout managers in one example. For that reason, this section will contain three separate code examples. The first will focus on FlowLayout, BorderLayout, and GridLayout; the second will demonstrate GridBagLayout; and the third will demonstrate CardLayout.

Every container in Java has a default layout manager. The manager is automatically referred to whenever the container needs to change its appearance. If the default manager does not perform the required operation, a different one can be used. The Java AWT contains five layout managers ranging from simple (FlowLayout and GridLayout) to special-purpose (BorderLayout and CardLayout) to very flexible (GridBagLayout).

FlowLayout is the default layout manager for all Panels. It will place the components from left to right, centered in the row. A new row is created as needed. Figure 6-8 shows a simple example of how components are placed in a panel with FlowLayout.

GridLayout displays components in the requested number of rows and columns. All the components will be of equal size.

BorderLayout is the default layout manager for all windows, such as Dialogs and Frames. It has five areas that are used to hold components: north, south, east, west, and center. The area locations are similar to the traditional map coordinates: north = top, south = bottom, west = left, east = right, and center is in the center. All extra space is placed in the center area. Figure 6-9 illustrates the positioning of components with BorderLayout.

CardLayout is used when a container can contain different components at different times. It can be thought of as a container that contains several different "cards." Only one card is visible at a time, and you can flip through the cards as needed. This is useful when the state of a choice can determine what is displayed.

GridBagLayout is a flexible layout manager that aligns components vertically and horizontally, without requiring that the components be the same size. Each GridBagLayout uses a rectangular grid of cells, with each component occupying one or more cells, called its *display area*.

Figure 6-8 Placing components with FlowLayout

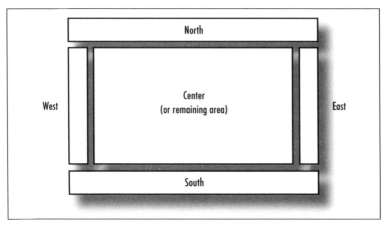

Figure 6-9 Positioning components with BorderLayout

6.8a How Do I Use FlowLayout, BorderLayout, and GridLayout?

Steps

1. Create the applet source file. Create a new file called LayoutApp1.java and enter the following source:

```java
import java.awt.*;
import java.applet.Applet;

/*
 * The applet class
 */
public class LayoutApp1 extends Applet {

/*
 * A panel to hold several other panels that will contain
 * the choice lists and button
 */
Panel p = new Panel();

/*
 * A panel to hold the row choice list and label
 */
Panel rowpanel = new Panel();

/*
 * A panel to hold the column choice list and label
 */
Panel colpanel = new Panel();
```

```
/*
 * A panel to hold the row spacing choice list and label
 */
Panel row_panel = new Panel();

/*
 * A panel to hold the column spacing choice list and label
 */
Panel col_panel = new Panel();

/*
 * A panel to hold the buttons
 */
Panel butpanel = new Panel();

/*
 * The choice list for the number of rows
 */
Choice x = new Choice();

/*
 * The choice list for the number of columns
 */
Choice y = new Choice();

/*
 * The choice list for the row spacing
 */
Choice px = new Choice();

/*
 * The choice list for the column spacing
 */
Choice py = new Choice();

int column = 1;
int row = 1;
int xspace = 0;
int yspace = 0;

/*
 * Called when the applet is loaded
 * Initializes the applet and creates the user interface
 */
public void init() {

    this.setLayout(new BorderLayout());
    p.setLayout(new FlowLayout());
    rowpanel.setLayout(new BorderLayout());
    colpanel.setLayout(new BorderLayout());
    row_panel.setLayout(new BorderLayout());
    col_panel.setLayout(new BorderLayout());
    add("North", p);
    add("Center", butpanel);
```

continued on next page

continued from previous page

```
p.add(new Button("display"));   //Add "display" button.
p.add(rowpanel);  //Add panel to hold row label and choice list.
p.add(colpanel);  //Add panel to hold column label and choice list.
p.add(row_panel); //Add panel to hold row spacing label and choice
➥list.
p.add(col_panel); //Add panel to hold col spacing label and choice
➥list.

/* Create the choice list for the number of rows.*/
x.addItem("1");
x.addItem("2");
x.addItem("3");
x.addItem("4");
x.addItem("5");
// Add the choice list to the bottom (South) of the rowpanel Panel
rowpanel.add("South", x);
// Create a label for the choice list and add it to the top (North)
// of the rowpanel Panel
Label rowlabel = new Label ("  Rows  ",1);
rowpanel.add("North", rowlabel);

// Create the choice list for the number of columns.
y.addItem("1");
y.addItem("2");
y.addItem("3");
y.addItem("4");
y.addItem("5");
// Add the choice list to the bottom (South) of the colpanel Panel.
colpanel.add("South", y);
// Create a label for the choice list and add it to the top (North)
// of the colpanel Panel.
Label collabel = new Label ("  Cols  ",1);
colpanel.add("North", collabel);

/* Create the choice list for the row spacing (padding). */
px.addItem("0");
px.addItem("1");
px.addItem("2");
px.addItem("3");
px.addItem("4");
// Add the choice list to the bottom (South) of the row_panel Panel.
row_panel.add("South", px);
// Create a label for the choice list and add it to the top (North)
// of the row_panel Panel.
Label row_label = new Label (" Row Sp ",1);
row_panel.add("North", row_label);

/* Create the choice list for the column spacing (padding). */
py.addItem("0");
py.addItem("1");
py.addItem("2");
py.addItem("3");
py.addItem("4");
// Add the choice list to the bottom (South) of the col_panel Panel.
```

```
    col_panel.add("South", py);
    // Create a label for the choice list and add it to the top (North)
    // of the col_panel Panel.
    Label col_label = new Label (" Col Sp ",1);
    col_panel.add("North", col_label);

    showButton(row, column, yspace, xspace);
}

public void update (Graphics g){

    paintAll(g);
}

/*
 * Called when an action event occurs
 * @param evt - the event object
 * @param arg - the target object
 */
public boolean action(Event evt, Object arg) {

    if (evt.target instanceof Button) {
        String label = (String)arg;
        if (label.equals("display")){
            butpanel.removeAll();
            showButton(row, column, yspace, xspace);
            this.repaint();
            p.repaint();
        }
    } else if (evt.target.equals (x)) {
        String label = (String)arg;
        try {
            row = Integer.valueOf (label).intValue();
        } catch (NumberFormatException e) {
        }

    } else if (evt.target.equals (y)){
        String label = (String)arg;
        try {
            column = Integer.valueOf (label).intValue();
        } catch (NumberFormatException e) {
        }
    } else if (evt.target.equals (px)){
        String label = (String)arg;
        try {
            xspace = Integer.valueOf (label).intValue();
        } catch (NumberFormatException e) {
        }
    } else if (evt.target.equals (py)){
        String label = (String)arg;
        try {
            yspace = Integer.valueOf (label).intValue();
        } catch (NumberFormatException e) {
        }
```

continued on next page

continued from previous page

```
    }
    return true;
}

/*
 * Called whenever the "display" button is pressed
 * Creates the buttons that represent the choice list selections
 * @param r - the number of rows
 * @param c - the number of rows
 * @param rs - the row spacing
 * @param cs - the column spacing
 */
public void showButton(int r,int c,int rs,int cs){

    int i,j;
    int count = 0;
    butpanel.setLayout(new GridLayout(r,c,rs,cs));

    for (i=0; i<c; i+=1) {
        for (j=0; j<r; j+=1) {
            count+=1;
            butpanel.add("South",new Button("Button "+ count));
        } // end for i
    } // end for j
} // end showButton

/*
 * Application entry point
 * @param args - command line arguments
 */
public static void main(String args[]) {

    Frame f = new Frame("Layout App 1");
    LayoutApp1 layoutapp = new LayoutApp1();
    layoutapp.init();
    layoutapp.start();
    f.add("Center", layoutapp);
    f.resize(300, 300);
    f.show();
}
}
```

2. Create an HTML document that contains the applet. Create a new file called howto68a.html as follows:

```
<html>
<head>
<title>Layout Applet 1</title>
</head>
<applet code="LayoutApp1.class" width=300 height=300>
</applet>
<hr size=4>

</html>
```

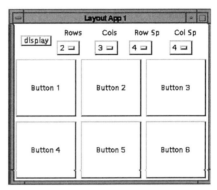

Figure 6-10 The LayoutApp1
applet

3. Compile and test the applet. Compile the source using javac or the makefile
provided. Test the applet using the Appletviewer by entering the following
command:

`APPLETVIEWER howto68a.html`

LayoutApp1.java may also be run as an application by typing

`java LayoutApp1`

When LayoutApp1 is executed, a window will open. At the top of the window will be a button labeled "display" and four choice lists. Each choice list
has a label above it describing its function. The choice list labeled "Rows" is
used to select the number of rows; the list labeled "Cols" is used to select
the number of columns; and "Row Sp" and "Col Sp" are used to select the
spacing between rows and columns, respectively. The remainder of the window will be occupied by a single button. Use the choice lists to select the
number of rows, columns, and spacing between rows and columns. Press
the "display" button to display the button pad with the specified number of
rows, columns, and spacing. Figure 6-10 shows an example of the running
applet.

How It Works

The LayoutApp1 application/applet contains one class, the *LayoutApp1* class, which
is the applet itself. The *LayoutApp1* class extends Applet because it is an applet. The
applet contains six containers. The main container (this) is the applet, and the layout is set to BorderLayout with *setLayout(new BorderLayout( ))*. Two panels, *p* and
butpanel, are added to the main container with FlowLayout and GridLayout, respectively. The panel p is added to the top (North), and butpanel is added to the

center (Center). The butpanel is added to the center, because in a BorderLayout all the extra space is added to the center. A button and four panels (all with BorderLayout) are then added to panel p. Since p uses FlowLayout, the button and panels added to it are placed from left to right. Within each of the four panels is placed a label and a choice list. The label is added to the top and the choice list to the bottom. This is done to give the choice lists a label describing their function. Figure 6-11 shows the layout of LayoutApp1 with each panel and component.

The *showButton()* method is used to create the buttons in the butpanel panel. The butpanel layout is set to GridLayout with the specified number of rows, columns, and spacing from the choice lists. The buttons are then added within two *for* loops to create the proper number of buttons.

Tables 6-6 to 6-8 show the constructors, methods, and variables for FlowLayout, BorderLayout, and GridLayout managers, respectively.

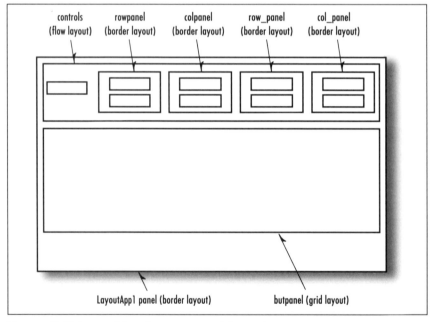

Figure 6-11 LayoutApp1 component layout

METHOD	DESCRIPTION
FlowLayout()	Constructs a new Flow Layout with a centered alignment
FlowLayout(int)	Constructs a new Flow Layout with the specified alignment
FlowLayout(int, int, int)	Constructs a new Flow Layout with the specified alignment and gap values
addLayoutComponent layout	Adds the specified component to the layoutContainer
(String, Component)	
(Container)	Lays out the container
minimumLayoutSize(Container)	Returns the minimum dimensions needed to lay out the components contained in the specified target container
preferredLayoutSize(Container)	Returns the preferred dimensions for this layout given the components in the specified target container
removeLayoutComponent(Component)	Removes the specified component from the layout
toString()	Returns the String representation of this FlowLayout's values
CENTER	The right alignment variable
LEFT	The left alignment variable
RIGHT	The right alignment variable

Table 6-6 FlowLayout constructors, methods, and variables

METHOD	DESCRIPTION
BorderLayout()	Constructs a new Border Layout
BorderLayout(int, int)	Constructs a Border Layout with the specified gaps
addLayoutComponent(String, Component)	Adds the specified named component to the layout
layoutContainer(Container)	Lays out the specified container
minimumLayoutSize(Container)	Returns the minimum dimensions needed to lay out the components contained in the specified target container
preferredLayoutSize(Container)	Returns the preferred dimensions for this layout given the components in the specified target container
removeLayoutComponent(Component)	Removes the specified component from the layout
toString()	Returns the String representation of this BorderLayout's values

Table 6-7 BorderLayout constructors and methods

METHOD	DESCRIPTION
GridLayout(int, int)	Creates a Grid Layout with the specified rows and columns
GridLayout(int, int, int, int)	Creates a Grid Layout with the specified rows, columns, horizontal gap, and vertical gap
addLayoutComponent(String, Component)	Adds the specified component with the specified name to the layout
layoutContainer(Container)	Lays out the container in the specified panel
minimumLayoutSize(Container)	Returns the minimum dimensions needed to lay out the components contained in the specified panel
preferredLayoutSize(Container)	Returns the preferred dimensions for this layout given the components in the specified panel
removeLayoutComponent(Component)	Removes the specified component from the layout
toString()	Returns the String representation of this GridLayout's values

Table 6-8 GridLayout constructors and methods

This example uses an *action()* method to catch events. The only events that are of interest are if the "display" button was pressed, or if one of the choice lists was selected. The button event is handled when the event.target, *evt*, is a button and the button label is equal to "display." The choice list events are handled when the evt.target is equal to the instance of the choice list. In this example the evt.target.equals (<instance name>) expression is used. The expression could have been evt.target == <instance name> and the result would have been the same.

Comments

When components are added to containers, the order they are added is not always important. For GridLayout and FlowLayout, components are added from left to right until a new row is required, and therefore the order they are added is important. In BorderLayout, components are added to the specified area, so the order they are added is not important.

6.8b   How Do I Use GridBagLayout?

Steps

1. Create the applet source file. Create a new file called LayoutApp2.java and enter the following source:

```
import java.awt.*;
import java.applet.Applet;

/**
 * A class that describes a Choice list for the number of rows
```

```
 */
class rowChoice extends Choice{
    public rowChoice() {
        super();
    }
}

/**
 * A class that describes a Choice list for the number of columns
 */
class columnChoice extends Choice{
    public columnChoice() {
        super();
    }
}

/**
 * A class that describes a Choice list for the row spacing
 */
class pxChoice extends Choice{
    public pxChoice() {
        super();
    }
}

/**
 * A class that describes a Choice list for the column spacing
 */
class pyChoice extends Choice{
    public pyChoice() {
        super();
    }
}

/**
 * A class that describes a panel with a GridBagLayout that contains
 * the labels and choice lists for rows, columns, row spacing, and
 * column spacing
 */
class GridBagPanel extends Panel {

    public GridBagPanel() {
        GridBagLayout p = new GridBagLayout();
        GridBagConstraints c = new GridBagConstraints();
        setLayout(p);

        /* weightx & weighty are set to 0 by default. This causes
           the components to clump together in the center of the
           container and not resize if the container is resized.
         */
        c.fill = GridBagConstraints.BOTH; // Fill the display area
        ➥entirely.
        c.gridheight = 2;          // Make "display" button 2 rows high.
        Button button = new Button("display");
```

continued on next page

continued from previous page

```
            p.setConstraints(button, c);
            add(button);

            c.gridheight = 1;        // Make all remaining components 1 row
        ➡high.
            /* Create a label for the row choice list. */
            Label rowlabel = new Label ("   Rows   ",1);
            p.setConstraints(rowlabel, c);
            add(rowlabel);

            /* Create a label for the column choice list. */
            Label collabel = new Label ("   Cols   ",1);
            p.setConstraints(collabel, c);
            add(collabel);

            /* Create a label for the row spacing choice list. */
            Label row_label = new Label (" Row Sp ",1);
            p.setConstraints(row_label, c);
            add(row_label);

            /* Create a label for the column spacing choice list. */
            Label col_label = new Label (" Col Sp ",1);
            c.gridwidth = GridBagConstraints.REMAINDER;   // End row
            p.setConstraints(col_label, c);
            add(col_label);

            /* Create the choice list for the number of rows. */
            c.gridwidth = 1;
            rowChoice x = new rowChoice();
            x.addItem("1");
            x.addItem("2");
            x.addItem("3");
            x.addItem("4");
            x.addItem("5");
            p.setConstraints(x, c);
            add(x);

            /* Create the choice list for the number of columns. */
            columnChoice y = new columnChoice();
            y.addItem("1");
            y.addItem("2");
            y.addItem("3");
            y.addItem("4");
            y.addItem("5");
            p.setConstraints(y, c);
            add(y);

            /* Create the choice list for the row spacing (padding). */
            pxChoice px = new pxChoice();
            px.addItem("0");
            px.addItem("1");
            px.addItem("2");
            px.addItem("3");
            px.addItem("4");
```

```
        p.setConstraints(px, c);
        add(px);

        /* Create the choice list for the column spacing (padding). */
        pyChoice py = new pyChoice();
        py.addItem("0");
        py.addItem("1");
        py.addItem("2");
        py.addItem("3");
        py.addItem("4");
        c.gridwidth = GridBagConstraints.REMAINDER;   // End row
        p.setConstraints(py, c);
        add(py);

    } // GridBagPanel method
} // GridBagPanel class

/*
 * The applet class
 */
public class LayoutApp2 extends Applet {

    GridBagPanel gridbagpanel = new GridBagPanel();
    Panel butpanel = new Panel();

    int column = 1;
    int row = 1;
    int xspace = 0;
    int yspace = 0;

/*
 * Called when the applet is loaded
 * Creates the user interface
 */
    public void init() {

        String st;

        this.setLayout(new BorderLayout());
        this.add("Center", butpanel);
        this.add("North", gridbagpanel);
        showButton(row, column, yspace, xspace);

    } // init()

    public void update (Graphics g){
        paintAll(g);
    } // update()

/*
 * Called when an action event occurs
 * @param evt - the event object
 * @param arg - the target object
 */
```

continued on next page

continued from previous page

```java
    public boolean action(Event evt, Object arg) {
        if (evt.target instanceof Button) {
            String label = (String)arg;
            if (label.equals("display")){
                butpanel.removeAll();
                showButton(row, column, yspace, xspace);
                repaint();
            }
        } else if (evt.target instanceof rowChoice){
            String row_label = (String)arg;
            try {
                row = Integer.valueOf (row_label).intValue();
            } catch (NumberFormatException e) {
            }

        } else if (evt.target instanceof columnChoice){
            String column_label = (String)arg;
            try {
                column = Integer.valueOf (column_label).intValue();
            } catch (NumberFormatException e) {
            }

        } else if (evt.target instanceof pxChoice){
            String xspace_label = (String)arg;
            try {
                xspace = Integer.valueOf (xspace_label).intValue();
            } catch (NumberFormatException e) {
            }

        } else if (evt.target instanceof pyChoice){
            String yspace_label = (String)arg;
            try {
                yspace = Integer.valueOf (yspace_label).intValue();
            } catch (NumberFormatException e) {
            }

        }
        return true;
    }

/*
 * Called when the display button is pressed
 * @param r - the number of rows to display
 * @param c - the number of columns to display
 * @param rs - the row spacing
 * @param cs - the column spacing
 */
    public void showButton(int r,int c,int rs,int cs){
        int i,j;
        int count = 0;
```

```
        butpanel.setLayout(new GridLayout(r,c,rs,cs));

        for (i=0; i<c; i+=1){
            for (j=0; j<r; j+=1){
                count+=1;
                butpanel.add("South",new Button("Button "+ count));
            } // for i
        } // for j
    } // mshowButton

/*
 * Application entry point
 * @param args - command line arguments
 */
    public static void main(String args[]) {
        Frame f = new Frame("Layout App 1");
        LayoutApp2 layoutapp = new LayoutApp2();
        layoutapp.init();
        layoutapp.start();
        f.add("Center", layoutapp);
    f.resize(300, 300);
    f.show();
    } // main()
} // Class LayoutApp2
```

2. Create an HTML document that contains the applet. Create a new file called howto68b.html as follows:

```
<html>
<head>
<title>Layout Applet 2</title>
</head>
<applet code="LayoutApp2.class" width=300 height=300>
</applet>
<hr size=4>

</html>
```

3. Compile and test the applet. Compile the source using javac or the makefile provided. Test the applet using the Appletviewer by entering the following command:

```
APPLETVIEWER howto68b.html
```

LayoutApp2.java may also be run as an application by typing

```
java LayoutApp2
```

When LayoutApp2 is executed, a window will open and will look very similar to the example in section 6.8a. The only noticeable visual difference is that the "display" button is two rows high. The functionality is identical to example 6.8a. Figure 6-12 shows an illustration of the running applet.

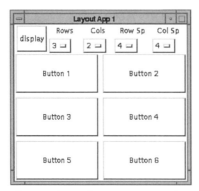

Figure 6-12 The LayoutApp2
applet

How It Works

The LayoutApp2 application/applet contains six classes. There is a separate class for each choice list, a *GridBagPanel* class for the panel that will hold the button panel, and the LayoutApp1 class, which is the applet itself.

A class was defined for each choice list. Each class simply extends the *Choice* class and declares a constructor. These classes were defined to allow for the choice lists to be handled in the event handler as separate classes. This is not required, but it is included to illustrate the possibilities.

The *GridBagPanel* class extends *Panel* and is used to add the "display" button and choice lists. The layout manager for the panel is set to *GridBagLayout*. Each component managed by a *GridBagLayout* is associated with a GridBagConstraints instance that specifies how the component is laid out within its display area. How a *GridBagLayout* places a set of components depends on each component's GridBagConstraints and minimum size, as well as the preferred size of the components' container.

To use a *GridBagLayout* effectively, you must customize one or more of its component's GridBagConstraints. You customize a GridBagConstraints object by setting one or more of its instance variables. The instance variables are as follows:

- *gridx, gridy* These specify the cell at the upper left of the component's display area, where the upper-leftmost cell has address *gridx* = 0, *gridy* = 0.

  Use GridBagConstraints.RELATIVE (the default value) to specify that the component be placed just to the right of (for *gridx*) or just below (for *gridy*) the component that was added to the container just before this component was added.

- *gridwidth, gridheight* These specify the number of cells in a row (for *gridwidth*) or column (for *gridheight*) in the component's display area. The default value is 1. Use GridBagConstraints.REMAINDER to specify that the component be the last one in its row (for *gridwidth*) or column (for *gridheight*). Use GridBagConstraints.RELATIVE to specify that the component be the next to last one in its row (for *gridwidth*) or column (for *gridheight*).

fill This is used when the component's display area is larger than the component's requested size to determine whether (and how) to resize the component. Valid values are GridBagConstraint.NONE (the default), GridBagConstraint.HORIZONTAL (make the component wide enough to fill its display area horizontally, but don't change its height), GridBagConstraint.VERTICAL (make the component tall enough to fill its display area vertically, but don't change its width), and GridBagConstraint.BOTH (make the component fill its display area entirely).

ipadx, ipady These specify the internal padding: how much to add to the minimum size of the component. The width of the component will be at least its minimum width plus *ipadx**2 pixels (since the padding applies to both sides of the component). Similarly, the height of the component will be at least the minimum height plus *ipady**2 pixels.

insets This specifies the external padding of the component—the minimum amount of space between the component and the edges of its display area.

anchor This is used when the component is smaller than its display area to determine where (within the area) to place the component. Valid values are GridBagConstraints.CENTER (the default), GridBagConstraints.NORTH, GridBagConstraints.NORTHEAST, GridBagConstraints.EAST, GridBagConstraints.SOUTHEAST, GridBagConstraints.SOUTH, GridBagConstraints.SOUTHWEST, GridBagConstraints.WEST, and GridBagConstraints.NORTHWEST.

weightx, weighty These are used to determine how to distribute space — this is important for specifying resizing behavior. Unless you specify a weight for at least one component in a row (*weightx*) and column (*weighty*), all the components clump together in the center of their container. This is because when the weight is zero (the default), the GridBagLayout puts any extra space between its grid of cells and the edges of the container.

In this example the "display" button has constraints of *gridheight* = 2 and *fill* = GridBagConstraints.BOTH. All other constraints are their default values. This will cause the button to have a display area two rows high and to fill the entire display area. The result is a single button two rows high. All remaining components have *gridheight* = 1. The col_label Label and py choice list have *gridwidth* = GridBagConstraints.REMAINDER, which will cause them to fill the remainder of the row. It is important to reset the gridwidth to something else before the next component is added. If it is not, it will retain the REMAINDER setting, and every additional button will be an entire row long.

The *LayoutApp2* class is the applet itself and extends Applet. The main panel layout manager is set to *BorderLayout*, and the *Gridbagpanel* is added to the top (North) and the butpanel to the center (Center). As seen before, *BorderLayout* places all remaining space in the center, so butpanel will occupy most of the main panel.

The *showButton()* method is used to add the selected button to the button panel. This method sets the layout manager of butpanel to *GridLayout* with the row, column, row spacing, and column spacing values taken from the choice lists values. This is identical to example 6.8a.

Table 6-9 shows the constant values for GridBagConstraints. Table 6-10 shows the constructors and methods for *GridBagLayout*.

CONSTANT		
BOTH	REMAINDER	gridwidth
CENTER	SOUTH	gridx
EAST	SOUTHEAST	gridy
HORIZONTAL	SOUTHWEST	insets
NONE	VERTICAL	ipadx
NORTH	WEST	ipady
NORTHEAST	anchor	weightx
NORTHWEST	fill	weighty
RELATIVE	gridheight	

Table 6-9 GridBagConstraints

METHOD	DESCRIPTION
GridBagLayout()	Creates a Gridbag Layout
DumpConstraints(GridBagConstraints)	Prints the layout constraints
DumpLayoutInfo(GridBagLayoutInfo)	Prints the layout information
addLayoutComponent(String, Component)	Adds the specified component with the specified name to the layout
getConstraints(Component)	Retrieves the constraints for the specified component
layoutContainer(Container)	Lays out the container in the specified panel
lookupConstraints(Component)	Retrieves the constraints for the specified component
minimumLayoutSize(Container)	Returns the minimum dimensions needed to lay out the components contained in the specified panel

METHOD	DESCRIPTION
preferredLayoutSize(Container)	Returns the preferred dimensions for this layout given the components in the specified panel
removeLayoutComponent(Component)	Removes the specified component from the layout
setConstraints(Component, GridBagConstraints)	Sets the constraints for the specified component
toString()	Returns the String representation of this GridBagLayout's values

Table 6-10 GridBagLayout constructors and methods

6.8c   How Do I Use CardLayout?

Steps

1. Create the applet source file. Create a new file called CalcButton.java and enter the following source:

```
import java.awt.*;
import java.applet.Applet;

/*
 * A class that holds the two keypad definitions and
 * extends panel
 */
class CardPanel extends Panel {

/*
 * A method that returns a panel that contains
 * a "standard" calculator keypad
 */
    Panel standard() {
        Panel p = new Panel();
        p.setLayout(new GridLayout(5,4,2,2));
        p.add(new Button("7"));
        p.add(new Button("8"));
        p.add(new Button("9"));
        p.add(new Button("/"));
        p.add(new Button("4"));
        p.add(new Button("5"));
        p.add(new Button("6"));
        p.add(new Button("x"));
        p.add(new Button("1"));
        p.add(new Button("2"));
        p.add(new Button("3"));
        p.add(new Button("-"));
        p.add(new Button("."));
        p.add(new Button("0"));
        p.add(new Button("+/-"));
        p.add(new Button("+"));
        p.add(new Button("C"));
```

continued on next page

continued from previous page

```
            p.add(new Label(""));
            p.add(new Label(""));
            p.add(new Button("="));
            return p;

    }


/*
 * A method that returns a panel that contains
 * a "scientific" calculator keypad
 */
    Panel scientific() {
        Panel p = new Panel();
        p.setLayout(new GridLayout(5,6,2,2));
        p.add(new Button("sin"));
        p.add(new Button("Exp"));
        p.add(new Button("7"));
        p.add(new Button("8"));
        p.add(new Button("9"));
        p.add(new Button("/"));
        p.add(new Button("cos"));
        p.add(new Button("log"));
        p.add(new Button("4"));
        p.add(new Button("5"));
        p.add(new Button("6"));
        p.add(new Button("x"));
        p.add(new Button("tan"));
        p.add(new Button("ln"));
        p.add(new Button("1"));
        p.add(new Button("2"));
        p.add(new Button("3"));
        p.add(new Button("-"));
        p.add(new Button("1/x"));
        p.add(new Button("x^y"));
        p.add(new Button("."));
        p.add(new Button("0"));
        p.add(new Button("+/-"));
        p.add(new Button("+"));
        p.add(new Label(""));
        p.add(new Label(""));
        p.add(new Button("C"));
        p.add(new Label(""));
        p.add(new Label(""));
        p.add(new Button("="));
        return p;

    }


/*
 * The CardPanel class constructor
 */
    CardPanel() {
    setLayout(new CardLayout());
        add("Standard", standard());
```

```
            add("Scientific", scientific());
    }

    public Dimension preferredSize() {
    return new Dimension(200, 100);
    }
}

/*
 * The applet class
 */
public class CalcButton extends Applet {
    CardPanel cards;

/*
 * Called when the applet is loaded
 * Creates the user interface
 */
    public void init() {
    setLayout(new BorderLayout());
    add("Center", cards = new CardPanel());
    Panel p = new Panel();
    p.setLayout(new FlowLayout());
        add("South", p);
        p.add(new Button("Standard"));
        p.add(new Button("Scientific"));
    }

/*
 * Called when an action event occurs
 * @param evt - the event object
 * @param arg - the target object
 */
    public boolean action(Event evt, Object arg) {
        if (evt.target instanceof Button) {
            String label = (String)arg;
            if (label.equals("Standard")) {
                ((CardLayout)cards.getLayout()).show(cards,label);
            } else if (label.equals("Scientific")) {
                ((CardLayout)cards.getLayout()).show(cards,label);
            }
            return true;
        }
            return false;
    }

/*
 * Application entry point
 * @param args - command line arguments
 */
    public static void main(String args[]) {
        Frame f = new Frame("Calculator Button");
        CalcButton calcbutton = new CalcButton();
        calcbutton.init();
        calcbutton.start();
```

continued on next page

continued from previous page

```
            f.add("Center", calcbutton);
            f.resize(200, 200);
        f.show();
        }

}
```

2. Create an HTML document that contains the applet. Create a new file called howto68c.html as follows:

```
<html>
<head>
<title>Calculator Button Panel</title>
</head>
<applet code="CalcButton.class" width=200 height=200>
</applet>
<hr size=4>

</html>
```

3. Compile and test the applet. Compile the source using javac or the makefile provided. Test the applet using the Appletviewer by entering the following command:

```
APPLETVIEWER howto68c.html
```

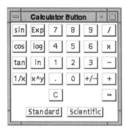

Figure 6-13 The CalcButton applet

CalcButton.java may also be run as an application by typing

```
java CalcButton
```

When CalcButton is executed, a window will open with a button pad that looks very similar to the calculator of example 6.1. Below the button pad are two buttons labeled "Standard" and "Scientific." When the Scientific button is pressed, the button pad will change to one that could be used for a scientific calculator. The standard pad can then be displayed by pressing the Standard button. Figure 6-13 shows an illustration of the running applet.

How It Works

The CalcButton application/applet contains two classes. The *CardPanel* class contains the definitions of the two panels that will be used, while the *CalcButton* class is the applet itself.

This example will use *CardLayout* to display a choice of two possible button pads. *CardLayout* can be thought of as having a deck of cards. Each card can contain a different layout manager and completely different components. The cards can only be viewed one at a time, but they can be flipped through in any order. Figure 6-14 shows an illustration of two different panels, with only one being visible at a time.

The *CalcButton* class extends Applet because it is the applet. This class adds the panel cards to the center of the main panel and a panel p to the bottom of the main panel. *Panel* p uses FlowLayout, and two buttons are placed in the panel. An event handler is used to capture action events. The only event of interest is that of a button press. If the button pressed has a label of "Standard," then the *CardLayout.show* method is called with "Standard" (or the button label) as an argument. Similarly, if the "Scientific" button is pressed, *CardLayout.show* is called with that button label as an argument.

The *CardLayout* class has several methods that can be called. This example illustrated using *show(<CardLayout panel>, <panel to show>)*. The other methods available are shown in Table 6-11.

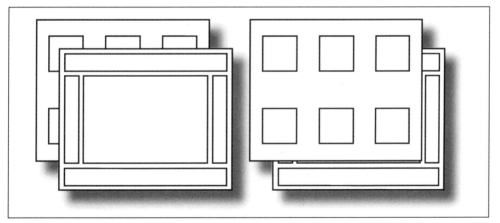

Figure 6-14 CardLayout display concept

The *CardPanel* class in the example extends panel. This class contains three methods. The *standard()* and *scientific()* methods return a *Panel* and are used to set up the different "cards." They each create a new panel, set the layout manager, and add the components to the panel. The *CardPanel()* constructor method sets the layout to *CardLayout* and adds the two cards.

METHOD	DESCRIPTION
CardLayout()	Creates a new Card Layout
CardLayout(int, int)	Creates a Card Layout with the specified gaps
addLayoutComponent(String, Component)	Adds the specified component with the specified name to the layout
first(Container)	Flips to the first card
last(Container)	Flips to the last card of the specified container
layoutContainer(Container)	Performs a layout in the specified panel
minimumLayoutSize(Container)	Calculates the minimum size for the specified panel
next(Container)	Flips to the next card of the specified container
preferredLayoutSize(Container)	Calculates the preferred size for the specified panel
previous(Container)	Flips to the previous card of the specified container
removeLayoutComponent(Component)	Removes the specified component from the layout
show(Container, String)	Flips to the specified component name in the specified container
toString()	Returns the String representation of this CardLayout's values

Table 6-11 CardLayout methods

Comments

Instead of using one of the AWT's layout managers, it is possible to write your own. Before you do this, make sure that no existing layout manager will work. To create a custom layout manager, a class must be created that implements the LayoutManager interface, which defines the five methods all layout managers require. These five methods are *addLayoutComponent( )*, *layoutContainer( )*, *minimalLayoutSize( )*, *preferredLayoutSize( )*, and *removeLayoutComponent( )*. LayoutManagers don't actually draw the components placed in them, they invoke the *resize( )*, *move( )*, and *reshape( )* methods of each component. In addition, absolute positioning may also be used, and that will be discussed in section 6.9.

COMPLEXITY
INTERMEDIATE

6.9 How do I...
Use absolute positioning?

Problem

I know how to use layout managers to place components in a panel. Sometimes the layout managers don't provide the desired look. I would like to place a component at a specified location with a specified size. How do I use absolute positioning?

Technique

Components can be positioned without using a layout manager by specifying the absolute position for the components. With absolute positioning the location and size of the components can be specified in the coordinates of the container.

Steps

1. Create the applet source file. Create a new file called AbsPosition.java and enter the following source:

```java
import java.awt.*;
import java.applet.Applet;

/*
 * The applet class
 */

public class AbsPosition extends Applet {
    Panel controls = new Panel();
    Panel butpanel = new Panel();
    Scrollbar sbvert;
    Scrollbar sbhoriz;
    Scrollbar sbwidth;
    Scrollbar sbheight;
    TextField tfvert;
    TextField tfhoriz;
    TextField tfwidth;
    TextField tfheight;
    int width = 20;
    int height = 20;
    int vert = 20;
    int horz = 20;
    int min = 20;
    int max = 400;
    Button but1;

/* Called when the applet is loaded
 * Creates the user interface
 */
    public void init() {
    // Set layout of main panel to BorderLayout.
        this.setLayout(new BorderLayout());
    // Set layout of controls panel to GridLayout with 3 rows and 4
    // columns
    // and the horizontal and vertical spacing to 5.
        controls.setLayout(new GridLayout(3,4,5,5));
    // Set layout of butpanel to null. This is so we can use absolute
    // positioning.
    butpanel.setLayout(null);
        add("South", controls);  // Add controls to bottom of main panel.
        add("Center", butpanel); // Add butpanel to middle of main panel.
```

continued on next page

continued from previous page

```
// Create TextfFields for the scrollbars with an 8-character display.
    tfwidth = new TextField (8);
    tfheight = new TextField (8);
    tfvert = new TextField (8);
    tfhoriz = new TextField (8);

//  Set up the scrollbars to be oriented horizontally, have an initial
// value of min, paging size of 1, min value of min, and max value of
   max.
// The paging size is the step amount of the scrollbar.
    sbhoriz = new Scrollbar (Scrollbar.HORIZONTAL, min, 1, min, max);
    sbvert = new Scrollbar (Scrollbar.HORIZONTAL, min, 1, min, max);
    sbwidth = new Scrollbar (Scrollbar.HORIZONTAL, min, 1, min, max);
    sbheight = new Scrollbar (Scrollbar.HORIZONTAL, min, 1, min, max);

// Add a label for each Scrollbar.
// These will fill up row one of the GridLayout.
controls.add(new Label(" Horizontal ",1 ));
controls.add(new Label(" Vertical ", 1 ));
controls.add(new Label(" Width ",1 ));
controls.add(new Label(" Height ", 1 ));

// Add the TextFields.
// This will fill up row 2 of the GridLayout.
controls.add (tfhoriz);
controls.add (tfvert);
controls.add (tfwidth);
controls.add (tfheight);

// Add the Scrollbars.
// This will fill up row 3 of the GridLayout.
controls.add(sbhoriz);
controls.add(sbvert);
controls.add(sbwidth);
controls.add(sbheight);

// Set the TextField to the value of the Scrollbar.
tfhoriz.setText(String.valueOf(sbwidth.getValue()));
tfvert.setText(String.valueOf(sbheight.getValue()));
tfwidth.setText(String.valueOf(sbwidth.getValue()));
tfheight.setText(String.valueOf(sbheight.getValue()));

but1 = new Button("one"); // Create a new Button with label "one."

butpanel.add(but1);   // Add but1 to the butpanel panel.

// Draw but1 with the initial values of horz, vert, width, and height.
// reshape draws the button in the panel at the horizontal and vertical
// position specified, and the button is of size width and height.
but1.reshape(horz, vert, width, height);
} // init

/*
 * The update method
 */
```

```
public void update (Graphics g){
    paintAll(g);
}

/*
 * The paint method
 * Redraws the button with the values from the sliders
 */
public void paint ( Graphics g) {

but1.reshape((int)getValue(tfhoriz), (int)getValue(tfvert),
    (int)getValue(tfwidth), (int)getValue(tfheight));
}

/** Gets the current value in the text field
  * That's guaranteed to be the same as the value
  * in the scroller (subject to rounding, of course).
  */
double getValue(TextField textField) {
double f;
try {
    f = Double.valueOf(textField.getText()).doubleValue();
} catch (java.lang.NumberFormatException e) {
    f = 0.0;
}
return f;
}


/*
 * Respond to user actions.
 * @param evt - the event object
 */
public boolean handleEvent(Event evt) {
    if (evt.target.equals (sbwidth)) {
        tfwidth.setText(String.valueOf(sbwidth.getValue()));
        repaint();

    } else if (evt.target.equals (sbheight)) {
        tfheight.setText(String.valueOf(sbheight.getValue()));
        repaint();

} else if (evt.target.equals (sbhoriz)) {
        tfhoriz.setText(String.valueOf(sbhoriz.getValue()));
        repaint();

} else if (evt.target.equals (sbvert)) {
        tfvert.setText(String.valueOf(sbvert.getValue()));
        repaint();

    } else if ((evt.target.equals (tfwidth))
                && (evt.id == Event.ACTION_EVENT)) {
        setSliderValue(sbwidth, getValue(tfwidth));
        tfwidth.setText(String.valueOf(sbwidth.getValue()));
        repaint();
```

continued on next page

continued from previous page

```
        } else if ((evt.target.equals (tfheight))
                && (evt.id == Event.ACTION_EVENT)) {
            setSliderValue(sbheight, getValue(tfheight));
            tfheight.setText(String.valueOf(sbheight.getValue()));
        repaint();

        } else if ((evt.target.equals (tfhoriz))
                && (evt.id == Event.ACTION_EVENT)) {
            setSliderValue(sbhoriz, getValue(tfhoriz));
            tfhoriz.setText(String.valueOf(sbhoriz.getValue()));
        repaint();

        } else if ((evt.target.equals (tfvert))
                && (evt.id == Event.ACTION_EVENT)) {
            setSliderValue(sbvert, getValue(tfvert));
            tfvert.setText(String.valueOf(sbvert.getValue()));
        repaint();

        } else if (evt.target instanceof Button) {
        repaint();
    }
        return false;
    }


    /*
     * Set the slider value.
     * @param slider - the scrollbar instance
     * @param f - the value to set the scrollbar
     */
    void setSliderValue(Scrollbar slider, double f) {
    int sliderValue = (int)f;
        if (sliderValue > max)
        sliderValue = max;
    if (sliderValue < min)
        sliderValue = min;
        slider.setValue(sliderValue);
    }

    /* Application entry point
     * @param args - command line arguments
     */
    public static void main(String args[]) {
        Frame f = new Frame("Absolute Positioning");
        AbsPosition abs = new AbsPosition();
        abs.init();
    f.resize(500, 700);
        f.add("Center", abs);
    f.show();
    }

}
```

2. Create an HTML document that contains the applet. Create a new file called howto69.html as follows:

```
<html>
<head>
<title>Absolute Positioning</title>
</head>
<applet code="AbsPosition.class" width=500 height=450>
</applet>
<hr size=4>


</html>
```

3. Compile and test the applet. Compile the source using javac or the makefile provided. Test the applet using the Appletviewer by entering the following command:

```
APPLETVIEWER howto69.html
```

AbsPosition.java may also be run as an application by typing

```
java AbsPosition
```

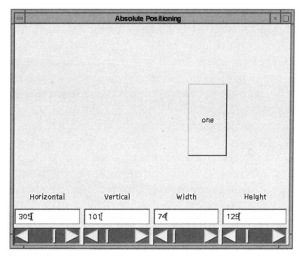

Figure 6-15 Absolute positioning

When AbsPosition is executed, a window will open with four scrollbars or sliders at the bottom and a button near the top. The sliders are labeled: "Horizontal," "Vertical," "Width," and "Height." The sliders can be moved to vary the value, or a value may be typed in the text field above the slider.

The range for each slider is from 20 to 400. As the sliders are moved, the corresponding value of the button will automatically change. For example, if the "Vertical" slider is moved, the vertical position of the button will change; if the "Width" slider is moved, the width of the button will change; and so on. Figure 6-15 shows an example of the running applet.

How It Works

The AbsPosition application/applet contains only one class, *AbsPosition*, which is the applet itself. The main panel layout is set to *BorderLayout*. Two panels are added to the main panel, controls to the South, and butpanel to the Center. Controls uses *GridLayout* with three rows, four columns, and a row and column spacing of five. The layout manager for butpanel is set to null to specify not to use a layout manager.

The controls panel has four Labels, four textFields, and four scrollbars. The labels are used to give the scrollbars a title, and the textfields indicate each scrollbar's value. The textfields also allow for a value to be entered from the keyboard.

A Button, but1, is added to the butpanel panel. The *reshape()* method is used to specify the button's horizontal and vertical position, width, and height. The *reshape()* method is contained in the component class and takes four integers as input; the horizontal and vertical positions, the width, and the height. The component is reshaped to the specified bounding box. The positions are measured from the container's upper-left corner.

The *handleEvent()* method is overridden to capture only the events required. The events that are required are any of the four scrollbars, and any of the four textfields. If a scrollbar event occurs, the corresponding textfield is set to the scrollbar value and *reshape()* is called. If a textfield event occurs, the scrollbar and textfield are set to the inputted value and *reshape()* is called. The scrollbar value is set by using the *setSliderValue()* method. This method verifies that the value is not out of the range of the scrollbar. If it is out of range, the value is set to either min or max. When a textfield event occurs, the scrollbar value is set first in case the value is out of range. The textfield is then set to correct the value entered if it was out of range.

Comments

Absolute positioning should be used with caution when designing applets/applications for platform-independence. On different platforms, components can have different sizes depending on the window manager.

COMPLEXITY
ADVANCED

6.10 How do I...
Create windows?

Problem

When I use the Appletviewer, I can print debugging information to the console. Not all browsers have Java consoles, so if I run an applet inside a browser, the output to System.out may not appear on the console. I want to create a debugging window that I can use in an applet in place of the console. I want to be able to print text in the window. Scrollbars would also be helpful. I could use a text area for holding the text output and maintaining scrollbars. I don't know how to create windows. How do I create windows?

Technique

Windows can be created in Java by using the *Frame* class. The frame class creates an empty window that can hold components (widgets and panels). The title of the frame can be specified by using the Frame constructor with a title or setting the title by calling *Frame.SetTitle()*.

Widgets and panels can be added to the frame by invoking the *Frame.add()* method with the component as an argument. Several events are unique to windows. These include Event.WINDOW_DESTROY, Event.WINDOW_ICONIFY, and Event.WINDOW_MOVE. The EventApp example can be used to determine which events are delivered for different actions.

Steps

1. Create the applet source file. Create a new file called Fonts.java and enter the following source:

```
import java.applet.Applet;
import java.awt.*;

/*
 * The applet class
 */
public class Fonts extends Applet {

/*
 * The maximum number of fonts to look for
 */
final int MaxFonts = 10;
```

continued on next page

continued from previous page

```
/*
 * Width and height of the panel
 */
int width, height;

/*
 * Array to hold the system font names
 */
String fontName[];

/*
 * Array of fonts, holds normal, italic, and bold versions
 */
Font theFonts[] = new Font[3 * MaxFonts];

/*
 * The number of fonts actually found
 */
int nfonts = 0;

/*
 * Instance of debugging window for printing
 * debug messages
 */
DebugWin debugWin;

/*
 * Called when the applet is loaded
 * Create the debug window and get system fonts.
 */
public void init () {

    int i;
    Dimension d = size ();

    width = d.width;
    height = d.height;

    debugWin = new DebugWin ();

    debugWin.println ("Width = "+width);
    debugWin.println ("height = "+height);

    fontName = Toolkit.getDefaultToolkit().getFontList ();

    nfonts = fontName.length;

    debugWin.println ("Number of fonts = "+fontName.length);

    if (nfonts > MaxFonts) nfonts = MaxFonts;
    for (i=0; i<nfonts; i+=1) {

        debugWin.println ("Font "+i+" is "+fontName[i]);
```

```
            theFonts[3*i + 0] = new Font (fontName[i], Font.PLAIN, 12);
            theFonts[3*i + 1] = new Font (fontName[i], Font.BOLD, 12);
            theFonts[3*i + 2] = new Font (fontName[i], Font.ITALIC, 12);
        }
}

/**
 * Paint the font names.
 * @param g - destination graphics object
 */
public void paint (Graphics g) {

    int i;

    for (i=0; i<nfonts; i+=1) {
        g.setFont (theFonts[3*i + 0]);
        g.drawString (fontName[i], 10, 20*i+30);
        g.setFont (theFonts[3*i + 1]);
        g.drawString ("Bold", 70, 20*i+30);
        g.setFont (theFonts[3*i + 2]);
        g.drawString ("Italic", 150, 20*i+30);
    }
}

/**
 * Application entry point
 * @param args - command line arguments
 */
public static void main (String args[]) {

    Frame f = new Frame ("Fonts");
    Fonts fonts = new Fonts ();

    f.resize (200, 200);
    f.add ("Center", fonts);
    f.show ();
    fonts.init ();
}

}
```

2. Create the applet source file. Create a new file called DebugWin.java and enter the following source:

```
import java.awt.*;
import java.io.*;

/*
 * A class to implement a simple debug output
 * text window
 */
public class DebugWin extends Frame {

/*
 * End point of the text area, used for inserting text.
```

continued on next page

continued from previous page

```
 */
int endPosition;

/*
 * The TextArea object used for displaying text
 */
private    TextArea t;

/*
 * The constructor creates the window
 * and adds the text area.
 */
public DebugWin()
{
    setTitle ("Debugging window");

    Font f = new Font("Courier", Font.PLAIN, 12);
    setFont(f);
    setBackground(Color.white);

    t = new TextArea ("", 24, 80);
    t.setEditable (true);
    endPosition = 0;
    add ("Center", t);

    resize(300,200);
    pack();
    show();
}

/**
 * A method to add text to the end of the text area
 * @param s - text to enter
 */
public void print (String s) {

    t.insertText (s, endPosition);
    endPosition += s.length ();
}

/**
 * A method to add text to the end of the text area
 * with a new line
 * @param s - text to enter
 */
public void println (String s) {

    t.insertText (s+"\n", endPosition);
    endPosition += s.length () + 1;
}

/**
 * Writes contents of the text area to a file
 * @param s - name of the file to write
```

```java
    */
public void write (String s) {

    FileOutputStream out = null;

    try {
        out = new FileOutputStream(s);
    } catch (Exception e) {
        println ("Error in opening file" + s);
        return;
    }

    PrintStream psOut = new PrintStream (out);

    psOut.print (t.getText());

    try {
        out.close ();
    } catch (IOException e) {
        println ("Unable to close "+s);
    }
}

/*
 * Handle events that have occurred.
 * @param evt - the event object
 */
public boolean handleEvent(Event evt) {

    String filename;

    switch(evt.id)
    {
        case Event.WINDOW_DESTROY:
            dispose ();
            return true;
    }

    return false;
}

}
```

3. Create an HTML document that contains the applet. Create a new file called howto610.html as follows:

```html
<html>
<head>
<title>Creating Windows</title>
</head>
<applet code="Fonts.class" width=200 height=200>
</applet>
<hr size=4>


</html>
```

4. Compile and test the applet. Compile the source using javac or the makefile provided. Test the applet using the Appletviewer by entering the following command:

`APPLETVIEWER howto610.html`

Fonts.java may also be run as an application by typing

`java Fonts`

When Fonts is executed, two windows appear. The first window displays the fonts available in bold and italic styles as in How-To 3.6. The second window displays debugging information such as how many fonts were found and the name of the fonts. Figure 6-16 shows an example of the running applet.

Figure 6-16 Creating windows

How It Works

The Fonts applet is used as a driver applet for the debug window. It is similar to the applet introduced in How-To 3.6.

The *init()* method of the *Fonts* class creates an instance of DebugWin by invoking its constructor. The font list is retrieved and the number of fonts is printed in the debug window by calling the *DebugWin.println()* method. The font names are also printed by the *DebugWin.println()* method.

The DebugWin constructor extends *Frame* so that a window can be created. The window is actually created by an implicit call to the Frame constructor. The title of the window is set by calling the *Frame.setTitle()* method. The font and background color are set for aesthetics; the default values could have been used with no consequence. A noneditable text area is created with no initial text, 24 rows, and 80 columns.

The text area is then added to the center of the window frame. The window is resized by calling *Frame.show()* with width and height as arguments. The default frame size is typically the entire desktop, which is usually not desirable. The window is displayed by calling *Frame.show()*.

Two *print* methods are defined: *print* and *println*. They both add string text to the end of the text area for display. The only difference is that *println* adds a newline at the end for convenience.

A *write* method is also included that writes the entire contents of the text area to a file. The name of the file is given by the argument to *write()*.

The *handleEvent()* method catches window close events by looking for Event. WINDOW_DESTROY. The window is destroyed by calling the *Frame.dispose()* method. The window will disappear when this method is called.

Comments

A nice extension to the *DebugWin* class is to add all of the functionality found in PrintStream.

COMPLEXITY
ADVANCED

6.11 How do I...
Create dialogs?

Problem

I found the SpreadSheet example in section 6.5 very useful. I want to extend the SpreadSheet to add user interaction with dialogs. I want to implement both Modal and Modeless dialogs. I would like to use the ModalDialogs for an AboutDialog that displays information about the program and also to display error messages such as missing parentheses or an improperly formed formula. How do I use dialogs?

Technique

Dialogs are actually a subclass of the Window class. Dialogs are created by invoking a Dialog constructor. The Dialog constructor takes the parentframe as an argument along with the title of the dialog and a flag. If the flag is set to True, the Dialog is created as a modal dialog. If it is set to False, the Dialog is modeless. The easiest way to implement dialogs is to create a class that extends Dialog. The constructor of the extended class must call the Dialog constructor using the super call. Events within the Dialog must be handled by overriding the *handleEvent()* method as shown in previous examples. When the dialog is completed, such as when the user presses the OK button, the dialog is destroyed by invoking the *dispose()* method.

Steps

1. Create the applet source file. Create a new file called SpreadSheet.java and enter the following source:

```java
import java.awt.*;
import java.applet.*;


/*
 * The applet class
 */
public class SpreadSheet extends Panel {

/*
 * The text entry field
 */
TextField textField;

/*
 * Instance of the sheet panel
 */
Sheet sheet;

/*
 * Initialize the application.
 * @param f - parent frame
 */
public void init (Frame f) {

    setLayout(new BorderLayout());

    textField = new TextField ("", 80);
    sheet = new Sheet (10, 5, 400, 200, textField, f);
    add ("North", textField);
    add ("Center", sheet);
}

/*
 * Check for return keypresses.
 */
public boolean handleEvent(Event e) {

    if ((e.target instanceof TextField)
        && (e.id == Event.ACTION_EVENT)) {

        sheet.enter (textField.getText ());
        return true;
    }
    return false;
}

/*
 * Application entry point
 * @param args - command line arguments
 */
```

```
public static void main (String args[]) {

    Frame f = new Frame ("SpreadSheet");

    SpreadSheet spreadSheet = new SpreadSheet ();

    spreadSheet.init (f);

    f.resize (440, 330);
    f.add ("Center", spreadSheet);
    f.show ();

    AboutDialog ab = new AboutDialog (f);
    ab.show();
}

}
```

2. Create the applet source file. Create a new file called Sheet.java and enter the following source:

```
import java.awt.*;

/*
 * The panel that holds the cells
 */
public class Sheet extends Panel {

/*
 * The number of rows and columns in the spreadsheet
 */
int rows;
int cols;

/*
 * Width and height of the panel
 */
int width;
int height;

/*
 * The array of cells
 */
Cell cells[][];

/*
 * Offsets into the panel where the cells are displayed
 */
int xoffset;
int yoffset;

/*
 * The row and column selected by a mouse click
 */
```

continued on next page

continued from previous page

```java
int selectedRow = 0;
int selectedCol = 0;

/*
 * The text entry field
 */
TextField textField;

/*
 * The parent frame
 */
Frame frame;

/*
 * Constructor
 * Create all the cells and init them.
 * @param r - number of rows
 * @param c - number of columns
 * @param w - width of the panel
 * @param h - height of the panel
 * @param t - instance of text entry field
 */
public Sheet (int r, int c, int w, int h, TextField t, Frame f) {

    int i, j;

    rows = r;
    cols = c;
    width = w;
    height = h;
    xoffset = 30;
    yoffset = 30;
    textField = t;
    frame = f;

    cells = new Cell[rows][cols];
    for (i=0; i<rows; i+=1) {
        for (j=0; j<cols; j+=1) {
            cells[i][j] = new Cell (cells, rows, cols, f);
        }
    }
}

/*
 * A mapping array for converting column indexes to characters
 */
static String charMap[] = {
    "a", "b", "c", "d", "e", "f", "g", "h", "i", "j",
    "k", "l", "m", "n", "o", "p", "q", "r", "s", "t",
    "u", "v", "w", "x", "y", "z"
};

/*
```

```
 * Paint each cell.
 * @param g - destination graphics object
 */
public void paint (Graphics g) {

    int i, j;
    int x, y;
    int w, h;
    double val;
    String s;
    boolean error;

    w = width / cols;
    h = height / rows;

    x = 0;
    g.setColor (Color.black);
    for (i=0; i<rows; i+=1) {
        y = (i * height / rows) + yoffset;
        g.drawString (String.valueOf (i+1), x, y+h);
    }
    y = yoffset-2;
    for (j=0; j<cols; j+=1) {
        x = (j * width / cols) + xoffset+(w/2);
        g.drawString (charMap[j], x, y);
    }

    for (i=0; i<rows; i+=1) {
        for (j=0; j<cols; j+=1) {
            s = cells[i][j].evalToString ();
            x = (j * width / cols) + xoffset + 2;
            y = (i * height / rows) + yoffset - 2;
            if (i == selectedRow && j == selectedCol) {
                g.setColor (Color.yellow);
                g.fillRect (x, y, w-1, h-1);
            } else {
                g.setColor (Color.white);
                g.fillRect (x, y, w-1, h-1);
            }
            g.setColor (Color.black);
            g.drawString (s, x, y+h);
        }
    }
}

/*
 * Called to recalculate the entire spreadsheet
 */
void recalculate () {

    int i, j;

    for (i=0; i<rows; i+=1) {
        for (j=0; j<cols; j+=1) {
```

continued on next page

continued from previous page

```
                cells[i][j].evaluate ();
        }
    }
}

/*
 * Handle mouse down events.
 * @param evt - event object
 * @param x - mouse x position
 * @param y - mouse y position
 */
public boolean mouseDown (Event evt, int x, int y) {

    int w = width / cols;
    int h = height / rows;

    int sr = (y-yoffset)/h;
    int sc = (x-xoffset)/w;

    if (sr < 0 || sr >= rows || sc < 0 || sc > cols) return true;

    selectedRow = sr;
    selectedCol = sc;
    repaint ();
    textField.setText (cells[selectedRow][selectedCol].text);
    return true;
}

/*
 * Called to enter a text into a selected cell
 * @param s - the string to enter
 */
void enter (String s) {

    cells[selectedRow][selectedCol].enter (s);
    recalculate ();
    repaint ();
}

}
```

3. Create the applet source file. Create a new file called Scroll.java and enter the following source:

```
import java.awt.*;

/**
 * A class that handles scrolling text
 */
class Scroll {

/*
 * X and y coordinates of starting point
 */
```

```
int xstart, ystart;

/*
 * Width and height of bounding panel
 */
int width, height;

/*
 * The text to be scrolled
 */
String text;

/*
 * X and y velocities, respectively
 */
int deltaX, deltaY;

/*
 * The current x and y position of the text
 */
int xpos, ypos;

/*
 * The color of the text
 */
Color color;

/**
 * Class constructor just saves arguments
 * @param x, y - starting coordinates
 * @param dx, dy - x and y velocities
 * @param w, h - width and height of bounding panel
 * @param t - the text string
 * @param c - color of the text
 */
public Scroll (int x, int y, int dx, int dy, int w, int h, String t, Color
c) {

    xstart = x;
    ystart = y;
    width = w;
    height = h;
    text = t;
    deltaX = dx;
    deltaY = dy;
    color = c;
    xpos = xstart;
    ypos = ystart;
}

/*
 * Draw the text at the current position.
 * Advance the position of and reinitialize outside bounding panel
 * @param g - destination graphics object
 */
```

continued on next page

continued from previous page

```
void paint (Graphics g) {

    g.setColor (color);
    g.drawString (text, xpos, ypos);
    xpos += deltaX;
    ypos += deltaY;

    FontMetrics fm = g.getFontMetrics ();
    int textw = fm.stringWidth (text);
    int texth = fm.getHeight ();
    if (deltaX < 0 && xpos < -textw) xpos = xstart;
    if (deltaX > 0 && xpos > width) xpos = xstart;
    if (deltaY < 0 && ypos < 0) ypos = ystart;
    if (deltaY > 0 && ypos > height+texth) ypos = ystart;
}

}
```

4. Create the applet source file. Create a new file called Cell.java and enter the following source:

```
import java.awt.*;

/*
 * Defines an individual cell
 */
public class Cell {

/*
 * Token types returned by Lex()
 */
static final int NUMBER = 1;
static final int EQUALS = 2;
static final int PLUS = 3;
static final int MINUS = 4;
static final int STAR = 5;
static final int SLASH = 6;
static final int TEXT = 7;
static final int EOT = 8;
static final int LEFT = 9;
static final int RIGHT = 10;
static final int UNKN = 11;
static final int FORMULA = 12;
static final int REFERENCE = 13;

/*
 * What is in this cell
 */
int type;

/*
 * The numeric value, if this cell is numeric
 */
double value;
```

```
/*
 * Numeric value for this token
 */
double lexValue;

/*
 * Index into input string (used for parsing)
 */
int lexIndex;

/*
 * Token value returned from Lex()
 */
int token;

/*
 * The text contents of this cell
 */
String text;
int textLength;
int textIndex;

/*
 * Reference to all cells in spreadsheet
 */
Cell cells[][];

/*
 * Error flag, set if parse error detected
 */
boolean error;

/*
 * Used to force rereading of tokens
 */
boolean lexFlag;

/*
 * Number of rows and columns in the spreadsheet
 * Used for bounds checking
 */
int cols;
int rows;

/*
 * The parent frame
 */
Frame frame;

public Cell (Cell cs[][], int r, int c, Frame f) {

    cells = cs;
    rows = r;
    cols = c;
```

continued on next page

continued from previous page

```
    frame = f;
    text = "";
    lexFlag = true;
    type = UNKN;
}

/*
 * Called to get the numeric value of this cell
 */
double evaluate () {

    resetLex ();
    error = false;
    switch (type) {
        case FORMULA:
        Lex ();
        value = Level1 ();
        if (error) return 0;
        return value;

        case NUMBER:
        value = lexValue;
        return value;

        case UNKN:
        return 0;
    }
    error = true;
    return 0;
}

/*
 * Returns the string representation of the value
 */
String evalToString () {

    String s;

    if (type == TEXT || type == UNKN) return text;
    s = String.valueOf (value);
    if (error) return "Error";
    else return s;
}

/*
 * Called to enter a string into this cell
 */
void enter (String s) {

    text = s;
    textLength = text.length ();
    resetLex ();
    error = false;
    switch (Lex ()) {
```

```
        case EQUALS:
        type = FORMULA;
        break;

        case NUMBER:
        type = NUMBER;
        value = lexValue;
        break;

        default:
        type = TEXT;
        break;
    }
}

/*
 * Top level of the recursive descent parser
 * Handles plus and minus
 */
double Level1 () {

    boolean ok;
    double x1, x2;

    x1 = Level2 ();
    if (error) return 0;

    ok = true;
    while (ok) switch (Lex ()) {
        case PLUS:
        x2 = Level2 ();
        if (error) return 0;
        x1 += x2;
        break;

        case MINUS:
        x2 = Level2 ();
        if (error) return 0;
        x1 -= x2;
        break;

        default:
        Unlex ();
        ok = false;
        break;
    }
    return x1;
}

/*
 * Handle multiply and divide.
 */
double Level2 () {

    boolean ok;
```

continued on next page

continued from previous page

```
    double x1, x2;

    x1 = Level3 ();
    if (error) return 0;

    ok = true;
    while (ok) switch (Lex ()) {
        case STAR:
        x2 = Level3 ();
        if (error) return 0;
        x1 *= x2;
        break;

        case SLASH:
        x2 = Level3 ();
        if (error) return 0;
        x1 /= x2;
        break;

        default:
        Unlex ();
        ok = false;
        break;
    }
    return x1;
}

/*
 * Handle unary minus, parenthesis, constants, and cell references.
 */
double Level3 () {

    double x1, x2;

    switch (Lex ()) {
        case MINUS:
        x2 = Level1 ();
        if (error) return 0;
        return -x2;

        case LEFT:
        x2 = Level1 ();
        if (error) return 0;
        if (Lex () != RIGHT) {
            ErrorDialog er = new ErrorDialog (frame,
                "Missing right parenthesis");
            er.show ();
            error = true;
            return 0;
        }
        return x2;

        case NUMBER:
        case REFERENCE:
```

```
            return lexValue;
        }
        ErrorDialog er = new ErrorDialog (frame,
            "Formula syntax error");
        er.show ();
        error = true;
        return 0;
}

/*
 * Reset the lexical analyzer.
 */
void resetLex () {

    lexIndex = 0;
    lexFlag = true;
}

/*
 * Push a token back for rereading.
 */
void Unlex () {

    lexFlag = false;
}

/*
 * Returns the next token
 */
int Lex () {

    if (lexFlag) {
        token = lowlevelLex ();
    }
    lexFlag = true;
    return token;
}

/*
 * Returns the next token in the text string
 */
int lowlevelLex () {

    char c;
    String s;

    do {
        if (lexIndex >= textLength) return EOT;
        c = text.charAt (lexIndex++);
    } while (c == ' ');
    switch (c) {
        case '=':
        return EQUALS;
```

continued on next page

continued from previous page

```
        case '+':
        return PLUS;

        case '-':
        return MINUS;

        case '*':
        return STAR;

        case '/':
        return SLASH;

        case '(':
        return LEFT;

        case ')':
        return RIGHT;
    }

    if (c >= '0' && c <= '9') {
        s = "";
        while ((c >= '0' && c <= '9') || c == '.' ||
            c == '-' || c == 'e' || c == 'E') {
            s += c;
            if (lexIndex >= textLength) break;
            c = text.charAt (lexIndex++);
        }
        lexIndex -= 1;
        try {
            lexValue = Double.valueOf (s).doubleValue();
        } catch (NumberFormatException e) {
            ErrorDialog er = new ErrorDialog (frame,
                "Number syntax error");
            er.show ();
            error = true;
            return UNKN;
        }
        return NUMBER;
    }
    if (c >= 'a' && c <= 'z') {
        int col = c - 'a';
        int row;
        s = "";
        if (lexIndex >= textLength) {
            error = true;
            return UNKN;
        }
        c = text.charAt (lexIndex++);
        while (c >= '0' && c <= '9') {
            s += c;
            if (lexIndex >= textLength) break;
            c = text.charAt (lexIndex++);
        }
```

```
            lexIndex -= 1;
            try {
                row = Integer.valueOf (s).intValue() - 1;
            } catch (NumberFormatException e) {
                ErrorDialog er = new ErrorDialog (frame,
                    "Missing row number");
                er.show ();
                error = true;
                return UNKN;
            }
            if (row >= rows || col >= cols) {
                ErrorDialog er = new ErrorDialog (frame,
                    "Row or Column number out of range");
                er.show ();
                error = true;
                return REFERENCE;
            }
            lexValue = cells[row][col].evaluate();
            if (cells[row][col].error) error = true;
            return REFERENCE;
        }
        return TEXT;
    }
}
```

5. Create the applet source file. Create a new file called AboutDialog.java and enter the following source:

```
import java.awt.*;

/*
 * A class for displaying information
 * dialog about the application
 */
public class AboutDialog extends Dialog {

/*
 * Instances of scrolling text
 */
Scroll left, right;

/**
 * Constructor creates the dialog
 * @param parent - parent window frame
 */
public AboutDialog (Frame parent)
{
    super (parent, "About Dialog", true);
    Panel p = new Panel();
    p.add(new Button("OK"));
    add("South", p);

    setFont (new Font ("Dialog", Font.BOLD + Font.ITALIC, 24));
```

continued on next page

continued from previous page

```
    int w = 200;
    int h = 150;

    resize(w, h);

    left = new Scroll (w, 50, -5, 0, w, h, "Super...", Color.red);
    right = new Scroll (0, 75, 5, 0, w, h, "Spread Sheet!", Color.green);
}

/**
 * Paint the scrolling text and force
 * a repaint every 50 ms.
 * @param g - destination graphics context
 */
public void paint (Graphics g) {

    left.paint (g);
    right.paint (g);
    repaint (50);
}

/**
 * Destroy the dialog when the OK
 * button is pressed.
 * @param evt - event object
 */
public boolean handleEvent(Event evt)
{
    switch(evt.id)
    {
        case Event.ACTION_EVENT:
        {
            if("OK".equals(evt.arg))
            {
                dispose ();
                return true;
            }
        }
    }
    return false;
}
}

/*
 * Class creates a dialog for displaying
 * error messages.
 */
class ErrorDialog extends Dialog {

/*
 * error text to display
 */
String text;
```

```
/**
 * Constructor creates dialog and saves text string
 * @param parent - parent window frame
 * @param t - text to display
 */
public ErrorDialog (Frame parent, String t) {

    super (parent, "Error", false);

    text = t;
    Panel p = new Panel();
    p.add(new Button("OK"));
    add("South", p);

    setFont (new Font ("Dialog", Font.BOLD, 14));

    int w = 250;
    int h = 150;

    resize(w, h);
}

/**
 * Draw the text string.
 * @param g - destination graphics context
 */
public void paint (Graphics g) {

    g.drawString (text, 10, 100);
}

/**
 * Dispose of the dialog when the
 * OK button is pressed.
 * @param evt - event object
 */
public boolean handleEvent(Event evt) {

    switch(evt.id)
    {
        case Event.ACTION_EVENT:
        {
            if("OK".equals(evt.arg))
            {
                dispose ();
                return true;
            }
        }
    }
    return false;
}

}
```

6. Compile and test the application. Compile the source using javac or the makefile provided. SpreadSheet.java can only be run as an application by typing

`java SpreadSheet`

When SpreadSheet is executed, a spreadsheet will be displayed similar to How-To 6.5, except a dialog box will be open with text scrolling. This dialog can be closed by clicking the OK button. If an error occurs, a dialog box will open with an error message printed in it. Similarly, the box can be closed by clicking the OK button. Figure 6-17 shows an example of the running applet.

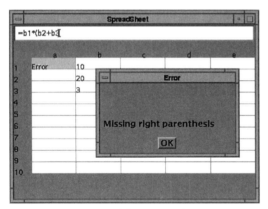

Figure 6-17 SpreadSheet application

How It Works

The SpreadSheet is very similar to that of How-To 6.5. The main difference is that it must be run as an application only. This is because a parent frame is required. Applets reside in panels that do not require a frame. The SpreadSheet program uses two types of dialogs: the AboutDialog and the ErrorDialog. The AboutDialog is displayed when the user first starts the program. The ErrorDialog is displayed when an error such as a syntax error in a formula or a computational error has occurred. Most of the application is identical to that of How-To 6.5. One important difference is that the frame containing the application is passed to all methods. This frame is passed as the first argument to the Dialog constructor. When the program is first started, the AboutDialog constructor is invoked. The AboutDialog constructor first invokes a Dialog constructor by calling *super()*. The first argument to *super()* is the parent frame.

The second argument is the title, which is "About Dialog," and the third argument is a flag. If the flag is set to True, the dialog is modal. In this case the AboutDialog is modal. AboutDialog creates an additional panel that will contain an OK button. This is added to the bottom of the dialog by using the *add()* method. The constructor then creates a new font and resizes itself. The *Scroll* class, which was introduced in Chapter 3, is used to make the dialog more interesting by creating scrolling text in different colors. Events that are sent to the dialog are handled by overriding the *handleEvent()* method. This has the same syntax as in other examples. If the OK button is pressed, the dialog is destroyed by calling the *dispose()* method. The ErrorDialog is very similar to the AboutDialog. The main difference is that it takes a string in addition to the parent frame as arguments to its constructor. This string is displayed in the center of the dialog as an error message. A single OK button is added to the bottom of the dialog. This is used to cancel the dialog after the user has read the message. The ErrorDialog is used in several places in the SpreadSheet. It is used twice in the *LevelThree* method in the *Cell* class. It is first used to alert the user that the right parenthesis is missing in a formula. It is also used to show a formula syntax error. The ErrorDialog is also used several times in the *lowlevelLex* method. It is shown when a syntax error is detected, a row number is missing from a cell reference, or when a row or a column number is out of range.

Comments

Modal and Modeless dialogs are very similar. The only difference is their behavior. This is largely handled by the Java runtime system. Modeless dialogs are created in the same way that ModalDialogs were created. Table 6-12 lists all the methods available in the dialog class.

METHOD	DESCRIPTION
Dialog(Frame, boolean)	Constructs an initially invisible Dialog
Dialog(Frame, String, boolean)	Constructs an initially invisible Dialog with a title
addNotify()	Creates the frame's peer
getTitle()	Gets the title of the Dialog
isModal()	Returns True if the Dialog is modal
isResizable()	Returns True if the user can resize the frame
paramString()	Returns the parameter String of this Dialog
setResizable(boolean)	Sets the resizable flag
setTitle(String)	Sets the title of the Dialog

Table 6-12 Dialog class constructors and methods

COMPLEXITY
ADVANCED

6.12 How do I...
Use file dialogs?

Problem

I would like to write a simple text editor. I plan to use the *TextArea* class to implement most of the function. I know that other graphical interface systems have methods to implement dialogs and save dialogs as a standard mechanism. This simplifies programming considerably. I would like to implement File Dialogs in Java.

Technique

Java supports File Dialogs in much the same way as X Window, Macintosh, and Windows. In fact, the File Dialog system supported in Java includes two types: Open and Save dialogs. They are actually the same class. The only difference is that a constant tells Java which type of dialog to use.

Steps

1. Create the applet source file. Create a new file called Scroll.java and enter the following source:

```java
import java.awt.*;

/**
 * A class that handles scrolling text
 */
class Scroll {

/*
 * X and y coordinates of starting point
 */
int xstart, ystart;

/*
 * Width and height of bounding panel
 */
int width, height;

/*
 * The text to be scrolled
 */
String text;

/*
 * X and y velocities, respectively
 */
```

```
int deltaX, deltaY;

/*
 * The current x and y position of the text
 */
int xpos, ypos;

/*
 * The color of the text
 */
Color color;

/**
 * Class constructor just saves arguments
 * @param x, y - starting coordinates
 * @param dx, dy - x and y velocities
 * @param w, h - width and height of bounding panel
 * @param t - the text string
 * @param c - color of the text
 */
public Scroll (int x, int y, int dx, int dy, int w, int h, String t, Color
➥c) {

    xstart = x;
    ystart = y;
    width = w;
    height = h;
    text = t;
    deltaX = dx;
    deltaY = dy;
    color = c;
    xpos = xstart;
    ypos = ystart;
}

/*
 * Draw the text at the current position.
 * Advance the position of and reinitialize outside bounding panel.
 * @param g - destination graphics object
 */
void paint (Graphics g) {

    g.setColor (color);
    g.drawString (text, xpos, ypos);
    xpos += deltaX;
    ypos += deltaY;

    FontMetrics fm = g.getFontMetrics ();
    int textw = fm.stringWidth (text);
    int texth = fm.getHeight ();
    if (deltaX < 0 && xpos < -textw) xpos = xstart;
    if (deltaX > 0 && xpos > width) xpos = xstart;
    if (deltaY < 0 && ypos < 0) ypos = ystart;
    if (deltaY > 0 && ypos > height+texth) ypos = ystart;
}

}
```

continued from previous page

2. Create the applet source file. Create a new file called NotePad.java and
enter the following source:

```java
import java.awt.*;
import java.io.*;

/*
 * A simple text editor application
 */
public class NotePad extends Frame {

/*
 * TextArea is used to hold content.
 */
private    TextArea t;

/*
 * Instances of FileDialog
 */
private FileDialog openDialog;
private FileDialog saveDialog;

/*
 * The menu bar
 */
private MenuBar mbar;

/*
 * Constructor creates application window and
 * menu bar.
 */
public NotePad ()
{
    super ("NotePad Editor");

    Font f = new Font("Courier", Font.PLAIN, 12);
    setFont(f);
    setBackground(Color.white);

    mbar = new MenuBar();
    Menu m = new Menu("File");
    m.add(new MenuItem("New"));
    m.add(new MenuItem("Open"));
    m.add(new MenuItem("Save"));
    m.add(new MenuItem("Save As"));
    m.addSeparator();
    m.add(new MenuItem("Quit"));
    mbar.add(m);

    m = new Menu("Help");
    m.add(new MenuItem("Help!!!!"));
    m.addSeparator();
    m.add(new MenuItem("About..."));
    mbar.add(m);
```

```
        t = new TextArea ("", 24, 80);
        t.setEditable (true);
        add ("Center", t);

        openDialog = new FileDialog(this, "Open File...", FileDialog.LOAD);
        saveDialog = new FileDialog(this, "Save File...", FileDialog.SAVE);

        setMenuBar(mbar);
        resize(300,200);
        pack();
        show();
}

/**
 * Reads text from a file and enters it into the text area
 * @param s - name of file to read
 */
public void read (String s) {

    String line;
    int i =0;
    FileInputStream in = null;
    DataInputStream dataIn = null;

    try {
        in = new FileInputStream(s);
        dataIn = new DataInputStream (in);
    } catch(Throwable e) {
        System.out.println("Error in opening file");
        return;
    }

    try {
        while ((line = dataIn.readLine()) != null)
        {
            line += "\n";
            t.insertText (line, i);
            i += line.length ();
        }
    } catch(IOException e) {
        System.out.println("Error in reading file");
    }

    try {
        in.close ();
    } catch (IOException e) {
        System.out.println (e);
    }
}

/**
 * Writes text from the text area to a file
 * @param s - name of file to write
 */
public void write(String s) {
```

continued on next page

continued from previous page

```
    FileOutputStream out = null;

    try {
        out = new FileOutputStream(s);
    } catch (Exception e) {
        System.out.println("Error in opening file");
        return;
    }

    PrintStream psOut = new PrintStream (out);

    psOut.print (t.getText());

    try {
        out.close ();
    } catch (IOException e) {
        System.out.println (e);
    }
}

/**
 * Handle user events.
 * @param evt - event object
 */
public boolean handleEvent (Event evt) {

    String filename;

    switch(evt.id)
    {
        System.out.println(evt.target.toString());
        case Event.WINDOW_DESTROY:
            System.exit(0);
            return true;

        case Event.ACTION_EVENT:
            if(evt.target instanceof MenuItem)
            {
                if (evt.arg.equals("Open")) {

                    openDialog.show();
                    filename = openDialog.getFile();
                    read(filename);
                    return true;
                }
                if (evt.arg.equals("Save As")) {

                    saveDialog.show();
                    filename = saveDialog.getFile();
                    write(filename);
                    return true;
                }
                if(evt.arg.equals("Quit")) {
                    System.exit(0);
```

```
                    }
                    if (evt.arg.equals("About...")) {
                        AboutDialog ab = new AboutDialog(this);
                        ab.show();
                        return true;
                    }
                }
                break;
        }

        return false;
    }

    /**
     * Application entry point
     * @param args - command line arguments
     */
    public static void main(String args[])
    {
        new NotePad();
    }
}

/*
 * A class for displaying information
 * dialog about the application
 */
class AboutDialog extends Dialog {

    /*
     * Instances of scrolling text
     */
    Scroll left, right;

    /**
     * Constructor creates the dialog.
     * @param parent - parent window frame
     */
    public AboutDialog(NotePad parent) {

        super(parent, "About Dialog", true);
        Panel p = new Panel();
        p.add(new Button("OK"));
        add("South", p);

        setFont (new Font ("Dialog", Font.BOLD + Font.ITALIC, 24));

        int w = 200;
        int h = 150;

        resize(w, h);

        left = new Scroll (w, 50, -5, 0, w, h, "About...", Color.red);
        right = new Scroll (0, 75, 5, 0, w, h, "Dialog!", Color.green);
```

continued on next page

continued from previous page

```
}

/**
 * Paint the scrolling text and force
 * a repaint every 50 ms.
 * @param g - destination graphics context
 */
public void paint (Graphics g) {

    left.paint (g);
    right.paint (g);
    repaint (50);
}

/**
 * Destroy the dialog when the OK
 * button is pressed.
 * @param evt - event object
 */
public boolean handleEvent(Event evt) {

    switch(evt.id)
    {
        case Event.ACTION_EVENT:
        {
            if("OK".equals(evt.arg))
            {
                dispose ();
                return true;
            }
        }
    }
    return false;
}

}
```

4. Compile and test the applet. Compile the source using javac or the makefile provided. Test the applet by entering the following command:

```
java NotePad
```

NotePad can only be run as an application. When NotePad is executed, a window will open with a simple notepad program within it. Figure 6-18 shows an example of the running applet.

How It Works

The NotePad program contains two classes: the *NotePad* class itself and the *AboutDialog* class.

The *NotePad* class is the main program. The *AboutDialog* class is used to show an about ModalDialog that is displayed when the user selects the About menu item.

The *NotePad* class extends *Frame* because it will be used as a stand-alone application. *FileDialog* has no meaning in applets, because applets cannot read from the local hard disk directly. The *NotePad* class creates a text area T; two file Dialogs, one called openDialog and one called saveDialog; and a menu bar (mbar). The NotePad constructor sets the window title by invoking the Frames constructor using *super()*. The constructor then creates a new font, sets the background color, and creates a menu bar with menu items similar to previous examples. It also creates the text area used for editing and sets it to be editable. This is added to the center of the Frame. The openDialog and saveDialog variables are also initialized by invoking the constructor for *FileDialog*. The same constructor is used for both openDialog and saveDialog. The only difference is the file constant in the argument list. For openDialog the constant is FileDialog.LOAD, and for saveDialog it is FileDialog.SAVE. When the user selects the Open menu item from the File menu, the openDialog is displayed by invoking the *openDialog.show()* method. The file name is returned by invoking the *getFile()* method in OpenDialog. FileDialogs are modal. All events are handled by the *FileDialog* class and will not be passed to the application. When the user clicks on OK or CANCEL, FileDialog will return the file name or null if no file is specified. After a file name is returned, the file is read in using the *read()* method in the *NotePad* class. A similar function occurs if the user selects the Save As menu item from the File menu. In this case the saveDialog is displayed by calling the *show()* method. The file name is returned by using the *getFile()* method, which is very similar to the *openDialog* method. Text from the text area is written to the file by using the *write()* method in the *NotePad* class. If the user selects the About menu

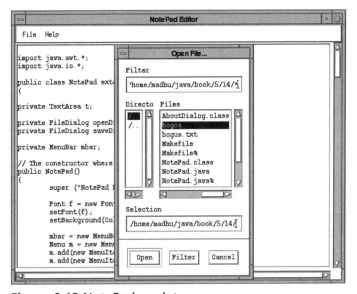

Figure 6-18 NotePad applet

item, the *AboutDialog* is displayed. The *AboutDialog* displays information about the program and handles events similar to examples in previous sections. The methods contained in *FileDialog* are listed in Table 6-13.

METHOD	DESCRIPTION
FileDialog(Frame, String)	Creates a File Dialog for loading a file
FileDialog(Frame, String, int)	Creates a File Dialog with the specified title and mode
addNotify()	Creates the frame's peer
getDirectory()	Gets the directory of the Dialog
getFile()	Gets the file of the Dialog
getFilenameFilter()	Gets the filter
getMode()	Gets the mode of the File Dialog
paramString()	Returns the parameter String of this File Dialog
setDirectory(String)	Sets the directory of the Dialog to the specified directory
setFile(String)	Sets the file for this Dialog to the specified file
setFilenameFilter(FilenameFilter)	Sets the filter for this Dialog to the specified filter
LOAD	The file load variable
SAVE	The file save variable

Table 6-13 FileDialog constructors and methods

ADVANCED GRAPHICS

ADVANCED GRAPHICS

How do I...

In Chapter 3, the techniques needed to draw basic graphical elements such as lines and polygons were presented. This chapter concentrates on advanced graphics manipulations. Java supports the ability to load images from the server so that they may be presented on the client in a manner that allows far greater control than is available with HTML alone. Many web developers have used server pushes to effect animation, but the method is crude, unpredictable, and slow. Java is deterministic, and with experience, can be used to implement interactive games, display real-time data, and animate images for a variety of purposes.

In this chapter image loading, drawing, scaling, and animation will be demonstrated.

7.1   Display a Series of Images

This example demonstrates how to load images from a server and cycle through them with a mouse click. The example uses a button that allows the user to skip to the next image.

7.2   Resize an Image

Resizing an image is a nice feature that allows an image to be displayed at any desired size. This example loads an image and presents buttons for making the image smaller and bigger. The buttons are used to resize the image accordingly.

7.3   Drag an Image with the Mouse

Dragging an image with the mouse is commonly necessary in graphical user interfaces. This example will load an image and allow it to be dragged with the mouse.

7.4   Implement Double Buffering

Drawing images on top of each other using techniques from How-To 7.1 are sufficient to effect convincing animation. Unfortunately, the results can be disappointing. Unwanted flicker and temporal distortion due to drawing latency can degrade performance. This example demonstrates the use of double buffering to produce high quality animation.

7.5   Layer Graphics

This example demonstrates the illusion of depth by layering images on top of each other. Several images are loaded which can be layered with respect to each other by "bring to front" and "send to back" buttons.

7.6   Display Part of an Image

There are many instances when only part of an image must be displayed. This example implements several image transition effects like "barn door open" and venetian blind. It can be used to save web page space and draw attention to banner advertisements.

7.7   Create Images from Pixel Values

In addition to loading images from a server, it may be necessary to construct images from pixel values. In this example, the Mandelbrot set is calculated and converted to an image object for display.

7.8   Access Pixels in an Image

Many applications require access to pixel values in an image object. This example extracts pixels from an image for use as the initial conditions in Conway's "game of life."

COMPLEXITY
BEGINNING

7.1   How do I...
Display a series of images?

Problem

I want to write an applet that loads a series of images and displays in sequence when I press a button. This may be used to show the user a series of thumbnail images that are representatives of larger images. I know how to create buttons and handle button events, but I don't know how to display a series of images. How do I display a series of images?

Technique

To display an image, an applet must first load it from the server. This is accomplished by using the *Applet.getImage()* method. *getImage()* takes a URL or server file name as an argument and returns an *Image* object. The image can then be drawn by using one of the *drawImage()* methods available from the *Graphics* class. In this example, four images are loaded in an array of type Image and successively drawn in response to a button press.

Steps

1. Create the applet source file. Create a new file called ImageApp.java as follows:

```
import java.awt.*;
import java.applet.Applet;

/*
 * Display a series of images.
 */
public class ImageApp extends Applet {
```

continued on next page

continued from previous page

```
/*
 * The number of images to load
 */
final int NumImages = 6;

/*
 * An array to hold the images
 */
Image imgs[] = new Image[NumImages];

/*
 * Which image is currently displayed
 */
int which = 0;

/*
 * init method runs when applet is loaded or reloaded.
 */
public void init() {

    setLayout(new BorderLayout());

    Panel p = new Panel ();
    add("South", p);
    p.add (new Button("Next Image"));
    for (int i=0; i < NumImages; i+=1) {
        String name = "Globe"+(i+1)+".gif";
        imgs[i] = getImage (getDocumentBase(),name);
    }
}

/**
 * paint method is called by update.
 * Draw the current image.
 * @param g - destination graphics object
 */
public void paint (Graphics g) {

    g.drawImage (imgs[which], 10, 10, this);
}

/**
 * Switch to next image when button is pressed
 * @param evt - event object
 * @param arg - target object
 */
public boolean action(Event evt, Object arg) {

    if ("Next Image".equals (arg)) {      // Our button press
        which += 1;
        which %= NumImages;      // Wrap around to zero.
        repaint ();      // Causes update as soon as possible
```

```
        return true;      // We got the event.
    }
    return false;      // This was not our event.
}
}
```

2. Create an HTML document that contains the applet. Create a new file called howto71.html as follows:

```
<html>
<head>
<title>ImageApp</title>
</head>
<hr size=4>
This is a simple image display applet
<hr size=4>
<applet code="ImageApp.class" width=200 height=200>
</applet>
<hr size=4>
</html>
```

3. Compile and test the applet. Compile the Java source file ImageApp.java using javac or the makefile provided. This example will load six images called Globe1.gif, Globe2.gif, Globe3.gif, and so on. When the applet is executed by using Appletviewer, an image should appear in the upper-left corner along with a Next Image button at the bottom. Clicking on Next Image should cycle through all six images. Figure 7-1 shows the image as it is displayed by Appletviewer. If for some reason the image does not appear, make sure it is in the same directory as the applet class (ImageApp.class) and is not corrupted in some way. If the image cannot be loaded, the applet will continue without warning.

Figure 7-1 Displaying an image

How It Works

Image is a class used to hold an image. It is contained in awt.imgs as an array of type *Image*; four elements are used for this example. The *init()* method creates a new panel at the bottom (south) and adds a button. The *start()* method retrieves each of the four images using the *getImage()* method. There are several *getImage()* methods that take URL as an argument. *GetDocumentBase()* returns the current URL base where the applet resides, so that only the file name of an image relative to the current document base is needed. The *drawImage()* method takes *Image*, position, and *ImageObserver* as arguments in order to draw the image. *this* (the applet) is specified as the ImageObserver argument. The *action()* method tests for a button press, increments the array index, and forces an update by calling *repaint ()*.

Comments

It is important to note that the image is not actually loaded with the *getImage()* call. An image is loaded asynchronously when it is needed. Images are only loaded once and kept in memory for future display or use. If you watch carefully when the applet is loaded, the first four image updates are not instantaneous. This is because the Java runtime routines are drawing the image as it is being loaded. After they are all loaded, the drawing time is not noticeable.

COMPLEXITY
BEGINNING

7.2   How do I...
Resize an image?

Problem

Images often need to be scaled to a size different from the way they are stored on disk. For example, two different-sized images need to be displayed as the same size, or I want to simulate in/out motion by making an image smaller/bigger. I know how to load and display images, but I don't know how to scale them. How do I resize an image?

Technique

How-to 7.1 used a *drawImage()* method to display an image. Another *drawImage()* method can scale an image to arbitrary dimensions. The image is retrieved with *getImage()* as before. A version of *drawImage()* that takes width and height as parameters can be used to scale and display the image.

Steps

1. Create the applet source file. Create a new file called ImageSize.java as
follows:

```java
import java.awt.*;
import java.applet.Applet;

/*
 * An applet that allows an image to be resized
 */
public class ImageSize extends Applet {

/*
 * The image to draw
 */
Image img;

/*
 * The current width and height of the image
 */
double width, height;

/*
 * The image size scale factor
 */
double scale = 1.0;

/*
 * Set to True if an image load error occurs.
 */
boolean error = false;

/*
 * Called when the applet is loaded or reloaded
 */
public void init() {

    setLayout(new BorderLayout());
    Panel p = new Panel ();
    add("South", p);
    p.add (new Button("Smaller"));
    p.add (new Button("Bigger"));

    MediaTracker tracker = new MediaTracker (this);

    img = getImage (getDocumentBase(), "T1.gif");
    tracker.addImage (img, 0);
    showStatus ("Getting image: T1.gif");
    try {
```

continued on next page

continued from previous page

```
        tracker.waitForID (0);
    } catch (InterruptedException e) { }
    width = img.getWidth (this);
    height = img.getHeight (this);
}

public void paint (Graphics g) {
    double w, h;

    // If an error occurred, draw a message.
    if (error) {
        g.drawString ("Unable to draw image T1.gif", 10, 50);
        return;
    }

    w = scale * width;
    h = scale * height;

    // If we don't have the size yet, we shouldn't draw.
    if (w < 0 || h < 0) { w=75; h=75; } //return;

    // Explicitly specify width (w) and height (h).
    g.drawImage (img, 10, 10, (int) w, (int) h, this);
}

public boolean action(Event evt, Object arg) {
    if ("Smaller".equals (arg)) {
        scale *= 0.9;      // Make it 10% smaller.
        repaint ();
        return true;
    }
    if ("Bigger".equals (arg)) {
        scale *= 1.1;      // Make it 10% bigger.
        repaint ();
        return true;
    }
    return false;
}
}
```

2. Create an HTML document that contains the applet. Create a new file called
howto72.html as follows:

```
<html>
<head>
<title>ImageSize</title>
</head>
A simple applet that demonstrates image scaling
<hr size=4>
<applet code="ImageSize.class" width=200 height=200>
</applet>
<hr size=4>
</html>
```

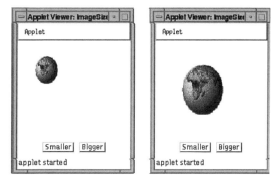

Figure 7-2 Resizing an image

3. Compile and test the applet. Compile ImageSize.java and test it using the Appletviewer. This example requires an image called T1.gif that must reside in the same directory as ImageSize.class. This image file can also be found on the CD-ROM. An image should appear in the upper-left corner as before, along with two buttons marked "Smaller" and "Bigger" at the bottom. Press either of the buttons to change the size of the image. Figure 7-2 shows the applet before and after the image has been resized.

How It Works

A version of *drawImage()* that takes width and height as parameters is used to scale and display the image. The scale factor is initialized to 1.0. When the user presses one of the buttons, scale is either increased or decreased by 10 percent and an update is forced. When the *paint()* method is called, the width and height are both multiplied by scale and supplied as arguments to *drawImage()*.

Comments

Note that *drawImage()* takes only integer types for width and height. Floating-point values must be typecast appropriately, as shown in the example code. Large scale factors can be time-consuming, so use them with care.

7.3 How do I...
Drag an image with the mouse?

Problem

Drag-and-drop is a common operation in graphical user interfaces. Mouse control of image placement can also be used in graphical games. How do I drag an image with the mouse?

Technique

The method *drawImage()* requires the x and y screen coordinates of the upper-left corner of the image. The *mouseDown()* and *mouseDrag()* methods both return the x and y positions of the mouse pointer. These are used to specify the drawing coordinates.

Steps

1. Create the applet source file. Create a new file called ImageMove.java as follows:

```
import java.awt.*;
import java.applet.Applet;

/*
 * The applet class
 */
public class ImageMove extends Applet {

/*
 * The image to be displayed
 */
Image img;

/*
 * The width and height of the image
 */
int width, height;

/*
 * xpos, ypos are the coordinates of the upper left of the image.
 */
int xpos=10, ypos=10;

/*
```

```
 * dx, dy are the deltas from the mouse point to xpos, ypos.
 */
int dx, dy;

/*
 * Called when the applet is loaded
 * Load the image and use media tracker so that
 * the width and height are available immediately.
 */
public void init () {

    MediaTracker tracker = new MediaTracker (this);

    img = getImage (getDocumentBase(), "T1.gif");
    tracker.addImage (img, 0);
    showStatus ("Getting image: T1.gif");
    try {
        tracker.waitForID (0);
    } catch (InterruptedException e) { }
    width = img.getWidth (this);
    height = img.getHeight (this);
}

/*
 * Paint the image in the new location.
 * @param g - destination graphics object
 */
public void paint (Graphics g) {

    g.setColor (Color.white);
    g.fillRect (xpos, ypos, width, height);
    g.drawImage (img, xpos, ypos, this);
}

/*
 * Get the offset from the first click.
 * @param evt - event object
 * @param x, y - x and y position of the mouse
 */
public boolean mouseDown (Event evt, int x, int y) {

    dx = x - xpos;
    dy = y - ypos;
    return true;
}

/*
 * Adjust the new position and repaint the image.
 * @param evt - event object
 * @param x, y - x and y position of the mouse
 */
public boolean mouseDrag (Event evt, int x, int y) {

    if (dx < width && dx >= 0 && dy < height && dy >= 0) {
```

continued on next page

continued from previous page

```
        xpos = x - dx;
        ypos = y - dy;
        repaint ();
    }
    return true;
}
}
```

2. Create an HTML document that contains the applet. Create a new file called howto73.html as follows:

```html
<html>
<head>
<title>ImageMove</title>
</head>
Use the mouse to move the image.
<hr size=4>
<applet code="ImageMove.class" width=200 height=200>
</applet>
<hr size=4>
</html>
```

3. Compile and test the applet. Compile ImageMove.java and use the Appletviewer to run the applet. This example requires an image called T1.gif that must reside in the same directory as the ImageMove.class to run the applet. This image file can be found on the CD-ROM. When the applet is run, an image should appear in the upper left. Use the mouse to move the image around. Figure 7-3 shows the applet after the image has been moved.

Figure 7-3 Moving an image

How It Works

Only one class is defined, the applet itself. The *start()* method loads the image from the server by invoking *Applet.getImage()* with the document base and file name relative to the applet directory as arguments. The *mouseDown()* method is called in response to a mouse down event. In this case, the relative distance from the mouse down point to the image origin is saved so that the image does not jump when it is moved. The *mouseDrag()* method is called in response to mouse drag events. The new position of the image is calculated and an update is forced by invoking *update()*. The *paint()* method simply draws the image at the new position by calling *Graphics.draw Image()*.

COMPLEXITY
ADVANCED

7.4 How do I...
Implement double buffering?

Problem

I want to write an applet that shows several images bouncing off the edge of the applet panel. I know how to load the images and move them. The problem is that the animation flickers and doesn't appear smooth. I want to use an off-screen object to implement double buffering. How do I implement double buffering?

Technique

From the previous examples, animation may appear straightforward. It can be done by using only the methods previously discussed, but may yield unwanted effects, like visible drawing latency and flicker. This becomes unsatisfactory when there are many images moving simultaneously. A good animation should be smooth and flicker free.

The drawing latency and flicker problems are solved by maintaining an off-screen image, drawing into it, and copying it to the screen when necessary. This is commonly referred to as *double buffering*. The screen copy is done very quickly by the Java runtime. This is because rectangular-block transfer routines are highly optimized on all windowing systems. Double buffering delivers crisp performance even at low frame rates.

Uniform update rates are also needed to give the illusion of smooth motion. This can be accomplished by using the thread mechanisms available to Java applets.

In this example, several balls appear to bounce off the sides of a box. The principles demonstrated here can be used as the basis for games or particle simulations.

Steps

1. Create the applet source file. Create a new file called Bounce.java as follows:

```java
import java.awt.*;
import java.applet.Applet;
import java.awt.image.ImageObserver;

/*
 * A class describing a single ball
 */
class Ball {

/*
 * The image for this ball
 */
Image img;

/*
 * x position and velocity
 */
double x, dx;

/*
 * y position and velocity
 */
double y, dy;

/*
 * Initialize the position and velocity
 * to random values.
 */
void random () {

    x = 10 + 380*Math.random ();
    y = 10 + 200*Math.random ();
    dx = 5 - 10*Math.random ();
    dy = 5 - 10*Math.random ();
}

/**
 * Calculate the next position of this ball,
 * and make sure it bounces off the edge of the panel.
 * @param d - dimension of the bounding panel
 */
void compute (Dimension d) {

    if (x <= 0 || x > d.width) dx = -dx;       // Bounce horizontally
    if (y <= 0 || y > d.height) dy = -dy;      // Bounce vertically
    x += dx;
    y += dy;
```

```
}

/**
 * Draw the ball image.
 * @param g - destination graphics object
 * @param obs - parent image observer
 */
public void paint (Graphics g, ImageObserver obs) {
    g.drawImage (img, (int) x-10, (int) y-10, obs);
}
}

/*
 * The panel containing the bouncing balls
 */
class BouncePanel extends Panel implements Runnable {

/*
 * The number of balls
 */
final int nballs = 4;

/*
 * The array holding all the balls
 */
Ball balls[] = new Ball[10];

/*
 * Off-screen image
 */
Image offimg;

/*
 * Size of off-screen image
 */
Dimension offsize;

/*
 * Graphics object associated with off-screen image
 */
Graphics offg;

/*
 * Thread for periodic updating
 */
Thread thread;

/*
 * The thread recalculates each ball position and
 * redraws it.
 */
public void run() {

    offsize = size();
```

continued on next page

continued from previous page

```java
    offimg = createImage (offsize.width, offsize.height);
    offg = offimg.getGraphics();
    while (true) {
        for (int i=0; i<nballs; i+=1) {
            balls[i].compute (offsize);
        }
        repaint ();
        try {
            Thread.sleep (25);
        } catch (InterruptedException e) {
            break;
        }
    }
}

/**
 * Override update to avoid erase flicker.
 * @param g - destination graphics object
 */
public synchronized void update (Graphics g) {

    offg.setColor (Color.lightGray);
    offg.fillRect (0, 0, offsize.width, offsize.height);

    for (int i = 0 ; i < nballs ; i++)
        balls[i].paint (offg, this);
    offg.setColor (Color.black);
    offg.drawRect (0, 0, offsize.width-1, offsize.height-1);
    g.drawImage(offimg, 0, 0, this);
}

/*
 * Start the update thread.
 */
public void start() {

    thread = new Thread(this);
    thread.start();
}

/*
 * Stop the update thread.
 */
public void stop() {

    thread.stop();
}
}

/*
 * The applet proper
 */
public class Bounce extends Applet {

/*
```

```
 * Instance of BouncePanel
 */
BouncePanel panel;

/*
 * An array containing the images for the balls
 */
Image img[] = new Image[4];

/*
 * Called when the applet is loaded
 * Create an instance of bounce panel and add the Start button
 * and load images.
 */
public void init() {

    setLayout(new BorderLayout());

    panel = new BouncePanel ();
    add ("Center", panel);
    Panel p = new Panel ();
    add ("South", p);
    p.add (new Button("Start"));

    img[0] = getImage (getDocumentBase(), "whiteball.gif");
    img[1] = getImage (getDocumentBase(), "redball.gif");
    img[2] = getImage (getDocumentBase(), "blueball.gif");
    img[3] = getImage (getDocumentBase(), "greenball.gif");
    for (int i=0; i<panel.nballs; i+=1) {
        panel.balls[i] = new Ball ();
        panel.balls[i].img = img[i & 3];
    }
}

/*
 * Called when the applet is started
 * Just start the bounce panel update thread.
 */
public void start() {

    panel.start();
}

/*
 * Called when the applet is stopped
 */
public void stop() {

    panel.stop();
}

/*
 * Handle Start button press by randomizing balls.
 * @param evt - event object
```

continued on next page

continued from previous page

```
 * @param arg - target object
 */
public boolean action(Event evt, Object arg) {

    if ("Start".equals(arg)) {
        for (int i=0; i<panel.nballs; i+=1)
            panel.balls[i].random ();
        return true;
    }
    return false;
}
}
```

2. Create an HTML document that contains the applet. Create a new file called howto74.html as follows:

```
<html>
<head>
<title>Bounce</title>
</head>
Bouncing balls example.
<hr size=4>
<applet code="Bounce.class" width=400 height=400>
</applet>
<hr size=4>
</html>
```

3. Compile and test the applet. Compile Bounce.java and use the Appletviewer to run the applet. Click the Start button at the bottom of the screen. You should see four balls bouncing off the sides of the box in random directions and rates. The balls are actually GIF images (whiteball.gif, redball.gif, blueball.gif, and greenball.gif) that need to reside in the same directory as the applet. Figure 7-4 shows an example of the running applet.

How It Works

In the spirit of object-oriented programming, a *Ball* class is defined. It contains all the parameters necessary for describing a ball: position (x, y), velocity (dx, dy), screen representation (img), *compute()* method, *paint()* method, and method to randomize the position and velocity $(random())$.

The *compute()* method increments the x and y positions by dx and dy each time it is called. If the ball's position exceeds the panel bounds, the corresponding velocity is reversed to give the effect of ideal bouncing.

The *paint()* method draws the ball at its current position into the graphics context given by parameter *g*. The ball's *paint()* method does not know where it is drawing, that is, it may or may not be drawing to the screen.

BouncePanel is a thread that does most of the work. Its *run()* method is called when a thread is started. The *run()* method creates an off-screen image by calling

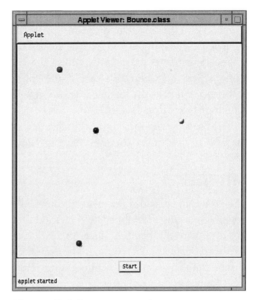

Figure 7-4 Bounce applet

createImage( ) with the screen dimensions as parameters. This off-screen image has a graphics object associated with it, which can be obtained by calling its *getGraphics( )* method. This graphics context is needed to draw into the off-screen image. Drawing into an off-screen graphics object is no different from drawing on screen; all drawing goes into off-screen memory instead of on screen. After the off-screen image has been drawn, it can then be displayed on the screen. Figure 7-5 shows an illustration of a screen image and an off-screen image. The off-screen image is drawn into a buffer without affecting the on-screen image. The off-screen image can then be displayed on the screen. The *run( )* method then loops forever. For each

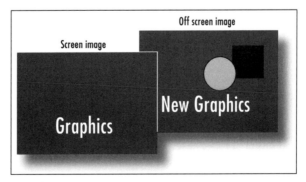

Figure 7-5 Double buffering

iteration, it updates the positions of all the balls by calling their respective *compute()* methods, forces a screen update, and sleeps for 25 milliseconds.

When a screen update occurs, the *update()* method is called. The *update()* method erases the off-screen image by filling it with the background color (lightGray) using *fillRect()*. It then calls each of the ball's *paint()* methods with the off-screen graphics context as the target context. Finally, the off-screen image is drawn on the screen by using *drawImage()*.

The *Bounce* class does all the initialization and loading of images. It also instructs the balls to randomize themselves when the Start button is pressed.

Comments

This example overrides the *update()* method instead of the *paint()* method. This is done because the default *update()* method fills the panel with the background color first and then calls *paint()*. Since we are drawing over the entire panel from the off-screen image, this is not required. The default *update()* also results in unwanted flicker.

The frame rate for this example is not 25 milliseconds as you might guess from the 25 millisecond sleep time. The frame rate depends somewhat on the performance of the client. This is due to time taken in the *compute()* method of the *BouncePanel*. This can be solved, however, by creating another thread whose only function is to provide a strict timing signal, a software interrupt of sorts. The new code might look like this:

```
// Thread to provide a 25 millisecond trigger
class Trigger extends Thread {
    public boolean startFlag= false;

    public void run () {
        while (true) {
            startFlag = true;
            try {
                sleep (25);
            } catch (InterruptedException e) {
                break;
            }
        }
    }
}
```

The *BouncePanel* class would have to be modified to look like this:

```
Trigger trigger = new Trigger ();

public void run() {
    offsize = size();
    offimg = createImage (offsize.width, offsize.height);
    offg = offimg.getGraphics();
    while (true) {
        if (trigger.startFlag) {
            trigger.startFlag= false;
            for (int i=0; i<nballs; i+=1) {
```

```
        balls[i].compute (offsize);
    }
    repaint ();
}
}
}
```

The advantage here is that the applet will run at the same speed on any platform, assuming it meets minimum performance requirements. The latter form is more complicated, but must be used if uniform performance is necessary.

> **NOTE**
>
> A resized image can be stored for later use by creating an off-screen image and drawing a scaled image into it. This new image can be used without the performance degradation caused by resizing.

COMPLEXITY
ADVANCED

7.5 How do I...
Layer graphics?

Problem

I want to write an image manipulation program. I want to have the ability to select an image with the mouse and either bring it to the front, or send it to the back. I learned how to draw images and move them with the mouse in previous examples in this chapter, but now I need to learn how to layer images. How do I layer graphics?

Technique

Images can be drawn on top of each other. The first image drawn appears to be in the back, whereas the last image drawn appears in the front. This gives the illusion of depth.

Steps

1. Create the applet source file. Create a new file called LayerApp.java and enter the following source:

```
import java.awt.*;
import java.applet.Applet;
import java.awt.image.*;

/*
```

continued on next page

continued from previous page

```
 * Class for handling one image
 */
class Picture {

/*
 * Position of the image
 */
int xpos, ypos;

/*
 * Width and height of the image
 */
int width, height;

/*
 * The image itself
 */
Image image;
ImageObserver obs;

/**
 * Constructor saves arguments
 * @param img - the image
 * @param x, y - initial position
 * @param o - imageObserver of parent
 */
public Picture (Image img, int x, int y, ImageObserver o) {

    image = img;
    xpos = x;
    ypos = y;
    obs = o;
    width = image.getWidth (obs);
    height = image.getHeight (obs);
}

/**
 * Determine if the point is inside this image.
 * @param x, y - coordinate of point
 */
boolean inside (int x, int y) {

    if (x < xpos || x > (xpos+width)) return false;
    if (y < ypos || y > (ypos+height)) return false;
    return true;
}

/**
 * Set the current postion of the image.
 * @param x, y - position to set
 */
void setPosition (int x, int y) {
```

```
    xpos = x;
    ypos = y;
}

/**
 * Draw the image.
 * Draw a green border around the image if
 * highlight is True.
 * @param g - destination graphics object
 * @param highlight - draw border
 */
void paint (Graphics g, boolean highlight) {

    if (highlight) {
        g.setColor (Color.green);
        g.fillRect (xpos-5, ypos-5, width+10, height+10);
    }
    g.drawImage (image, xpos, ypos, obs);
}
}

/*
 * The applet
 */
public class LayerApp extends Applet {

/*
 * The number of picture objects
 */
final int NPictures = 4;

/*
 * An array containing the picture objects
 */
Picture pictures[] = new Picture[NPictures];

/*
 * The user-selected picture
 */
int selectedPic = -1;

/*
 * Offsets from mouse to image origin
 */
int dx, dy;

/*
 * Off-screen image for double buffering
 */
Image offimg;

/*
 * Off-screen graphics context associated with
 * off-screen image
```

continued on next page

continued from previous page

```
 */
Graphics offg;

/*
 * Dimension of off-screen image
 */
Dimension offsize;

/*
 * Called when the applet is loaded
 */
public void init() {

    setLayout(new BorderLayout());

    Panel p = new Panel ();
    add ("South", p);
    p.add (new Button("Bring to front"));
    p.add (new Button("Send to back"));

    int i;
    Image img;
    String name;
    MediaTracker tracker = new MediaTracker (this);

    offsize = size();
    offimg = createImage (offsize.width, offsize.height);
    offg = offimg.getGraphics();

    for (i=0; i<NPictures; i+=1) {
            if (i < 2) name = "T"+(i+1)+".jpg";
            else name = "T"+(i+1)+".gif";
        img = getImage (getDocumentBase(), name);
        tracker.addImage (img, i);
        showStatus ("Getting image: "+name);
        try {
            tracker.waitForID (i);
        } catch (InterruptedException e) { }
        pictures[i] = new Picture (img, i*10, i*20, this);
    }
}

/**
 * Reverse the order of update for efficiency.
 * @param g - destination graphics object
 */
public void paint (Graphics g) {

    update (g);
}

/**
```

```
 * Override update to avoid erase flicker.
 * @param g - destination graphics object
 */
public void update (Graphics g) {

    int i;

    offg.setColor (Color.black);
    offg.fillRect (0, 0, offsize.width, offsize.height);
    for (i=0; i<NPictures; i+=1) {
        if (i == selectedPic) pictures[i].paint (offg, true);
        else pictures[i].paint (offg, false);
    }
    g.drawImage(offimg, 0, 0, this);
}

/**
 * Determine which image the user clicked on.
 * @param evt - event object
 * @param x, y - mouse position
 */
public boolean mouseDown (Event evt, int x, int y) {

    int i;

    selectedPic = -1;
    for (i=NPictures-1; i>=0; i-=1) {
        if (pictures[i].inside (x, y)) {
            selectedPic = i;
            dx = x - pictures[i].xpos;
            dy = y - pictures[i].ypos;
            break;
        }
    }
    return true;
}

/**
 * Drag the selected image.
 * @param evt - event object
 * @param x, y - mouse position
 */
public boolean mouseDrag (Event evt, int x, int y) {

    int i;

    if (selectedPic < 0) return true;
    for (i=NPictures-1; i>=0; i-=1) {

        pictures[selectedPic].setPosition (x - dx, y - dy);
        repaint ();
    }
    return true;
}
```

continued on next page

continued from previous page

```
/**
 * Draw the image after the user drops it.
 * @param evt - event object
 * @param x, y - mouse position
 */
public boolean mouseUp (Event evt, int x, int y) {

    repaint ();
    return true;
}

/**
 * Reorder the images depending on which button is pressed.
 * @param evt - event object
 * @param arg - target object
 */
public boolean action(Event evt, Object arg) {

    int i;
    Picture temp;

    if ("Bring to front".equals(arg)) {
        if (selectedPic < 0) return true;
        temp = pictures[selectedPic];
        for (i=selectedPic; i<NPictures-1; i+=1) {
            pictures[i] = pictures[i+1];
        }
        pictures[NPictures-1] = temp;
        selectedPic = NPictures - 1;
        repaint ();
        return true;
    }
    if ("Send to back".equals(arg)) {
        if (selectedPic < 0) return true;
        temp = pictures[selectedPic];
        for (i=selectedPic; i>0; i-=1) {
            pictures[i] = pictures[i-1];
        }
        pictures[0] = temp;
        selectedPic = 0;
        repaint ();
        return true;
    }
    return false;
}
}
```

2. Create an HTML document that contains the applet. Create a new file called howto75.html as follows:

```
<head>
```

```
<title>Layer App</title>
</head>
<applet code="LayerApp.class" width=400 height=400>
</applet>
<hr size=4>
</body>
```

3. Compile and test the applet. Compile the source using javac or the makefile provided. Test the applet using the Appletviewer by entering the following command:

`APPLETVIEWER howto65.html`

When the applet is started, a window will open with four images displayed and two buttons labeled "Bring to front" and "Send to back." Each image can be moved with the mouse. An image can also be sent to back or brought to front. To do so, select the image and then press the desired button. Figure 7-6 shows an example of the output.

How It Works

The program contains two classes: the *Picture* class and the *LayerApp* class.

The *Picture* class contains the information of an image. It contains the position on the screen of the image, its width and height, and the image itself. The *Image* constructor initializes these values and saves them. The *Picture* class contains a method *inside()*. The method *inside()* returns True for a given x,y position if it is inside the rectangle containing the image. The *setPosition()* method sets the origin of the image given the position. The *Picture.paint()* method takes two arguments: the Graphics

Figure 7-6 LayerApp applet

context and a Boolean variable *Highlight*. If *Highlight* is True, a rectangle slightly larger than the image is drawn first, then the image itself is drawn.

The *LayerApp* class is the applet itself. It contains an array of pictures and an *int* variable, *selectedPic*, which holds the index of the selected picture. It also contains an off-screen image and an off-screen graphics context maintained to implement double buffering.

The *init()* method creates a new panel and adds two buttons at the bottom: Bring To Front and Send To Back.

The *start()* method creates the off-screen image and the off-screen graphics context. It then loads the images using the *getImage()* method and initializes the picture array. *MediaTracker* is used to wait for image loading. The *MediaTracker* class is a utility class that traces the status of media objects, like images.

The *update()* method is overridden to avoid unnecessary flickering. The *update()* method erases the off-screen image and draws all the pictures into the off-screen image. The off-screen image is then drawn onto the screen.

The *mouseDown()* method determines which picture was selected by using the *Picture.inside()* method. It iterates from the last image drawn and continues to the first. It saves the selected image index in *selectedPic* and returns immediately. The loop runs from the last image to the first, because the mouse point may be inside two images. The front image is always selected before the rear image.

The *mouseDrag()* method sets the position of the selected image. If no image is selected, it returns immediately. After an image has been moved, an update is forced by calling re*paint()*.

The *mouseUp()* method simply forces an *update()*.

The *action()* method handles button presses. If the Bring To Front button is pressed, the array of pictures is shuffled so that the selected picture is at the end of the array. A similar action is performed if the Send To Back button is pressed. In this case the selected image is moved to the beginning of the array.

COMPLEXITY
ADVANCED

7.6   How do I...
Display part of an image?

Problem

I want to write a program to draw images with transition effects, such as a "barn door open," venetian blind, and checkerboard. This would make advertisements more interesting to the viewer. To do this, I need to draw only parts of an image. How do I draw part of an image?

Technique

The easiest way to draw part of an image is to use clipping. A graphics object can be created with a clipping rectangle specified. This graphics context is created almost identically to the panel's graphics context. The only difference is that all graphics drawn into this context will be clipped. To draw part of an image, the new graphics context must be created with the coordinates and width and height of the section of the image that needs to be drawn.

Steps

1. Create the applet source file. Create a new file called Advertiser.java and enter the following source:

```java
import java.util.*;
import java.awt.*;
import java.applet.Applet;

/*
 * A class that performs the banner animation
 */
class Banner extends Panel implements Runnable {

/*
 * An instance of the applet for
 * invoking methods from advertiser class
 */
Advertiser advertiser;

/*
 * Instance of thread used for animation
 */
Thread thread;

/*
 * The next banner image to be displayed
 */
Image theImage;

/*
 * Width and height of the new banner image
 */
int img_width, img_height;

/*
 * Off-screen image for double buffering
 */
Image offscreen;

/*
 * offg1 is the graphics object associated with
 * off-screen image. offg2 is the clipped version
```

continued on next page

continued from previous page

```
 * of offg1.
 */
Graphics offg1, offg2;

/*
 * xstart, ystart - x and y coordinate of clipping rectangle
 * width, height - width and height of clipping rectangle
 * effect_type - the effect type applied to the next image
 */
int xstart, ystart, width, height, effect_type;

/**
 * Constructor just saves instance of the applet
 * @param advertiser - instance of advertiser applet
 */
Banner (Advertiser advertiser) {

    this.advertiser = advertiser;
}

/*
 * Thread that calls repaint() every 25 ms
 * to effect animation.
 */
public void run() {

    Dimension d = size();
    offscreen = createImage (d.width, d.height);
    offg1 = offscreen.getGraphics ();
    offg1.setFont (getFont ());
    offg1.setColor (Color.gray);
    offg1.fillRect (0, 0, d.width, d.height);
    while (true) {
        repaint ();
        try {
            Thread.sleep (25);
        } catch (InterruptedException e) {
            break;
        }
    }
}

/**
 * Override update() method to avoid erase flicker.
 * This is where the drawing is done.
 * @param g - destination graphics object
 */
public synchronized void update(Graphics g) {

    int i, x, y, w, h;
    switch (effect_type) {
        case 0:
        offg1.drawImage (theImage, 0, 0, null);
```

```
        break;

        case 1:          // Barn-door open
        if (xstart > 0) {
            xstart -= 5;
            width += 10;
            offg2 = offg1.create (xstart, 0, width, height);
            offg2.drawImage (theImage, -xstart, 0, null);
        } else offg1.drawImage (theImage, 0, 0, null);
        break;

        case 2:          // Venetian blind
        if (height < 10) {
            height += 1;
            for (y=0; y<img_height; y+=10) {
                offg2 = offg1.create (0, y, width, height);
                offg2.drawImage (theImage, 0, -y, null);
            }
        } else offg1.drawImage (theImage, 0, 0, null);
        break;

        case 3:          // Checkerboard
        if (width <= 20) {
            if (width <= 10) {
                i = 0;
                for (y=0; y<img_height; y+=10) {
                    for (x=(i&1)*10; x<img_width; x+=20) {
                        offg2 = offg1.create (x, y, width, 10);
                        offg2.drawImage (theImage, -x, -y, null);
                    }
                    i += 1;
                }
            } else {
                i = 1;
                for (y=0; y<img_height; y+=10) {
                    for (x=(i&1)*10; x<img_width; x+=20) {
                        offg2 = offg1.create (x, y, width-10, 10);
                        offg2.drawImage (theImage, -x, -y, null);
                    }
                    i += 1;
                }
            }
            width += 5;
        } else offg1.drawImage (theImage, 0, 0, null);
        break;
    }
    g.drawImage (offscreen, 0, 0, null);
}

/**
 * Initialize variables for clipping rectangle
 * depending on effect type.
 * @param which - the effect type for next image
 * @param img - the next image
```

continued on next page

continued from previous page

```java
 */
public void effect (int which, Image img) {

    img_width = img.getWidth (null);
    img_height = img.getHeight (null);
    theImage = img;
    switch (which) {
        case 0:
        break;

        case 1:          // Barn door
        xstart = img_width >> 1;
        width = 0;
        height = img_height;
        break;

        case 2:
        width = img_width;
        height = 0;
        break;

        case 3:
        width = 0;
        break;
    }
    effect_type = which;
}

/*
 * Start the repaint thread.
 */
public void start() {

    thread = new Thread(this);
    thread.start();
}

/*
 * Stop the repaint thread.
 */
public void stop() {

    thread.stop();
}
}

/*
 * The advertiser class proper
 */
public class Advertiser extends Applet implements Runnable {

/*
 * Instance of Banner
 */
```

```
Banner panel;

/*
 * Instance of thread for cycling effects
 * for each new image
 */
Thread thread;

/*
 * The total number of images
 */
int NBanners;

/*
 * The array of images
 */
Image img[] = new Image[10];

/*
 * The delay (dwell) time in milliseconds for each image
 */
int delay[] = new int[10];

/*
 * The effect type for each image
 */
int effect[] = new int[10];

/*
 * Called when applet is loaded
 * Add the banner panel, load images, and parse applet
 * parameters.
 */
public void init() {

    int i;
    setLayout(new BorderLayout());

    panel = new Banner (this);
    add("Center", panel);
    NBanners = 0;
    MediaTracker tracker = new MediaTracker (this);

    for (i=1; i<=10; i+=1) {
        String param, token;
        int j, next;

        param = getParameter ("T"+i);
        if (param == null) break;

        StringTokenizer st = new StringTokenizer (param, " ,");
```

continued on next page

continued from previous page

```
            token = st.nextToken ();
            img[NBanners] = getImage (getDocumentBase(), token);
            tracker.addImage (img[NBanners], i);
            showStatus ("Getting image: "+token);
            try {
                tracker.waitForID (i);
            } catch (InterruptedException e) { }

            token = st.nextToken ();
            delay[NBanners] = Integer.parseInt (token);

            token = st.nextToken ();
            effect[NBanners] = Integer.parseInt (token);

            NBanners += 1;
        }
    }

    /*
     * Thread which starts the next image transition
     */
    public void run () {

        int current = 0;

        while (true) {
            panel.effect (effect[current], img[current]);
            try {
                Thread.sleep (delay[current]);
            } catch (InterruptedException e) { }
            current += 1;
            current %= NBanners;
        }
    }

    /*
     * Called when applet is started
     * Starts both threads
     */
    public void start() {

        panel.start();
        thread = new Thread(this);
        thread.start();
    }

    /*
     * Called when applet is stopped
     * Stops all threads
     */
    public void stop() {

        panel.stop();
        thread.stop();
```

2. Create an HTML document that contains the applet. Create a new file called howto76.html as follows:

```
<head>
<title>Java Advertiser</title>
</head>
<applet code="Advertiser.class" width=262 height=50>
<param name=T1 value="T1.gif,1000,0">
<param name=T2 value="T2.gif,3000,1">
<param name=T3 value="T3.gif,3000,2">
<param name=T4 value="T4.gif,3000,3">
</applet>
<hr size=4>
</body>
```

3. Compile and test the applet. Compile the source using javac or the makefile provided. The applet requires four images to reside in the same directory as the applet class files. Test the applet using the Appletviewer by entering the following command:

```
APPLETVIEWER howto76.html
```

The applet will open and one image at a time is displayed for 1,000 milliseconds. The transition from one image to the next can be one of four possibilities. Figure 7-7 shows an example of the output.

How It Works

The Advertiser applet contains two classes, both of which run as independent threads. The first class is *Banner*. *Banner* does the actual drawing of the images. Its *run()* method creates an off-screen image and a graphic context of offg1. It continuously repaints the screen every 25 milliseconds.

A method known as *clipping* is used to display only part of an image. Clipping is simply displaying a certain area of an image. In Figure 7-8, the large gray rectangle can be thought of as an image. The smaller white rectangle can represent any portion of that image. For example, if you only wanted to display the white rectangle, clipping would be used to display only that area.

Figure 7-7 Advertiser applet

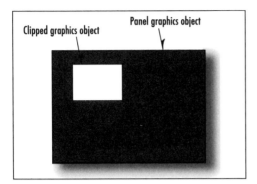

Figure 7-8 Clipping of an image

The *update()* method draws the current image in various ways depending on the effect_type. If no effect is selected, the current image is drawn into the off-screen graphics context. If "barn door open" is selected, a new graphics context is created, Offg2. This new graphics context is created with a clipping rectangle specified. The clipping rectangle starts in the middle of the image and grows outward with each call.

If the venetian blind effect is selected, off-screen graphics contexts are created repeatedly with different positions and sizes. The positions are fixed but the sizes grow. This is done in such a way that a venetian blind effect is produced. The checkerboard effect is created in a similar way. In this case a clipping rectangle is created for each square of the checkerboard. After each iteration of an effect, the off-screen image is drawn on the screen.

The *effect()* method initializes the effect_type and the image. Also, the variables *xstart* and *width* are initialized depending on the effect_type. The *start()* method creates a thread from the *Banner* and starts it. The *stop()* method stops the thread.

The Advertiser applet also runs as a thread. The *Init()* method creates a new panel for the *Banner* and adds it to the center. Next it loads the images into an array, along with information about the transition effect for this image and the time duration. This information is extracted from applet parameters. The applet expects the parameter names to be T1, T2,...T10. The value of each parameter contains the name of the image file, the time duration in milliseconds, and the effect_type as an integer between 0 and 3. More effects such as a "barn door close" can be easily added.

The *run()* method continuously invokes the *effect()* method with the effect_type and the current image. It then sleeps for a time determined by the delay array. The *Run()* method cycles through all images forever.

The *start()* method starts the panel and applet's threads. The *stop()* method stops the panel and applet's threads.

Comments

Clipping is a convenient way of drawing parts of an image. In fact this method can be used to extract individual pixels of an image. This can be very inefficient. There are better ways of extracting pixels of an image, and they will be discussed in How-Tos 7.7 and 7.8.

Clipping could also be used to simulate animation, such as the effect of a ball rolling. The traditional method of animating a ball would involve creating several images of a ball that is rolling but not moving. All the images would be loaded into the applet and displayed one at a time. Each image would have to be moved slightly to simulate the motion of the rolling ball. An alternative solution would be to create a larger image that contains images of the ball as it rotates and translates. This larger image could be loaded, and only one instance of the ball displayed at a time. The second method is more efficient, because it only requires a single file to be loaded into the applet. This saves time opening and closing additional files. It also turns out that the single file will be smaller than the sum of all the smaller files. This technique will be demonstrated in How-To 8.5.

COMPLEXITY
ADVANCED

7.7 How do I...
Create images from pixel values?

Problem

I want to write a program to calculate the Mandelbrot set and display it. I know how to calculate the set and create a two-dimensional array of values. To display the set, I need to create an image from these values. How do I create an image from the pixel values?

Technique

Images can be created from pixel values by use of the *createImage()* method in conjunction with *MemoryImageSource*. The pixels are supplied to *MemoryImageSource* as a single-dimensional array of integers. The pixel values contain the red, green, and blue components of the pixel. The dimensions of the image are also given to *MemoryImageSource*. The number of elements in the pixel array is the width times the height of the image to be created.

Steps

1. Create the applet source file. Create a new file called Mandelbrot.java and enter the following source:

```
import java.applet.Applet;
import java.awt.*;
```

continued on next page

continued from previous page

```java
import java.awt.image.*;

/*
 * A class for generating and displaying the
 * Mandelbrot set
 */
public class Mandelbrot extends Panel {

/*
 * The maximum number of colors for
 * each pixel
 */
final int MaxColors = 256;

/*
 * The width and height of the image
 */
int mWidth, mHeight;

/*
 * The array of pixel values
 */
int pixels[];

/*
 * The set values
 */
int mandelSet[];

/*
 * The image produced by the set
 */
Image theImage = null;

/*
 * The mapping function from set values to pixel values
 */
int pixMap[] = new int[MaxColors];

/*
 * A flag used for recalculating
 */
boolean startCalculate = false;

/*
 * Instance of MandelRect class
 */
MandelRect mandelRect;

/*
 * The control buttons
 */
Button startButton;
```

```
Button zoomButton;

/*
 * Called when the applet is loaded
 * Initialize the pixmap array and add user interface
 */
public void init () {

    mWidth = 100;
    mHeight = 100;
    pixels = new int [mWidth * mHeight];
    mandelSet = new int [mWidth * mHeight];

    mandelRect = new MandelRect (mWidth, mHeight);

    int red, green, blue;
    int i;

    pixMap[0] = 0xffffffff;
    for (i=1; i<MaxColors-1; i+=1) {
        red = i;
        green = (i<128) ? i << 1 : 255-(i<<1);
        blue = MaxColors-i;
        pixMap[i] = (255 << 24) | (red << 16) | (green << 8) | blue;
    }
    pixMap[MaxColors-1] = 0xff000000;

    setLayout(new BorderLayout());

    startButton = new Button ("Start over");
    zoomButton = new Button ("Zoom in");

    Panel p = new Panel ();
    p.setLayout (new FlowLayout ());
    p.add (startButton);
    p.add (zoomButton);
    add ("South", p);
}

/*
 * Called when the applet is started
 * Forces a recalculation of the set
 */
public void start () {

    startCalculate = true;
    repaint ();
}

/*
 * Call update for efficiency.
 * @param g - destination graphics object
 */
```

continued on next page

continued from previous page

```
public void paint (Graphics g) {

    update (g);
}

/**
 * Override default update() method to avoid erase flicker.
 * @param g - destination graphics object
 */
public void update (Graphics g) {

    if (startCalculate) {
        calculate ();
        startCalculate = false;
    }
    if (theImage != null) g.drawImage (theImage, 0, 0, this);
    else repaint (1000);
    mandelRect.paint (g);
}

/*
 * Perform the actual set calculation.
 */
void calculate () {

    int i, index;
    double width, height;
    double row, col;
    double zr, zi, cr, ci, tzr, tzi;
    double hFactor, vFactor;
    double x, y;

    theImage = null;

    x = mandelRect.mandelX;
    y = mandelRect.mandelY;
    width = (double) mandelRect.imgWidth;
    height = (double) mandelRect.imgHeight;
    hFactor = mandelRect.mandelWidth/width;
    vFactor = mandelRect.mandelHeight/height;

    index = 0;
    for (row=0; row<height; row+=1) {
        for (col=0; col<width; col+=1) {
            zr = 0;
            zi = 0;
            cr = x + col * hFactor;
            ci = y + row * vFactor;
            for (i=1; i<64; i+=1) {
                tzr = zr*zr - zi*zi + cr;
                tzi = 2*zr*zi + ci;
                zr = tzr;
                zi = tzi;
                if (zr*zr + zi*zi > 4.0) break;
```

```
            }
            mandelSet[index++] = (i << 2)-1;
        }
    }

    for (i=0; i<mWidth*mHeight; i+=1) {
        pixels[i] = pixMap[mandelSet[i]];
    }

    theImage = createImage (
        new MemoryImageSource(mWidth, mHeight, pixels, 0, mWidth));
}

/**
 * Save the start position of the zoom rectangle.
 * @param evt - event object
 * @param x, y - position of the mouse
 */
public boolean mouseDown (Event evt, int x, int y) {

    mandelRect.setXY (x, y);
    return true;
}

/**
 * Draw the zoom rectangle.
 * @param evt - event object
 * @param x, y - position of the mouse
 */
public boolean mouseDrag (Event evt, int x, int y) {

    mandelRect.setWidthHeight (x, y);
    mandelRect.setPaintRect (true);
    repaint ();
    return true;
}

/**
 * Draw the zoom rectangle.
 * @param evt - event object
 * @param x, y - position of the mouse
 */
public boolean mouseUp (Event evt, int x, int y) {

    mandelRect.setWidthHeight (x, y);
    mandelRect.setPaintRect (true);
    repaint ();
    return true;
}

/**
 * Handle button presses.
 * @param evt - event object
```

continued on next page

continued from previous page

```
 * @param arg - target object
 */
public boolean action(Event evt, Object arg) {

    if (evt.target == startButton) {
        mandelRect = new MandelRect (mWidth, mHeight);
        startCalculate = true;
        repaint ();
        return true;
    }
    if (evt.target == zoomButton) {
        startCalculate = true;
        mandelRect.setPaintRect (false);
        mandelRect.scaleSet ();
        repaint ();
        return true;
    }
    return false;
}

/**
 * Application entry point
 * Create window and new set.
 * @param args - command line arguments
 */
public static void main (String args[]) {

    Frame f = new Frame ("Mandelbrot set");
    Mandelbrot mandel = new Mandelbrot ();

    mandel.init ();
    f.resize (210, 275);
    f.add ("Center", mandel);
    f.show ();
    mandel.start ();
}
}
```

2. Create the applet source file. Create a new file called MandelRect.java and enter the following source:

```
import java.awt.*;

/*
 * A helper class to manage the zoom rectangle
 */
public class MandelRect {

/*
 * The coordinates of the zoom rectangle
 * in screen space
 */
int x;
int y;
```

```
int width;
int height;

/*
 * The final image width and height
 */
int imgWidth;
int imgHeight;

/*
 * The coordinates of the zoom rectangle
 * in set space
 */
double mandelX;
double mandelY;
double mandelWidth;
double mandelHeight;

/*
 * Set to True if the zoom rectangle should be painted.
 */
boolean paintRect;

/**
 * Constructor initializes variables.
 * @param iW - final image width
 * @param iH - final image height
 */
public MandelRect (int iW, int iH) {

    imgWidth = iW;
    imgHeight = iH;
    paintRect = false;

    mandelX = -1.75;
    mandelY = -1.125;
    mandelWidth = 2.25;
    mandelHeight = 2.25;
}

/**
 * Set the top left of the zoom rectangle in screen space.
 * @param ix, iy - top left corner of zoom rectangle
 */
void setXY (int ix, int iy) {

    x = ix;
    y = iy;
}

/**
 * Set the width, height of the zoom rectangle in screen space
 * @param ix, iy - bottom right corner of zoom rectangle
 */
```

continued on next page

continued from previous page

```java
void setWidthHeight (int ix, int iy) {

    width = ix - x;
    height = iy - y;
}

/*
 * Translate screen coordinates to set coordinates.
 */
void scaleSet () {

    int tx, ty, tw, th;

    tx = x;
    ty = y;
    tw = width;
    th = height;
    if (tw < 0) {
        tw = -width;
        tx = x-tw;
    }
    if (th < 0) {
        th = -height;
        ty = y-th;
    }
    mandelX = mandelX + (mandelWidth) * ((double) tx)/((double) imgWidth);
    mandelY = mandelY + (mandelHeight) * ((double) ty)/((double)
    ➥imgHeight);
    mandelWidth = mandelWidth * ((double) tw)/((double) imgWidth);
    mandelHeight = mandelHeight * ((double) th)/((double) imgHeight);
}

/**
 * Set the paintRect flag.
 * @param p - True means zoom rectangle should be painted
 */
void setPaintRect (boolean p) {

    paintRect = p;
}

/**
 * Paint the zoom rectangle if necessary.
 * @param g - destination graphics object
 */
void paint (Graphics g) {

    if (paintRect == false) return;

    int tx, ty, tw, th;

    tx = x;
```

```
        ty = y;
        tw = width;
        th = height;
        if (tw < 0) {
            tw = -width;
            tx = x-tw;
        }
        if (th < 0) {
            th = -height;
            ty = y-th;
        }
        g.setColor (Color.white);
        g.drawRect (tx, ty, tw, th);
    }
}
```

3. Create an HTML document that contains the applet. Create a new file called howto77.html as follows:

```html
<html>
<head>
<title>Mandelbrot Set</title>
</head>
<applet code="Mandelbrot.class" width=200 height=200>
</applet>
<hr size=4>

</html>
```

4. Compile and test the applet. Compile the source using javac or the makefile provided. Test the applet using the Appletviewer by entering the following command:

```
APPLETVIEWER howto77.html
```

Figure 7-9 shows an example of the output.

Figure 7-9
Mandelbrot applet

How It Works

The Mandelbrot applet contains only the *Mandelbrot* class itself. The *init()* method creates an array of pixels specified by the width and height. The top, left, bottom, and right are the coordinates in the space of the Mandelbrot set. A pixmap array is created to map values in the set to pixel values. The mapping of set values to pixel values is a subject for study in itself. For purposes of simplicity, an arbitrary algorithm was chosen for assigning pixel values. A button is added at the bottom of the panel which is used to reset the set coordinates to their original values.

The *start()* method calculates a new set by invoking the *calculate()* method. It then draws the set by forcing an update. The *update()* method draws the image if it exists. If the image does not exist, for example, the calculation is not complete, the image is not drawn, and a *repaint()* is forced one second later.

The *calculate()* method performs the set calculation based on standard algorithms. Before the calculation is started, the image is set to null. This will keep the previous image from being displayed. The inner loop of the iteration is only performed for the number of colors available in the pixmap. This does not yield a very interesting image, but it is straightforward. After the pixel array is created, the image is created by calling create image with *MemoryImageSource()* as an argument. *MemoryImageSource()* takes the width and height of the image along with the pixel array starting point and format as arguments.

The *mouseDown()* event calculates the top and left coordinates of the new set based on the mouse position. The *mouseUp()* method calculates the right and the bottom coordinates of the set. Next it calculates the new set based on the new set coordinates. It then repaints the image.

The *action()* method handles button presses. If the user presses the Start Over button, the set coordinates are reset to the original values, and set is recalculated and displayed. A *main()* method is also included that creates a frame and an instance of the applet in the event that the program is executed as a stand-alone application.

Comments

This example is an excellent demonstration of performance. Clearly, Java does not perform as well as an equivalent compiled C or C++ program. The performance is not a limitation of the Java language or the AWT; it is due to the implementation of the Java interpreter. This will most likely be addressed by Just In Time compilers (JIT).

Note that memoryimagesource is contained in Java.awt.image; therefore Java.awt.image.* is imported.

7.8 How do I...
Access pixels in an image?

Problem

I want to write an applet that simulates Conway's classic game of life. I have the algo-rithm for advancing the generations and plotting the cells. I want to enter the starting conditions as a GIF image. I know how to load images, but I need to extract the pix-els in the image. How do I access pixels in an image?

Technique

Pixels can be extracted from an Image via the *PixelGrabber* class. *PixelGrabber* delivers some or all of the pixels in an image given the image; the rectangle containing the pixels to deliver; an integer array to hold the pixel values, offset into the array; and the distance from one row of pixels to the next in the array.

Each pixel in the integer array is described by a 24-bit RGB value. The pixels are delivered by the *PixelGrabber.grabPixels( )* method. This method throws InterruptedException, which must be caught.

Steps

1. Create the source file. Create a file called LifeApp.java and enter the follow-ing source:

```
import java.util.*;
import java.awt.*;
import java.awt.image.ImageObserver;
import java.awt.image.PixelGrabber;

/*
 * Class that manages a generation
 */
class LifeGenerator {

/*
 * Array containing packed cells
 * n - number of elements in the CellList array
 */
int CellList[], n;
int a[];
int b[];
```

continued on next page

continued from previous page

```java
int c[];

/*
 * The current generation number
 */
int generations;

/*
 * Background and foreground colors
 */
Color background;
Color foreground;

int statusheight;
int displaywidth;
int displayheight;

int originx;
int originy;

int maxcells;

static int countmsk=0x1f;
static int posmsk=0x7fffffe0;
static int maxval=0x7fffffff;

String statusLine;
String loading;

int scroll;

/*
 * The rules of life
 */
static boolean rules[]={
    false, false,
    false, false,
    false, true,
    true,  true,
    false, false,
    false, false,
    false, false,
    false, false,
    false, false
};

/*
 * Constructor initializes variables.
 */
public LifeGenerator() {

    n=0;
    generations=0;
    maxcells=0;
```

```
        background=Color.white;
        foreground=Color.black;

        originx=0;
        originy=0;

        loading=null;
        scroll=10;

        statusLine=new String("");
}

public void loading(String init_loading) {

        loading=init_loading;
}

public void setScroll(int init_scroll) {

        scroll=init_scroll;
}

public void setColors(Color init_background, Color init_foreground) {

        background=init_background;
        foreground=init_foreground;
}

public void setDisplaySize(int width, int height) {

        statusheight=35;

        displaywidth=width;
        displayheight=height-statusheight;
}

/**
 * Translate the origin.
 * @param dx, dy - offsets to translate
 */
public void translate(int dx, int dy) {

        originx+=dx;
        originy+=dy;
}

public void recenter(int x, int y) {

        translate(displaywidth/2-x, displayheight/2-y);
}

public void approachcenter(int x, int y) {

        translate((displaywidth/2-x)/scroll,
```

continued on next page

continued from previous page

```
            (displayheight/2-y)/scroll);
}

public void findPattern() {

    if (n>0) {
        int packed=CellList[n/2];
        int plotx=(((packed>>5)&0x1fff)-(1<<12))*2+originx;
        int ploty=((packed>>18)-(1<<12))*2+originy;
        recenter(plotx, ploty);
    }
}

/**
 * Print status message.
 * @param g - destination graphics object
 */
public void updateStatusLine(Graphics g) {

    g.setColor(background);
    g.drawString(statusLine,0,displayheight+15);

    if (loading!=null) {
        statusLine="Loading: " + loading;
    } else {
        statusLine="Generations: " + generations + "  Cells: " + n;
    }
    g.setColor(foreground);
    g.drawString(statusLine,0,displayheight+15);
}

void resizeIfNeeded(int cellcount) {

    int tmp[];
    int i;

    if (cellcount>maxcells) {

        int newsize=2*cellcount;

        tmp=new int[newsize];
        for (i=0; i<maxcells; i++) tmp[i]=CellList[i];
        CellList=tmp;

        tmp=new int[newsize];
        for (i=0; i<maxcells; i++) tmp[i]=a[i];
        a=tmp;

        tmp=new int[newsize];
        for (i=0; i<maxcells; i++) tmp[i]=b[i];
        b=tmp;

        tmp=new int[newsize];
```

```
            for (i=0; i<maxcells; i++) tmp[i]=c[i];
            c=tmp;

            maxcells=newsize;
        }
    }

    static int combineLists(int a[], int na, int b[], int nb, int c[]) {

        int i,j,nc;
        i=0; j=0; nc=0;
        a[na]=maxval;
        b[nb]=maxval;
        while (i<na || j<nb) {
            if ((a[i]^b[j])<=countmsk) {
                c[nc++]=(a[i++]&countmsk)+b[j++];
            } else if (a[i]<b[j]) {
                c[nc++]=a[i++];
            } else {
                c[nc++]=b[j++];
            }
        }
        return nc;
    }

    static void extractCenterCells(int list[], int n, int counts[]) {

        int i=0, j=0;

        while (i<n) {
            if ((list[i]^counts[j])<=countmsk) {
                counts[j]--;
                i++;
                j++;
            } else j++;
        }
    }

    static int Cell(int x, int y, int value) {

        return ((y+(1<<12))<<18) +((x+(1<<12))<<5) + value;
    }

    /**
     * Plot an individual cell.
     * @param packed - a set of packed cells
     * @param g - destination graphics object
     */
    void plotCell(int packed, Graphics g) {

        int plotx=(((packed>>5)&0x1fff)-(1<<12))*2+originx;
        int ploty=((packed>>18)-(1<<12))*2+originy;

        if (plotx > 3 && plotx < displaywidth-5 &&
```

continued on next page

continued from previous page

```
            ploty > 3 && ploty < displayheight-5 ) {
            g.fillRect(plotx, ploty, 2, 2);
        }
}

/**
 * Paint the current generation.
 * @Param g - destination graphics object
 */
public void paintAll(Graphics g) {

    g.clearRect(0,0,displaywidth, displayheight+statusheight);
    g.drawRect(0,0,displaywidth-1, displayheight-1);

    g.setColor(foreground);
    for (int i=0; i<n; i++) {
        plotCell(CellList[i],g);
    }
    updateStatusLine(g);
}

int nextGen(int counts[], int ncounts, int list[], Graphics g) {

    int nlist=0;
    for (int i=0; i<ncounts; i++) {
        int count=counts[i]&countmsk;
        if (rules[count]) {
            list[nlist++]=(counts[i]&posmsk)+2;
            if ((count&1)==0) {
                g.setColor(foreground);
                plotCell(counts[i],g);
            }
        } else {
            if ((count&1)==1) {
                g.setColor(background);
                plotCell(counts[i],g);
            }
        }
    }
    return nlist;
}

public void generate(Graphics g) {

    int na, nb, nc;

    for (na=0; na<n; na++) a[na]=CellList[na]-(1<<18);
    resizeIfNeeded(n+na);
    nb=combineLists(CellList,n,a,na,b);

    for (na=0; na<n; na++) a[na]=CellList[na]+(1<<18);
    resizeIfNeeded(na+nb);
```

```
        nc=combineLists(a,na,b,nb,c);

        for (na=0; na<nc; na++) a[na]=c[na]-(1<<5);
        resizeIfNeeded(na+nc);
        nb=combineLists(a,na,c,nc,b);

        for (na=0; na<nc; na++) a[na]=c[na]+(1<<5);
        resizeIfNeeded(na+nb);
        nc=combineLists(a,na,b,nb,c);

        extractCenterCells(CellList, n, c);

        n=nextGen(c, nc, CellList, g);

        generations++;
    }

    /**
     * Load a new initial image.
     * @param img - the image to load
     * @param imgobs - the image observer
     */
    public boolean loadLifePattern(Image img, ImageObserver imgobs) {

        int w=img.getWidth(imgobs);
        int h=img.getHeight(imgobs);

        if (w<0 || h<0) return false;

        originx= (displaywidth-w*2)/2;
        originy= (displayheight-h*2)/2;

        int[] pixels = new int[w * h];

        PixelGrabber pg = new PixelGrabber(img, 0, 0, w, h, pixels, 0, w);

        try {
            pg.grabPixels();
        } catch (InterruptedException e) {
            return false;
        }

        int i,j;

        int pix0= pixels[0];
        int pix1= -1;
        int count1= 0;

        for (i=0; i<h; i++) {
            for (j=0; j<w; j++) {
                if (pixels[i*w+j]!=pix0) {
                    pix1= pixels[i*w+j];
                    count1++;
                }
```

continued on next page

continued from previous page

```
            }
        }

    /* Figure out which pixel color denotes a live cell. */

    if (pix0==0xffffff) {}
    else if (pix1==0xffffff || count1 > w*h-count1) {
        pix1=pix0;
        count1=w*h-count1;
    }

    resizeIfNeeded(count1);

    n=0;
    for (i=0; i<h; i++) {
        for (j=0; j<w; j++) {
            if (pixels[i*w+j]==pix1) {
                CellList[n++]=Cell(j,i,2);
            }
        }
    }

    return true;
}
}

/*
 * The applet class
 */
public class LifeApp extends java.applet.Applet implements Runnable {

LifeGenerator LifeList;

/*
 * The thread controlling generations
 */
Thread killme=null;
int speed=50;
boolean neverPainted=true;
int count=0;

/*
 * The image name text field
 */
TextField patfield;
Button pausebutton;
boolean generating=false;
int stepsleft=0;
int scrollfraction=5;

/*
```

```
 * Called when applet is loaded
 * Create user interface and parse applet parameters.
 */
public void init() {

    setLayout(new FlowLayout(FlowLayout.RIGHT, 0, size().height-30));
    add(pausebutton=new Button("Start"));
    add(new Button("Step"));
    add(new Button("Recenter"));
    add(new Button("Load:"));

    String patname=getParameter("pattern");
    if (patname==null) patname="gun30";

    if (getParameter("started")!=null) {
        pausebutton.setLabel("Stop");
        generating=true;
    }

    String pstring;

    if ((pstring=getParameter("speed"))!=null) {
        speed=Integer.valueOf(pstring).intValue();
    }

    if ((pstring=getParameter("scrollfraction"))!=null) {
        scrollfraction=Integer.valueOf(pstring).intValue();
    }

    add(patfield=new TextField(patname,8));

    LifeList=null;
}

/*
 * Called when applet is started
 * Start the life thread.
 */
public void start() {

    if (killme==null) {
        killme=new Thread(this);
        killme.start();
    }
}

/*
 * Called when the applet is stopped
 * Stop the life thread.
 */
public void stop() {

    killme=null;
```

continued on next page

continued from previous page

```
}

public boolean mouseDown(Event ev, int x, int y) {

    LifeList.approachcenter(x,y);
    LifeList.paintAll(getGraphics());

    return true;
}

public boolean action(Event ev, Object arg) {

    boolean acted=true;
    boolean damage=true;

    if (ev.target instanceof Button) {
        String label=(String)arg;
        if (label.equals("Stop")) {
            pausebutton.setLabel("Start");
            generating=false;
        } else if (label.equals("Start")) {
            pausebutton.setLabel("Stop");
            generating=true;
        } else if (label.equals("Step")) {
            stepsleft=1;
            if (generating) {
                pausebutton.setLabel("Start");
                generating=false;
            }
            damage=false;
        } else if (label.equals("Recenter")) {
            LifeList.findPattern();
        } else if (label.equals("Load:")) {
            stop();
            LifeList=null;
            start();
        } else acted=false;
    } else acted=false;

    if (acted && damage) LifeList.paintAll(getGraphics());

    return acted;
}

/**
 * Add .gif to the file name.
 * @param patname - base file name
 */
static String makeGifName(String patname) {

    int i=patname.indexOf(".");
    String base=(i<0)?patname:patname.substring(0,i);
    return base.concat(".gif");
```

```
}

/**
 * Load new image file.
 * @parame patname - name of image file
 */
void loadNew(String patname) {

    Image img=getImage(getCodeBase(), makeGifName(patname));
    LifeList.loading(patname);
    LifeList.paintAll(getGraphics());

    while(killme!=null && !LifeList.loadLifePattern(img, this)) {
        try {
            Thread.sleep(200);
        } catch (InterruptedException e) {}
    }

    LifeList.loading(null);
    LifeList.paintAll(getGraphics());
}

/*
 * Life thread
 * Causes new generations to be created
 */
public void run() {

    Graphics g=getGraphics();

    if (LifeList==null) {
        LifeList = new LifeGenerator();
        LifeList.setColors(getBackground(), Color.black);
        LifeList.setScroll(scrollfraction);
        LifeList.setDisplaySize(size().width, size().height);
        loadNew(patfield.getText());
    }

    while (killme != null) {
        try {
            Thread.sleep(speed);
        } catch (InterruptedException e) {}
        repaint();
    }
    killme=null;
}

/**
 * Paint the current generation.
 * @param g - destination graphics object
 */
public void paint(Graphics g) {

    LifeList.paintAll(g);
```

continued on next page

continued from previous page

```
}

/**
 * Override update to avoid erase flicker.
 * @param g - destination graphics object
 */
public void update(Graphics g) {

    if (generating || stepsleft-- > 0) {
        LifeList.generate(g);
        LifeList.updateStatusLine(g);
    }
}
}
```

2. Create an HTML file containing the applet. Create a file called
howto78.html and enter the following text:

```
<html>
<head>
<title>Life</title>
</head>
<applet code="LifeApp.class" width=500 height=300>
<param name=pattern value=acorn>
</applet>
<hr size=4>

</html>
```

3. Compile and test the applet. Compile the applet and test it using the
Appletviewer. Several test images are provided on the CD-ROM. Figure 7-
10 shows an example of the running applet.

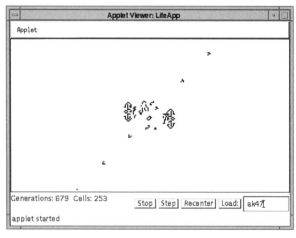

Figure 7-10 LifeApp applet

How It Works

LifeApp contains two classes: *LifeGenerator* and *LifeApp*. *LifeGenerator* implements Conway's life algorithm, extracts the image pixels, advances generations, and draws the new generations. *LifeApp* is the applet itself. *LifeApp* manages *LifeGenerator* by loading a starting image, causes *LifeGenerator* to advance one generation, and handles user events.

The cells are contained by an integer array CellList in the *LifeGenerator* class. The cells are represented by packed bits for efficiency. Generations are advanced by calling the *generate()* method, which plots new cells using rules specified by Conway. The method *loadLifePattern()* takes an image and extracts the pixel by using PixelGrabber. All the pixels are extracted into the array pixels.

The *LifeApp()* method is the applet itself. It implements Runnable in order to create a separate thread for invoking generations. The *init()* method creates the buttons and text fields for the user interface and adds them to the applet panel. The *start()* and *stop()* methods start and stop the thread, respectively. The *action* method handles user events.

The *loadNew()* method loads a new GIF image by calling the *Applet.getImage()* method. It then loads the image into *LifeGenerator*.

The *run()* method first creates an instance of *LifeGenerator* and enters an infinite loop that forces *LifeGenerator* to advance and display new generations.

CHAPTER 8
MULTIMEDIA

MULTIMEDIA

How do I...

In Chapter 3 and 7, the techniques needed to draw graphical elements were presented. This chapter concentrates on bringing your programs alive with sound. Java supports the ability to load sounds from the server so that they may be presented on the client in a manner that allows far greater control than is available with HTML alone. Sound is a very important aspect when developing high impact applications.

In this chapter audio playing and coordination with animation will be addressed. How to use image cliping to perform animation will also be demonstrated.

8.1 Play Sounds

This example demonstrates how to play sounds in Java. Sounds are important when trying to grab attention or to have fun with a game. This example creates a phone dialer application. A button pad similar to the telephone keypad is created. Whenever a button is pressed, the corresponding touch tone is played.

8.2 Play Sounds in a Loop

Playing sounds in a loop is useful when implementing music to be played in the background. When a sound is played in a loop, a very small file can be played for an arbitrary length of time. This example shows an animation sequence of four balls bouncing around the screen while music is played in the background.

8.3   Play Several Sounds Simultaneously

Audio support in Java uses native sound drivers. On most platforms, several audio clips can be played simultaneously. In this example, a drumbeat plays in the background. Several electric guitar chords can be played over the drums.

8.4   Coordinate Animation and Sound

Coordinating animation and sound is a necessity for games. This example will create an invader game where the user controls the gunship that shoots the invaders. Sound is coordinated when the game starts, when an invader is destroyed, and when the player is shot by an invader.

8.5   Use Clipping to Perform Animation

This How-To demonstrates an alternative method for performing simple animation that is much quicker than loading many images. A single image that contains several small images is used to animate a ball rolling.

COMPLEXITY
ADVANCED

8.1   How do I...
Play sounds?

Problem

I want to write a program to play the telephone touch tones. I want to create a keypad with the telephone buttons on it. When a button is pressed, I want the appropriate tone to be played on the computer speaker. I know how to create buttons and handle button events, but I don't know how to play sounds. How do I play sounds?

Technique

Sound clips are contained in a class called *AudioClip*. An AudioClip is loaded by invoking the *getAudioClip()* method with the name of the sound file as an argument. The AudioClip is played by invoking its *play()* method.

Steps

1. Create the applet source file. Create a new file called Dialer.java and enter the following source:

```
import java.awt.*;
import java.applet.*;

/*
 * The dialer applet
 */
```

```
public class Dialer extends Applet {

/*
 * Array of sound clips for each tone
 * 0 = 0, 9 = 9, 11 = *, 12 = #
 *
 */
AudioClip touchTones[] = new AudioClip[12];

/*
 * Called when the applet is loaded
 * Load audio clips and add the keypad panel.
 */
public void init () {

    int i;
    String name;
    Keypad   keypad;

    for (i=0; i<10; i+=1) {
        name = "touchtone."+i+".au";
        showStatus ("Getting "+name);
        touchTones[i] = getAudioClip (getCodeBase(), name);
    }
    name = "touchtone.star.au";
    showStatus ("Getting "+name);
    touchTones[10] = getAudioClip (getCodeBase(), name);

    name = "touchtone.pound.au";
    showStatus ("Getting "+name);
    touchTones[11] = getAudioClip (getCodeBase(), name);

    setLayout(new BorderLayout());

    add ("Center", keypad = new Keypad (touchTones));
}
}

/*
 * The keypad is a separate panel for no important reason.
 */
class Keypad extends Panel {

/*
 * Keep the array of tones around.
 */
AudioClip touchTones[];

/*
 * Constructor creates user interface.
 * @param tones - array of audio tones
 */
Keypad (AudioClip tones[]) {
```

continued on next page

continued from previous page

```
    touchTones = tones;
    Button   b;
    Font     font = new Font ("Times", Font.BOLD, 14);
    Color    functionColor = new Color (255, 0, 0);
    Color    miscColor = new Color (0, 0, 255);
    setFont (font);

    add ("South", b = new NumberButton ("1", touchTones[1]));
    add ("South", b = new NumberButton ("2", touchTones[2]));
    add ("South", b = new NumberButton ("3", touchTones[3]));

    add ("South", b = new NumberButton ("4", touchTones[4]));
    add ("South", b = new NumberButton ("5", touchTones[5]));
    add ("South", b = new NumberButton ("6", touchTones[6]));

    add ("South", b = new NumberButton ("7", touchTones[7]));
    add ("South", b = new NumberButton ("8", touchTones[8]));
    add ("South", b = new NumberButton ("9", touchTones[9]));

    add ("South", b = new Button ("*"));
    b.setBackground (miscColor);
    add ("South", b = new NumberButton ("0", touchTones[0]));
    add ("South", b = new Button ("#"));
    b.setBackground (miscColor);

    setLayout (new GridLayout (4, 3, 4, 4));
}

/**
 * Handle button presses.
 * @param ev - event object
 * @param arg - target object
 */
public boolean action (Event ev, Object arg) {

    if (ev.target instanceof Button) {
        String label = (String) arg;

        if (label.equals("*")) touchTones[10].play ();
        else if (label.equals("#"))   touchTones[11].play ();;
        return true;
    }
    return false;
}
}

/*
 * Handle number buttons.
 */
class NumberButton extends Button {

/*
 * Background color for this button
```

```
 */
static  Color    color = new Color (255, 99, 71);          // Tomato

/*
 * The tone for this button
 */
AudioClip myTone;

/**
 * Constructor just saves the arguments and changes the color.
 * @param label - title of the button
 * @param tone - tone for this button
 */
NumberButton (String label, AudioClip tone) {

    myTone = tone;
    setBackground (color);
    setForeground (Color.black);
    setLabel (label);
}

/**
 * Play the tone when the button is pressed.
 * @param e - event object
 */
public boolean handleEvent (Event e) {

    myTone.play ();
    return (true);
}
}
```

2. Create an HTML document that contains the applet. Create a new file called howto81.html as follows:

```
<html>
<head>
<title>Touchtone Dialer</title>
</head>
<applet code="Dialer.class" width=200 height=200>
</applet>
<hr size=4>

</html>
```

3. Compile and test the applet. Compile the source using javac or the makefile provided. Dialer requires several sound files. These files are included on the CD-ROM. Test the applet using the Appletviewer by entering the following command:

APPLETVIEWER howto81.html

The applet will create a number pad similar to that of a telephone. Pressing the buttons will cause the corresponding tone to be played. Figure 8-1 shows an example of the output.

Figure 8-1 Dialer applet

How It Works

The Dialer applet contains an array of audio clips called touchTones. This array contains the tones for the digits, star, and pound sign found on a standard telephone keypad. The *init()* method loads these audio clips into the array by invoking the *getAudioClip()* method. The keypad is a separate panel that is added to the center of the applet panel.

The *Keypad* class creates the keypad buttons in its constructor. The class also contains the array of touch tones that is initialized by the constructor. Each number button is created by invoking the number button constructor with the label of the button and its associated touch tone as arguments. When a number button is pressed, the tone for that button is played by invoking the *AudioClip.play()* method. The star and pound keys are handled separately, but a similar function is performed. Table 8-1 lists the *AudioClip* methods.

Comments

getAudioClip(), like *getImage()*, is part of the Applet class. It can take an absolute URL as an argument, or take a current document base and a relative path as arguments. The latter is used in this example.

METHOD	DESCRIPTION
loop	Starts playing the audio clip in a loop.
play	Starts playing the audio clip. Each time this method is called, the clip is restarted from the beginning.
stop	Stops playing the audio clip.

Table 8-1 getAudioClip methods

COMPLEXITY
ADVANCED

8.2 How do I...
Play sounds in a loop?

Problem

I would like to play some background noise while an applet is running. I have a small audio file, and it would be nice to just continuously loop through the sound. I know how to play sounds, but how do I play sounds in a loop?

Technique

The Bounce animation example from How-To 7.4 will be used here with music playing in the background. A small sound file (AU format) will be continuously looped through and played while the applet is running. Sound clips are contained in a class called AudioClip in the applet package. An AudioClip is loaded by invoking the *getAudioClip( )* method with the name of the sound file as an argument. The AudioClip is played in a loop by invoking its *loop* method.

Steps

1. Create the applet source file. Create a new file called Bounce.java and enter the following source:

```
import java.awt.*;
import java.applet.*;
import java.awt.image.ImageObserver;

/*
 * A class describing a single ball
 */
class Ball {

/*
 * The image for this ball
 */
Image img;

/*
 * x position and velocity
 */
double x, dx;     // x position and velocity

/*
 * y position and velocity
 */
```

continued on next page

continued from previous page

```
 */
double y, dy;     // y position and velocity

/*
 * Initialize the position and velocity
 * to random values.
 */
void random () {
    x = 10 + 380*Math.random ();
    y = 10 + 200*Math.random ();
    dx = 5 - 10*Math.random ();
    dy = 5 - 10*Math.random ();
}


/**
 * Calculate the next position of this ball,
 * and make sure it bounces off the edge of the panel.
 * @param d - dimension of the bounding panel
 */
void compute (Dimension d) {
    if (x <= 0 || x > d.width) dx = -dx;     // Bounce horizontally
    if (y <= 0 || y > d.height) dy = -dy;     // Bounce vertically
    x += dx;
    y += dy;
}


/**
 * Draw the ball image.
 * @param g - destination graphics object
 * @param obs - parent image observer
 */
public void paint (Graphics g, ImageObserver obs) {

    g.drawImage (img, (int) x-10, (int) y-10, obs);
}
}


/*
 * The panel containing the bouncing balls
 */
class BouncePanel extends Panel implements Runnable {

/*
 * The number of balls
 */
final int nballs = 4;

/*
 * The array holding all the balls
 */
Ball balls[] = new Ball[10];

/*
 * Off-screen image
```

```
  */
Image offimg;

/*
 * Size of off-screen image
 */
Dimension offsize;

/*
 * Graphics object associated with off-screen image
 */
Graphics offg;

/*
 * Thread for periodic updating
 */
Thread thread;

/*
 * The thread recalculates each ball position and
 * redraws it.
 */
public void run() {

    offsize = size();
    offimg = createImage (offsize.width, offsize.height);
    offg = offimg.getGraphics();
    while (true) {
        for (int i=0; i<nballs; i+=1) {
            balls[i].compute (offsize);
        }
        repaint ();
        try {
            Thread.sleep (25);
        } catch (InterruptedException e) {
            break;
        }
    }
}


/**
 * Override update to avoid erase flicker.
 * @param g - destination graphics object
 */
public synchronized void update (Graphics g) {

    offg.setColor (Color.lightGray);
    offg.fillRect (0, 0, offsize.width, offsize.height);

    for (int i = 0 ; i < nballs ; i++)
        balls[i].paint (offg, this);
    offg.setColor (Color.black);
    offg.drawRect (0, 0, offsize.width-1, offsize.height-1);
    g.drawImage(offimg, 0, 0, this);
}
```

continued on next page

continued from previous page

```
/*
 * Start the update thread.
 */
public void start() {

    thread = new Thread(this);
    thread.start();
}

/*
 * Stop the update thread.
 */
public void stop() {

    thread.stop();
}
}

/*
 * The applet proper
 */
public class Bounce extends Applet {

/*
 * Instance of BouncePanel
 */
BouncePanel panel;

/*
 * An array containing the images for the balls
 */
Image img[] = new Image[4];

/*
 * The audio clip to be played in a loop
 */
AudioClip sound;

/*
 * Called when the applet is loaded
 * Create an instance of bounce panel and add the Start button
 * and load images.
 */
public void init() {

    setLayout(new BorderLayout());

    panel = new BouncePanel ();
    add ("Center", panel);
    Panel p = new Panel ();
    add ("South", p);
    p.add (new Button("Start"));
    p.add (new Button("Stop"));
    sound = getAudioClip(getCodeBase(),  "sound.au");
```

```
    img[0] = getImage (getDocumentBase(), "whiteball.gif");
    img[1] = getImage (getDocumentBase(), "redball.gif");
    img[2] = getImage (getDocumentBase(), "blueball.gif");
    img[3] = getImage (getDocumentBase(), "greenball.gif");
    for (int i=0; i<panel.nballs; i+=1) {
        panel.balls[i] = new Ball ();
        panel.balls[i].img = img[i & 3];
    }
}

/*
 * Called when the applet is started
 * Just start the bounce panel update thread.
 */
public void start () {

    panel.start();
    sound.loop ();
}

/*
 * Called when the applet is stopped
 */
public void stop() {

    panel.stop();
    sound.stop ();
}

/*
 * Handle Start button press by randomizing balls.
 * @param evt - event object
 * @param arg - target object
 */
public boolean action(Event evt, Object arg) {

    if ("Start".equals(arg)) {
        for (int i=0; i<panel.nballs; i+=1)
            panel.balls[i].random ();
        sound.loop ();
        return true;
    }
    if ("Stop".equals(arg)) {
        panel.stop ();
        sound.stop ();
        return true;
    }
    return false;
}
}
```

2. Create an HTML document that contains the applet. Create a new file called howto82.html as follows:

```
<html>
<head>
```

continued on next page

continued from previous page

```
<title>Bounce</title>
</head>
Bouncing balls example.
<hr size=4>
<applet code="Bounce.class" width=400 height=400>
</applet>
<hr size=4>
</html>
```

3. Compile and test the applet. Compile the source using javac or the makefile provided. Test the applet using the Appletviewer by entering the following command:

```
APPLETVIEWER howto82.html
```

When Bounce is executed, a frame will open and have Start and Stop buttons at the bottom. If you press Start, you should see four balls bouncing off the sides of the box in random directions and rates, as in example 7.4. The difference in this example is that music is being played in the background. Figure 8-2 shows an example of the output.

The sound is contained in the sound.au file that must reside in the same directory as the applet. The balls are actually GIF images (whiteball.gif, redball.gif, blueball.gif, and greenball.gif) that need to reside in the same directory as the applet.

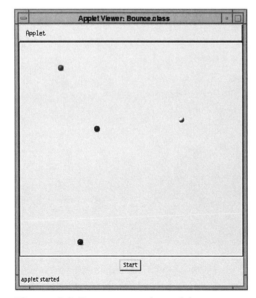

Figure 8-2 Bounce applet with background music

How It Works

This example is identical to the Bounce example of example 7.4, except for the addition of the sound. An AudioClip, sound, is declared, and the file sound.au is loaded into the class with the *getAudioClip()* method. The *getAudioClip()* method needs the URL and file name as parameters. The URL is supplied with the *getCodeBase()* method that returns the URL of the applet itself. The file name sound.au is supplied as the file. To start playing the sound in a loop, the *loop()* method is called for the sound. This occurs in the event handler when the Start button is pressed. When the Stop button is pressed, the *sound.stop()* method is called to stop the sound from playing.

COMPLEXITY
ADVANCED

8.3 How do I...
Play several sounds simultaneously?

Problem

I would like to create an applet that can play several guitar chords. I have the chords as AU files. I also have a drumbeat sound file I would like to play in the background, so I can play the chords over it. I know how to play sounds, but how do I play sounds simultaneously?

Technique

As seen in the previous example, sound clips are contained in a class called AudioClip in the applet package. An AudioClip is loaded by invoking the *GetAudioClip* method with the name of the sound file as an argument. The AudioClip is played by invoking its *play* method. The AudioClip is played in a loop by invoking its *loop* method.

Steps

1. Create the applet source file. Create a new file called Guitar.java and enter the following source:

```
import java.awt.*;
import java.applet.*;

/*
 * The applet class
 */
public class Guitar extends Applet {
```

continued on next page

continued from previous page

```
/*
 * The guitar chords
 */
AudioClip chords[] = new AudioClip[7];

/*
 * The drum clip
 */
AudioClip drum;
String chordnames[] = {"a", "c", "d", "low_e", "high_e", "g", "chaa"};
String drumbeat  = "drum";

/*
 * Called when the applet is loaded
 * Load all sounds and add user interface.
 */
public void init () {

    String name;
    int i;
    Panel keyboard = new Panel();
    Panel controls = new Panel();

    this.setLayout(new BorderLayout());
    keyboard.setLayout(new FlowLayout());
    controls.setLayout(new FlowLayout());
    add ("Center", keyboard);
    add ("South", controls);

    for (i=0; i<7; i+=1) {
        name = chordnames[i]+".au";
        showStatus ("Getting " + name);
        chords[i] = getAudioClip (getCodeBase(), name);
        keyboard.add (new Button (chordnames[i]));
    }
    showStatus ("Getting " + drumbeat + ".au");
    drum = getAudioClip (getCodeBase(), drumbeat + ".au");

    controls.add (new Button ("Start"));
    controls.add (new Button ("Stop"));
}

/*
 * Handle button presses.
 * @param ev - event object
 * @param arg - target object
 */
public boolean action (Event ev, Object arg) {

    String label;
    if (ev.target instanceof Button) {
        label = (String)arg;
```

```
        if (label == "a") {
            chords[0].play ();
            return true;
        } else if (label == chordnames[1]) {
            chords[1].play ();
            return true;
        } else if (label == chordnames[2]) {
            chords[2].play ();
            return true;
        } else if (label == chordnames[3]) {
            chords[3].play ();
            return true;
        } else if (label == chordnames[4]) {
            chords[4].play ();
            return true;
        } else if (label == chordnames[5]) {
            chords[5].play ();
            return true;
        } else if (label == chordnames[6]) {
            chords[6].play ();
            return true;
        } else if (label == "Start") {
            drum.loop ();
            return true;
        } else if (label == "Stop") {
            drum.stop ();
            return true;
        }
    }
    return false;
}
}
```

2. Create an HTML document that contains the applet. Create a new file called howto83.html as follows:

```
<html>
<head>
<title>Guitar</title>
</head>
<applet code="Guitar.class" width=200 height=200>
</applet>
<hr size=4>

</html>
```

3. Compile and test the applet. Compile the source using javac or the makefile provided. Test the applet using the Appletviewer by entering the following command:

```
APPLETVIEWER howto83.html
```

This example requires several sound files that need to reside in the same directory as the applet. These files can be found on the CD and are named a.au, c.au, d.au, low_e.au, high_e.au, g.au, chaa.au, and drum.au.

Figure 8-3 Guitar
applet

When the applet is executed, a window will open with seven buttons, each labeled with the name of the chord. Pressing the buttons will play the chord. At the bottom are two buttons labeled "Start" and "Stop." The Start button will start the drumbeat playing in the background. The Stop button will stop the drumbeat from playing. Figure 8-3 shows an example of the output.

How It Works

An AudioClip is declared and the file sound.au is loaded into the class with the *getAudioClip()* method. The *getAudioClip()* method needs the URL and file name as parameters. The URL is supplied with the *getCodeBase()* method that returns the URL of the applet itself. The file name sound.au is supplied as the file. To play the sound, the *play()* method is called for the sound. This occurs in the event handler when a chord button is pressed. To start playing the sound in a loop, the *loop()* method is called for the sound. This occurs in the event handler when the Start button is pressed. When the Stop button is pressed, the *sound.stop()* method is called to stop the sound from playing. While the drumbeat is playing in the background, the chords can be played simultaneously.

8.4 How do I...
Coordinate animation and sound?

Problem

I want to write a video game that has sound in it. I want sounds to be played when a target or the player is hit. I know how to animate graphics and play sounds, but I need to know how to coordinate them. How do I coordinate animation and sound?

Technique

Sounds can be played asynchronously. This means that the audio clip can be invoked in response to a target or player being hit. When either of these events is detected, the *play()* method can be invoked to coordinate animation and sound.

Steps

1. Create the applet source file. Create a new file called InvaderApp.java and enter the following source:

```
import java.awt.*;
import java.applet.Applet;
import java.awt.image.*;

/**
 * A class that describes a target "invader"
 * This hold a single invader.
 */
class Invader {

/*
 * This invader's position and velocity
 */
double x, y, dx, dy;

/*
 * This invader's missile position and velocity
 * Only one missile allowed per invader
 */
int mx, my, mdy;
```

continued on next page

continued from previous page

```
/*
 * The images for an invader
 */
Image img[] = new Image[4];

/*
 * inplay is True if this invader has not been killed.
 */
boolean inplay;

/*
 * fired is set True when this invader fires a missile.
 */
boolean fired = false;

/*
 * state is used to cycle through the four images
 * of this invader.
 */
double state;

/*
 * value is the score value, it depends on the speed.
 */
int value;

/*
 * Initialize position and speed for this invader.
 */
void random (int speed, int w, int h) {

    x = 10 + (w-20)*Math.random ();
    y = 10 + ((h>>1)-20)*Math.random ();
    dx = (speed>>1) - speed*Math.random ();
    dy = (speed>>1) - speed*Math.random ();
    inplay = true;
    state = 3 * Math.random ();
    fired = false;
    mdy = 20;
    value = speed * 10;
}

/*
 * Calculate new invader and missile position.
 * Also fires a missile at random
 * @param w - panel width
 * @param h - panel height
 */
void compute (int w, int h) {

    if (x <= 0 || x > w) dx = -dx;
    if (y <= 0 || y > h>>1) dy = -dy;
    if (my > h-20) fired = false;
    if (fired) my += mdy;
```

```
        else my = 0;
        if (inplay && !fired && Math.random () > 0.99) {
            fired = true;
            mx = (int) x; my = (int) y+25;
        }
        x += dx; y += dy;
}

/*
 * Paint invader and missile (if it has been fired).
 * @param g - destination graphics object
 * @param obs - imageobserver associated with this graphics context
 */
public void paint (Graphics g, ImageObserver obs) {

    int whichImage;

    if (inplay) {
        whichImage = (int) state;
        g.drawImage (img[whichImage & 0x3], (int) x-25,
            (int) y-25, obs);
        state += .25;
    }
    if (fired) {
        g.setColor (Color.green);
        g.drawLine ((int) mx, (int) my, (int) mx, (int) my-10);
    }
}

/*
 * Tests if the player's missile has hit this invader
 * Returns True if invader is hit
 * @param pmx - player's missile x position
 * @param pmy - player's missile y position
 */
boolean killer (int pmx, int pmy) {

    int deltaX, deltaY;

    if (!inplay) return false;
        deltaX = (int) Math.abs (x-pmx);
        deltaY = (int) Math.abs (y-pmy);
        if (deltaX < 20 && deltaY < 20) {
            inplay = false;
            return true;
        }
        return false;
}
}

/**
 * A class to describe the player, very similar to Invader,
 * except in reverse
 */
class Player {
```

continued on next page

continued from previous page

```
/*
 * Position of the player
 */
int x, y=-100;

/*
 * Position of the player's missile
 */
int mx, my, mdy = -20;

/*
 * Two different player images
 */
Image img1, img2;

/*
 * fired is True if player has fired a missile.
 * inplay is True if the game is not over.
 */
boolean fired = false, inplay=true;

/*
 * Called when a player fires a missile
 */
void fire () {

    if (fired || !inplay) return;
    mx = x; my = y;
    fired = true;
}

/*
 * Calculate next missile position.
 */
void compute () {

    if (my < 0) fired = false;
    if (fired) my += mdy;
    else my = y;
}

/**
 * Paint player and missile.
 * @param g - destination graphics object
 * @param obs - image observer
 */
public void paint (Graphics g, ImageObserver obs) {

    if (fired) {
        if (inplay) g.drawImage (img2, x-25, y, obs);
        g.setColor (Color.white);
        g.drawLine (mx, my, mx, my+10);
    } else if (inplay) g.drawImage (img1, x-25, y, obs);
}
```

```
/**
 * Returns True if the player has been killed
 * @param bmx, bmy - position of enemy missile
 */
boolean killer (int bmx, int bmy) {

    int dx, dy;

    if (!inplay) return false;
    dx = (int) Math.abs (x-bmx);
    dy = (int) Math.abs (y-bmy);
    if (dx < 20 && dy < 20) {
        return true;
    }
    return false;
}
}

/*
 * Much of the game logic is here.
 */
class Playfield extends Panel implements Runnable {

static final int PLAYER_HIT = 1;
static final int INVADER_HIT = 2;

InvaderApp invaderApp;

/*
 * The number of invaders in play
 */
int NInvaders=0;

/*
 * The maximum number of invaders possible
 */
final int MaxInvaders = 32;

/*
 * Array of invaders
 */
Invader invaders[] = new Invader[MaxInvaders];
Player player;

/*
 * Off-screen image for double buffering
 */
Image offscreen;

/*
 * Dimension of off-screen graphics image
 */
Dimension psize;
```

continued on next page

continued from previous page

```java
/*
 * Graphics object associated with off-screen image
 */
Graphics offgraphics;

/*
 * Game action thread
 */
Thread theThread;

/*
 * The playfield background color
 */
Color bgcolor = new Color (51, 0, 153);
int score, playerLives, playLevel;
Font font;

/**
 * Constructor saves instance of the applet
 * @param invaderApp - instance of the applet
 */
public Playfield (InvaderApp invaderApp) {

    this.invaderApp = invaderApp;
}

/*
 * Game action thread
 */
public void run() {

    psize = size();
    offscreen = createImage (psize.width, psize.height);
    offgraphics = offscreen.getGraphics ();
    font = new Font ("TimesRoman", Font.BOLD, 18);
    offgraphics.setFont (font);

    while (true) {
        compute ();
        repaint ();
        try {
            Thread.sleep(25);
        } catch (InterruptedException e) { }
    }
}

/*
 * Calculate new positions for all objects.
 */
synchronized void compute () {

    for (int i=0; i<NInvaders; i+=1) {
        invaders[i].compute (psize.width, psize.height);
        if (invaders[i].killer (player.mx, player.my)) {
```

```
                invaderApp.hit (INVADER_HIT);
                player.fired = false;
                score += invaders[i].value;
            }
            if (player.killer (invaders[i].mx, invaders[i].my)) {
                invaderApp.hit (PLAYER_HIT);
                invaders[i].fired = false;
                playerLives -= 1;
                if (playerLives < 1) player.inplay = false;
            }
        }
        player.compute ();
    }

    /**
     * Override default update.
     * Draw into off-screen image and then copy it to the screen.
     * @param g - destination graphics object
     */
    public synchronized void update(Graphics g) {

        offgraphics.setColor (bgcolor);
        offgraphics.fillRect (0, 0, psize.width, psize.height);

        for (int i = 0 ; i < NInvaders ; i++)
            if (invaders[i].inplay) invaders[i].paint (offgraphics, this);
        player.paint (offgraphics, this);

        offgraphics.setColor (Color.green);
        offgraphics.drawString ("Score", 10, 20);
        offgraphics.drawString (Integer.toString (score), 60, 20);
        offgraphics.drawString ("Level", psize.width>>1, 20);
        offgraphics.drawString (Integer.toString (playLevel),
            (psize.width>>1)+50, 20);
        offgraphics.drawString ("Lives", psize.width-80, 20);
        offgraphics.drawString (Integer.toString (playerLives),
            psize.width-30, 20);
        if (playerLives < 1) offgraphics.drawString ("Game Over",
            (psize.width>>1)-30, psize.height>>1);
        g.drawImage (offscreen, 0, 0, null);
    }

    /**
     * Fire the player's missile.
     * @param evt - event object
     * @param x, y - mouse position
     */
    public synchronized boolean mouseDown(Event evt, int x, int y) {

        player.fire ();
        return true;
    }

    /**
     * Move the player's position.
```

continued on next page

continued from previous page

```
 * @param evt - event object
 * @param x, y - mouse position
 */
public boolean mouseMove (Event evt, int x, int y) {

    player.x = x;
    player.y = psize.height-45;
    if (player.x < 20) player.x = 20;
    if (player.x > psize.width-20) player.x = psize.width-20;
    return true;
}

/*
 * Start the game thread.
 */
public void start() {

    theThread = new Thread (this);
    theThread.start ();
}

/*
 * Stop the game thread.
 */
public void stop() {

    theThread.stop ();
}
}

/*
 * The applet class
 */
public class InvaderApp extends Applet {

/*
 * The playfield instance
 */
Playfield panel;

/*
 * Temporary storage for images
 */
Image img[] = new Image[4];

/*
 * The speed of the game
 * The number of invaders in this round
 */
int speed, NInvadersInPlay;

/*
 * Called when the applet is loaded
 * Load the images.
```

```
    */
public void init() {

    int i;
    MediaTracker tracker = new MediaTracker (this);

    setLayout(new BorderLayout());

    panel = new Playfield (this);
    add("Center", panel);
    Panel p = new Panel();
    add("South", p);
    p.add(new Button("New Game"));

    showStatus ("Getting Invader images...");
    for (i=0; i<4; i+=1) {
        img[i] = getImage (getDocumentBase(), "T"+(i+1)+".gif");
        tracker.addImage (img[i], 0);
    }

    try {
        tracker.waitForID(0);
    } catch (InterruptedException e) { }

        for (i=0; i<panel.MaxInvaders; i+=1) {
        panel.invaders[i] = new Invader ();
        panel.invaders[i].inplay = false;
        panel.invaders[i].img[0] = img[0];
        panel.invaders[i].img[1] = img[1];
        panel.invaders[i].img[2] = img[2];
        panel.invaders[i].img[3] = img[3];
    }
    panel.player = new Player ();

    showStatus ("Getting player images...");
    panel.player.img1 = getImage (getDocumentBase(), "Player1.gif");
    panel.player.img2 = getImage (getDocumentBase(), "Player2.gif");

    tracker.addImage (panel.player.img1, 1);
    tracker.addImage (panel.player.img2, 1);
    try {
        tracker.waitForID (1);
    } catch (InterruptedException e) { }
    showStatus ("Ready to play!");
}

/*
 * Start the action thread.
 */
public void start() {

    panel.start();
}
```

continued on next page

continued from previous page

```
/*
 * Stop the action thread.
 */
public void stop() {

    panel.stop();
}

/*
 * Handle button presses.
 * @param evt - event object
 * @param arg - target object
 */
public boolean action(Event evt, Object arg) {

    if ("New Game".equals(arg)) {
        speed = 10;
        panel.player.inplay = true;
        panel.playerLives = 3;
        panel.score = 0;
        panel.playLevel = 1;
        NInvadersInPlay = 2 * panel.playLevel + 1;
        panel.NInvaders = NInvadersInPlay;
        for (int i=0; i<panel.NInvaders; i+=1)
            panel.invaders[i].random (speed,
                panel.psize.width, panel.psize.height);

        play (getCodeBase(), "gong.au");
        if (NInvadersInPlay >= panel.MaxInvaders)
            NInvadersInPlay = panel.MaxInvaders;
        return true;
    }
    return false;
}

/**
 * Play the appropriate sound when something was hit.
 * @param which - which sound to play
 */
public void hit (int which) {

    switch (which) {
        case Playfield.INVADER_HIT:
        NInvadersInPlay -= 1;
        if (NInvadersInPlay < 1) {
```

```
        play (getCodeBase(), "gong.au");
        panel.playLevel += 1;
        NInvadersInPlay = 2 * panel.playLevel + 1;
        speed += 4;
        panel.NInvaders = NInvadersInPlay;
        for (int i=0; i<panel.NInvaders; i+=1)
        panel.invaders[i].random (speed,
            panel.psize.width, panel.psize.height);
    } else {
        play (getCodeBase(), "drip.au");
    }
    break;

    case Playfield.PLAYER_HIT:
    play (getCodeBase(), "doh2.au");
    break;
    }
}
}
```

2. Create an HTML document that contains the applet. Create a new file called howto84.html as follows:

```
<html>
<head>
<title>InvaderApp</title>
</head>
<applet code="InvaderApp.class" width=600 height=400>
</applet>
<hr size=4>

</html>
```

3. Compile and test the applet. Compile the source using javac or the makefile provided. InvaderApp requires several sound and image files. These files are included on the CD-ROM. Test the applet using the Appletviewer by entering the following command:

```
APPLETVIEWER howto84.html
```

InvaderApp is a full-functional "video" game. Press the Start button to begin the game. The gunship can be moved left and right by just moving the mouse. To fire, press the mouse button. Figure 8-4 shows an example of the output.

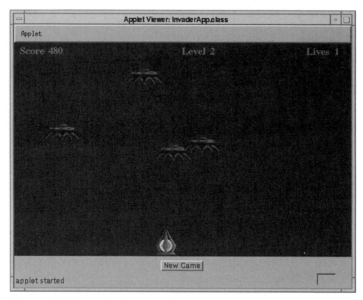

Figure 8-4 InvaderApp applet

How It Works

The InvaderApp program contains four classes: an *Invader* class, which describes a target invader; the *Player* class, which describes the player; the *PlayField* class, which is the main engine to the game; and the *InvaderApp* class, which manages the game.

The *Invader* class describes the single invader. It contains the invader position and velocity along with a missile position and velocity. It also contains four images for the invader that are cycled to make the invader more interesting. The *inPlay* variable is set to True if the invader has not been killed. The *fired* variable is set to True if the invader has fired a missile. The *state* variable is used to determine which image is displayed for this invader. The variable *value* is the score value for this invader.

The *random()* method initializes the position and velocity of this invader to random values. The velocity of the invader is dependent on the speed argument. The speed argument is determined by the play level in the applet. Higher play levels cause higher speeds. This makes the game challenging at higher levels. The score value is also dependent on the speed.

The *compute()* method calculates the next position for the invader. It also computes the position of the missile if it has been fired. If the missile has not been fired, it will be fired randomly. The invader's position is incremented by its velocity. If the invader encounters the boundary of the panel specified by the *w* and *h*, then the velocity in the respective direction is inverted. This gives the illusion of bouncing off the walls.

The *paint()* method paints the invader image and the invader's missile if it has been fired. The *killer()* method determines if the player's missile has hit this invader. The player's missile position is given by *pmx* and *pmy*. This is used to determine if the missile is within the rectangle bounding the invader. The method returns True if the invader has been hit.

The *Player* class is similar to the Invader class. It contains *paint()* and *killer()* methods that are analogous to those of the Invader class. The *fire()* method fires a missile from the current player position if it has not been fired already. A different player image is drawn if the player has fired a missile. This gives more life to the game. The *compute()* method only calculates the new missile position if a missile has been fired.

The *PlayField* class is a separate thread that contains the game engine itself. An array of invaders is maintained along with a single instance of player. An off-screen image and an off-screen image context are maintained to implement double buffering.

The *run()* method first creates the off-screen image and graphics context. It also sets the font. It then continuously computes the new invader and missile positions by calling *compute()*. The screen is updated by calling *repaint()*.

The *compute()* method invokes each invader's *compute()* method. It then tests if an invader has been hit by a player missile by calling the *Invader.killer()* method. If an invader has been hit, the sound for an invader being hit is played, the player's missile is eliminated, and *score* is incremented. A similar test is performed for the player. In this case a different sound is played, and the number of player lives is decreased.

The *update()* method overrides the default *update()* method to avoid unnecessary flickering. The invaders are drawn by calling the *Invader.paint()* methods for all invaders. The player is drawn by calling the *Player.paint()* method. The score, play level, and the number of player lives are drawn. All of this drawing is done in the off-screen image via the off-screen graphics context. The off-screen image is drawn on-screen.

If a *mouseDown()* event occurs, the *Player.fire()* method is invoked. If a *mouseEvent()* occurs, the player's position is set to the mouse x position. Care is taken to keep the player position within panel bounds.

The play field *start()* and *stop()* methods start and stop the play field thread, respectively.

The *InvaderApp* class manages the game. The *init()* method creates an instance of the play field panel and adds it to the center of the applet panel. A button is added at the bottom of the applet panel for starting a new game. The images for the invaders are loaded via the *getImage()* method. MediaTracker is used to wait for the images to load. The invaders are created and initialized. An instance of the player is created, and its images are loaded.

If the player presses the New Game button, the play field variables are initialized and the game is started.

Comments

The game can be improved in many ways. Different types of targets can be added, multiple missiles can be managed.

COMPLEXITY
ADVANCED

8.5   How do I...
Use clipping to perform animation?

Problem

I know how to simulate animation by displaying a series of images. However, this can mean substantial loading time due to the number of images needed. I would like to apply the clipping technique from section 7.6 to a single image to produce the effect of animation. How do I use clipping to perform animation?

Technique

As shown in section 7.6, the easiest way to draw part of an image is to use clipping. A graphics object can be created with a clipping rectangle specified. To draw part of an image, the new graphics context must be created with the coordinates, width, and height of the section of the image that needs to be drawn.

Steps

1. Create the applet source file. Create a new file called BallSpin.java and enter the following source:

```
import java.applet.*;
import java.awt.*;
import java.net.*;

/*
 * The applet class
 */
public class BallSpin extends Applet implements Runnable {

/*
 * The number of subimages in the entire image
 */
int nImages;

/*
 * The full-size image
 */
Image theImage;

/*
 * The animation thread
 */
Thread thread;
```

```
/*
 * The position of the displayed image
 */
int xOffset;
int yOffset;

/*
 * Offscreen image for double buffering
 */
Image offImage;

/*
 * Graphics object associated with the off-screen image
 */
Graphics offg;

/*
 * Dimension of the off-screen image
 */
Dimension offSize;

/*
 * The subimage to be drawn
 */
int whichImage;

/*
 * The dimension of each subimage
 */
Dimension imageDim = new Dimension ();

/*
 * Initializes the applet
 * Load the entire image.
 */
public void init () {

    int i;

    thread = null;

    offSize = size ();
    offImage = createImage (offSize.width, offSize.height);
    offg = offImage.getGraphics ();

    nImages = 7;
    imageDim.width = 48;
    imageDim.height = 53;

    MediaTracker tracker = new MediaTracker (this);

        String name = "ballspin.gif";
    theImage = getImage (getDocumentBase(), name);

    tracker.addImage (theImage, 100);
    showStatus ("Getting image: "+name);
```

continued on next page

continued from previous page

```
        try {
            tracker.waitForID (100);
        } catch (InterruptedException e) { }

        xOffset = nImages * 30;
        yOffset = 3 + offSize.height - imageDim.height;
        whichImage = nImages;
        repaint ();
        thread = new Thread (this);
        thread.start ();
}

/*
 * Start the animation.
 */
public void start () {

    xOffset = nImages * 30;
    yOffset = 3 + offSize.height - imageDim.height;
    whichImage = nImages;
    if (thread != null) thread.stop ();
    thread = new Thread (this);
    thread.start ();
}

/*
 * Stop the animation.
 */
public void stop () {

    if (thread != null) thread.stop ();
}

/**
 * Call update for efficiency.
 * @param g - destination graphics object
 */
public void paint (Graphics g) {

    update (g);
}

/**
 * Draw the subimage at xOffset, yOffset.
 * @param g - destination graphics object
 */
public void update (Graphics g) {

    Graphics offgClip;
```

```
        offg.setColor (Color.white);
        offg.fillRect (0, 0, offSize.width, offSize.height);
        offgClip = offg.create (xOffset, yOffset, imageDim.width,
            imageDim.height);
        offgClip.drawImage (theImage, 0 - (whichImage * imageDim.width),
            0, this);
        g.drawImage (offImage, 0, 0, this);
}

/*
 * Animation thread forces repaint every 100 ms.
 */
public void run () {

    int i;

    for (i=0; i<nImages; i+=1) {
        xOffset -= 30;
        whichImage -= 1;
        repaint ();
        try {
            Thread.sleep (100);
        } catch (InterruptedException e) { }
    }
}
}
```

2. Create an HTML document that contains the applet. Create a new file called howto85.html as follows:

```
<html>
<head>
<title>Single Image Animation</TITLE>
</head>
<applet code="BallSpin.class"  width=225 height=125>
</applet>
<hr size = 4)

</html>
```

3. Compile and test the applet. Compile the source using javac or the makefile provided. Test the applet using the Appletviewer by entering the following command:

`APPLETVIEWER howto87.html`

When BallSpin is executed, a window will open and a ball will roll from the right to the left. Figure 8-5 shows an example of the running applet.

Figure 8-5 Rolling ball applet

How It Works

The BallSpin applet loads a single GIF image which contains several sub images of a rolling ball. Clipping is used to draw these individual images in an animated fashion such that the ball appears to roll across the screen.

The applet *init( )* method creates an offscreen image for double-buffering. The complete image is loaded from the server by using the Applet.*getImage( )* method. MediaTracker is used to wait for the image to load. A status message is displayed during image load.

The *start( )* method initializes the image display location and starts a separate animation thread. The *stop( )* method simply stops the animation thread. The *paint( )* method calls the *update( )* method to avoid unnecessary flickering. The *run( )* method is the animation thread that calculates the new image position, forcing a *repaint( )* every 100 milliseconds.

The *update( )* method erases the offscreen image, offg, by filling it with the color white. A second graphics object, *offgClip*, is created as a copy of the offscreen image with a clipping rectangle defined as the dimensions of the sub images. The sub image is drawn into the clipped graphics object by invoking *Graphics.drawImage( )*. The variable *whichImage* is used to specify which sub image will be drawn. Finally, the offscreen image, *offImage*, is drawn to the screen by calling *Graphics.drawImage( )*.

Comments

The original purpose for this technique was to reduce the number of files that had to be downloaded by the applet, and thus speed up the loading time. As it turns out, that was not the only advantage. The single image containing all the images turned out to be considerably smaller than the sum of all the smaller images.

CHAPTER 9
NETWORKING

NETWORKING

How do I...

Networking is one of the strengths of the Java API. Classes and methods exist to access Internet sockets, create server sockets, get host names and addresses, and force web browsers to show specified documents. Socket connections can be made to arbitrary ports, but there are specific classes for accessing data via the HTTP port. Many applets may want to exploit these classes for server-to-client data transfer for reasons of efficiency and simplicity.

Most of these classes are found in the java.net package. This package must be imported in order to use the classes.

Applications can perform all networking operations. Applets are restricted to some extent for security reasons. Web browsers will typically allow connections to the server from which they were downloaded, but may not allow connections to other hosts.

9.1 Access a URL

This example demonstrates the mechanism for forcing web browsers to show specific documents. Both full-page and frame changes are supported.

The example extends the functionality of the example in section 6.6. In that example, advertiser banners were animated by using common transition effects. This example allows the user to click on a particular banner that will cause the browser to show the page corresponding to that advertisement.

9.2 Translate Host Names to Internet Addresses

This example uses methods in the InetAddress class. It is similar in function to the nslookup utility found on many UNIX platforms.

9.3 Create a Socket

This example determines if a remote host is running by attempting to open a specific port. If the port can be opened successfully, the remote host must be running.

9.4 Access a Stream

This example implements a simple Telnet application by opening the standard telnet port (port #23) and creating a simple terminal interface. It demonstrates the use of sockets.

9.5 Receive Data via HTTP

For server-to-client only data transfers, the HTTP port may be used. This example demonstrates data transfer via HTTP by implementing an application that allows the user to view the source of any document available on the Web. Techniques used in the application can be exploited to create a unique content handler.

9.6 Create a Server Socket

Server sockets are necessary for implementing client-server applications. In this example, the PhoneBook application introduced in Chapter 5 is modified to allow networked phone number access. Bidirectional data transfers are demonstrated.

9.7 Determine the Name of the Host Running My Applet

One interesting benefit of downloading applets to remote clients is the ability to determine the host's name and IP number. This can be useful for logging accesses and restricting execution of applets to particular machines or domains. This example will create an applet that will determine the name of the host that it is running on and send it back to the server for logging.

9.1 How do I...
Access a URL?

Problem

I found the adviser applet very useful. I want to make one improvement. I want to be able to force the web browser to show a predefined location when the user clicks on any of the advertiser banners. I want to specify the URLs as applet parameters. I want to be able to specify unique URLs for each advertiser banner. I know how to access mouse down events, but I do not know how to force the web browser to show a document. How do I force the browser to show a document?

Technique

The *showDocument()* method in the applet class forces web browsers, such as Netscape Navigator, to show a document, given a URL. The *showDocument()* method takes the URL object as an argument. URL is a class that describes a Web universal resource locator. A URL is created by using one of its constructors. One of the constructors takes a string as an argument. This string is of the format commonly used by popular web browsers.

The technique used by the previous advertiser example for specifying banner images and transition effects will be extended. One more field will be added to the parameters. That field will be the URL associated with that banner. When a user clicks on a particular banner, the *showDocument()* method will be invoked with the URL of the banner as an argument.

Steps

1. Create the applet source file. Create a new file called Advertiser.java and enter the following source:

```
import java.util.*;
import java.awt.*;
import java.applet.Applet;
import java.net.*;

/*
 * A class that performs the banner animation
 */
class Banner extends Panel implements Runnable {

/*
 * An instance of the applet for
```

continued on next page

continued from previous page

```
 * invoking methods from advertiser class
 */
Advertiser advertiser;

/*
 * Instance of thread used for animation
 */
Thread thread;

/*
 * The next banner image to be displayed
 */
Image theImage;

/*
 * Width and height of the new banner image
 */
int img_width, img_height;

/*
 * Off-screen image for double buffering
 */
Image offscreen;

/*
 * offg1 is the graphics object associated with
 * offscreen image. offg2 is the clipped version
 * of offg1.
 */
Graphics offg1, offg2;

/*
 * xstart, ystart - x and y coordinate of clipping rectangle
 * width, height - width and height of clipping rectangle
 * effect_type - the effect type applied to the next image
 */
int xstart, ystart, width, height, effect_type;

/**
 * Constructor just saves instance of the applet.
 * @param advertiser - instance of advertiser applet
 */
Banner (Advertiser advertiser) {

    this.advertiser = advertiser;
}

/*
 * Thread that calls repaint() every 25 ms
 * to effect animation
 */
public void run() {

    Dimension d = size();
```

```
        offscreen = createImage (d.width, d.height);
        offg1 = offscreen.getGraphics ();
        offg1.setFont (getFont ());
        offg1.setColor (Color.gray);
        offg1.fillRect (0, 0, d.width, d.height);
        while (true) {
            repaint ();
            try {
                Thread.sleep (25);
            } catch (InterruptedException e) {
                break;
            }
        }
    }
}

/**
 * Override update() method to avoid erase flicker.
 * This is where the drawing is done.
 * @param g - destination graphics object
 */
public synchronized void update(Graphics g) {

    int i, x, y, w, h;
    switch (effect_type) {
        case 0:
        offg1.drawImage (theImage, 0, 0, null);
        break;

        case 1:           // Barn door open
        if (xstart > 0) {
            xstart -= 5;
            width += 10;
            offg2 = offg1.create (xstart, 0, width, height);
            offg2.drawImage (theImage, -xstart, 0, null);
        } else offg1.drawImage (theImage, 0, 0, null);
        break;

        case 2:           // Venetian blind
        if (height < 10) {
            height += 1;
            for (y=0; y<img_height; y+=10) {
                offg2 = offg1.create (0, y, width, height);
                offg2.drawImage (theImage, 0, -y, null);
            }
        } else offg1.drawImage (theImage, 0, 0, null);
        break;

        case 3:           // Checkerboard
        if (width <= 20) {
            if (width <= 10) {
                i = 0;
                for (y=0; y<img_height; y+=10) {
                    for (x=(i&1)*10; x<img_width; x+=20) {
                        offg2 = offg1.create (x, y, width, 10);
                        offg2.drawImage (theImage, -x, -y, null);
```

continued on next page

continued from previous page

```
                            }
                            i += 1;
                    }
            } else {
                    i = 1;
                    for (y=0; y<img_height; y+=10) {
                            for (x=(i&1)*10; x<img_width; x+=20) {
                                    offg2 = offg1.create (x, y, width-10, 10);
                                    offg2.drawImage (theImage, -x, -y, null);
                            }
                            i += 1;
                    }
            }
            width += 5;
        } else offg1.drawImage (theImage, 0, 0, null);
        break;
    }
    g.drawImage (offscreen, 0, 0, null);
}

/**
 * Initialize variables for clipping rectangle
 * depending on effect type.
 * @param which - the effect type for next image
 * @param img - the next image
 */
public void effect (int which, Image img) {

    img_width = img.getWidth (null);
    img_height = img.getHeight (null);
    theImage = img;
    switch (which) {
        case 0:
        break;

        case 1:          // Barn door
        xstart = img_width >> 1;
        width = 0;
        height = img_height;
        break;

        case 2:
        width = img_width;
        height = 0;
        break;

        case 3:
        width = 0;
        break;
    }
    effect_type = which;
}

/*
```

```
 * Start the repaint thread.
 */
public void start() {

    thread = new Thread(this);
    thread.start();
}

/*
 * Stop the repaint thread.
 */
public void stop() {

    thread.stop();
}
}

/*
 * The advertiser class proper
 */
public class Advertiser extends Applet implements Runnable {

/*
 * Instance of Banner
 */
Banner panel;

/*
 * Instance of thread for cycling effects
 * for each new image
 */
Thread thread;

/*
 * The total number of images
 */
int NBanners;

/*
 * The array of images
 */
Image img[] = new Image[10];

/*
 * The delay (dwell) time in milliseconds for each image
 */
int delay[] = new int[10];

/*
 * The effect type for each image
 */
int effect[] = new int[10];

/*
```

continued on next page

continued from previous page

```
 * The URL to go to for each image
 */
URL url[] = new URL[10];

/*
 * The index variable pointing to the
 * current image, delay time, and associated URL
 */
int current = 0;

/*
 * Called when applet is loaded
 * Add the banner panel, load images, and parse applet
 * parameters.
 */
public void init() {

    int i;
    setLayout(new BorderLayout());

    panel = new Banner (this);
    add("Center", panel);
    NBanners = 0;
    MediaTracker tracker = new MediaTracker (this);

    for (i=1; i<=10; i+=1) {
        String param, token;
        int j, next;

        param = getParameter ("T"+i);
        if (param == null) break;

        StringTokenizer st = new StringTokenizer (param, " ,");

        token = st.nextToken ();
        img[NBanners] = getImage (getDocumentBase(), token);
        tracker.addImage (img[NBanners], i);
        showStatus ("Getting image: "+token);
        try {
            tracker.waitForID (i);
        } catch (InterruptedException e) { }

        token = st.nextToken ();
        delay[NBanners] = Integer.parseInt (token);

        token = st.nextToken ();
        effect[NBanners] = Integer.parseInt (token);

        token = st.nextToken ();
        try {
            url[NBanners] = new URL (token);
        } catch (MalformedURLException e) {
            url[NBanners] = null;
```

```
            }

            NBanners += 1;
        }
    }

    /*
     * Thread that starts the next image transition
     */
    public void run () {

        while (true) {
            panel.effect (effect[current], img[current]);
            try {
                Thread.sleep (delay[current]);
            } catch (InterruptedException e) { }
            current += 1;
            current %= NBanners;
        }
    }

    /*
     * Called when applet is started
     * Start both threads.
     */
    public void start() {

        panel.start();
        thread = new Thread(this);
        thread.start();
    }

    /*
     * Called when applet is stopped
     * Stop all threads.
     */
    public void stop() {

        panel.stop();
        thread.stop();
    }

    /**
     * Called when user clicks in the applet
     * Force the browser to show the associated URL.
     * @param evt - event record
     * @param x, y - x and y coordinate of the mouse click
     */
    public boolean mouseDown (Event evt, int x, int y) {

        if (url[current] != null)
            getAppletContext().showDocument (url[current]);
        return true;
    }
}
```

2. Create an HTML document that contains the applet. Create a new file called howto91.html as follows:

```
<head>
<title>Java Advertiser</title>
</head>
<applet code="Advertiser.class" width=262 height=50>
<param name=T1 value="T1.gif,1000,0,http://www.zdnet.com/~zdsubs/pcc/">
<param name=T2
value="T2.gif,3000,1,http://home.netscape.com/comprod/at_work/">
<param name=T3 value="T3.gif,3000,2,http://www.shoppingplanet.com/">
<param name=T4 value="T4.gif,3000,3,http://www.insight.com/web/zdad.html">
</applet>
<hr size=4>
</body>
```

3. Compile and test the applet. Compile the source using javac or the makefile provided. The applet must be accessed by a Java-supported browser such as Netscape Navigator. The applet should be placed on a web server accessible from a web browser. When the applet is executed, an advertiser banner will be running similarly to example 7.6. Click on an ad when it is visible, and the browser will go to that web page. Figure 9-1 shows a snapshot of the running applet.

How It Works

The advertiser applet is very similar to that of Chapter 7. It contains two classes: the *Banner* class and the *Advertiser* class. The *Banner* class runs as a separate thread and implements the banner transition effects. As in Chapter 7, four transition effects are supported.

The *Advertiser* class is the applet itself and also runs as a separate thread. It manages the *Banner* class by directing it to perform transition effects defined by the user

Figure 9-1 Advertiser applet

in the applet parameters. The *init()* method creates an instance of the *Banner* class and adds it to the center of the appletís panel. The *init()* method then parses up to ten applet parameters. The number of applet parameters can be altered to suit the programmer. Each parameter is retrieved by using the *getParameter()* method. Next a *StringTokenizer* object is used to split the parameter into four fields. The first three fields are the same as in Chapter 6. The last field is a standard URL. The URL string in the parameter is used to create a URL object by invoking the URL constructor. The URL constructor throws *malformedURLException*, which must be caught and handled. The URLs are maintained in an array paralleling the arrays holding the images, effect types, and the display times. The variable *NBanners* keeps the total number of banners.

The *run()* method constantly invokes the *Banner.effect()* method with the current effect type and the current image as arguments. The variable *current* contains the index of the current banner displayed. The *start()* and *stop()* methods simply start and stop the threads used in the applet.

The *mouseDown()* method is called when the user clicks in the applet. When the user clicks on a banner, the *showDocument()* method is invoked with the current URL as an argument. This causes the web browser to show the document specified by the URL.

Comments

showDocument() is a method in the AppletContext interface, which defines the services and information an applet can obtain from the browser it is running in. The method *Applet.getAppletContext()* returns the AppletContext for an applet.

There are several forms of *showDocument()*; they are listed in Table 9-1. The version of *showDocument()* used in this example causes destruction of the applet, because the page containing it will be eliminated when the document is displayed. The applet can display a page in a separate Frame by using the version of *showDocument()* that takes a target Frame as an argument. It is interesting to note that a hidden applet could be created in a Frame of zero size. Or the applet could be displayed in a separate window, such as a navigation window separate from the browser window.

METHOD	DESCRIPTION
showDocument(URL url)	Replaces the Web page currently being viewed with the given URL. This method may be ignored by applet contexts that are not browsers.
showDocument(URL url, String target)	Requests that the browser or Appletviewer show the Web page indicated by the URL argument. The target argument indicates where to display the frame. The target argument is interpreted as follows: "_self" : show in the current frame; "_parent" : show in the parent frame; "_top" : show in the top-most frame; "_blank" : show in a new unnamed top-level window; name : show in a new top-level window named name.

Table 9-1 showDocument methods

9.2 How do I...
Translate host names to internet addresses?

Problem

I want to write an application, similar to the UNIX nslookup utility, that determines the Internet address associated with a host name. I know how to accept user input using an editable TextField and displaying results in a noneditable TextArea. I want to use these techniques to implement the lookup application. To print the Internet addresses, I need to translate host names to Internet addresses. How do I translate host names to Internet addresses?

Technique

The class *InetAddress* contains several methods for dealing with Internet addresses. This class is declared final, so it cannot be extended. The static *getByName( )* method returns an *InetAddress* class, given a string containing a host name. The *InetAddress.toString()* method can be used to create a string representation in the familiar decimal dot notation. User input is taken from an editable TextField, and output is displayed in a noneditable TextArea by using techniques from Chapter 5.

Steps

1. Create the application source file. Create a new file called Lookup.java and enter the following source:

```
import java.awt.*;
import java.net.*;

/*
 * Look up application class
 */
public class Lookup extends Frame {

/*
 * Text field for host name
 */
TextField nameField;

/*
 * Text area for displaying Internet addresses
 */
TextArea addrArea;
```

```
/*
 * Instance of InetAddress needed for name->address
 * translation
 */
InetAddress inetAddr;

/*
 * Insertion point in the Internet address
 * text area
 */
int insertIndex;

/*
 * Constructor creates user interface.
 */
public Lookup () {

    super ("Lookup");

    setLayout (new BorderLayout ());

    Panel editPanel = new Panel ();
    editPanel.setLayout (new BorderLayout ());
    editPanel.add ("North", new Label ("Host name"));
    nameField = new TextField ("", 32);
    editPanel.add ("Center", nameField);

    add ("North", editPanel);

    Panel areaPanel = new Panel ();
    areaPanel.setLayout (new BorderLayout ());
    addrArea = new TextArea ("", 24, 32);
    addrArea.setEditable (false);
    areaPanel.add ("North", new Label ("Internet address"));
    areaPanel.add ("Center", addrArea);

    add ("Center", areaPanel);

    insertIndex = 0;

    resize (300, 200);
    show ();
}

/**
 * Handle return key event.
 * Performs name->address translation and
 * prints inside the text area
 * @param evt - event object
 * @param arg - object receiving the event
 */
public boolean action (Event evt, Object arg) {
```

continued on next page

continued from previous page

```java
        if (evt.target.equals (nameField)) {
            String name = nameField.getText ();
            try {
                inetAddr = InetAddress.getByName (name);
                String str = inetAddr.toString () + "\n";
                addrArea.insertText (str, insertIndex);
                insertIndex += str.length ();
            } catch (UnknownHostException ex) {
                String str = name + "/ No such host\n";
                addrArea.insertText (str, insertIndex);
                insertIndex += str.length ();
            }

            return true;
        }
        return false;
    }

/**
 * Application entry point
 * @param args - command line arguments
 */
public static void main (String args[])
{
    new Lookup ();
}
}
```

2. Compile and test the application. Compile the source using javac or the makefile provided. Lookup.java must be run as an application by typing

`java Lookup`

When Lookup is executed, a window will open with a text field and a text area. Type the host name desired and press [ENTER]. The IP address for the host name will be determined and printed in the text area. Figure 9-2 shows a snapshot of the running application.

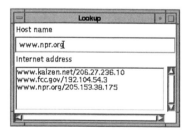

Figure 9-2 Lookup application

How It Works

The Lookup application contains only one class, the application itself. The *main()* method, which is called when the application is executed, simply creates an instance of the *Lookup* class. The *Lookup* class extends Frame similarly to previous application examples. The *Lookup* constructor invokes the Frame constructor with the Frame title as an argument. The *setTitle()* method could have been called instead.

Two Panels are created, one containing a TextField and one containing the TextArea. The first Panel contains a Label at the top and a TextField in the center. The second Panel contains a Label at the top and a noneditable TextArea at the center. This second Panel is added to the center of the Frame. *BorderLayout* is used for both the Frame and the Panels.

The *action()* method is called when the user enters a host name in the TextField and presses ENTER. The text within the TextField is retrieved by using the *TextField.getText()* method and passed as an argument to the *InetAddress.getByName()* method. This returns an instance of *InetAddress*. This instance of *InetAddress* is used to retrieve the Internet address as a string in decimal dot notation by using the *InetAddress.toString()* method. The Internet address is displayed in the TextArea by invoking the *insertText()* method. An insert index is maintained to keep track of the insert position in the TextArea.

InetAddress.getByName() throws *UnknownHostException* if the host name given does not exist. This exception must be caught and handled. In this example, the message 'no such host' is printed.

Comments

The *InetAddress* class is declared final so that it cannot be extended. This is done for security reasons.

COMPLEXITY
ADVANCED

9.3   How do I...
Create a socket?

Problem

I want to write an application that will determine if a remote host is running. If I can open an Internet socket on a known port, like the telnet port, that will tell me that the remote machine is running. I can use a TextField to take the host name as input and a TextArea to print the results. I don't know how to open a socket. How do I open a socket?

Technique

The java.net package contains a class for handling Internet sockets. It is called *Socket*. A constructor is defined for creating a socket given the host name and port number. The host name is of type *string*, and the port number is of type *int*. To open a socket, an instance of *Socket* must be declared and then created by using the *Socket* constructor.

Steps

1. Create the application source file. Create a new file called Ping.java and enter the following source:

```java
import java.awt.*;
import java.io.*;
import java.net.*;

/*
 * Application class
 */
public class Ping extends Frame implements Runnable {

/*
 * Instance of Socket used for determining
 * if remote host is alive.
 */
Socket socket;

/*
 * Host name text entry field
 */
TextField addrField;

/*
 * The Stop button
 */
Button stopButton;

/*
 * The text area for printing remote
 * host status
 */
TextArea content;

/*
 * Thread used to decouple user activity
 * from socket activity
 */
Thread thread;

/*
```

```
 * Text area insert position
 */
int insertPos;

/*
 * Constructor creates user interface.
 */
public Ping () {

    int i;

    setTitle ("View Source");
    setLayout(new BorderLayout());

    addrField = new TextField ("", 20);
    stopButton = new Button ("Stop");
    content = new TextArea ("", 24, 80);
    content.setEditable (false);
    insertPos = 0;

    Panel p = new Panel ();
    p.setLayout (new FlowLayout ());
    p.add (addrField);
    p.add (stopButton);

    add ("North", p);
    add ("Center", content);

    thread = new Thread (this);

    resize (400, 300);
    show ();
}

/**
 * Handle action events.
 * Return keypress starts socket open thread.
 * Stop button press stops socket thread.
 * @param evt - event object
 * @param obj - object receiving this event
 */
public boolean action (Event evt, Object obj) {

    if (evt.target == addrField) {
        thread.stop ();
        thread = new Thread (this);
        thread.start ();
        return true;
    }
    if (evt.target == stopButton) {
        thread.stop ();
    }
    return false;
```

continued on next page

continued from previous page

```
}

/*
 * Socket open thread
 * Tries to open the telnet port (23)
 */
public void run () {

    String name;

    name = addrField.getText ();
        try {
                try {
                        socket = new Socket (name, 23);
                } catch (UnknownHostException e) {
                        insertString (name+" :unknown host\n");
                        return;
                }
        } catch (IOException e2) {
                insertString ("Unable to open socket\n");
                return;
        }

    insertString (name + " is alive\n");
    try {
        socket.close ();
        } catch (IOException e2) {
                insertString ("IOExeption closing socket\n");
                return;
        }
}

/**
 * Helper method for adding text to the end
 * of the text area
 * @param s - text to add
 */
void insertString (String s) {

    content.insertText (s, insertPos);
    insertPos += s.length ();
}

/**
 * Application entry point
 * @param args - command line arguments
 */
public static void main (String args[]) {

    new Ping ();
}
}
```

3. Compile and test the application. Compile the source using javac or the makefile provided. Test the application by entering the following command:

```
java Ping
```

When Ping is executed, a window will open with an editable text field. Enter a host name in the text field and press ENTER. A message should soon appear in the center text area reporting the status of the remote host. Figure 9-3 shows an example of the running application. This program will run only as an application.

How It Works

There is only one source file, Ping.java. It contains only one class, *Ping*. *Ping* extends Frame so that it creates a window Frame for drawing. It also implements Runnable so that a separate thread can be used for opening the socket. This allows the user to stop the open attempt if a host does not respond.

An instance of class *Socket* is defined along with a TextField, a TextArea, a Stop button, and a Thread. The variable insertPos maintains the current insert position for the TextArea.

The *Ping* constructor creates the user interface with a separate Panel for the host name TextField and the Stop button. This Panel is added to the top of the application Frame. The TextArea is added to the center of the application Frame. An instance of the thread is created for use later.

The *action()* method overrides the default *action()* method for handling action events. If the user enters a new host name and presses ENTER, the thread currently running is stopped, and a new thread is created and started.

The *run()* method contains the code for the thread. When it starts, it gets the host name from the TextField using *TextField.getText()* and attempts to open a socket with

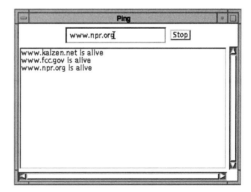

Figure 9-3 Ping application

the given host name and port number 23. This version of the *Socket* constructor throws *UnknownHostException*, which must be caught. If this exception occurs, the host name along with "unknown host" is displayed. The *Socket* constructor also throws IOException in the event that a network-related error occurred. This must also be caught. An error message is displayed in this case.

If no exceptions are thrown, the socket was successfully opened, meaning the remote host is running with a waiting telnet daemon. A "host is alive" message is printed, and the socket is closed by using the *Socket.close()* method. *Socket.close()* throws *IOException*, which must be caught. An error message is printed in this case for completeness.

The *insertString()* method inserts a given string at the end of the TextArea. It adds the length of the string to insertPos to maintain the end position of the text.

Comments

The UNIX ping utility performs more sophisticated communication tests to determine if a host is running. This program is sufficient for most cases, but will fail if a telnet daemon is not running or not responding. The program could be extended to test for other ports like time, mail, and http.

COMPLEXITY
ADVANCED

9.4   How do I...
Access a stream?

Problem

I want to write a Telnet program. I want to have a TextField at the top in which I can enter the host name and a terminal-like area at the bottom. I know how to handle keystrokes and how to print characters. I learned how to open a socket from example 9.3, but I need to read and write data to the socket. How do I access a stream?

Technique

To access a stream, a socket must first be opened. This is easily done by using the techniques of example 9.3. Once the socket is open, the input and output streams associated with the socket can be accessed by invoking the *Socket.getInputStream()* and the *Socket.getOutputStream()* methods, respectively. These methods do not take any arguments. Data is transferred by using the methods found in the *InputStream* and *OutputStream* classes.

Steps

1. Create the application source file. Create a new file called Telnet.java and enter the following source:

```java
import java.awt.*;
import java.io.*;
import java.net.*;

/*
 * Class for the "terminal" panel
 */
class Content extends Panel implements Runnable {

/*
 * The maximum number of characters for one line
 */
final int MaxChars = 128;

/*
 * The current line of text
 */
String text;

/*
 * Off-screen image for double buffering
 */
Image offImage;

/*
 * Off-screen graphics object associated with offImage
 */
Graphics offg;

/*
 * Size of this panel
 */
Dimension panelSize;

/*
 * The socket used for communication to the remote host
 */
Socket socket;

/*
 * Input stream instance
 */
InputStream in;

/*
 * Output stream instance
 */
```

continued on next page

continued from previous page

```
OutputStream out;

/*
 * Thread used to decouple user activity
 * from socket activity
 */
Thread thread;

/*
 * Host name text entry field
 */
TextField addrField;

/*
 * Set to True if local echo should be done.
 */
boolean echoKeys;

/**
 * Constructor saves variables and creates thread.
 * @param t - address text field
 */
public Content (TextField t) {

    text = "";
    thread = new Thread (this);
    addrField = t;
    echoKeys = false;
}

/**
 * Request the keyboard focus if mouse is clicked.
 * @param evt - event object
 * @param x, y - x and y position of mouse
 */
public boolean mouseDown (Event evt, int x, int y) {

    requestFocus ();
    return true;
}

/**
 * If a key is pressed, send it to the remote host.
 * Echo the character if necessary.
 * @param evt - event object
 * @param key - the key pressed
 */
public boolean keyDown (Event evt, int key) {

    writeChar (key);
    if (echoKeys) insertChar (key);
    return true;
```

```
}

/**
 * Print a character in the content "terminal" area.
 * @param c - the character to insert
 */
void insertChar (int c)
{
    int textLength;
    panelSize = size ();

    switch (c) {
        case '\n':
            offg.copyArea (0, 20, panelSize.width, panelSize.height,
            0, -20);
            offg.clearRect (0, panelSize.height-20, panelSize.width,
            20);
            text = "";
            break;

        default:
            text += (char)c;
            offg.drawString (text, 10, panelSize.height-10);
            break;
    }

    repaint ();
}

/**
 * Inserts a string into content area
 * @param s - string to insert
 */
void insertString (String s) {

    int i;

    for (i=0; i<s.length(); i+=1) insertChar (s.charAt (i));
}

/**
 * Copy off-screen image to the screen.
 * @param g - destination graphics object
 */
public void update (Graphics g) {

    g.drawImage (offImage, 0, 0, this);
}

/**
 * Save panel size and create off-screen image.
 */
```

continued on next page

continued from previous page

```java
void init () {

    panelSize = size ();
    offImage = createImage (panelSize.width, panelSize.height);
    offg = offImage.getGraphics ();
}

/**
 * Read a character from the remote host.
 */
int readChar () {

    int c;

    try {
        c = in.read ();
    } catch (IOException e) {
        c = ' ';
    }
    return c;
}

/**
 * Write a character to the remote host.
 * @param c - character to write
 */
void writeChar (int c) {

    try {
        out.write (c);
        out.flush ();
    } catch (IOException e) {
    }
}

/**
 * Thread that waits for characters from remote host
 */
public void run () {

    try {
        try {
            socket = new Socket (addrField.getText (), 23);
        } catch (UnknownHostException e) {
            insertString ("Unknown host\n");
            return;
        }
    } catch (IOException e2) {
        insertString ("Unable to open socket\n");
        return;
    }

    try {
        in = socket.getInputStream ();
```

```
        out = socket.getOutputStream ();
    } catch (IOException e) {
        insertString ("Unable to open streams\n");
        return;
    }

    while (true) {

        int c;
        int cmd;
        int opt;

        c = readChar ();
        if (c == -1) {
        // Error during read. Most likely the connection is closed.
            break;
        }

        if (c == 255) {
        // Process Telnet IAC message.
            cmd = readChar ();
            switch (cmd) {
                case 250:
                    // Ignore SB data from other side
                    opt = readChar();
                    while (readChar () != 240);
                            break;

                case 251:    // WILL <option>
                    opt = readChar();
                    break;

                case 252:    // WON'T <option>
                    opt = readChar();
                    break;

                case 253:    // DO <option>
                    opt = readChar();

                    switch (opt) {
                        case 1:          // Local echo
                            if (cmd == 251) echoKeys = true;
                            else if (cmd == 252) echoKeys = false;
                            break;

                        case 24:    // Terminal type
                            // Send IAC, WILL terminal type
                                    writeChar (255);
                            writeChar (251);
                            writeChar (24);
                            // Send IAC, SB terminal-type IS "dumb" IAC

                            writeChar (255);
```

SE

continued on next page

continued from previous page

```
                                writeChar (250);
                                writeChar (24);
                                writeChar (0);
                                writeChar ((int) 'd');
                                writeChar ((int) 'u');
                                writeChar ((int) 'm');
                                writeChar ((int) 'b');
                                        writeChar (255);
                                        writeChar (240);
                                break;

                    default:
                    // For all other options, respond with
                    // IAC WON'T <opt>.
                        writeChar(255);
                        writeChar(252);
                        writeChar(opt);
                        break;
                    }
                break;

            case 254:    // DON'T <option>
                opt = readChar();

                // Send IAC WON'T <opt>.
                writeChar(255);
                writeChar(252);
                writeChar(opt);
                break;

            default:
                // Don t know what to do
                break;
            }

        }
        if (c >= ' ' && c <= '~') {
            insertChar (c);
        }
        else {
            switch (c) {
                case 8:
                case 10:
                case 13:
                    insertChar (c);
                    break;
            }
        }
    }
}
}

/**
```

```
 * Application class
 */
public class Telnet extends Frame {

/*
 * Remote host Internet host name
 */
TextField addrField;

Button openButton;
Button closeButton;

/*
 * Instance of content
 */
Content content;

/*
 * Constructor
 * Creates user interface and instance of content
 */
public Telnet () {

    int i;

    setTitle ("Telnet");
    setLayout(new BorderLayout());

    addrField = new TextField ("", 20);

    resize (500, 500);

    Panel p1 = new Panel ();
    p1.setLayout (new FlowLayout ());
    p1.add (new Label ("Address"));
    p1.add (addrField);
    p1.add (openButton = new Button ("Open"));
    p1.add (closeButton = new Button ("Close"));

    add ("North", p1);

    content = new Content (addrField);
    add ("Center", content);

    show ();
    content.init ();
}

/**
 * Handle open and return key strikes.
 * @param evt - event object
 * @param arg - object receiving event
 */
```

continued on next page

continued from previous page

```java
public boolean action (Event evt, Object arg) {

    if (evt.target == openButton || evt.target == addrField) {
        content.thread.stop ();
        content.thread = new Thread (content);
        content.thread.start ();
    }

    return true;
}

/**
 * Application entry point
 * @param args - command line arguments
 */
public static void main (String args[]) {

    new Telnet ();
}
}
```

2. Compile and test the application. Compile the source using javac or the makefile provided.

Telnet.java must be run as an application by typing

`java Telnet`

When Telnet is executed, a window will open with an editable text field on top and a blank area in the center. Enter a host name in the text field and press [ENTER]. If a telnet connection is successfully made, the remote host will respond in the center area. Figure 9-4 shows an example of the running applet.

How It Works

Telnet.java contains two classes: *Content* and *Telnet*. The *Content* class runs as a separate thread, manages data transfer to the host, and displays text from the telnet session. The *Telnet* class contains the *main()* method and manages the content thread.

The *Content* class contains a variable, *text,* which is a string representation of the current line of text. The characters in the string come from either the keyboard or the remote host. An off-screen image is maintained for smooth repainting. Other variables include an instance of *Socket, InputStream,* and *OutputStream* for reading and writing data to the socket, a thread, an instance of the host name TextField, and a flag for implementing local echo.

The *Content* constructor clears the current line of text, creates an instance of Thread, saves the host name TextField passed to it from the *Telnet* class, and sets local echo to False. The host name TextField is needed to access the host name when a session is started.

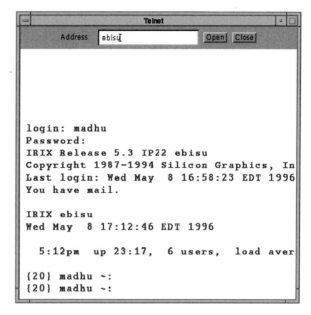

Figure 9-4 Telnet application

The *mouseDown( )* method overrides the default *mouseDown( )* method and requests focus for this Panel. This is used when a session is started to allow the user to move the focus from the host name TextField to the content area.

The *keyDown( )* method takes input keystrokes and sends them to the remote host by calling *writeChar( )*. It also displays these characters if local echo is enabled by calling *insertChar( )*.

The *insertChar( )* method adds the character passed to it to the current line of text. This line is drawn on the bottom of the off-screen image by using *drawImage( )*, and a repaint is forced. Line feeds are handled differently. When *insertChar( )* detects a line feed, it scrolls all lines up one line using the *Graphics.copyArea( )* method. The bottom line is erased by calling *Graphics.clearRect( )*. The current line of text is also discarded.

The *insertString( )* method inserts a string into the content area by calling the *insertChar( )* method for each character in the string argument.

The *readChar( )* and *writeChar( )* methods read and write single characters to the remote host. These methods will block if no characters are available from the remote host, or the output buffer is full.

The *run( )* method manages data transfer. It is called when the *Telnet* class starts the *Content* thread. The *run( )* method first tries to open a socket to the remote host using the *Socket* constructor. If an error occurs, the *run( )* method returns and the thread dies. The input and output streams associated with the socket are obtained by calling *Socket.getInputStream( )* and *Socket.getOutputStream( )*, respectively. These are saved for use in *readChar( )* and *writeChar( )*.

If no errors occur, the *run()* method enters an infinite loop in which it waits for characters from the remote host. Printable characters along with line feeds are printed by calling *insertChar()*. A number of special characters control a variety of telnet options. Details of the protocol may be found in text detailing Internet protocols or in Internet RFCs.

The *Telnet* class creates the user interface and an instance of the *Content* class. It handles TextField and button events by stopping the *Content* thread, creating a new one, and starting it.

COMPLEXITY
ADVANCED

9.5 How do I...
Receive data via HTTP?

Problem

I want to write an application that will show the document source, given a URL. I want to enter the URL in a TextField and display the document source corresponding to that URL in a noneditable TextArea. I know how to program the user interface, but I do not know how to access data via HTTP. How do I access data via HTTP?

Technique

Reading data via HTTP is similar to reading data from any other data input stream. First a URL must be created by using the *URL* constructor. A URL connection must be created by using the *openConnection()* method in the *URL* class. The input stream associated with *URLConnection* can be retrieved by using the *GetInputStream()* method. At this point data can be read from the data input stream by using methods contained in the *Data InputStream* class.

A separate thread is used to isolate stream activity from user input. In this way data can be read asynchronously. If the user presses the Stop button, stream activity can be terminated.

Steps

1. Create the application source file. Create a new file called ViewSource.java and enter the following source:

```
import java.awt.*;
import java.io.*;
import java.net.*;

/*
 * Application class
 */
```

```java
public class ViewSource extends Frame implements Runnable {

String s;

/*
 * The URL to get data from
 */
URL u;

/*
 * Connection to URL
 */
URLConnection uc;

/*
 * URL input text field
 */
TextField location;

/*
 * Text area for displaying document source
 */
TextArea content;

/*
 * Separate thread is used to read the document
 */
Thread thread;

/*
 * Content area insert position
 */
int insertPos = 0;

/**
 * Constructor creates user interface.
 */
public ViewSource () {

    int i;

    setTitle ("View Source");
    setLayout(new BorderLayout());

    location = new TextField ("", 20);
    content = new TextArea ("", 24, 80);
    content.setEditable (false);

    Panel p = new Panel ();
    p.setLayout (new FlowLayout ());
    p.add (location);
    p.add (new Button ("Stop"));

    add ("North", p);
```

continued on next page

continued from previous page

```
    add ("Center", content);

    thread = new Thread (this);

    resize (400, 300);
    show ();
}

/**
 * Handle return key strikes and Stop button.
 * @param e - event object
 */
public boolean handleEvent(Event e) {

    if ((e.target instanceof TextField)
        && (e.id == Event.ACTION_EVENT)) {

        thread.stop ();
        content.replaceText ("", 0, insertPos);
        thread = new Thread (this);
        thread.start ();

        return true;
    }
    if ((e.target instanceof Button)
        && (e.id == Event.ACTION_EVENT)) {

        thread.stop ();

        return true;
    }
    return false;
}

/*
 * Thread that reads data from the URL and displays
 * it in the content area
 */
public void run () {

    try {
        u = new URL (location.getText ());
    } catch (MalformedURLException e) {
    }

    try {
        uc = u.openConnection();
    } catch (IOException e) {
    }

    DataInputStream in = null;
    try {
        in = new DataInputStream (new BufferedInputStream (
            uc.getInputStream()));
    } catch(IOException e) {
```

```
    }

    String line;

    insertPos = 0;
    try {
        while ((line = in.readLine()) != null)
        {
            line += "\n";
            content.insertText (line, insertPos);
            insertPos += line.length ();
        }
    } catch(IOException e) {
        System.out.println("Error in reading file");
    }
}

/**
 * Application entry point
 * @param args - command line arguments
 */
public static void main (String args[]) {

    new ViewSource ();
}
}
```

2. Compile and test the application. Compile the source using javac or the makefile provided. Test the application by typing

```
java ViewSource
```

When *ViewSource* is executed, a window will open with an editable text field on top and a noneditable text area in the middle. Enter the complete URL (including http://) in the text field and press ENTER. If all goes well, the document source should appear in the noneditable text area. Figure 9-5 shows an example of the running application.

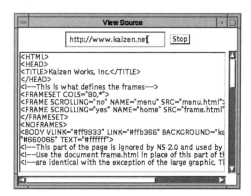

Figure 9-5 ViewSource application

How It Works

The ViewSource application contains only one class, the application itself. The class extends Frame in order to create a window Frame for itself. The class implements Runnable so that a separate thread for stream access can be created.

The *ViewSource* constructor first sets the window title and then sets the layout for the Frame as BorderLayout. A Panel is created to contain a TextField for the document URL and a Stop button. This Panel uses FlowLayout to keep the TextField and the Button on one line. This Panel is added to the top of the Frame. A noneditable TextArea is created and is placed in the center of the Frame. The TextArea is used to display the document source. Finally the variable thread is initialized with a valid instance of Thread.

The *handleEvent()* method responds to user-generated events. When the user enters a URL in the TextField and presses ENTER, the stream-reading thread is stopped, and the TextArea is erased. A new stream-reading thread is created and started. If the user presses the Stop button, the stream-reading thread is simply stopped.

The *run()* method first creates an instance of *URL* using the URL entered by the user in the TextField as an argument. The *URL* constructor throws *MalformedURLException*, which must be caught. Next, a *URLConnection* is created by invoking the *URL.openConnection()* method. This throws IOException. Next, the data input stream associated with the *URLConnection* is retrieved by using the *getInputStream()* method. This also throws *IOException*. Finally, data is read from the input stream via the *readLine()* method in the *DataInputStream class*. This also throws *IOException*. This data is inserted into the TextArea for display.

COMPLEXITY
INTERMEDIATE

9.6   How do I...
Create a server socket?

Problem

The PhoneBook application in Chapter 6 is very useful if names and numbers can be kept on a local hard disk. I would like to make a networked version of the application. The phone book file would be kept on a remote server. The application client would connect to a server program, which sends the contents of the file to the PhoneBook application. The server program should also be able to save the file if the user wants to update the phone book.

I know how to create sockets and access streams, but I need to create a server program that listens on a unique port for connections to the client. I need to send and receive data from the socket. I don't know how to create a server socket. How do I create a server socket?

Technique

Two programs are necessary: the client and the server. The client is very similar to the PhoneBook application in Chapter 6. The only significant difference is that data is read and written to a socket as opposed to a file. The server uses the *ServerSocket* class contained in the java.net package. *ServerSocket* contains an *accept()* method that listens to a specified port and establishes a socket connection when the client opens a socket with the same port number. The *accept()* method returns a Socket object when a connection is made. The connection may be closed from either end by calling *Socket.close()*.

Steps

1. Create the client source file. Create a new file called PhoneBook.java and enter the following source:

```java
import java.applet.Applet;
import java.awt.*;
import java.io.*;
import java.net.*;
import java.util.StringTokenizer;

/**
 * Phone book application class
 * Demonstrates the use of server sockets
 */
public class PhoneBook extends Frame {

/*
 * The port for reading the phone book data from
 */
final int InPort = 7000;

/*
 * The port for writing the phone book data
 */
final int OutPort = 7001;

/*
 * The maximum number of phone numbers
 */
final int MaxNumbers = 25;

/*
 * An instance of list box
 */
List phoneList;

/*
 * The button instances
```

continued on next page

continued from previous page

```
 */
Button addButton;
Button deleteButton;
Button findButton;
Button saveButton;

/*
 * The text field instances
 */
TextField nameField;
TextField phoneField;
TextField emailField;

/*
 * An array of strings that holds all of the
 * phone numbers
 */
String data[] = new String[MaxNumbers];
int NNumbers = 15;

/*
 * The name of the remote host serving the data
 */
String hostName;

/*
 * Constructor
 * Add all user interface components
 * and read data from socket.
 * Display names in the list box.
 */
public PhoneBook (String host) {

    int i;

    setTitle ("Phone book");
    setLayout (new BorderLayout ());

    Panel buttonPanel = new Panel ();
    buttonPanel.setLayout (new FlowLayout ());
    buttonPanel.add (findButton = new Button ("Find name"));
    buttonPanel.add (addButton = new Button ("Add"));
    buttonPanel.add (deleteButton = new Button ("Delete"));
    buttonPanel.add (saveButton = new Button ("Save"));

    Panel fieldPanel = new Panel ();
    fieldPanel.setLayout (new GridLayout (6, 1, 5, 5));
    fieldPanel.add (new Label ("Name"));
    fieldPanel.add (nameField = new TextField ("", 32));
    fieldPanel.add (new Label ("Phone number"));
    fieldPanel.add (phoneField = new TextField ("", 32));
    fieldPanel.add (new Label ("Email address"));
```

```
    fieldPanel.add (emailField = new TextField ("", 32));

    phoneList = new List (5, false);

    Socket fs = null;

    hostName = host;
    if (hostName == null) hostName = "synapses";
        try {
                fs = new Socket (hostName, InPort);
        } catch (Exception e) {
                System.out.println ("Unable to open socket");
                System.exit (1);
        }

    DataInputStream ds = null;

        try {
        ds = new DataInputStream (fs.getInputStream ());
    } catch (IOException e) {
        System.out.println (e);
                System.exit (1);
        }

    NNumbers = 0;
    for (i=0; i<MaxNumbers; i+=1) {
                try {
                        data[i] = ds.readLine ();
                        if (data[i] == null) break;
            NNumbers += 1;
                } catch (IOException e) {
                        System.out.println ("Exception caught reading
file.");
                        break;
                }
        StringTokenizer st = new StringTokenizer (data[i], ":\t");
        phoneList.addItem (st.nextToken ());
    }
        try {
                fs.close ();
        } catch (IOException e) {
                System.out.println ("Exception caught closing socket.");
        }

    add ("North", buttonPanel);
    add ("South", fieldPanel);
    add ("Center", phoneList);

    resize (300, 400);
    show ();
}

/*
```

continued on next page

continued from previous page

```
 * Handle button presses and list box select events.
 */
public boolean action (Event evt, Object arg) {

    int i;
    StringTokenizer st;
    String dname;
    String tname;

    tname = nameField.getText ();
    if (evt.target == findButton || evt.target == nameField) {
        for (i=0; i<NNumbers; i+=1) {
            st = new StringTokenizer (data[i], ":\t");
            dname = st.nextToken ();
            if (contains (tname, dname)) {
                phoneList.select (i);
                nameField.setText (dname);
                phoneField.setText (st.nextToken ());
                emailField.setText (st.nextToken ());
                break;
            }
        }
        return true;
    }

    if (evt.target == addButton) {
        if (NNumbers < MaxNumbers) {
            tname = nameField.getText ();
            dname = tname + ":" + phoneField.getText() +
                ":" + emailField.getText();
            data[NNumbers] = dname;
            NNumbers += 1;
            phoneList.addItem (tname);
        }
        return true;
    }

    if (evt.target == deleteButton) {
        i = phoneList.getSelectedIndex ();
        phoneList.delItem (i);
        for (; i<NNumbers-1; i+=1) data[i] = data[i+1];
        NNumbers -= 1;
        nameField.setText ("");
        phoneField.setText ("");
        emailField.setText ("");
        return true;
    }

    if (evt.target == saveButton) {
        Socket fs = null;

            try {
            fs = new Socket (hostName, OutPort);
        } catch (Exception e) {
```

```
            System.out.println ("Unable to open socket");
            System.exit (1);
        }
        PrintStream ps = null;
        try {
            ps = new PrintStream (fs.getOutputStream ());
        } catch (Exception e) {
            System.out.println (e);
            System.exit (1);
        }

        for (i=0; i<NNumbers; i+=1) {
            ps.println (data[i]);
                }
        try {
            fs.close ();
        } catch (IOException e) {
            System.out.println (e);
        }
        return true;
    }

    if (evt.target == phoneList) {
        i = phoneList.getSelectedIndex ();
        st = new StringTokenizer (data[i], ":\t");
        nameField.setText (st.nextToken ());
        phoneField.setText (st.nextToken ());
        emailField.setText (st.nextToken ());
        return true;
    }

    return false;
}

/*
 * contains method is a fuzzy string compare that returns True
 * if either string is completely contained in the other one.
 *      String s1, s2 - two strings to compare
 */
boolean contains (String s1, String s2) {

        int i;
        int l1 = s1.length ();
        int l2 = s2.length ();

        if (l1 < l2) {
                for (i=0; i<=l2-l1; i+=1)
                        if (s1.regionMatches (true, 0, s2, i, l1))
                                return true;
        }
        for (i=0; i<=l1-l2; i+=1)
                if (s2.regionMatches (true, 0, s1, i, l2))
```

continued on next page

continued from previous page

```
                          return true;

         return false;
}

/**
 * Application entry point
 * The first command line argument is the remote host name.
 * @param args - command line arguments
 */
public static void main (String args[]) {

    if (args.length == 1) new PhoneBook (args[0]);
    else new PhoneBook (null);
}
}
```

2. Create the server source file. Create a new file called PhoneServer.java and
enter the following source:

```
import java.net.*;
import java.io.*;

/*
 * The server side of the application
 * creates instances of InServer and OutServer.
 */
public class PhoneServer {

static final int OutPort = 7000;
static final int InPort = 7001;

/**
 * Application entry point
 * @param args - command line arguments
 */
public static void main (String args[]) {

    OutServer outServer = new OutServer (OutPort);
    InServer inServer = new InServer (InPort);
}
}

/*
 * Class creates a server socket for writing data to
 * the client.
 */
class OutServer implements Runnable {

/*
 * Instance of ServerSocket
 */
```

```
ServerSocket server = null;

/*
 * The actual socket used for writing
 */
Socket socket = null;

/*
 * A PrintStream is used for writing.
 */
PrintStream stream = null;
int thePort;

/*
 * A separate thread is used to wait for a
 * socket accept.
 */
Thread thread;

/**
 * Constructor starts the thread
 * @param port - the port to listen to
 */
public OutServer (int port) {

    thePort = port;
    thread = new Thread (this);
    thread.start ();
}

/*
 * The thread that waits for socket
 * connections and writes data to the client
 */
public void run () {

    try {
        server = new ServerSocket (thePort);
    } catch (Exception e) {
        System.out.println (e);
        System.exit (1);
    }

    while (true) {
        try {
            socket = server.accept ();
        } catch (Exception e) {
            System.out.println (e);
            System.exit (1);
        }
        try {
            stream = new PrintStream (socket.getOutputStream ());
        } catch (Exception e) {
```

continued on next page

continued from previous page

```
                System.out.println (e);
                System.exit (1);
        }

        FileInputStream fs = null;

            try {
            fs = new FileInputStream ("PhoneBook.txt");
        } catch (Exception e) {
            System.out.println (e);
            System.exit (1);
        }
        DataInputStream ds = new DataInputStream (fs);
        while (true) {
            try {
                String s = ds.readLine ();
                if (s == null) break;
                stream.println (s);
                    } catch (IOException e) {
                System.out.println (e);
                break;
            }
        }
        try {
            fs.close ();
            socket.close ();
        } catch (IOException e) {
            System.out.println (e);
        }
    }
}
}

/*
 * Class creates a server socket for reading data from
 * the client.
 */
class InServer implements Runnable {

/*
 * Instance of ServerSocket
 */
ServerSocket server = null;

/*
 * The actual socket used for reading
 */
Socket socket = null;

/*
 * A DataInputStream is used for reading.
 */
DataInputStream stream = null;
```

```
int thePort;

/*
 * A separate thread is used to wait for a
 * socket accept.
 */
Thread thread;

/**
 * Constructor starts the thread.
 * @param port - the port to listen to
 */
public InServer (int port) {

    thePort = port;
    thread = new Thread (this);
    thread.start ();
}

/*
 * The thread that waits for socket
 * connections and reads data from the client
 */
public void run () {

    try {
        server = new ServerSocket (thePort);
    } catch (Exception e) {
        System.out.println (e);
        System.exit (1);
    }

    while (true) {
        try {
            socket = server.accept ();
        } catch (Exception e) {
            System.out.println (e);
            System.exit (1);
        }
        try {
            stream = new DataInputStream (socket.getInputStream ());
        } catch (Exception e) {
            System.out.println (e);
            System.exit (1);
        }

        FileOutputStream fs = null;

            try {
            fs = new FileOutputStream ("PhoneBook.txt");
        } catch (Exception e) {
            System.out.println (e);
            System.exit (1);
        }
```

continued on next page

continued from previous page

```
        PrintStream ds = new PrintStream (fs);
        while (true) {
            try {
                String s = stream.readLine ();
                if (s == null) break;
                ds.println (s);
                    } catch (IOException e) {
                System.out.println (e);
                break;
            }
        }
        try {
            fs.close ();
            socket.close ();
        } catch (IOException e) {
            System.out.println (e);
        }
    }
}
}
```

3. Compile and test the application. Compile the source using javac or the makefile provided. Test the application by first starting the server and then start the client. Start the server by typing

`java PhoneServer`

This should be run in the background. Start the client by typing

`java PhoneBook <server hostname>`

When the application is started, a window with a list box and several buttons and text fields should appear. Names and phone numbers should appear in the list box. Names, numbers, and e-mail addresses can be modified; new numbers can be added also. Figure 9-6 shows an example of the running application.

How It Works

The client and server use two sockets: one for client-to-server transfers, and one for server-to-client transfers. This is done to simplify the end of transmission. When either side has completed its data transfer, it closes the socket. The other side sees this as an end of file.

The client is contained in the file PhoneBook.java. It is similar to PhoneBook.java found in the list box example of How-To 6.7. The primary difference is in the data reading and writing. The PhoneBook constructor tries to open a socket to the server given by the command line argument. It uses the server-to-client port. If it succeeds, a *DataInputStream* is created from the socket input stream. A *DataInputStream* is used because it contains a *readLine()* method. The data is read into an array like before.

Figure 9-6 PhoneServer
application

When all data is read, *readLine()* returns null because the server closes the socket. The client then closes its socket.

When the client saves the phone book, it tries to open a socket using the client-to-server port. If it succeeds, it creates a PrintStream from the socket output stream. PrintStream is used because it contains a *println()* method. The data from the data array is written to the socket, and when it is finished, the socket is closed. The server sees this as an end of file and closes its socket.

The server is contained in the file PhoneServer.java. It contains three classes: the *PhoneServer* class, which contains the *main()* method; the *OutServer* class, which handles server-to-client transfers; and the *InServer* class, which handles client-to-server transfers. Both *InServer* and *OutServer* are run as independent threads.

The *main()* method in the *PhoneServer* class creates instances of *InServer* and *OutServer*. *InServer* uses *InPort* as its socket port. *OutServer* uses *OutPort* as its socket port.

An *OutServer* contains instances of *ServerSocket*, *Socket*, *PrintStream*, and *Thread*. The *OutServer* constructor simply creates a new thread and starts it.

The *run()* method first creates a *ServerSocket* by invoking the *ServerSocket* constructor with the port number as an argument. The *ServerSocket* constructor throws an *IOException*, which must be caught. An exception is raised if the specified port is in use. The *run()* method then enters an infinite loop in which it waits for a connection by calling *ServerSocket.accept()*. This method will block until a connection is made by the client. When a connection is made, *ServerSocket.accept()* returns a *Socket*, which is a connection to the client. A *PrintStream* associated with the socket is created, and the PhoneBook.txt file is opened for reading. The data is read from the PhoneBook.txt file and written to the socket using *DataStream.readLine()* and *PrintStream.println()*, respectively.

When end of file is detected, the socket and the file are closed. The socket closure will look like an end of file to the client. When this is all complete, the *run()* method calls *ServerSocket.accept()* again to wait for another connection.

The *InServer* class is similar to the *OutServer* class. The only difference is the port number it listens to and the direction of data flow. The *run()* method contained in the *InServer* class waits for a connection, creates a *DataInputStream* associated with the socket, and opens the PhoneBook.txt file for writing. Data is read from the socket and written to the file. When an end of file is detected from the socket, both the socket and the file are closed. The *run()* method then waits for another connection and the cycle repeats.

Comments

A single socket could have been used instead of using two. A protocol would have to be defined to specify the direction of data transfer.

This implementation is more or less "connectionless," meaning connections are made only when data is transferred. This allows many clients to be served by a single server. The alternative is to maintain a connection until the client has finished all transactions, that is, the client application exits.

One improvement would be to spawn threads when a connection is made. This would allow multiple clients to connect simultaneously. Clearly, file locking would have to be done during file access to avoid unpredictable results.

Some security measures should be considered before this application is put into general use, as anyone could add or delete records from the phone book. A password field is one solution.

COMPLEXITY
INTERMEDIATE

9.7 How do I...
Determine the name of the host running my applet?

Problem

I want to know who has run my applets. I want to write an applet that will determine the name of the host that it is running on and send it back to the server for logging. I know how to create a server that can wait for a connection and save data, but I don't know how to determine the host the applet is running on. How do I determine the name of the host running my applet?

Technique

The InetAddress class contains a static method called *getLocalHost()*. This method returns an InetAddress that is the address of the local host, which is the host running the applet. The method *InetAddress.toString()* can be used to return the name and IP numbers contained in the InetAddress as a string.

The name can be sent to the host and logged by creating a server using ServerSocket to listen to a specific port, similar to example 9.6. When the server makes a connection and receives the name, it appends it to a file with a time stamp.

Steps

1. Create the applet source file. Create a new file called HostName.java and enter the following source:

```java
import java.applet.Applet;
import java.awt.*;
import java.io.*;
import java.net.*;

/*
 * the applet class for determining the name
 * of the host running the applet
 */
public class HostName extends Applet {

final int logPort = 7000;

/*
 * the client name running this applet
 */
String hostName;

/*
 * called when the applet is loaded
 * get local host name and report it to the
 * server
 */
public void init () {

    try {
        hostName = InetAddress.getLocalHost().toString ();
    } catch (UnknownHostException e) {
        hostName = "Unknown Host";
    }

    Socket fs = null;

        try {
```

continued on next page

continued from previous page

```
        fs = new Socket (this.getCodeBase().getHost(), logPort);
    } catch (Exception e) {
        System.out.println (e);
    }

    PrintStream ps = null;
    try {
        ps = new PrintStream (fs.getOutputStream ());
    } catch (Exception e) {
        System.out.println (e);
        System.exit (1);
    }

    ps.println (hostName);
    try {
        fs.close ();
    } catch (IOException e) {
        System.out.println (e);
    }

    repaint (1000);
}

/**
 * just draw the name of the local host
 * @param g - destination graphics object
 */
public void paint (Graphics g) {

    g.drawString (hostName, 10, 50);
}

}
```

2. Create the server source file. Create a new file called LogServer.java and enter the following source:

```
import java.net.*;
import java.io.*;
import java.util.Date;

/*
 * The server side of the application
 * Creates instance of InServer
 */
public class LogServer {

static final int InPort = 7000;

/**
 * Application entry point
 * @param args - command line arguments
 */
```

```
public static void main (String args[]) {

    InServer inServer = new InServer (InPort);
}
}

/*
 * Class creates a server socket for reading data from
 * the client.
 */
class InServer implements Runnable {

/*
 * The maximum number of data lines
 */
final int MaxData = 50;

/*
 * Instance of ServerSocket
 */
ServerSocket server = null;

/*
 * The actual socket used for reading
 */
Socket socket = null;

/*
 * A DataInputStream is used for reading.
 */
DataInputStream stream = null;
int thePort;

/*
 * A separate thread is used to wait for a
 * socket accept.
 */
Thread thread;

/*
 * The array of strings holds the data sent
 * from the client applet.
 */
String data[] = new String[MaxData];

/**
 * Constructor starts the thread.
 * @param port - the port to listen to
 */
public InServer (int port) {

    thePort = port;
```

continued on next page

continued from previous page

```
        thread = new Thread (this);
        thread.start ();
}

/*
 * The thread that waits for socket
 * connections and reads data from the client
 * and saves it into a file.
 */
public void run () {

    try {
        server = new ServerSocket (thePort);
    } catch (Exception e) {
        System.out.println (e);
        System.exit (1);
    }

    while (true) {
        try {
            socket = server.accept ();
        } catch (Exception e) {
            System.out.println (e);
            System.exit (1);
        }
        try {
            stream = new DataInputStream (socket.getInputStream ());
        } catch (Exception e) {
            System.out.println (e);
            System.exit (1);
        }

        FileInputStream fi = null;

            try {
            fi = new FileInputStream ("LogFile.txt");
        } catch (Exception e) {
                    System.out.println (e);
                    System.exit (1);
            }
            DataInputStream di = new DataInputStream (fi);

        int NLines = 0;
        int i;

        for (i=0; i<MaxData; i+=1) {
                    try {
                            data[i] = di.readLine ();
                            if (data[i] == null) break;
                NLines += 1;
                    } catch (IOException e) {
                            System.out.println (e);
                            break;
                    }
```

```
        }
            try {
                    fi.close ();
            } catch (IOException e) {
                    System.out.println (e);
            }

        FileOutputStream fs = null;

            try {
            fs = new FileOutputStream ("LogFile.txt");
        } catch (Exception e) {
            System.out.println (e);
            System.exit (1);
        }
        PrintStream ds = new PrintStream (fs);

        if (NLines >= MaxData) NLines = MaxData - 1;

        for (i=0; i<NLines; i+=1) {
            ds.println (data[i]);
        }
        try {
            String s = stream.readLine ();
            ds.println (s + "\t" + new Date ());
        } catch (IOException e) {
            System.out.println (e);
        }
        try {
            fs.close ();
            socket.close ();
        } catch (IOException e) {
            System.out.println (e);
        }
    }
}
}
```

3. Create an HTML document that contains the applet. Create a new file called howto97.html as follows:

```
<html>
<head>
<title>HostName</title>
</head>
<applet code="HostName.class" width=200 height=200>
</applet>
<hr size=4>

</html>
```

4. Compile and test the applet. Compile the source using javac or the makefile provided. Start the server first by typing

```
java LogServer
```

5. Test the applet using a Java-supported web browser or the Applet Viewer by entering the following command:

```
appletviewer howto97.html
```

HostName.java may also be tested as an application by typing

```
java HostName <servername>
```

When HostName is executed, a window will open displaying the local host name. Figure 9-7 shows a snapshot of the running applet.

How It Works

The HostName applet gets the local host name in the *init( )* method by calling *InetAddress.getLocalHost().toString()*. This returns a string that is the name of the local host running the applet with the IP address. This method throws *UnknownHostException*, which must be caught.

Once the local host name is known, a socket is opened to the remote server for logging. A PrintStream is created from the socket so that *println( )* can be used to send the data to the server. The host name is written and the socket is closed.

A *paint( )* method is also included, which prints the host name in the applet panel using *Graphics.drawString( )*.

The *LogServer* class creates an instance of *InServer*, which is a class similar to that in example 9.6. *InServer* implements *Runnable* so that it may run as a separate thread. The *InServer* constructor creates an instance of *Thread* and starts it.

The *run( )* method creates a ServerSocket listening on port InPort. It then enters an infinite loop that first waits for a connection using the *ServerSocket.accept( )* method. After a connection is made, the log file is opened for reading, read into an array, and closed. The file is opened again for writing, and the array is written back. The data from the socket is read by using *DataInputStream.readLine( )* and written to the file along with the current date. The file and the socket are then closed.

Figure 9-7 HostName applet

Comments

This applet could be used to log other data in addition to host name and IP numbers. An editable TextArea could be added to the applet in which the user could enter comments or other information that needs to be logged.

Other uses include limiting use of an applet to a set of machines or a particular domain. This can be useful in preventing unauthorized distribution of an applet.

CHAPTER 10
MISCELLANEOUS AND ADVANCED TOPICS

10

MISCELLANEOUS AND ADVANCED TOPICS

How do I...

All of the previous chapters covered features of the Java language and the most significant classes. This chapter covers lesser-used classes and addresses some of the issues concerning native methods and applets.

10.1   Use the Vector Class

The examples in previous chapters used fixed-length arrays. This is adequate for many applications, but often data size is not known at compile time. Linked lists could be used to handle dynamic data, as is done in other programming languages. Another, possibly more robust method, is the use of the Java vector class. The vector class creates dynamic arrays. The DrawApp application of Chapter 3 is modified to accommodate arbitrarily large amounts of data.

10.2   Create a Stack

Stacks are an important data structure used in modern programming. You could easily define a stack class with *push()* and *pop()* methods. This is not necessary, as a stack class is defined in the util package. In this example a reverse Polish notation calculator is demonstrated, which is a standard application requiring a stack.

10.3   Link Java to Other Code

There are times when the standard classes provided are not sufficient or may be too slow when interpreted. Hardware control is an example of where Java alone is not sufficient. There are mechanisms for linking native code (usually compiled C or C++) to Java. This example uses native C code to significantly improve the performance of the Mandelbrot applet/application introduced in Chapter 7.

10.4   Communicate Between Applets

Many times a single web page will contain several Java applets. It is possible for one applet to affect another applet on the same page. This How-To demonstrates communicating between applets with a scrolling text marquee that displays a string from another applet.

10.5   Translate Between Unicode and ASCII

Unlike C and C++, the standard character set used in Java is Unicode. Fortunately, the Unicode character set is very close to the ASCII character for English. This application will translate files from Unicode to ASCII and vice versa.

10.6   Keep My Applets from Being Stolen

Applets available on the Web are easily copied and duplicated for use elsewhere. A Java developer may want to limit the proliferation of applets in some way. This example demonstrates a possible method for doing so.

COMPLEXITY

ADVANCED

10.1   How do I...
Use the Vector class?

Problem

I liked the DrawApp program first introduced in Chapter 3. In that example, the number of objects that could be stored and drawn was limited to a fixed value. Although this value could be made arbitrarily large, a growable array would be more efficient. I know how to allocate fixed arrays, but I don't know how to create growable or dynamic arrays. I understand that the Vector class in the java.util package manages dynamic arrays, but I don't know how to use it. How do I use the *Vector* class?

Technique

The *Vector* class allows the Java programmer to allocate dynamic arrays that can grow on demand. Arbitrary objects can be stored in a *Vector*. A *Vector* can be sized manually, but it will automatically resize itself as needed. The initial size and incremental increase can be defined in the Vector constructor.

Steps

1. Create the application source file. Create a new file called DrawApp.java and enter the following source:

```java
import java.applet.Applet;
import java.awt.*;
import java.io.*;
import java.util.*;

/**
 * Class describing a shape
 */
class Shape {

/**
 * Constants for the shape type
 */
static final int rectType = 1;
static final int ovalType = 2;
static final int arcType = 3;
static final int polyType = 4;

/*
 * The shape type
 */
int type;

/*
 * Color for this shape
 */
Color color;
static final int MaxPoints = 10;

/*
 * Arrays of x and y points for this shape
 */
int xp[] = new int[MaxPoints];
int yp[] = new int[MaxPoints];

/*
 * The number of points in this shape
 */
int npoints;
```

continued on next page

continued from previous page

```java
/**
 * Shape constructor
 * Saves parameters
 * @param tp - shape type
 * @param n - number of points
 * @param pts[] - array of endpoints
 * @param c - color of the shape
 */
public Shape (int tp, int n, int pts[], Color c) {

    int i;
    type = tp;
    color = c;
    npoints = n < MaxPoints ? n : MaxPoints;
    if (type == polyType) {
        npoints >>= 1;
        for (i=0; i<npoints; i+=1) {
            xp[i] = pts[i << 1];
            yp[i] = pts[(i << 1) +1];
        }
    } else {
        for (i=0; i<npoints; i+=1)
            xp[i] = pts[i];
    }
}


/**
 * Draw the shape
 * @param g - destination graphics object
 */
void paint (Graphics g) {

    g.setColor (color);
    switch (type) {

    case rectType:
        g.drawRect (xp[0], xp[1], xp[2], xp[3]);
        break;

    case ovalType:
        g.drawOval (xp[0], xp[1], xp[2], xp[3]);
        break;

    case arcType:
        g.drawArc (xp[0], xp[1], xp[2], xp[3], xp[4], xp[5]);
        break;

    case polyType:
        g.drawPolygon (xp, yp, npoints);
        break;
    }
}
}
```

```java
/**
 * Application class proper
 */
public class DrawApp extends Panel {

/*
 * The maximum number of shapes allowed
 */
static final int MaxShapes = 25;

/*
 * nshapes - the number of shapes read in
 * nlines - the line number in the input file
 */
static int nshapes, nlines = 0;

/*
 * Vector object containing shapes
 */
static Vector shapeVector;

/**
 * Invoke paint() method for each shape.
 * @param g - destination graphics object
 */
public void paint (Graphics g) {

    Shape sh;

    int i;
    for (i=0; i<nshapes; i+=1) {
        sh = (Shape) shapeVector.elementAt (i);
        sh.paint (g);
    }
}

/**
 * Application entry point
 * @param args - command line arguments
 */
public static void main (String args[]) {

    String buf;
    FileInputStream fs=null;
    int i, type = 0;

    shapeVector = new Vector (100, 100);
    if (args.length != 1) {
        System.out.println ("usage: java DrawApp <file>");
        System.exit (1);
    }

/*
 * Try to open the file name specified by args[0].
 */
```

continued on next page

continued from previous page

```java
    try {
        fs = new FileInputStream (args[0]);
    } catch (Exception e) {
        System.out.println (e);
        System.exit (1);
    }

/*
 * Create a DataInputStream associated with FileInputStream fs.
 */
    DataInputStream ds = new DataInputStream (fs);
    String token;
    Color color = Color.white;
    int pts[] = new int[2 * Shape.MaxPoints];

    while (true) {
        try {
            buf = ds.readLine ();        // Read 1 line.
            if (buf == null) break;
        } catch (IOException e) {
            System.out.println (e);      // No newlines are in buf.
            break;
        }
        nlines += 1;
        StringTokenizer st = new StringTokenizer (buf);
        token = st.nextToken ();
        if (token.equals ("white")) {
            color = Color.white;
            token = st.nextToken ();
        } else if (token.equals ("lightgray")) {
            color = Color.white;
            token = st.nextToken ();
        } else if (token.equals ("gray")) {
            color = Color.gray;
            token = st.nextToken ();
        } else if (token.equals ("darkgray")) {
            color = Color.darkGray;
            token = st.nextToken ();
        } else if (token.equals ("black")) {
            color = Color.black;
            token = st.nextToken ();
        } else if (token.equals ("red")) {
            color = Color.red;
            token = st.nextToken ();
        } else if (token.equals ("pink")) {
            color = Color.pink;
            token = st.nextToken ();
        } else if (token.equals ("orange")) {
            color = Color.orange;
            token = st.nextToken ();
        } else if (token.equals ("yellow")) {
            color = Color.yellow;
            token = st.nextToken ();
```

```
    } else if (token.equals ("green")) {
        color = Color.green;
        token = st.nextToken ();
    } else if (token.equals ("magenta")) {
        color = Color.magenta;
        token = st.nextToken ();
    } else if (token.equals ("cyan")) {
        color = Color.cyan;
        token = st.nextToken ();
    } else if (token.equals ("blue")) {
        color = Color.blue;
        token = st.nextToken ();
    } else {
        System.out.println ("Unknown color: "+token);
        System.out.println ("Line "+nlines);
        System.exit (1);
    }

    int npoints = 0;
    if (token.equals ("rect")) {
        npoints = getInt (st, pts, 4);
        type = Shape.rectType;
    } else if (token.equals ("oval")) {
        npoints = getInt (st, pts, 4);
        type = Shape.ovalType;
    } else if (token.equals ("arc")) {
        npoints = getInt (st, pts, 6);
        type = Shape.arcType;
    } else if (token.equals ("poly")) {
        npoints = getInt (st, pts, Shape.MaxPoints);
        type = Shape.polyType;
    } else {
        System.out.println ("Unknown shape: "+token);
        System.out.println ("Line "+nlines);
        System.exit (1);
    }
    shapeVector.addElement (new Shape (type, npoints, pts, color));
    nshapes += 1;
}
/*
 * Close can throw an exception also, catch it for completeness.
 */
    try {
        fs.close ();
    } catch (IOException e) {
        System.out.println (e);
    }

    Frame f = new Frame ("Drawing shapes");
    DrawApp drawApp = new DrawApp ();

    f.resize (410, 430);
    f.add ("Center", drawApp);
    f.show ();
}
```

continued on next page

continued from previous page

```
/**
 * Parse points
 * @param st - StringTokenizer for current line
 * @param pts[] - array of points to be returned
 * @param nmax - maximum number of points to accept
 */
static int getInt (StringTokenizer st, int pts[], int nmax) {

    int i;
    String token;

    for (i=0; i<nmax; i+=1) {
        if (st.hasMoreTokens () == false) break;
        token = st.nextToken ();
        try {
            pts[i] = Integer.valueOf (token).intValue ();
        } catch (NumberFormatException e) {
            System.out.println (e);
            System.out.println ("line "+nlines);
            System.exit (1);
        }
    }
    return i;
}
}
```

2. Compile and test the application. Compile the source using javac or the makefile provided.

DrawApp.java must be run as an application by typing

```
java DrawApp testfile
```

When DrawApp is executed, a window will open, read in the file testfile, and draw several line objects in the window. Figure 10-1 shows an example of the running application.

How It Works

The bulk of the DrawApp application is identical to that of How-To 3.3. The main difference is the replacement of the shapes array with a Vector called shapeVector. shapeVector holds objects of type Shape.

A Vector is a growable array. Each Vector tries to optimize storage management by maintaining a capacity and a capacityIncrement. The capacity is always at least as large as the Vector size. It is usually larger, because as elements are added to the Vector, the Vector's storage increases in chunks the size of capacityIncrement. Setting the capacity to what you want before inserting a large number of objects will reduce the amount of incremental reallocation. You can safely ignore the capacity, and the Vector will still work correctly.

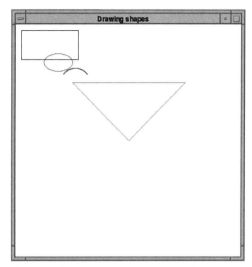

Figure 10-1 DrawApp application

The *main( )* method opens the file containing the shape definitions. The application then reads from the file one line at a time and assigns the appropriate value to color. A new element is then added to shapeVector containing the Shape constructor. Table 10-1 contains the constructors and methods contained in the Vector class. The number of shapes is then incremented and another line is read. This is repeated until the end of the file is reached or an exception occurs in FileInputStream.

The *paint( )* method retrieves the shapes from shapeVector with the *elementAt( )* method. The *elementAt( )* method returns the element at the specified index. The shape is stored in the Shape sh and then displayed.

METHOD	DESCRIPTION
Vector(int, int)	Constructs an empty vector with the specified storage capacity and the specified capacityIncrement
Vector(int)	Constructs an empty vector with the specified storage capacity
Vector()	Constructs an empty vector
addElement(Object)	Adds the specified object as the last element of the vector
capacity()	Returns the current capacity of the vector
clone()Clones this vector	Returns True if the specified object is
contains(Object)	a value of the collection
copyInto(Object[])	Copies the elements of this vector into the specified array
elementAt(int)	Returns the element at the specified index
elements()	Returns an enumeration of the elements

continued on next page

continued from previous page

METHOD	DESCRIPTION
ensureCapacity(int)	Ensures that the vector has at least the specified capacity
firstElement()	Returns the first element of the sequence
indexOf(Object)	Searches for the specified object, starting from the first position, and returns an index to it
indexOf(Object, int)	Searches for the specified object, starting at the specified position, and returns an index to it
insertElementAt(Object, int)	Inserts the specified object as an element at the specified index
isEmpty()	Returns True if the collection contains no values
lastElement()	Returns the last element of the sequence
lastIndexOf(Object)	Searches backwards for the specified object, starting from the last position, and returns an index to it
lastIndexOf(Object, int)	Searches backwards for the specified object, starting from the specified position, and returns an index to it
removeAllElements()	Removes all elements of the vector
removeElement(Object)	Removes the element from the vector
removeElementAt(int)	Deletes the element at the specified index
setElementAt(Object, int)	Sets the element at the specified index to be the specified object
setSize(int)	Sets the size of the vector
size()	Returns the number of elements in the vector
toString()	Converts the vector to a string
trimToSize()	Trims the vector's capacity down to size
capacityIncrement	The size of the increment
elementCount	The number of elements in the buffer
elementData	The buffer where elements are stored

Table 10-1 Vector class constructors and methods

COMPLEXITY
ADVANCED

10.2   How do I...
Create a stack?

Problem

I found the calculator applet/application introduced in Chapter 6 useful. That example created an infix-style calculator. I would like to use much of the code in that application and modify it so that I can make a reverse Polish notation (RPN) calculator. The algorithms for implementing an RPN-style calculator are straightforward, but a stack (last-in, first-out data structure) is needed. I noticed that a Stack class is included in the java.util package. If that can be used, much of the coding can be minimized. How do I use the *Stack* class?

Technique

The Stack class contained in the java.util package is relatively straightforward. The constructor does not take any arguments. Methods for pushing and popping are defined, as expected. Arbitrary objects can be pushed onto the stack.

The Stack class extends the Vector class, which implements a growable array, so stack size allocation and management are not necessary.

Steps

1. Create the applet source file. Create a new file called Calc.java and enter the following source:

```java
import java.util.*;
import java.awt.*;
import java.applet.*;

class Value {
    double value;
}

/**
 * An RPN calculator
 */
public class Calc extends Applet {

TextField display;
String input;
Stack stack;
Value v1 = new Value ();
Value v2 = new Value ();
Value v3 = new Value ();

/**
 *   Initialize the Calc applet.
 */
public void init () {

    setLayout(new BorderLayout());

    input = "";

    stack = new Stack ();

    display = new TextField ();
    display.setEditable (false);

    Keypad    keypad = new Keypad();
```

continued on next page

continued from previous page

```java
      add ("North", display);
      add ("Center", keypad);
}


/**
 * Handle the calculator functions.
 */
public boolean action (Event ev, Object arg) {

     if (ev.target instanceof Button) {

          String label = (String)arg;
          if (label.equals("C")) {
               input = "";
               display.setText (input);
               return true;
          }
          else if (label.equals(".")) {
               input += label;
               display.setText (input);
               return true;
          }
          else if (label.equals("+")) {
               v1 = (Value) stack.pop ();
               v2.value = Double.valueOf (input).doubleValue();
               v3.value = v1.value + v2.value;
               stack.push (v3);
               display.setText (String.valueOf (v3.value));
               input = "";
               return true;
          }
          else if (label.equals("-")) {
               v1 = (Value) stack.pop ();
               v2.value = Double.valueOf (input).doubleValue();
               v3.value = v1.value - v2.value;
               stack.push (v3);
               display.setText (String.valueOf (v3.value));
               input = "";
               return true;
          }
          else if (label.equals("x")) {
               v1 = (Value) stack.pop ();
               v2.value = Double.valueOf (input).doubleValue();
               v3.value = v1.value * v2.value;
               stack.push (v3);
               display.setText (String.valueOf (v3.value));
               input = "";
               return true;
          }
          else if (label.equals("/")) {
               v1 = (Value) stack.pop ();
               v2.value = Double.valueOf (input).doubleValue();
               v3.value = v1.value / v2.value;
               stack.push (v3);
```

```
                display.setText (String.valueOf (v3.value));
                input = "";
                return true;
            }
            else if (label.equals("+/-")) {
                return true;
            }
            else if (label.equals("Enter")) {
                try {
                    v1.value = Double.valueOf (input).doubleValue();
                } catch (NumberFormatException e) {
                    System.out.println (e);
                }
                stack.push (v1);
                input = "";
                return true;
            }
            else {
                input += label;
                display.setText (input);
                return true;
            }
        }
        return false;
    }

    /**
     * This allows the class to be used either as an applet
     * or as a stand-alone application.
     */
    public static void main (String args[]) {

        Frame f = new Frame ("Calculator");
        Calc calc = new Calc ();

        calc.init ();

        f.resize (210, 200);
        f.add ("Center", calc);
        f.show ();
    }
}

/* ------------------------------------------------ */

/**
 * The keypad handles the input for the calculator
 * and writes to the display.
 */
class Keypad extends Panel {

/**
 * Initialize the keypad, add buttons, set colors, etc.
 */
public Keypad (){
```

continued on next page

continued from previous page

```
Button   b = new Button();
Font     font = new Font ("Times", Font.BOLD, 14);
Color    functionColor = new Color (255, 255, 0);
Color    numberColor = new Color (0, 255, 255);
Color    equalsColor = new Color (0, 255, 0);
setFont (font);
setLayout (new GridLayout (5, 4, 4, 4));

b.setForeground (Color.black);

add (b = new Button ("7"));
b.setBackground (numberColor);
add (b = new Button ("8"));
b.setBackground (numberColor);
add (b = new Button ("9"));
b.setBackground (numberColor);
add (b = new Button ("/"));
b.setBackground (functionColor);

add (b = new Button ("4"));
b.setBackground (numberColor);
add (b = new Button ("5"));
b.setBackground (numberColor);
add (b = new Button ("6"));
b.setBackground (numberColor);
add (b = new Button ("x"));
b.setBackground (functionColor);

add (b = new Button ("1"));
b.setBackground (numberColor);
add (b = new Button ("2"));
b.setBackground (numberColor);
add (b = new Button ("3"));
b.setBackground (numberColor);
add (b = new Button ("-"));
b.setBackground (functionColor);

add (b = new Button ("."));
b.setBackground (functionColor);
add (b = new Button ("0"));
b.setBackground (numberColor);
add (b = new Button ("+/-"));
b.setBackground (functionColor);
add (b = new Button ("+"));
b.setBackground (functionColor);

add (b = new Button ("C"));
b.setBackground (functionColor);
add (new Label (""));
add (new Label (""));
add (b = new Button ("Enter"));
b.setBackground (equalsColor);

   }
}
```

2. Create an HTML document that contains the applet. Create a new file called howto102.html as follows:

```html
<html>
<head>
<title>Calculator</title>
</head>
<applet code="Calc.class" width=200 height=200>
</applet>
<hr size=4>

</html>
```

3. Compile and test the applet. Compile the source using javac or the makefile provided. Test the applet using the Appletviewer by entering the following command:

```
APPLETVIEWER howto102.html
```

Calc.java may also be run as an application by typing

```
java Calc
```

When Calc is executed, a window will open that contains a calculator very similar to that of How-To 6.1. The main difference is that this calculator has an Enter button instead of an = button. This calculator functions as a simple RPN calculator. Figure 10-2 shows an example of the running applet.

How It Works

The source file contains three classes: *Value*, *Calc*, and *KeyPad*. The *Value* class simply holds a single floating-point value. This is the type of object that will be placed on the stack. The *Calc* class is the applet itself, and the *KeyPad* class is a panel that holds the buttons representing the calculator keypad.

The *Value* class is needed because the *Stack* class works with variables of type Object. The basic type *double* does not extend Object, which will cause a type mismatch error with the *Stack.push()* and the *Stack.pop()* methods. The class Double could have been used instead. Table 10-2 lists the constructors and methods contained in the *Stack* class.

Figure 10-2 RPN calculator

The *Calc* class is the applet/application class proper. It contains a *main()* method in the event that the program is executed as an application. It also extends Applet so that it may be executed as an applet.

The *init()* method is the first method called when the program is used as an applet. The *main* method also calls the *init()* method after an application frame is created and displayed. The *init()* method in the *Calc* class first sets the layout of the applet panel to BorderLayout and then creates an instance of *Stack* using the *Stack()* constructor. No arguments are necessary; the stack will be sized dynamically as necessary. A TextField is used to display the user entry and also the results. The TextField is noneditable, requiring all input to be taken from the keypad. The TextField is added to the top (north) of the applet panel. An instance of *KeyPad* is created and added to the center of the applet panel. The variable input is a string representation of the current input.

The *action()* method handles action events. An action event is generated when the user presses a button. If a digit is pressed, the digit is added to the end of the input variable, which is then displayed by calling *TextEdit.setText()*. The input variable is cleared if the clear ("C") button is pressed. The Enter button converts the input string into a *double* using *Double.valueOf()* and stores it in a temporary variable *v1*. This temporary variable is then pushed onto the stack via the *Stack.push()* method. Operator buttons, like +, -, *, and /, cause one value to be popped off the stack by using the *Stack.pop()* method and used as the left value to the operator. The right value is the input string, which must be converted to a *double* via *Double.valueOf()*. The result is pushed back onto the stack and also displayed.

The *KeyPad* class extends Panel and is used to organize the buttons of the keypad. The buttons are arranged using GridLayout and added in sequence.

METHOD	DESCRIPTION
Stack()	–
empty()	Returns True if the stack is empty
peek()	Peeks at the top of the stack
pop()	Pops an item off the stack
push(Object)	Pushes an item onto the stack
search(Object)	Sees if an object is on the stack

Table 10-2 Stack class constructor and methods

COMPLEXITY
ADVANCED

10.3 How do I...
Link Java to other code?

Problem

I liked the Mandelbrot application from Chapter 7. The only complaint is that the calculation time was too slow in the Java interpreter. I would like to implement the calculation in native code for speed. I know how to write C code, but I don't know how to link it with Java. How do I link Java to other code?

Technique

Java supports native code linking at the method level. To link a native method, it must be declared in a Java class as native. This informs the compiler that the code will be loaded at runtime and will not be defined here. Next, the native code must be written. The C language is a good candidate, because the javah tool creates C header files and stub code. After the sources are compiled, the native code must be loaded at runtime. This is accomplished by invoking the *System.load()* method with the native code object as file and argument. Native methods may access arguments and return Java objects like any other method.

Steps

1. Create the Mandelbrot.java source file. Create a new file called Mandelbrot.java and enter the following source:

```
import java.applet.Applet;
import java.awt.*;
import java.awt.image.*;

/*
 * A class for generating and displaying the
 * Mandelbrot set
 */
public class Mandelbrot extends Panel {

/*
 * The maximum number of colors for
 * each pixel
 */
final int MaxColors = 256;
```

continued on next page

continued from previous page

```
/*
 * The width and height of the image
 */
int mWidth, mHeight;

/*
 * The array of pixel values
 */
int pixels[];

/*
 * The set values
 */
int mandelSet[];

/*
 * The image produced by the set
 */
Image theImage = null;

/*
 * The mapping function from set values to pixel values
 */
int pixMap[] = new int[MaxColors];

/*
 * A flag used for recalculating
 */
boolean startCalculate = false;

/*
 * Instance of MandelRect class
 */
MandelRect mandelRect;

/*
 * The control buttons
 */
Button startButton;
Button zoomButton;

/*
 * Called when the applet is loaded
 * Initialize the pixmap array and add user interface.
 */
public void init () {

    mWidth = 200;
    mHeight = 200;
    pixels = new int [mWidth * mHeight];
    mandelSet = new int [mWidth * mHeight];

    mandelRect = new MandelRect (mWidth, mHeight);
```

```
    int red, green, blue;
    int i;

    pixMap[0] = 0xffffffff;
    for (i=1; i<MaxColors-1; i+=1) {
        red = i;
        green = (i<128) ? i << 1 : 255-(i<<1);
        blue = MaxColors-i;
        pixMap[i] = (255 << 24) | (red << 16) | (green << 8) | blue;
    }
    pixMap[MaxColors-1] = 0xff000000;

    setLayout(new BorderLayout());

    startButton = new Button ("Start over");
    zoomButton = new Button ("Zoom in");

    Panel p = new Panel ();
    p.setLayout (new FlowLayout ());
    p.add (startButton);
    p.add (zoomButton);
    add ("South", p);
}

/*
 * Called when the applet is started
 * Forces a recalculation of the set
 */
public void start () {

    startCalculate = true;
    repaint ();
}

/*
 * Call update for efficiency
 * @param g - destination graphics object
 */
public void paint (Graphics g) {

    update (g);
}

/**
 * Override default update() method to avoid erase flicker.
 * @param g - destination graphics object
 */
public void update (Graphics g) {

    if (startCalculate) {
        calculate ();
        startCalculate = false;
    }
    if (theImage != null) g.drawImage (theImage, 0, 0, this);
    else repaint (1000);
```

continued on next page

continued from previous page

```
    mandelRect.paint (g);
}

/**
 * The definition for the native method
 * @param m - instance of MandelRect
 * @param p - returned pixel array
 */
native void ccalc (MandelRect m, int p[]);

/*
 * Create image from pixel values.
 */
void calculate () {

    int i;

    theImage = null;

    ccalc (mandelRect, mandelSet);

    for (i=0; i<mWidth*mHeight; i+=1) {
        pixels[i] = pixMap[mandelSet[i]];
    }
    theImage = createImage (
        new MemoryImageSource(mWidth, mHeight, pixels, 0, mWidth));
}

/**
 * Save the start position of the zoom rectangle.
 * @param evt - event object
 * @param x, y - position of the mouse
 */
public boolean mouseDown (Event evt, int x, int y) {

    mandelRect.setXY (x, y);
    return true;
}

/**
 * Draw the zoom rectangle.
 * @param evt - event object
 * @param x, y - position of the mouse
 */
public boolean mouseDrag (Event evt, int x, int y) {

    mandelRect.setWidthHeight (x, y);
    mandelRect.setPaintRect (true);
    repaint ();
    return true;
}
```

```
/**
 * Draw the zoom rectangle.
 * @param evt - event object
 * @param x, y - position of the mouse
 */
public boolean mouseUp (Event evt, int x, int y) {

    mandelRect.setWidthHeight (x, y);
    mandelRect.setPaintRect (true);
    repaint ();
    return true;
}

/**
 * Handle button presses.
 * @param evt - event object
 * @param arg - target object
 */
public boolean action(Event evt, Object arg) {

    if (evt.target == startButton) {
        mandelRect = new MandelRect (mWidth, mHeight);
        startCalculate = true;
        repaint ();
        return true;
    }
    if (evt.target == zoomButton) {
        startCalculate = true;
        mandelRect.setPaintRect (false);
        mandelRect.scaleSet ();
        repaint ();
        return true;
    }
    return false;
}

/**
 * Application entry point
 * Create window and new set.
 * @param args - command line arguments
 */
public static void main (String args[]) {

    Frame f = new Frame ("Mandelbrot set");
    Mandelbrot mandel = new Mandelbrot ();

    System.load ("/home/madhu/java/book/8/3/ccalc");
    mandel.init ();
    f.resize (210, 275);
    f.add ("Center", mandel);
    f.show ();
    mandel.start ();
}
}
```

continued on next page

2. Create the MandelRect.java source file. Create a new file called
MandelRect.java and enter the following source:

```java
import java.awt.*;

/*
 * A helper class to manage the zoom rectangle
 */
public class MandelRect {

/*
 * The coordinates of the zoom rectangle
 * in screen space
 */
int x;
int y;
int width;
int height;

/*
 * The final image width and height
 */
int imgWidth;
int imgHeight;

/*
 * The coordinates of the zoom rectangle
 * in set space
 */
double mandelX;
double mandelY;
double mandelWidth;
double mandelHeight;

/*
 * Set to True if the zoom rectangle should be painted.
 */
boolean paintRect;

/**
 * Constructor initializes variables.
 * @param iW - final image width
 * @param iH - final image height
 */
public MandelRect (int iW, int iH) {

    imgWidth = iW;
    imgHeight = iH;
    paintRect = false;

    mandelX = -1.75;
    mandelY = -1.125;
    mandelWidth = 2.25;
    mandelHeight = 2.25;
}
```

```
/**
 * Set the top left of the zoom rectangle in screen space.
 * @param ix, iy - top left corner of zoom rectangle
 */
void setXY (int ix, int iy) {

    x = ix;
    y = iy;
}

/**
 * Set the width, height of the zoom rectangle in screen space
 * @param ix, iy - bottom right corner of zoom rectangle
 */
void setWidthHeight (int ix, int iy) {

    width = ix - x;
    height = iy - y;
}

/*
 * Translate screen coordinates to set coordinates.
 */
void scaleSet () {

    int tx, ty, tw, th;

    tx = x;
    ty = y;
    tw = width;
    th = height;
    if (tw < 0) {
        tw = -width;
        tx = x-tw;
    }
    if (th < 0) {
        th = -height;
        ty = y-th;
    }
    mandelX = mandelX + (mandelWidth) * ((double) tx)/((double) imgWidth);
    mandelY = mandelY + (mandelHeight) * ((double) ty)/((double)
imgHeight);
    mandelWidth = mandelWidth * ((double) tw)/((double) imgWidth);
    mandelHeight = mandelHeight * ((double) th)/((double) imgHeight);
}

/**
 * Set the paintRect flag.
 * @param p - True means zoom rectangle should be painted
 */
void setPaintRect (boolean p) {

    paintRect = p;
}
```

continued on next page

continued from previous page

```
/**
 * Paint the zoom rectangle if necessary.
 * @param g - destination graphics object
 */
void paint (Graphics g) {

    if (paintRect == false) return;

    int tx, ty, tw, th;

    tx = x;
    ty = y;
    tw = width;
    th = height;
    if (tw < 0) {
        tw = -width;
        tx = x-tw;
    }
    if (th < 0) {
        th = -height;
        ty = y-th;
    }
    g.setColor (Color.white);
    g.drawRect (tx, ty, tw, th);
}
}
```

3. Create the native code source file. Create a new file called ccalc.c and enter the following source:

```
# include "Mandelbrot.h"
# include "MandelRect.h"

/**
 * Native method performing Mandelbrot set calculation
 * @param _P_ - handle to Mandelbrot class
 * @param rect - handle to MandelRect class
 * @param mSet - handle to pixel array where set is stored
 */
void Mandelbrot_ccalc (struct HMandelbrot *_P_, struct HMandelRect *rect,
    HArrayOfInt *mSet)
{
    int i;
    double row, col;
    double zr, zi, cr, ci, tzr, tzi;
    double hFactor, vFactor;
    ClassMandelRect *mandelRect;
    long *mandelSet;
    double width, height;
    double x, y;
```

```
/*
 * Dereference the handles.
 */
    mandelSet = unhand (mSet)->body;
    mandelRect = unhand (rect);

    x = mandelRect->mandelX;
    y = mandelRect->mandelY;
    width = mandelRect->imgWidth;
    height = mandelRect->imgHeight;
    hFactor = mandelRect->mandelWidth/((double) width);
    vFactor = mandelRect->mandelHeight/((double) height);

    for (row=0; row<height; row+=1) {
        for (col=0; col<width; col+=1) {
            zr = 0;
            zi = 0;
            cr = x + col * hFactor;
            ci = y + row * vFactor;
            for (i=1; i<64; i+=1) {
                tzr = zr*zr - zi*zi + cr;
                tzi = 2*zr*zi + ci;
                zr = tzr;
                zi = tzi;
                if (zr*zr + zi*zi > 4.0) break;
            }
            *mandelSet++ = (i << 2)-1;
        }
    }
}
```

4. Compile and test the applet. Compile the source using the makefile provided. The makefile contains commands for creating C header files and C stub files needed for compiling and linking. The makefile provided is valid only for UNIX platforms with the GNU C compiler (gcc). Other platforms and C compilers will require unique compilation flags for generating shared objects.

This example is an application exclusively because it uses native methods. It may be executed by typing the following:

`java Mandelbrot`

When Mandelbrot is executed, a window will open with the Mandelbrot set displayed after some calculation time. The mouse may be used to select a zoom region. Figure 10-3 shows an example of the running application.

Figure 10-3
Mandelbrot with
natice codewide x
16p6 high

How It Works

Three source files are created: MandelRect.java, Mandelbrot.java, and ccalc.c. The MandelRect.java file contains the *MandelRect* class, which is used mainly for translating screen coordinates to coordinates in the Mandelbrot space. It also draws the zoom rectangle during mouse drag events. This file is unchanged from How-To 7.7. The Mandelbrot.java file contains the *Mandelbrot* class, which is the application class proper. It manages the calculation and screen updates, and handles user events. The ccalc.c file contains the native C code that performs the set calculation.

The *Mandelbrot* class is similar to that of How-To 7.7. The major difference is the addition of the native method declaration and the loading of the native code shared object. The *Mandelbrot.calculate()* method calls the *ccalc()* method to perform the set calculation. An instance of MandelRect and the MandelSet array are passed as arguments. The *ccalc* method is really not a Java method; it is a reference to native code.

The native code was compiled as a shared object and must be loaded at runtime. This is done in the *Mandelbrot.init()* method. The shared object is loaded by invoking the *System.load()* method with the name of the shared-object file as an argument. The *System.load()* method expects an absolute path for the shared-object file. The alternative is to use the *SystemloadLibrary()* method, which searches the standard library path. This assumes that the shared-object file is in the standard library path.

The native code itself is written in C. It could be written in other languages like C++ or possibly assembler. C was chosen because of its simplicity and also because the javah tool creates C header files and stub files. The native C function has the class name prepended to it. A prototype of the function will appear as a header file called Mandelbrot.h.

The arguments to the C function include a handle to the *Mandelbrot* class in addition to handles to arguments declared in the native method definition. The arguments are *handles,* which are pointers to structure pointers. To access the data, the unhand( ) preprocessor macro may be used. The unhand( ) macro is defined in the interpreter.h header file found in the include directory of the JDK distribution. The result of unhand( ) applied to a class handle is a structure pointer to the class. The result of unhand( ) applied to an array handle is also a structure pointer. The body member in an array structure is the array itself. After pointers have been dereferenced to access the data, the set is calculated by using a typical Mandelbrot set algorithm.

Comments

Native methods can only be used in Java applications. The reason is security. Java applets are limited such that a client machine cannot be attacked. Native methods are not restricted, so they may do irreparable harm to client machines.

COMPLEXITY
ADVANCED

10.4 How do I...
Communicate between applets?

Problem

I have a web page that contains a scrolling marquee. I would like the user to be able to input the text to be scrolled in a TextField. I would also like the TextField to be a separate applet so I can place it independently of the marquee. How do I communicate between applets?

Technique

For an applet to call a method in a different applet, the applets need to be given a name with the *name* parameter in the HTML file. A reference to another applet on the same page is obtained, in the java source code, by use of the *getApplet( )* method. This creates a reference to the applet, and it can be referred to as if it were just another object.

Steps

1. Create the applet source file. Create a new file called ScrollApp.java and enter the following source:

```
import java.applet.*;
import java.awt.*;

class Scroll {

int xstart, ystart;
```

continued on next page

continued from previous page

```
int width, height;
String text;
int deltaX, deltaY;
int xpos, ypos;
Color color;

/**
    *Text scrolls in different directions.
    *@param xpos - initial x position
    *@param ypos - initial y position
    *@param deltax - velocity in x direction
    *@param deltay - velocity in y direction
    *@param width - bounding point for window panel width
    *@param height - bounding point for window panel height
    *@param text - text that is scrolled on the window
    *@para color - color of the text
    */
public Scroll (int x, int y, int dx, int dy, int w, int h, String t, Color
c) {

    xstart = x;
    ystart = y;
    width = w;
    height = h;
    text = t;
    deltaX = dx;
    deltaY = dy;
    color = c;
    xpos = xstart;
    ypos = ystart;
}

/**
    *Entry point for an applet
    *@param g - graphics context
    */
void paint (Graphics g) {

    g.setColor (color);
    g.drawString (text, xpos, ypos);
    xpos += deltaX;
    ypos += deltaY;

    FontMetrics fm = g.getFontMetrics ();
    int textw = fm.stringWidth (text);
    int texth = fm.getHeight ();
    if (deltaX < 0 && xpos < -textw) xpos = xstart;
    if (deltaX > 0 && xpos > width) xpos = xstart;
    if (deltaY < 0 && ypos < 0) ypos = ystart;
    if (deltaY > 0 && ypos > height+texth) ypos = ystart;
}
} // class Scroll


public class ScrollApp extends Applet implements Runnable{
```

```
int width, height;
Scroll left;
String text = " ";
Font font = new Font("Helvetica",1,24);
Thread thread;

public void init () {

    Dimension d = size ();

    width = d.width;
    height = d.height;
    left = new Scroll (400, 30, -5, 0, width, height,
            text, Color.red);

} // init()


public void start() {

    thread = new Thread(this);
    thread.start();
} // start()

public void run() {

    while (true) {
        try {
            Thread.sleep(100);
        } catch (InterruptedException e) { }
        repaint();
    }
} // run()

public void stop() {

    thread.stop();
} // stop()

/**
   *Entry point for an applet
   *@param g - graphics context
   */
public void paint (Graphics g) {

    setBackground(Color.white);
    g.setFont(font);
    left.paint (g);
} // paint()

/*
 * Method that updates the text being scrolled
 * @param newtext - the new text to scroll
 */
```

continued on next page

continued from previous page

```java
public void updateText (String newtext) {

    left = new Scroll (400, 30, -5, 0, width, height,
            newtext, Color.red);
}

} // class ScrollApp
```

2. Create the applet source file. Create a new file called TextInput.java and enter the following source:

```java
import java.awt.*;
import java.applet.*;
import java.util.*;

/*
 * The applet class
 */
public class TextInput extends Applet {

TextField textfield = new TextField(25);
String mytext = " ";

/*
 * Called when the applet is loaded
 * Create the user interface.
 */
public void init() {

        Font font = new Font("TimesRoman", Font.ITALIC, 24);
        Graphics g;
        g = getGraphics();

        g.setFont(font);

        textfield.setEditable (true);
    this.setLayout(new BorderLayout());
        add("Center", textfield);
}


/*
 * Check for return keypresses and send text to
 * the other applet.
 */
public boolean handleEvent(Event evt) {

        if ((evt.target instanceof TextField)
                && (evt.id == Event.ACTION_EVENT)){
                mytext = textfield.getText();
                Applet receiver =
```

```
getAppletContext().getApplet("receiver");
                ((ScrollApp)receiver).updateText(mytext);
                repaint();
                return true;
        }
        return false;
    }
}
```

3. Create an HTML document that contains the applet. Create a new file called howto104.html as follows:

```
<html>
<head>
<title>Communicating Between Applets</title>
</head>
<h2>The Scrolling Text Marquee</h2>
<blockquote> Enter the text to be scrolled in the text field
and press Enter.  The text will begin to scroll across the
screen.  The text in the text field can be modified at
any time and the scrolling text will change as soon as the
Enter key is pressed. <p>
The text field and the scrolling marquee are actually two
separate applets. </blockquote>
<hr size = 4>
<applet code="ScrollApp.class" width=400 height=50
 name = "receiver">
</applet>
<hr size = 4>
<p>
Enter the text to scroll
<applet code ="TextInput.class" width = 150 height = 40
 name = "sender" align = center>
</applet>
<p>
<hr size=4>

</html>
```

4. Compile and test the applet. Compile the source using javac or the makefile provided. Test the applet using the Appletviewer by entering the following command:

`APPLETVIEWER howto104.html`

When the Appletviewer is used, the applets will be opened in two separate windows. Text can be entered into the TextField, and it will be displayed in the marquee. These applets need to be used in a web page to illustrate the intended use. Figure 10-4 shows an example of the running applets in the Netscape browser.

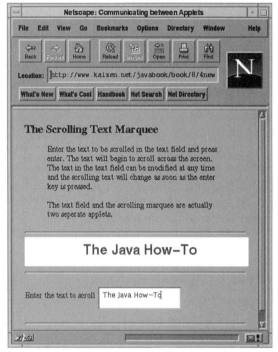

Figure 10-4 Communicating between applets

How It Works

In this example, a method from one applet is called by a second applet. To do this, the applets must be given a name in the HTML file. This is simply done by using

```
name  =   <name>
```

within the <applet> tag. In this example, the ScrollApp applet was named receiver and TextInput was named sender.

The ScrollApp applet is very similar to that of example 3.5. The only significant difference is that the *updateText( )* method was added. This method takes a string as an argument. The string is then used to create a new instance of the class *Scroll*. This method is used when text is keyed into the TextInput applet.

The TextInput applet contains only one class, the applet itself. An editable TextField is created and added to the center of the panel. The *handleEvent( )* method is used to handle an event if it is an instance of a TextField. If this is so, the text entered is placed in the string mytext. This string must then be passed to the ScrollApp applet. The string will be passed by calling the *updateText( )* method with *mytext* as a parameter.

To get a reference of another applet on the same page, the *getApplet( )* method is used with the applet's name as a parameter. The applet's name is the name given in the HTML file. This creates a reference to that applet. That applet can then be thought of as just another object.

COMPLEXITY
ADVANCED

10.5 How do I...
Translate between Unicode and ASCII?

Problem

I know that Java supports Unicode characters. I want to write an application that translates ASCII files to Unicode files and vice versa. The program should run as a command line utility like many of the UNIX utilities. I know how to access command line arguments and how to read and write files. I don't know how to translate between Unicode and ASCII. How do I translate between Unicode and ASCII?

Technique

The basic character type used in Java is a 16-bit integer of type *char.* This was done to support Unicode, which requires this size. The venerable ASCII standard requires only 7 bits, which is normally stored in an 8-bit byte. In Java, an 8-bit quantity is of type *byte. Chars* may be cast in *bytes,* and *bytes* may be cast into *chars.* When using the Latin character set, no loss occurs, because the high byte of a Latin Unicode character is zero.

This example uses the methods in the *DataInputStream* class for reading characters and bytes. The methods in the *DataOuputStream* class are used for writing characters and bytes. The translation, if it can be called that, is done as a simple cast from one type to the other.

Steps

1. Create the application source file. Create a new file called Translate.java and enter the following source:

```
import java.io.*;

/*
 * Application class
 */
class Translate {

/*
 * Constants to define translation format
```

continued on next page

continued from previous page

```
*/
static final int FROM_ASCII = 0;
static final int FROM_UNICODE = 1;

static final int TO_ASCII = 3;
static final int TO_UNICODE = 4;

/*
 * Print a usage message if command line
 * parameters are bogus.
 */
static void usage () {
    System.out.print ("usage: java Translate -aut <in-file> -aut ");
    System.out.println ("<out-file>");
    System.out.println ("\t-a Ascii format");
    System.out.println ("\t-u Unicode format");
}

/**
 * Application entry point
 * @param args - command line arguments
 */
public static void main (String args[])
{
    int from = 0;
    int to = 0;
    String buf;
    FileInputStream fsIn = null;
    FileOutputStream fsOut = null;

    if (args.length != 4) {          // You must specify format, in, out.
        usage ();
        System.exit (1);
    }

/*
 * args[0] is a String, so we can use the equals (String) method for
 * comparisons.
 */
    if (args[0].equals ("-a")) from = FROM_ASCII; else
    if (args[0].equals ("-u")) from = FROM_UNICODE; else {
        usage ();
        System.exit (1);
    }

    try {
        fsIn = new FileInputStream (args[1]);
    } catch (Exception e) {
        System.out.println (e);
        System.exit (1);
    }

    if (args[2].equals ("-a")) to = TO_ASCII; else
    if (args[2].equals ("-u")) to = TO_UNICODE; else {
```

```
            usage ();
            System.exit (1);
        }

/*
 * FileOutputStream is the complement of FileInputStream.
 */
    try {
        fsOut = new FileOutputStream (args[3]);
    } catch (Exception e) {
        System.out.println (e);
        System.exit (1);
    }
    DataInputStream dsIn = new DataInputStream (fsIn);
    DataOutputStream dsOut = new DataOutputStream (fsOut);

    char aChar = ' ';
    boolean eofHit = false;

    while (true) {
        switch (from) {
            case FROM_ASCII:
            try {
                try {
                    aChar = (char) dsIn.readByte ();
                } catch (EOFException e) {
                    eofHit = true;
                }
            } catch (IOException e2) {
                System.out.println (e2);
            }
            break;

            case FROM_UNICODE:
            try {
                try {
                    aChar = dsIn.readChar ();
                } catch (EOFException e) {
                    eofHit = true;
                }
            } catch (IOException e2) {
                System.out.println (e2);
            }
            break;

            default:
            System.out.println ("Internal error #1");
            System.exit (1);
            break;
        }

        if (eofHit == true) break;

        switch (to) {
            case TO_ASCII:
```

continued on next page

continued from previous page

```
            try {
                dsOut.writeByte ((byte) aChar);
            } catch (IOException e) {
                System.out.println (e);
            }
            break;

            case TO_UNICODE:
            try {
                dsOut.writeChar (aChar);
            } catch (IOException e) {
                System.out.println (e);
            }
            break;

            default:
            System.out.println ("Internal error #2");
            System.exit (1);
            break;
        }
    }

/*
 * Not absolutely necessary to catch these individually
 * It keeps the compiler from issuing a warning about
 * IOException not caught.
 */
    try {
        fsIn.close ();
        fsOut.close ();
    } catch (IOException e) {
        System.out.println (e);
    }
}
}
```

2. Compile and test the application. Compile the source using javac or the makefile provided. Test the application by entering the following command:

```
java Translate -a a.test -u u.test
```

This example translates the ASCII file a.test to a Unicode file called u.test. The translation can be performed in either direction using the command line options of Translate. The Translate application takes command line parameters in the format:

```
Translate -au <infile> -au <outfile>
```

where -a specifies it is an ASCII file and -u as an Unicode file. A sample file in each format has been provided, named a.test (ASCII) and u.test (Unicode). Figure 10-5 shows an example of the running application.

Figure 10-5 Translate application

How It Works

The application contains only one class, the application itself. The *main()* method checks for four arguments: the input file type, the input file name, the output file type, and the output file name. If the number of arguments is incorrect or the file types are not correct, the program prints a usage table and exits. The input file type is saved in the variable *from,* the output file type is saved in the variable *to.*

The input file is opened by creating a *FileInputStream*, and the output file is opened by creating a *FileOutputStream*. The constructors for these classes throw exceptions that must be caught. *FileInputStream* and *FileOutputStream* are used to create a *DataInputStream* and a *DataOutputStream*, respectively. The constructors for these classes also throw exceptions that must be caught.

The program enters an infinite loop that reads characters or bytes from the input file depending on the value of the variable *from*. Characters are read by using *DataInputStream.readChar( )*, and bytes are read by using *DataInputStream. readByte()*. In either case the result is stored in a character variable *aChar.* In the case of *readByte( ),* casting to type *char* must be done. The *read* methods throw both EOFException and IOException, which must be caught. If an EOFException occurs, a flag is set and the program breaks out of the infinite loop. After a valid character or *byte* is read, it is written to the output file by using either *DataOutputStream.writeByte()* or *DataOutputStream.writeChar()*. These methods throw IOException, which must be caught. In the case of *writeByte( ),* casting to type *byte* must be done.

After the operation is complete, both files are closed, and the program exits.

COMPLEXITY

ADVANCED

10.6 How do I...
Keep my applets from being stolen?

Problem

I have developed a really cool applet that I want to post on the Web for people to run. I do not put the source file anywhere to be found, but people could steal the class files. With the class files they can post the applet on their own page or just run it at will. I would like to make my applet so it can only be used on my page. How do I keep my applets from being stolen?

Technique

Keeping people from stealing applets will become very important as the usefulness of the applets written increases. The technique to do this includes writing a CGI script that computes a key value and passes it to the applet as a parameter. The applet contains a similar function and compares the computed value with the applet parameter. This will ensure that the applet must be loaded from a server containing the launching CGI.

Steps

1. Create the applet source file. Create a new file called InvaderApp.java and enter the following source:

```java
import java.awt.*;
import java.applet.Applet;
import java.awt.image.*;
import java.util.Date;

/**
 * A class that describes a target "invader"
 * This hold a single invader.
 */
class Invader {

/*
 * This invader s position and velocity
 */
double x, y, dx, dy;

/*
 * This invader s missile position and velocity
 * Only one missile allowed per invader
 */
int mx, my, mdy;

/*
 * The images for an invader
 */
Image img[] = new Image[4];

/*
 * inplay is True if this invader has not been killed.
 */
boolean inplay;

/*
 * fired is set True when this invader fires a missile.
 */
boolean fired = false;
```

```
/*
 * state is used to cycle through the four images
 * of this invader.
 */
double state;

/*
 * value is the score value, it depends on the speed.
 */
int value;

/*
 * Initialize position and speed for this invader.
 */
void random (int speed, int w, int h) {

    x = 10 + (w-20)*Math.random ();
    y = 10 + ((h>>1)-20)*Math.random ();
    dx = (speed>>1) - speed*Math.random ();
    dy = (speed>>1) - speed*Math.random ();
    inplay = true;
    state = 3 * Math.random ();
    fired = false;
    mdy = 20;
    value = speed * 10;
}

/*
 * Calculate new invader and missile position.
 * Also fires a missile at random
 * @param w - panel width
 * @param h - panel height
 */
void compute (int w, int h) {

    if (x <= 0 || x > w) dx = -dx;
    if (y <= 0 || y > h>>1) dy = -dy;
    if (my > h-20) fired = false;
    if (fired) my += mdy;
    else my = 0;
    if (inplay && !fired && Math.random () > 0.99) {
        fired = true;
        mx = (int) x; my = (int) y+25;
    }
    x += dx; y += dy;
}

/*
 * Paint invader and missile (if it has been fired).
 * @param g - graphics context
 * @param obs - imageobserver associated with this graphics context
 */
public void paint (Graphics g, ImageObserver obs) {

    int whichImage;
```

continued on next page

continued from previous page

```
    if (inplay) {
        whichImage = (int) state;
        g.drawImage (img[whichImage & 0x3], (int) x-25,
            (int) y-25, obs);
        state += .25;
    }
    if (fired) {
        g.setColor (Color.green);
        g.drawLine ((int) mx, (int) my, (int) mx, (int) my-10);
    }
}

/*
 * Tests if the player s missile has hit this invader
 * Returns True if invader is hit
 * @param pmx - player s missile x position
 * @param pmy - player s missile y position
 */
boolean killer (int pmx, int pmy) {

int deltaX, deltaY;

if (!inplay) return false;
    deltaX = (int) Math.abs (x-pmx);
    deltaY = (int) Math.abs (y-pmy);
    if (deltaX < 20 && deltaY < 20) {
        inplay = false;
        return true;
    }
    return false;
}
}

/**
 * A class to describe the player, very similar to Invader,
 * except in reverse
 */
class Player {

/*
 * Position of the player
 */
int x, y=-100;

/*
 * Position of the player s missile
 */
int mx, my, mdy = -20;

/*
 * Two different player images
 */
Image img1, img2;
```

```
/*
 * fired is True if player has fired a missile.
 * inplay is True if the the game is not over.
 */
boolean fired = false, inplay=true;

/*
 * Called when a player fires a missile
 */
void fire () {

    if (fired || !inplay) return;
    mx = x; my = y;
    fired = true;
}

/*
 * Calculate next missile position.
 */
void compute () {

    if (my < 0) fired = false;
    if (fired) my += mdy;
    else my = y;
}

/**
 * Paint player and missile.
 * @param g - destination graphics object
 * @param obs - image observer
 */
public void paint (Graphics g, ImageObserver obs) {

    if (fired) {
        if (inplay) g.drawImage (img2, x-25, y, obs);
        g.setColor (Color.white);
        g.drawLine (mx, my, mx, my+10);
    } else if (inplay) g.drawImage (img1, x-25, y, obs);
}

/**
 * Returns True if the player has been killed
 * @param bmx, bmy - position of enemy missile
 */
boolean killer (int bmx, int bmy) {

    int dx, dy;

    if (!inplay) return false;
    dx = (int) Math.abs (x-bmx);
    dy = (int) Math.abs (y-bmy);
    if (dx < 20 && dy < 20) {
        return true;
    }
```

continued on next page

continued from previous page

```java
        return false;
}
}

/*
 * Much of the game logic is here.
 */
class Playfield extends Panel implements Runnable {

static final int PLAYER_HIT = 1;
static final int INVADER_HIT = 2;

InvaderApp invaderApp;

/*
 * The number of invaders in play
 */
int NInvaders=0;

/*
 * The maximum number of invaders possible
 */
final int MaxInvaders = 32;

/*
 * Array of invaders
 */
Invader invaders[] = new Invader[MaxInvaders];
Player player;

/*
 * Off-screen image for double buffering
 */
Image offscreen;

/*
 * Dimension of off-screen graphics image
 */
Dimension psize;

/*
 * Graphics object associated with off-screen image
 */
Graphics offgraphics;

/*
 * Game action thread
 */
Thread theThread;

/*
 * The play field background color
 */
Color bgcolor = new Color (51, 0, 153);
```

```
int score, playerLives, playLevel;
Font font;

/**
 * Constructor saves instance of the applet.
 * @param invaderApp - instance of the applet
 */
public Playfield (InvaderApp invaderApp) {

    this.invaderApp = invaderApp;
}

/*
 * Game action thread
 */
public void run() {

    psize = size();
    offscreen = createImage (psize.width, psize.height);
    offgraphics = offscreen.getGraphics ();
    font = new Font ("TimesRoman", Font.BOLD, 18);
    offgraphics.setFont (font);

    while (true) {
        compute ();
        repaint ();
        try {
            Thread.sleep(25);
        } catch (InterruptedException e) { }
    }
}

/*
 * Calculate new positions for all objects.
 */
synchronized void compute () {

    for (int i=0; i<NInvaders; i+=1) {
        invaders[i].compute (psize.width, psize.height);
        if (invaders[i].killer (player.mx, player.my)) {
            invaderApp.hit (INVADER_HIT);
            player.fired = false;
            score += invaders[i].value;
        }
        if (player.killer (invaders[i].mx, invaders[i].my)) {
            invaderApp.hit (PLAYER_HIT);
            invaders[i].fired = false;
            playerLives -= 1;
            if (playerLives < 1) player.inplay = false;
        }
    }
    player.compute ();
}

/**
 * Override default update.
```

continued on next page

continued from previous page

```
 * Draw into off-screen image and then copy it to the screen.
 * @param g - destination graphics object
 */
public synchronized void update(Graphics g) {

    offgraphics.setColor (bgcolor);
    offgraphics.fillRect (0, 0, psize.width, psize.height);

    for (int i = 0 ; i < NInvaders ; i++)
        if (invaders[i].inplay) invaders[i].paint (offgraphics, this);
    player.paint (offgraphics, this);

    offgraphics.setColor (Color.green);
    offgraphics.drawString ("Score", 10, 20);
    offgraphics.drawString (Integer.toString (score), 60, 20);
    offgraphics.drawString ("Level", psize.width>>1, 20);
    offgraphics.drawString (Integer.toString (playLevel),
        (psize.width>>1)+50, 20);
    offgraphics.drawString ("Lives", psize.width-80, 20);
    offgraphics.drawString (Integer.toString (playerLives),
        psize.width-30, 20);
    if (playerLives < 1) offgraphics.drawString ("Game Over",
        (psize.width>>1)-30, psize.height>>1);
    g.drawImage (offscreen, 0, 0, null);
}

/**
 * Fire the player missile.
 * @param evt - event object
 * @param x, y - mouse position
 */
public synchronized boolean mouseDown(Event evt, int x, int y) {

    player.fire ();
    return true;
}

/**
 * Move the player position.
 * @param evt - event object
 * @param x, y - mouse position
 */
public boolean mouseMove (Event evt, int x, int y) {

    player.x = x;
    player.y = psize.height-45;
    if (player.x < 20) player.x = 20;
    if (player.x > psize.width-20) player.x = psize.width-20;
    return true;
}

/*
 * Start the game thread.
 */
public void start() {
```

```
        theThread = new Thread (this);
        theThread.start ();
}

/*
 * Stop the game thread.
 */
public void stop() {

        theThread.stop ();
}
}

/*
 * The applet class
 */
public class InvaderApp extends Applet {

/*
 * The playfield instance
 */
Playfield panel;

/*
 * Temporary storage for images
 */
Image img[] = new Image[4];

/*
 * The speed of the game
 * The number of invaders in this round
 */
int speed, NInvadersInPlay;

/*
 * Set to True if verification passes.
 */
boolean canPlay;

/*
 * Called when the applet is loaded
 * Load the images.
 */
public void init() {

    int i;
    MediaTracker tracker = new MediaTracker (this);

    canPlay = Validate ();
    setLayout(new BorderLayout());

    panel = new Playfield (this);
    add("Center", panel);
    Panel p = new Panel();
    add("South", p);
    p.add(new Button("New Game"));
```

continued on next page

continued from previous page

```java
        showStatus ("Getting Invader images...");
        for (i=0; i<4; i+=1) {
            img[i] = getImage (getDocumentBase(), "T"+(i+1)+".gif");
            tracker.addImage (img[i], 0);
        }

        try {
            tracker.waitForID(0);
        } catch (InterruptedException e) { }

            for (i=0; i<panel.MaxInvaders; i+=1) {
            panel.invaders[i] = new Invader ();
            panel.invaders[i].inplay = false;
            panel.invaders[i].img[0] = img[0];
            panel.invaders[i].img[1] = img[1];
            panel.invaders[i].img[2] = img[2];
            panel.invaders[i].img[3] = img[3];
        }
        panel.player = new Player ();

        showStatus ("Getting player images...");
        panel.player.img1 = getImage (getDocumentBase(), "Player1.gif");
        panel.player.img2 = getImage (getDocumentBase(), "Player2.gif");

        tracker.addImage (panel.player.img1, 1);
        tracker.addImage (panel.player.img2, 1);
        try {
            tracker.waitForID (1);
        } catch (InterruptedException e) { }
        showStatus ("Ready to play!");
}

/*
 * Start the action thread.
 */
public void start() {

    panel.start();
}

/*
 * Stop the action thread.
 */
public void stop() {

    panel.stop();
}

/*
 * Handle button presses.
 * @param evt - event object
 * @param arg - target object
 */
public boolean action(Event evt, Object arg) {
```

```
    if ("New Game".equals(arg)) {
        speed = 10;
        panel.player.inplay = canPlay;
        panel.playerLives = canPlay ? 3 : 0;
        panel.score = 0;
        panel.playLevel = 1;
        NInvadersInPlay = 2 * panel.playLevel + 1;
        panel.NInvaders = NInvadersInPlay;
        for (int i=0; i<panel.NInvaders; i+=1)
            panel.invaders[i].random (speed,
                panel.psize.width, panel.psize.height);

        play (getCodeBase(), "gong.au");
        if (NInvadersInPlay >= panel.MaxInvaders)
            NInvadersInPlay = panel.MaxInvaders;
        return true;
    }
    return false;
}

/**
 * Play the appropriate sound when something was hit.
 * @param which - which sound to play
 */
public void hit (int which) {

    switch (which) {
        case Playfield.INVADER_HIT:
        NInvadersInPlay -= 1;
        if (NInvadersInPlay < 1) {
            play (getCodeBase(), "gong.au");
            panel.playLevel += 1;
            NInvadersInPlay = 2 * panel.playLevel + 1;
            speed += 4;
            panel.NInvaders = NInvadersInPlay;
            for (int i=0; i<panel.NInvaders; i+=1)
            panel.invaders[i].random (speed,
                panel.psize.width, panel.psize.height);
        } else {
            play (getCodeBase(), "drip.au");
        }
        break;

        case Playfield.PLAYER_HIT:
        play (getCodeBase(), "doh2.au");
        break;
    }
}

/**
 * Arbitrary encryption algorithm for verification
 * @param minute - the current minute
 * @param key - the key used in the launching CGI
 */
String Crypt (int minute, int key) {
```

continued on next page

continued from previous page

```
    int i;
    int code;
    String crypt = "";

    code = (key << 1) + 1;
    for (i=0; i<minute; i+=1) {
        if ((code & 0x80000000) != 0) {
            code <<= 1;
            code |= 1;
        } else code <<= 1;
        code += key;
    }
    for (i=0; i<8; i+=1) {
        crypt += code & 0xf;
        code >>= 4;
    }
    return crypt;
}

/*
 * Returns True if verification succeeds
 */
boolean Validate () {

    Date date = new Date ();
    String param = getParameter ("key");
    System.out.println (param);

    int minute = date.getMinutes ();

    if (param.equals(Crypt (minute, 0xc0defeed))) return true;
    minute -= 1;
    if (minute < 0) minute = 59;
    if (param.equals(Crypt (minute, 0xc0defeed))) return true;
    minute -= 1;
    if (minute < 0) minute = 59;
    if (param.equals(Crypt (minute, 0xc0defeed))) return true;
    return false;
}
}
```

2. Create a CGI script source file. Create a new file called Launch.java and
enter the following source:

```
import java.util.Date;

/*
 * a CGI application for launching the applet
 */
public class Launch {

/**
 * Encryption algorithm for generating a hash value
 * @param minute - the current minute
```

```
 * @param key - an arbitrary key used for encryption
 */
static String Crypt (int minute, int key) {

    int i;
    int code;
    String crypt = "";

    code = (key << 1) + 1;
    for (i=0; i<minute; i+=1) {
        if ((code & 0x80000000) != 0) {
            code <<= 1;
            code |= 1;
        } else code <<= 1;
        code += key;
    }
    for (i=0; i<8; i+=1) {
        crypt += code & 0xf;
        code >>= 4;
    }
    return crypt;
}

/**
 * Application entry point
 * Generates an encrypted hash value and passes it
 * to the applet as a parameter
 * @param args - command line arguments
 */
public static void main (String args[]) {

    Date date = new Date ();
    String param;

    int minute = date.getMinutes ();

    param = Crypt (minute, 0xc0defeed);

    System.out.println ("<html>\n<head>\n<title>Invader</title>\n</head>");
    System.out.println ("<applet code=\"InvaderApp.class\" ");
    System.out.println ("width=600 height=400>\n");
    System.out.println ("<param name=key value=\""+param+"\">");
    System.out.println ("</applet><hr size=4></html>");
}
}
```

3. Create an HTML document that contains the applet. Create a new file called howto106.html as follows:

```
<html>
<head>
<title>Invader</title>
</head>
<applet code="InvaderApp.class"
width=600 height=400>
```

continued on next page

continued from previous page

```
<param name=key value="105111211476">
</applet><hr size=4></html>
```

3. Compile and test the applet. Compile the source using javac or the makefile provided. Test the applet using the Appletviewer by entering the following command:

```
APPLETVIEWER howto106.html
```

InvaderApp may only be run as an applet because it requires applet parameters. When InvaderApp is executed, a window will open and the invader game will appear identical to How-To 8.4. If the security measures are met, the game will function normally. If the security measures are not met, the applet will seem like it is running, but will just say, "Game Over," similar to an arcade game before a quarter is inserted. Figure 10-6 shows an example of the applet if the security measures are not met.

How It Works

The applet is identical to the InvaderApp of example 8.4. The only difference is the addition of the security measures.

The applet contains a *Validate()* method that is used to validate the server running the applet. This method contains a fixed key value. It then uses the current minutes after the hour on the computer running the applet, obtained from the Date class, to perform a arbitrary manipulation on the key. The server running the applet uses a CGI script to perform the same function. The CGI script contains the same fixed key and performs the same manipulation with the current minutes after the hour on the server. The CGI script is used to create the param tag in the html file. The param name is "key," and the param value is set with the CGI script. The applet then compares the param value with the value it computed to see if they match. Since the current minute on the server and the local computer running the applet may not be the same, the *Validate()* method first will try the current minute. If it is not valid, it tries the previous minute. It does this twice. If it still does not match, the applet will not run.

This outlines the basic strategy that can be used to keep an applet from being stolen. The algorithm used to manipulate the fixed key value can be as simple or complex as you like. In this example, the time was used as part of the manipulation algorithm, since it always changes and makes it hard to crack the code. It is important to make sure the CGI script resides in a directory that users cannot directly access. With the correct CGI script the applet can then be used.

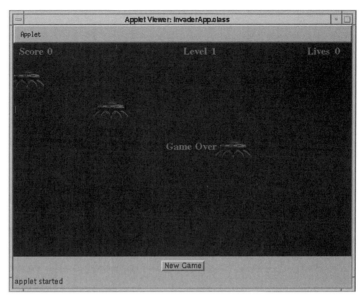

Figure 10-6 InvaderApp with security

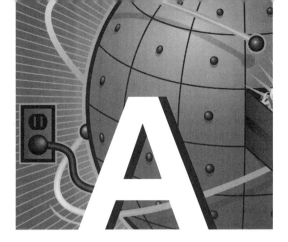

THE JAVA CLASS HIERARCHY

This appendix describes the eight Java class packages, which give programmers the fundamental routines required for most Java programming. Each package is explained briefly, then the hierarchy of classes within the package is given.

A.1 The java.applet Package

The java.applet package enables construction of applets. It also provides information about an applet's parent document and about other applets in that document, and enables sounds to be played.

```
java.applet

    Applet
        private AppletStub stub
        public final void setStub(AppletStub stub)
        public boolean isActive()
        public URL getDocumentBase()
        public URL getCodeBase()
        public String getParameter(String name)
        public AppletContext getAppletContext()
        public void resize(int width, int height)
        public void resize(Dimension d)
        public void showStatus(String msg)
        public Image getImage(URL url)
        public Image getImage(URL url, String name)
        public AudioClip getAudioClip(URL url)
        public AudioClip getAudioClip(URL url, String name)
        public String getAppletInfo()
        public String[][] getParameterInfo()
        public void play(URL url)
        public void play(URL url, String name)
        public void init()
        public void start()
        public void stop()
        public void destroy()

    AppletContext
        AudioClip getAudioClip(URL url)
        Image getImage(URL url)
        Applet getApplet(String name)
        Enumeration getApplets()
        void showDocument(URL url)
        public void showDocument(URL url, String target)
        void showStatus(String status)

    AppletStub
        boolean isActive()
        URL getDocumentBase()
        URL getCodeBase()
        String getParameter(String name)
        AppletContext getAppletContext()
        void appletResize(int width, int height)

    AudioClip
        void play()
        void loop()
        void stop()
```

A.2 The java.awt Package

The java.awt package is the Abstract Windowing Toolkit. It provides user interface features such as buttons, check boxes, scrollbars, and menus. It also provides the ability to define colors, fonts, images, polygons, and so on, and provides layout managers for controlling the layout of components within their container objects.

```
java.awt

    AWTError
        public AWTError(String msg)

    AWTException
        public AWTException(String msg)

    BorderLayout
        int hgap
        int vgap
        Component north
        Component west
        Component east
        Component south
        Component center
        public BorderLayout()
        public BorderLayout(int hgap, int vgap)
        public void addLayoutComponent(String name, Component comp)
        public void removeLayoutComponent(Component comp)
        public Dimension minimumLayoutSize(Container target)
        public Dimension preferredLayoutSize(Container target)
        public void layoutContainer(Container target)
        public String toString()

    Button
        String label
        public Button()
        public Button(String label)
        public synchronized void addNotify()
        public String getLabel()
        public void setLabel(String label)
        protected String paramString()

    Canvas
        public synchronized void addNotify()
        public void paint(Graphics g)

    CardLayout
        Hashtable tab = new Hashtable()
        int hgap
        int vgap
        public CardLayout()
        public CardLayout(int hgap, int vgap)
        public void addLayoutComponent(String name, Component comp)
        public void removeLayoutComponent(Component comp)
        public Dimension preferredLayoutSize(Container parent)
        public Dimension minimumLayoutSize(Container parent)
        public void layoutContainer(Container parent)
        void checkLayout(Container parent)
        public void first(Container parent)
        public void next(Container parent)
        public void previous(Container parent)
        public void last(Container parent)
```

continued on next page

continued from previous page

```
        public void show(Container parent, String name)
        public String toString()

CheckBox
        String label
        boolean state
        CheckboxGroup group
        void setStateInternal(boolean state)
        public Checkbox()
        public Checkbox(String label)
        public Checkbox(String label, CheckboxGroup group, boolean state)
        public synchronized void addNotify()
        public String getLabel()
        public void setLabel(String label)
        public boolean getState()
        public void setState(boolean state)
        public CheckboxGroup getCheckboxGroup()
        public void setCheckboxGroup(CheckboxGroup g)
        protected String paramString()

CheckBoxGroup
        Checkbox currentChoice = null
        public CheckboxGroup()
        public Checkbox getCurrent()
        public synchronized void setCurrent(Checkbox box)
        public String toString()

CheckBoxMenuItem
        boolean state = false
        public CheckboxMenuItem(String label)
        public synchronized void addNotify()
        public boolean getState()
        public void setState(boolean t)
        public String paramString()

Choice
        Vector pItems
        int selectedIndex = -1
        public Choice()
        public synchronized void addNotify()
        public int countItems()
        public String getItem(int index)
        public synchronized void addItem(String item)
        public String getSelectedItem()
        public int getSelectedIndex()
        public synchronized void select(int pos)
        public void select(String str)
        protected String paramString()

Color
        public final static Color white = new Color(255, 255, 255)
        public final static Color lightGray = new Color(192, 192, 192)
        public final static Color gray = new Color(128, 128, 128)
```

```
            public final static Color darkGray = new Color(64, 64, 64)
            public final static Color black = new Color(0, 0, 0)
            public final static Color red = new Color(255, 0, 0)
            public final static Color pink = new Color(255, 175, 175)
            public final static Color orange = new Color(255, 200, 0)
            public final static Color yellow = new Color(255, 255, 0)
            public final static Color green = new Color(0, 255, 0)
            public final static Color magenta= new Color(255, 0, 255)
            public final static Color cyan = new Color(0, 255, 255)
            public final static Color blue = new Color(0, 0, 255)
            private int pData
            private int value
            public Color(int r, int g, int b)
            public Color(int rgb)
            public Color(float r, float g, float b)
            public int getRed()
            public int getGreen()
            public int getBlue()
            public int getRGB()
            private static final double FACTOR = 0.7
            public Color brighter()
            public Color darker()
            public int hashCode()
            public boolean equals(Object obj)
            public String toString()
            public static Color getColor(String nm)
            public static Color getColor(String nm, Color v)
            public static Color getColor(String nm, int v)
            public static int HSBtoRGB(float hue, float saturation, float
            brightness)
            public static float[] RGBtoHSB(int r, int g, int b, float[]
            hsbvals)
            public static Color getHSBColor(float h, float s, float b)

    Component
        ComponentPeer peer
        Container parent
        int x
        int y
        int width
        int height
        Color foreground
        Color background
        Font font
        boolean visible = true
        boolean enabled = true
        boolean valid = false
        Component()
        public Container getParent()
        public ComponentPeer getPeer()
        public Toolkit getToolkit()
        public boolean isValid()
        public boolean isVisible()
        public boolean isShowing()
```

continued on next page

continued from previous page

```
public boolean isEnabled()
public Point location()
public Dimension size()
public Rectangle bounds()
public synchronized void enable()
public void enable(boolean cond)
public synchronized void disable()
public synchronized void show()
public void show(boolean cond)
public synchronized void hide()
public Color getForeground()
public synchronized void setForeground(Color c)
public Color getBackground()
public synchronized void setBackground(Color c)
public Font getFont()
public synchronized void setFont(Font f)
public synchronized ColorModel getColorModel()
public void move(int x, int y)
public void resize(int width, int height)
public void resize(Dimension d)
public synchronized void reshape(int x, int y, int width, int
height)
public Dimension preferredSize()
public Dimension minimumSize()
public void layout()
public void validate()
public void invalidate()
public Graphics getGraphics()
public FontMetrics getFontMetrics(Font font)
public void paint(Graphics g)
public void update(Graphics g)
public void paintAll(Graphics g)
public void repaint()
public void repaint(long tm)
public void repaint(int x, int y, int width, int height)
public void repaint(long tm, int x, int y, int width, int height)
public void print(Graphics g)
public void printAll(Graphics g)
public boolean imageUpdate(Image img, int flags,
int x, int y, int w, int h)
public Image createImage(ImageProducer producer)
public Image createImage(int width, int height)
public boolean prepareImage(Image image, ImageObserver observer)
public boolean prepareImage(Image image, int width, int
height,ImageObserver observer)
public int checkImage(Image image, ImageObserver observer)
public int checkImage(Image image, int width, int height,
ImageObserver
observer)
public synchronized boolean inside(int x, int y)
public Component locate(int x, int y)
public void deliverEvent(Event e)
public boolean postEvent(Event e)
```

```
    public boolean handleEvent(Event evt)
    public boolean mouseDown(Event evt, int x, int y)
    public boolean mouseDrag(Event evt, int x, int y)
    public boolean mouseUp(Event evt, int x, int y)
    public boolean mouseMove(Event evt, int x, int y)
    public boolean mouseEnter(Event evt, int x, int y)
    public boolean mouseExit(Event evt, int x, int y)
    public boolean keyDown(Event evt, int key)
    public boolean keyUp(Event evt, int key)
    public boolean action(Event evt, Object what)
    public void addNotify()
    public synchronized void removeNotify()
    public boolean gotFocus(Event evt, Object what)
    public boolean lostFocus(Event evt, Object what)
    public void requestFocus()
    public void nextFocus()
    protected String paramString()
    public String toString()
    public void list()
    public void list(PrintStream out)
    public void list(PrintStream out, int indent)

Container
    int ncomponents
    Component component[] = new Component[4]
    LayoutManager layoutMgr
    Container()
    public int countComponents()
    public synchronized Component getComponent(int n)
    public synchronized Component[] getComponents()
    public Insets insets()
    public Component add(Component comp)
    public synchronized Component add(Component comp, int pos)
    public synchronized Component add(String name, Component comp)
    public synchronized void remove(Component comp)
    public synchronized void removeAll()
    public LayoutManager getLayout()
    public void setLayout(LayoutManager mgr)
    public synchronized void layout()
    public synchronized void validate()
    public synchronized Dimension preferredSize()
    public synchronized Dimension minimumSize()
    public void paintComponents(Graphics g)
    public void printComponents(Graphics g)
    public void deliverEvent(Event e)
    public Component locate(int x, int y)
    public synchronized void addNotify()
    public synchronized void removeNotify()
    protected String paramString()
    public void list(PrintStream out, int indent)

Dialog
    boolean    resizable = true
    boolean modal
```

continued on next page

continued from previous page

```
        String title
        public Dialog(Frame parent, boolean modal)
        public Dialog(Frame parent, String title, boolean modal)
        public synchronized void addNotify()
        public boolean isModal()
        public String getTitle()
        public void setTitle(String title)
        public boolean isResizable()
        public void setResizable(boolean resizable)
        protected String paramString()

    Dimension
        public int width
        public int height
        public Dimension()
        public Dimension(Dimension d)
        public Dimension(int width, int height)
        public String toString()

    Event
        private int data
        public static final int SHIFT_MASK = 1 << 0
        public static final int CTRL_MASK = 1 << 1
        public static final int META_MASK = 1 << 2
        public static final int ALT_MASK = 1 << 3
        public static final int HOME = 1000
        public static final int END = 1001
        public static final int PGUP = 1002
        public static final int PGDN = 1003
        public static final int UP = 1004
        public static final int DOWN = 1005
        public static final int LEFT = 1006
        public static final int RIGHT = 1007
        public static final int F1 = 1008
        public static final int F2 = 1009
        public static final int F3 = 1010
        public static final int F4 = 1011
        public static final int F5 = 1012
        public static final int F6 = 1013
        public static final int F7 = 1014
        public static final int F8 = 1015
        public static final int F9 = 1016
        public static final int F10 = 1017
        public static final int F11 = 1018
        public static final int F12 = 1019
        private static final int WINDOW_EVENT = 200
        public static final int WINDOW_DESTROY = 1 + WINDOW_EVENT
        public static final int WINDOW_EXPOSE = 2 + WINDOW_EVENT
        public static final int WINDOW_ICONIFY = 3 + WINDOW_EVENT
        public static final int WINDOW_DEICONIFY = 4 + WINDOW_EVENT
        public static final int WINDOW_MOVED = 5 + WINDOW_EVENT
        private static final int KEY_EVENT = 400
        public static final int KEY_PRESS = 1 + KEY_EVENT
```

```
        public static final int KEY_RELEASE = 2 + KEY_EVENT
        public static final int KEY_ACTION = 3 + KEY_EVENT
        public static final int KEY_ACTION_RELEASE = 4 +

KEY_EVENT
        private static final int MOUSE_EVENT = 500
        public static final int MOUSE_DOWN = 1 + MOUSE_EVENT
        public static final int MOUSE_UP = 2 + MOUSE_EVENT
        public static final int MOUSE_MOVE = 3 + MOUSE_EVENT
        public static final int MOUSE_ENTER = 4 + MOUSE_EVENT
        public static final int MOUSE_EXIT = 5 + MOUSE_EVENT
        public static final int MOUSE_DRAG = 6 + MOUSE_EVENT
        private static final int SCROLL_EVENT = 600
        public static final int SCROLL_LINE_UP = 1 + SCROLL_EVENT
        public static final int SCROLL_LINE_DOWN = 2 + SCROLL_EVENT
        public static final int SCROLL_PAGE_UP = 3 + SCROLL_EVENT
        public static final int SCROLL_PAGE_DOWN = 4 + SCROLL_EVENT
        public static final int SCROLL_ABSOLUTE = 5 + SCROLL_EVENT
        private static final int LIST_EVENT = 700
        public static final int LIST_SELECT = 1 + LIST_EVENT
        public static final int LIST_DESELECT = 2 + LIST_EVENT
        private static final int MISC_EVENT= 1000
        public static final int ACTION_EVENT = 1 + MISC_EVENT
        public static final int LOAD_FILE = 2 + MISC_EVENT
        public static final int SAVE_FILE = 3 + MISC_EVENT
        public static final int GOT_FOCUS = 4 + MISC_EVENT
        public static final int LOST_FOCUS = 5 + MISC_EVENT
        public Object target
        public long when
        public int id
        public int x
        public int y
        public int key
        public int modifiers
        public int clickCount
        public Object arg
        public Event evt
        public Event(Object target, long when, int id, int x, int y, int
        key,int modifiers, Object arg)
        public Event(Object target, long when, int id, int x, int y, int
        key,
        int modifiers)
        public Event(Object target, int id, Object arg)
        public void translate(int x, int y)
        public boolean shiftDown()
        public boolean controlDown()
        public boolean metaDown()
        protected String paramString()
        public String toString()

FileDialog
        public static final int LOAD = 0
        public static final int SAVE = 1
        int mode
```

continued on next page

continued from previous page

```
        String dir
        String file
        FilenameFilter filter
        public FileDialog(Frame parent, String title)
        public FileDialog(Frame parent, String title, int mode)
        public synchronized void addNotify()
        public int getMode()
        public String getDirectory()
        public void setDirectory(String dir)
        public String getFile()
        public void setFile(String file)
        public FilenameFilter getFilenameFilter()
        public void setFilenameFilter(FilenameFilter filter)
        protected String paramString()

    FlowLayout
        public static final int LEFT     = 0
        public static final int CENTER     = 1
        public static final int RIGHT     = 2
        int align
        int hgap
        int vgap
        public FlowLayout()
        public FlowLayout(int align)
        public FlowLayout(int align, int hgap, int vgap)
        public void addLayoutComponent(String name, Component comp)
        public void removeLayoutComponent(Component comp)
        public Dimension preferredLayoutSize(Container target)
        public Dimension minimumLayoutSize(Container target)
        private void moveComponents(Container target, int x, int y, int
        width,
        int height, int rowStart, int rowEnd)
        public void layoutContainer(Container target)
        public String toString()

    Font
        public static final int PLAIN     = 0
        public static final int BOLD     = 1
        public static final int ITALIC     = 2
        private int pData
        private String family
        protected String name
        protected int style
        protected int size
        public Font(String name, int style, int size)
        public String getFamily()
        public String getName()
        public int getStyle()
        public int getSize()
        public boolean isPlain()
        public boolean isBold()
        public boolean isItalic()
        public static Font getFont(String nm)
```

```
    public static Font getFont(String nm, Font font)
    public int hashCode()
    public boolean equals(Object obj)
    public String toString()

FontMetrics
    protected Font font
    protected FontMetrics(Font font)
    public Font getFont()
    public int getLeading()
    public int getAscent()
    public int getDescent()
    public int getHeight()
    public int getMaxAscent()
    public int getMaxDescent()
    public int getMaxDecent()
    public int getMaxAdvance()
    public int charWidth(int ch)
    public int charWidth(char ch)
    public int stringWidth(String str)
    public int charsWidth(char data[], int off, int len)
    public int bytesWidth(byte data[], int off, int len)
    public int[] getWidths()
    public String toString()

Frame
    public static final int     DEFAULT_CURSOR = 0
    public static final int     CROSSHAIR_CURSOR = 1
    public static final int     TEXT_CURSOR = 2
    public static final int     WAIT_CURSOR = 3
    public static final int     SW_RESIZE_CURSOR = 4
    public static final int     SE_RESIZE_CURSOR = 5
    public static final int     NW_RESIZE_CURSOR = 6
    public static final int     NE_RESIZE_CURSOR = 7
    public static final int     N_RESIZE_CURSOR = 8
    public static final int     S_RESIZE_CURSOR = 9
    public static final int     W_RESIZE_CURSOR = 10
    public static final int     E_RESIZE_CURSOR = 11
    public static final int     HAND_CURSOR = 12
    public static final int     MOVE_CURSOR = 13
    String      title = "Untitled"
    Image       icon
    MenuBar     menuBar
    boolean     resizable = true
    Image       cursorImage
    int             cursorType = DEFAULT_CURSOR
    Color       cursorFg
    Color       cursorBg
    public Frame()
    public Frame(String title)
    public synchronized void addNotify()
    public String getTitle()
    public void setTitle(String title)
    public Image getIconImage()
```

continued on next page

continued from previous page

```
        public void setIconImage(Image image)
        public MenuBar getMenuBar()
        public synchronized void setMenuBar(MenuBar mb)
        public synchronized void remove(MenuComponent m)
        public synchronized void dispose()
        public boolean isResizable()
        public void setResizable(boolean resizable)
        public void setCursor(int cursorType)
        public int getCursorType()
        protected String paramString()

    Graphics
        protected Graphics()
        public abstract Graphics create()
        public Graphics create(int x, int y, int width, int height)
        public abstract void translate(int x, int y)
        public abstract Color getColor()
        public abstract void setColor(Color c)
        public abstract void setPaintMode()
        public abstract void setXORMode(Color c1)
        public abstract Font getFont()
        public abstract void setFont(Font font)
        public FontMetrics getFontMetrics()
        public abstract FontMetrics getFontMetrics(Font f)
        public abstract Rectangle getClipRect()
        public abstract void clipRect(int x, int y, int width, int height)
        public abstract void copyArea(int x, int y, int width, int height,
        int
        dx, int dy)
        public abstract void drawLine(int x1, int y1, int x2, int y2)
        public abstract void fillRect(int x, int y, int width, int height)
        public void drawRect(int x, int y, int width, int height)
        public abstract void clearRect(int x, int y, int width, int
        height)
        public abstract void drawRoundRect(int x, int y, int width, int
        height,
        int arcWidth, int arcHeight)
        public abstract void fillRoundRect(int x, int y, int width, int
        height,
        int arcWidth, int arcHeight)
        public void draw3DRect(int x, int y, int width, int height,
        boolean
        raised)
        public void fill3DRect(int x, int y, int width, int height,
        boolean
        raised)
        public abstract void drawOval(int x, int y, int width, int height)
        public abstract void fillOval(int x, int y, int width, int height)
        public abstract void drawArc(int x, int y, int width, int height,
        int
        startAngle, int arcAngle)
        public abstract void fillArc(int x, int y, int width, int height,
        int
        startAngle, int arcAngle)
```

```
public abstract void drawPolygon(int xPoints[], int yPoints[], int
nPoints)
public void drawPolygon(Polygon p)
public abstract void fillPolygon(int xPoints[], int yPoints[], int
nPoints)
public void fillPolygon(Polygon p)
public abstract void drawString(String str, int x, int y)
public void drawChars(char data[], int offset, int length, int x,
int
y)
public void drawBytes(byte data[], int offset, int length, int x,
int
y)
public abstract boolean drawImage(Image img, int x, int y,
ImageObserver observer)
public abstract boolean drawImage(Image img, int x, int y, int
width,
int height, ImageObserver observer)
public abstract boolean drawImage(Image img, int x, int y,
Color bgcolor,ImageObserver observer)
public abstract boolean drawImage(Image img, int x, int y,
int width, int height, Color bgcolor,ImageObserver observer)
public abstract void dispose()
public void finalize()
public String toString()

GridBagConstraints
public static final int RELATIVE = -1
public static final int REMAINDER = 0
public static final int NONE = 0
public static final int BOTH = 1
public static final int HORIZONTAL = 2
public static final int VERTICAL = 3
public static final int CENTER = 10
public static final int NORTH = 11
public static final int NORTHEAST = 12
public static final int EAST = 13
public static final int SOUTHEAST = 14
public static final int SOUTH = 15
public static final int SOUTHWEST = 16
public static final int WEST = 17
public static final int NORTHWEST = 18
public int gridx, gridy, gridwidth, gridheight
public double weightx, weighty
public int anchor, fill
public Insets insets
public int ipadx, ipady
int tempX, tempY
int tempWidth, tempHeight
int minWidth, minHeight
public GridBagConstraints ()
public Object clone ()
```

continued on next page

continued from previous page

```
GridBagLayout
      protected static final int MAXGRIDSIZE = 128
      protected static final int MINSIZE = 1
      protected static final int PREFERREDSIZE = 2
      protected Hashtable comptable
      protected GridBagConstraints defaultConstraints
      protected GridBagLayoutInfo layoutInfo
      public int columnWidths[]
      public int rowHeights[]
      public double columnWeights[]
      public double rowWeights[]
      public GridBagLayout ()
      public void setConstraints(Component comp, GridBagConstraints
      constraints)
      public GridBagConstraints getConstraints(Component comp)
      protected GridBagConstraints lookupConstraints(Component comp)
      public Point getLayoutOrigin ()
      public int [][] getLayoutDimensions ()
      public double [][] getLayoutWeights ()
      public Point location(int x, int y)
      public void addLayoutComponent(String name, Component comp)
      public void removeLayoutComponent(Component comp)
      public Dimension preferredLayoutSize(Container parent)
      public Dimension minimumLayoutSize(Container parent)
      public void layoutContainer(Container parent)
      public String toString()
      protected void DumpLayoutInfo(GridBagLayoutInfo s)
      protected void DumpConstraints(GridBagConstraints constraints)
      protected GridBagLayoutInfo GetLayoutInfo(Container parent, int
      sizeflag)
      protected void AdjustForGravity(GridBagConstraints constraints,
      Rectangle r)
      protected Dimension GetMinSize(Container parent, GridBagLayoutInfo
      info)
      protected void ArrangeGrid(Container parent)

Image
      public abstract int getWidth(ImageObserver observer)
      public abstract int getHeight(ImageObserver observer)
      public abstract ImageProducer getSource()
      public abstract Graphics getGraphics()
      public abstract Object getProperty(String name, ImageObserver
      observer)
      public static final Object UndefinedProperty = new Object()
      public abstract void flush()

Insets
      public int top
      public int left
      public int bottom
      public int right
      public Insets(int top, int left, int bottom, int right)
      public String toString()
```

```
        public Object clone()

Label
    public static final int LEFT     = 0
    public static final int CENTER    = 1
    public static final int RIGHT     = 2
    String label
    int alignment = LEFT
    public Label()
    public Label(String label)
    public Label(String label, int alignment)
    public synchronized void addNotify()
    public int getAlignment()
    public void setAlignment(int alignment)
    public String getText()
    public void setText(String label)
    protected String paramString()


LayoutManager
    void addLayoutComponent(String name, Component comp)
    void removeLayoutComponent(Component comp)
    Dimension preferredLayoutSize(Container parent)
    Dimension minimumLayoutSize(Container parent)
    void layoutContainer(Container parent)


List
    Vector      items = new Vector()
    int         rows = 0
    boolean     multipleSelections = false
    int         selected[] = new int[0]
    int         visibleIndex = -1
    public List()
    public List(int rows, boolean multipleSelections)
    public synchronized void addNotify()
    public synchronized void removeNotify()
    public int countItems()
    public String getItem(int index)
    public synchronized void addItem(String item)
    public synchronized void addItem(String item, int index)
    public synchronized void replaceItem(String newValue, int index)
    public synchronized void clear()
    public synchronized void delItem(int position)
    public synchronized void delItems(int start, int end)
    public synchronized int getSelectedIndex()
    public synchronized int[] getSelectedIndexes()
    public synchronized String getSelectedItem()
    public synchronized String[] getSelectedItems()
    public synchronized void select(int index)
    public synchronized void deselect(int index)
    public synchronized boolean isSelected(int index)
    public int getRows()
    public boolean allowsMultipleSelections()
    public void setMultipleSelections(boolean v)
    public int getVisibleIndex()
```

continued on next page

continued from previous page

```
            public void makeVisible(int index)
            public Dimension preferredSize(int rows)
            public Dimension preferredSize()
            public Dimension minimumSize(int rows)
            public Dimension minimumSize()
            protected String paramString()

     MediaTracker
            Component target
            MediaEntry head
            public MediaTracker(Component comp)
            public void addImage(Image image, int id)
            public synchronized void addImage(Image image, int id, int w, int
            h)
            public static final int LOADING = 1
            public static final int ABORTED = 2
            public static final int ERRORED = 4
            public static final int COMPLETE = 8
            static final int DONE = (ABORTED | ERRORED | COMPLETE)
            public boolean checkAll()
            public synchronized boolean checkAll(boolean load)
            public synchronized boolean isErrorAny()
            public synchronized Object[] getErrorsAny()
            public void waitForAll() throws

InterruptedException
            public synchronized boolean waitForAll(long ms)
            throws InterruptedException
            public int statusAll(boolean load)
            public boolean checkID(int id)
            public synchronized boolean checkID(int id, boolean load)
            public synchronized boolean isErrorID(int id)
            public synchronized Object[] getErrorsID(int id)
            public void waitForID(int id) throws InterruptedException
            public synchronized boolean waitForID(int id, long ms)
            throws InterruptedException
            public int statusID(int id, boolean load)
            synchronized void setDone()

     Menu
            Vector          items = new Vector()
            boolean         tearOff
            boolean         isHelpMenu
            public Menu(String label)
            public Menu(String label, boolean tearOff)
            public synchronized void addNotify()
            public synchronized void removeNotify()
            public boolean isTearOff()
            public int countItems()
            public MenuItem getItem(int index)
            public synchronized MenuItem add(MenuItem mi)
            public void add(String label)
            public void addSeparator()
            public synchronized void remove(int index)
```

```
        public synchronized void remove(MenuComponent item)

MenuBar
    Vector menus = new Vector()
    Menu helpMenu
    public MenuBar()
    public synchronized void addNotify()
    public void removeNotify()
    public Menu getHelpMenu()
    public synchronized void setHelpMenu(Menu m)
    public synchronized Menu add(Menu m)
    public synchronized void remove(int index)
    public synchronized void remove(MenuComponent m)
    public int countMenus()
    public Menu getMenu(int i)

MenuComponent
    MenuComponentPeer peer
    MenuContainer parent
    Font font
    public MenuContainer getParent()
    public MenuComponentPeer getPeer()
    public Font getFont()
    public void setFont(Font f)
    public void removeNotify()
    public boolean postEvent(Event evt)
    protected String paramString()
    public String toString()

MenuContainer
    Font getFont()
    boolean postEvent(Event evt)
    void remove(MenuComponent comp)

MenuItem
    boolean enabled = true
    String label
    public MenuItem(String label)
    public synchronized void addNotify()
    public String getLabel()
    public void setLabel(String label)
    public boolean isEnabled()
    public void enable()
    public void enable(boolean cond)
    public void disable()
    public String paramString()

Panel
    final static LayoutManager panelLayout = new FlowLayout()
    public Panel()
    public synchronized void addNotify()

Point
    public int x
```

continued on next page

continued from previous page

```
            public int y
            public Point(int x, int y)
            public void move(int x, int y)
            public void translate(int x, int y)
            public int hashCode()
            public boolean equals(Object obj)
            public String toString()

        Polygon
            public int npoints = 0
            public int xpoints[] = new int[4]
            public int ypoints[] = new int[4]
            Rectangle bounds = null
            public Polygon()
            public Polygon(int xpoints[], int ypoints[], int npoints)
            void calculateBounds(int xpoints[], int ypoints[], int npoints)
            void updateBounds(int x, int y)
            public void addPoint(int x, int y)
            public Rectangle getBoundingBox()
            public boolean inside(int x, int y)

        Rectangle
            public int x
            public int y
            public int width
            public int height
            public Rectangle()
            public Rectangle(int x, int y, int width, int height)
            public Rectangle(int width, int height)
            public Rectangle(Point p, Dimension d)
            public Rectangle(Point p)
            public Rectangle(Dimension d)
            public void reshape(int x, int y, int width, int height)
            public void move(int x, int y)
            public void translate(int x, int y)
            public void resize(int width, int height)
            public boolean inside(int x, int y)
            public boolean intersects(Rectangle r)
            public Rectangle intersection(Rectangle r)
            public Rectangle union(Rectangle r)
            public void add(int newx, int newy)
            public void add(Point pt)
            public void add(Rectangle r)
            public void grow(int h, int v)
            public boolean isEmpty()
            public int hashCode()
            public boolean equals(Object obj)
            public String toString()

        Scrollbar
            public static final int     HORIZONTAL = 0
            public static final int     VERTICAL   = 1
            int value
            int maximum
```

```
          int minimum
          int sVisible
          int orientation
          int lineIncrement = 1
          int pageIncrement = 10
          public Scrollbar()
          public Scrollbar(int orientation)
          public Scrollbar(int orientation, int value, int visible, int
          minimum,
          int maximum)
          public synchronized void addNotify()
          public int getOrientation()
          public int getValue()
          public void setValue(int value)
          public int getMinimum()
          public int getMaximum()
          public int getVisible()
          public void setLineIncrement(int l)
          public int getLineIncrement()
          public void setPageIncrement(int l)
          public int getPageIncrement()
          public void setValues(int value, int visible, int minimum, int
          maximum)
          protected String paramString()

     TextArea
          int     rows
          int     cols
          public TextArea()
          public TextArea(int rows, int cols)
          public TextArea(String text)
          public TextArea(String text, int rows, int cols)
          public synchronized void addNotify()
          public void insertText(String str, int pos)
          public void appendText(String str)
          public void replaceText(String str, int start, int end)
          public int getRows()
          public int getColumns()
          public Dimension preferredSize(int rows, int cols)
          public Dimension preferredSize()
          public Dimension minimumSize(int rows, int cols)
          public Dimension minimumSize()
          protected String paramString()

     TextComponent
          String text
          boolean editable = true
          int selStart
          int selEnd
          TextComponent(String text)
          public synchronized void removeNotify()
          public void setText(String t)
          public String getText()
          public String getSelectedText()
```

continued on next page

continued from previous page

```
            public boolean isEditable()
            public void setEditable(boolean t)
            public int getSelectionStart()
            public int getSelectionEnd()
            public void select(int selStart, int selEnd)
            public void selectAll()
            protected String paramString()

    TextField
        int cols
        char echoChar
        public TextField()
        public TextField(int cols)
        public TextField(String text)
        public TextField(String text, int cols)
        public synchronized void addNotify()
        public char getEchoChar()
        public boolean echoCharIsSet()
        public int getColumns()
        public void setEchoCharacter(char c)
        public Dimension preferredSize(int cols)
        public Dimension preferredSize()
        public Dimension minimumSize(int cols)
        public Dimension minimumSize()
        protected String paramString()

    Toolkit
        protected abstract ButtonPeer createButton(Button
        target)
        protected abstract TextFieldPeer createTextField(TextField target)
        protected abstract LabelPeer createLabel(Label target)
        protected abstract ListPeer createList(List target)
        protected abstract CheckboxPeer createCheckbox(Checkbox target)
        protected abstract ScrollbarPeer createScrollbar (Scrollbar target)
        protected abstract TextAreaPeer createTextArea (TextArea target)
        protected abstract ChoicePeer createChoice(Choice target)
        protected abstract FramePeer createFrame(Frame target)
        protected abstract CanvasPeer createCanvas(Canvas target)
        protected abstract PanelPeer createPanel(Panel target)
        protected abstract WindowPeer createWindow(Window target)
        protected abstract DialogPeer createDialog(Dialog target)
        protected abstract MenuBarPeer createMenuBar(MenuBar target)
        protected abstract MenuPeer createMenu(Menu target)
        protected abstract MenuItemPeer createMenuItem(MenuItem target)
        protected abstract FileDialogPeer createFileDialog(FileDialog
        target)
        protected abstract CheckboxMenuItemPeer createCheckboxMenuItem
        (CheckboxMenuItem target)
        public abstract Dimension getScreenSize()
        public abstract int getScreenResolution()
        public abstract ColorModel getColorModel()
        public abstract String[] getFontList()
        public abstract FontMetrics getFontMetrics(Font font)
        public abstract void sync()
```

```
    private static Toolkit toolkit
    public static synchronized Toolkit getDefaultToolkit()
    public abstract Image getImage(String filename)
    public abstract Image getImage(URL url)
    public abstract boolean prepareImage(Image image, int width, int
    height,ImageObserver observer)
    public abstract int checkImage(Image image, int width, int
    height,ImageObserver observer)
    public abstract Image createImage(ImageProducer producer)

Window
    String warningString
    Window()
    public Window(Frame parent)
    public synchronized void addNotify()
    public synchronized void pack()
    public synchronized void show()
    public synchronized void dispose()
    public void toFront()
    public void toBack()
    public Toolkit getToolkit()
    public final String getWarningString()
```

A.3 The java.awt.image Package

The java.awt.image package manages image data, such as setting the color model, cropping, color filtering, setting pixel values, and grabbing snapshots. It is important to note that the *Image* class is part of the java.awt package and not the java.awt.image package. Also the *java.awt.image* classes serve to manipulate images and are not the source of images. The *Applet.getImage()* method is the most common method for obtaining images.

```
java.awt.image

ColorModel
    protected int pixel_bits
    private static ColorModel RGBdefault
    public static ColorModel getRGBdefault()
    public ColorModel(int bits)
    public int getPixelSize()
    public abstract int getRed(int pixel)
    public abstract int getGreen(int pixel)
    public abstract int getBlue(int pixel)
    public abstract int getAlpha(int pixel)
    public int getRGB(int pixel)

CropImageFilter
    int cropX
    int cropY
    int cropW
    int cropH
    public CropImageFilter(int x, int y, int w, int h)
    public void setProperties(Hashtable props)
```

continued on next page

continued from previous page

```
        public void setDimensions(int w, int h)
        public void setPixels(int x, int y, int w, int h, ColorModel
        model, byte pixels[], int off, int scansize)
        public void setPixels(int x, int y, int w, int h, ColorModel
        model, int pixels[], int off, int scansize)

DirectColorModel
        private int red_mask
        private int green_mask
        private int blue_mask
        private int alpha_mask
        private int red_offset
        private int green_offset
        private int blue_offset
        private int alpha_offset
        private int red_bits
        private int green_bits
        private int blue_bits
        private int alpha_bits
        public DirectColorModel(int bits, int rmask, int gmask, int bmask)
        public DirectColorModel(int bits, int rmask, int gmask, int bmask,
        int amask)
        final public int getRedMask()
        final public int getGreenMask()
        final public int getBlueMask()
        final public int getAlphaMask()
        private int accum_mask = 0
        private void DecomposeMask(int mask, String componentName, int
        values[])
        private void CalculateOffsets()
        final public int getRed(int pixel)
        final public int getGreen(int pixel)
        final public int getBlue(int pixel)
        final public int getAlpha(int pixel)
        final public int getRGB(int pixel)

FilteredImageSource
        ImageProducer src
        ImageFilter filter
        public FilteredImageSource(ImageProducer orig, ImageFilter imgf)
        private Hashtable proxies
        public synchronized void addConsumer(ImageConsumer ic)
        public synchronized boolean isConsumer(ImageConsumer ic)
        public synchronized void removeConsumer(ImageConsumer ic)
        public void startProduction(ImageConsumer ic)
        public void requestTopDownLeftRightResend(ImageConsumer ic)

ImageConsumer
        void setDimensions(int width, int height)
        void setProperties(Hashtable props)
        void setColorModel(ColorModel model)
        void setHints(int hintflags)
        int RANDOMPIXELORDER = 1
```

```
int TOPDOWNLEFTRIGHT = 2
int COMPLETESCANLINES = 4
int SINGLEPASS = 8
int SINGLEFRAME = 16
void setPixels(int x, int y, int w, int h, ColorModel model, byte
pixels[], int off, int scansize)
void setPixels(int x, int y, int w, int h, ColorModel model, int
pixels[], int off, int scansize)
void imageComplete(int status)
int IMAGEERROR = 1
int SINGLEFRAMEDONE = 2
int STATICIMAGEDONE = 3
int IMAGEABORTED = 4
```

ImageFilter
```
    protected ImageConsumer consumer
    public ImageFilter getFilterInstance(ImageConsumer ic)
    public void setDimensions(int width, int height)
    public void setProperties(Hashtable props)
    public void setColorModel(ColorModel model)
    public void setHints(int hints)
    public void setPixels(int x, int y, int w, int h, ColorModel
    model, byte pixels[], int off, int scansize)
    public void setPixels(int x, int y, int w, int h, ColorModel
    model, int pixels[], int off, int scansize)
    public void imageComplete(int status)
    public void resendTopDownLeftRight(ImageProducer ip)
    public Object clone()
```

ImageObserver
```
    public boolean imageUpdate(Image img, int infoflags, int x, int y,
    int width, int height)
    public static final int WIDTH = 1
    public static final int HEIGHT = 2
    public static final int PROPERTIES = 4
    public static final int SOMEBITS = 8
    public static final int FRAMEBITS = 16
    public static final int ALLBITS = 32
    public static final int ERROR = 64
    public static final int ABORT = 128
```

ImageProducer
```
    public void addConsumer(ImageConsumer ic)
    public boolean isConsumer(ImageConsumer ic)
    public void removeConsumer(ImageConsumer ic)
    public void startProduction(ImageConsumer ic)
    public void requestTopDownLeftRightResend(ImageConsumer ic)
```

IndexColorModel
```
    private byte red[]
    private byte green[]
    private byte blue[]
    private byte alpha[]
```

continued on next page

continued from previous page

```
          private int map_size
          private int transparent_index
          public IndexColorModel(int bits, int size,byte r[], byte g[], byte
          b[])
          public IndexColorModel(int bits, int size, byte r[], byte g[],
          byte b[], int trans)
          public IndexColorModel(int bits, int size, byte r[], byte g[],
          byte b[], byte a[])
          public IndexColorModel(int bits, int size, byte cmap[], int start,
          boolean hasalpha)
          public IndexColorModel(int bits, int size, byte cmap[], int start,
          boolean hasalpha, int trans)
          final public int getMapSize()
          final public int getTransparentPixel()
          final public void getReds(byte r[])
          final public void getGreens(byte g[])
          final public void getBlues(byte b[])
          final public void getAlphas(byte a[])
          private void setTransparentPixel(int trans)
          final public int getRed(int pixel)
          final public int getGreen(int pixel)
          final public int getBlue(int pixel)
          final public int getAlpha(int pixel)
          final public int getRGB(int pixel)


     MemoryImageSource
          int width
          int height
          ColorModel model
          Object pixels
          int pixeloffset
          int pixelscan
          Hashtable properties
          public MemoryImageSource(int w, int h, ColorModel cm, byte[] pix,
          int off, int scan)
          public MemoryImageSource(int w, int h, ColorModel cm, byte[] pix,
          int off, int scan, Hashtable props)
          public MemoryImageSource(int w, int h, ColorModel cm, int[] pix,
          int off, int scan)
          public MemoryImageSource(int w, int h, ColorModel cm, int[] pix,
          int off, int scan, Hashtable props)
          private void initialize(int w, int h, ColorModel cm, Object pix,
          int off, int scan, Hashtable props)
          public MemoryImageSource(int w, int h, int pix[], int off, int
          scan)
          public MemoryImageSource(int w, int h, int pix[], int off, int
          scan, Hashtable props)
          private ImageConsumer theConsumer
          public synchronized void addConsumer(ImageConsumer ic)
          public synchronized boolean isConsumer(ImageConsumer ic)
          public synchronized void removeConsumer(ImageConsumer ic)
          public void startProduction(ImageConsumer ic)
```

```
    public void requestTopDownLeftRightResend(ImageConsumer ic)
    private void produce()

PixelGrabber
    ImageProducer producer
    int dstX
    int dstY
    int dstW
    int dstH
    int[] pixelbuf
    int dstOff
    int dstScan
    private boolean grabbing
    private int flags
    private final int GRABBEDBITS = (ImageObserver.FRAMEBITS |
    ImageObserver.ALLBITS)
    private final int DONEBITS = (GRABBEDBITS | ImageObserver.ERROR)
    public PixelGrabber(Image img, int x, int y, int w, int h, int[]
    pix, int off, int scansize)
    public PixelGrabber(ImageProducer ip, int x, int y, int w, int
    h,int[] pix, int off, int scansize)
    public boolean grabPixels() throws InterruptedException
    public synchronized boolean grabPixels(long ms) throws
    InterruptedException
    public synchronized int status()
    public void setDimensions(int width, int height)
    public void setHints(int hints)
    public void setProperties(Hashtable props)
    public void setColorModel(ColorModel model)
    public void setPixels(int srcX, int srcY, int srcW, int srcH,
    ColorModel model,byte pixels[], int srcOff, int srcScan)
    public void setPixels(int srcX, int srcY, int srcW, int srcH,
    ColorModel model, int pixels[], int srcOff, int srcScan)
    public synchronized void imageComplete(int status)

  RGBImageFilter
protected ColorModel origmodel
    protected ColorModel newmodel
    protected boolean canFilterIndexColorModel
    public void setColorModel(ColorModel model)
    public void substituteColorModel(ColorModel oldcm, ColorModel
    newcm)
    public IndexColorModel filterIndexColorModel(IndexColorModel icm)
    public void filterRGBPixels(int x, int y, int w, int h, int
    pixels[], int off, int scansize)
    public void setPixels(int x, int y, int w, int h, ColorModel
    model, byte pixels[], int off,int scansize)
    public void setPixels(int x, int y, int w, int h, ColorModel
    model, int pixels[], int off,int scansize)
    public abstract int filterRGB(int x, int y, int rgb)
```

A.4 The java.awt.peer Package

The java.awt.peer package consists of interface definitions that connect AWT components to their platform-specific implementation. The interfaces in this package must be supported by the GUI components on a specific platform.

The classes in the java.peer package are not included here, because they are typically not used by the Java programmer directly. They are of more importance to the porting of the Java runtime to other platforms.

A.5 The java.io Package

This package provides a set of input and output streams to read and write data to files, strings, and other sources.

java.io

```
BufferedInputStream
    protected byte buf[]
    protected int count
    protected int pos
    protected int markpos = -1
    protected int marklimit
    public BufferedInputStream(InputStream in)
    public BufferedInputStream(InputStream in, int size)
    private void fill() throws IOException
    public synchronized int read() throws IOException
    public synchronized int read(byte b[], int off, int len) throws
    IOException
    public synchronized long skip(long n) throws IOException
    public synchronized int available() throws IOException
    public synchronized void mark(int readlimit)
    public synchronized void reset() throws IOException
    public boolean markSupported()

BufferedOutputStream
    protected byte buf[]
    protected int count
    public BufferedOutputStream(OutputStream out)
    public BufferedOutputStream(OutputStream out, int size)
    public synchronized void write(int b) throws IOException
    public synchronized void write(byte b[], int off, int len) throws
    IOException
    public synchronized void flush() throws IOException

ByteArrayInputStream
    protected byte buf[]
    protected int pos
    protected int count
    public ByteArrayInputStream(byte buf[])
    public ByteArrayInputStream(byte buf[], int offset, int length)
    public synchronized int read()
    public synchronized int read(byte b[], int off, int len)
    public synchronized long skip(long n)
    public synchronized int available()
    public synchronized void reset()

ByteArrayOutputStream
    protected byte buf[]
    protected int count
    public ByteArrayOutputStream()
```

```
public ByteArrayOutputStream(int size)
public synchronized void write(int b)
public synchronized void write(byte b[], int off, int len)
public synchronized void writeTo(OutputStream out) throws
IOException
public synchronized void reset()
public synchronized byte toByteArray()[]
public int size()
public String toString()
public String toString(int hibyte)
```

DataInput
```
void readFully(byte b[]) throws IOException
void readFully(byte b[], int off, int len) throws IOException
int skipBytes(int n) throws IOException
boolean readBoolean() throws IOException
byte readByte() throws IOException
int readUnsignedByte() throws IOException
short readShort() throws IOException
int readUnsignedShort() throws IOException
char readChar() throws IOException
int readInt() throws IOException
long readLong() throws IOException
float readFloat() throws IOException
double readDouble() throws IOException
String readLine() throws IOException
String readUTF() throws IOException
```

DataInputStream
```
public DataInputStream(InputStream in)
public final int read(byte b[]) throws IOException
public final int read(byte b[], int off, int len) throws
IOException
public final void readFully(byte b[]) throws IOException
public final void readFully(byte b[], int off, int len) throws
IOException
public final int skipBytes(int n) throws IOException
public final boolean readBoolean() throws IOException
public final byte readByte() throws IOException
public final int readUnsignedByte() throws IOException
public final short readShort() throws IOException
public final int readUnsignedShort() throws IOException
public final char readChar() throws IOException
public final int readInt() throws IOException
public final long readLong() throws IOException
public final float readFloat() throws IOException
public final double readDouble() throws IOException
private char lineBuffer[]
public final String readLine() throws IOException
public final String readUTF() throws IOException
public final static String readUTF(DataInput in) throws IOException
```

DataOutput
```
void write(int b) throws IOException
```

continued on next page

continued from previous page

```
    void write(byte b[]) throws IOException
    void write(byte b[], int off, int len) throws IOException
    void writeBoolean(boolean v) throws IOException
    void writeByte(int v) throws IOException
    void writeShort(int v) throws IOException
    void writeChar(int v) throws IOException
    void writeInt(int v) throws IOException
    void writeLong(long v) throws IOException
    void writeFloat(float v) throws IOException
    void writeDouble(double v) throws IOException
    void writeBytes(String s) throws IOException
    void writeChars(String s) throws IOException
    void writeUTF(String str) throws IOException

DataOutputStream
    protected int written
    public DataOutputStream(OutputStream out)
    public synchronized void write(int b) throwsIOException
    public synchronized void write(byte b[], int off, int len)
    throws IOException
    public void flush() throws IOException
    public final void writeBoolean(boolean v) throws IOException
    public final void writeByte(int v) throws IOException
    public final void writeShort(int v) throws IOException
    public final void writeChar(int v) throws IOException
    public final void writeInt(int v) throws IOException
    public final void writeLong(long v) throws IOException
    public final void writeFloat(float v) throws IOException
    public final void writeDouble(double v) throws IOException
    public final void writeBytes(String s) throws IOException
    public final void writeChars(String s) throws IOException
    public final void writeUTF(String str) throws IOException
    public final int size()

EOFExeption
    public EOFException()
    public EOFException(String s)

File
    private String path
    public static final String separator = System.getProperty
    ("file.separator")
    public static final char separatorChar = separator.charAt(0)
    public static final String pathSeparator =
    System.getProperty("path.separator")
    public static final char pathSeparatorChar =
    pathSeparator.charAt(0)
    public File(String path)
    public File(String path, String name)
    public File(File dir, String name)
    public String getName()
    public String getPath()
    public String getAbsolutePath()
```

```
        public String getParent()
        private native boolean exists0()
        private native boolean canWrite0()
        private native boolean canRead0()
        private native boolean isFile0()
        private native boolean isDirectory0()
        private native long lastModified0()
        private native long length0()
        private native boolean mkdir0()
        private native boolean renameTo0(File dest)
        private native boolean delete0()
        private native String[] list0()
        public boolean exists()
        public boolean canWrite()
        public boolean canRead()
        public boolean isFile()
        public boolean isDirectory()
        public native boolean isAbsolute()
        public long lastModified()
        public long length()
        public boolean mkdir()
        public boolean renameTo(File dest)
        public boolean mkdirs()
        public String[] list()
        public String[] list(FilenameFilter filter)
        public boolean delete()
        public int hashCode()
        public boolean equals(Object obj)
        public String toString()

FileDescriptor
        private int fd
        public static final FileDescriptor in = initSystemFD(new
        FileDescriptor(),0)
        public static final FileDescriptor out = initSystemFD(new
        FileDescriptor(),1)
        public static final FileDescriptor err = initSystemFD(new
        FileDescriptor(),2)
        public native boolean valid()
        private static native FileDescriptor initSystemFD(FileDescriptor
        fdObj, int desc)

FileInputStream
        private FileDescriptor fd
        public FileInputStream(String name) throws FileNotFoundException
        public FileInputStream(File file) throws FileNotFoundException
        public FileInputStream(FileDescriptor fdObj)
        private native void open(String name) throws IOException
        public native int read() throws IOException
        private native int readBytes(byte b[], int off, int len) throws
        IOException
        public int read(byte b[]) throws IOException
        public int read(byte b[], int off, int len) throws IOException
        public native long skip(long n) throws IOException
```

continued on next page

continued from previous page

```
            public native int available() throws IOException
            public native void close() throws IOException
            public final FileDescriptor getFD() throws IOException
            protected void finalize() throws IOException

    FilenameFilter
            boolean accept(File dir, String name)
    FileNotFoundException
            public FileNotFoundException()
            public FileNotFoundException(String s)

    FileOutputStream
            private FileDescriptor fd
            public FileOutputStream(String name) throws IOException
            public FileOutputStream(File file) throws IOException
            public FileOutputStream(FileDescriptor fdObj)
            private native void open(String name) throws IOException
            public native void write(int b) throws IOException
            private native void writeBytes(byte b[], int off, int len) throws
            IOException
            public void write(byte b[]) throws IOException
            public void write(byte b[], int off, int len) throws IOException
            public native void close() throws IOException
            public final FileDescriptor getFD()  throws IOException
            protected void finalize() throws IOException

    FileInputStream
            protected InputStream in
            protected FilterInputStream(InputStream in)
            public int read() throws IOException
            public int read(byte b[]) throws IOException
            public int read(byte b[], int off, int len) throws IOException
            public long skip(long n) throws IOException
            public int available() throws IOException
            public void close() throws IOException
            public synchronized void mark(int readlimit)
            public synchronized void reset() throws IOException
            public boolean markSupported()

    FilterInputStream
            protected InputStream in
            protected FilterInputStream(InputStream in)
            public int read() throws IOException
            public int read(byte b[]) throws IOException
            public int read(byte b[], int off, int len) throws IOException
            public long skip(long n) throws IOException
            public int available() throws IOException
            public void close() throws IOException
            public synchronized void mark(int readlimit)
            public synchronized void reset() throws IOException
            public boolean markSupported()
```

```
FilterOutputStream
    protected OutputStream out
    public FilterOutputStream(OutputStream out)
    public void write(int b) throws IOException
    public void write(byte b[]) throws IOException
    public void write(byte b[], int off, int len) throws IOException
    public void flush() throws IOException
    public void close() throws IOException

InputStream
    public abstract int read() throws IOException
    public int read(byte b[]) throws IOException
    public int read(byte b[], int off, int len) throws IOException
    public long skip(long n) throws IOException
    public int available() throws IOException
    public void close() throws IOException
    public synchronized void mark(int readlimit)
    public synchronized void reset() throws IOException
    public boolean markSupported()

InterruptedIOException
    public InterruptedIOException()
    public InterruptedIOException(String s)
    public int bytesTransferred = 0

IOException
    public IOException()
    public IOException(String s)

LineNumberInputStream
    int pushBack = -1
    int lineNumber
    int markLineNumber
    public LineNumberInputStream(InputStream in)
    public int read() throws IOException
    public int read(byte b[], int off, int len) throws IOException
    public void setLineNumber(int lineNumber)
    public int getLineNumber()
    public long skip(long n) throws IOException
    public int available() throws IOException
    public void mark(int readlimit)
    public void reset() throws IOException

OutputStream
    public abstract void write(int b) throws IOException
    public void write(byte b[]) throws IOException
    public void write(byte b[], int off, int len) throws IOException
    public void flush() throws IOException
    public void close() throws IOException

PipedInputStream
    boolean closed = true
    Thread readSide
    Thread writeSide
    private byte buffer[] = new byte[1024]
```

continued on next page

continued from previous page

```
int in = -1
int out = 0
public PipedInputStream (PipedOutputStream src) throws IOException
public PipedInputStream ()
public void connect(PipedOutputStream src) throws IOException
synchronized void receive(int b) throws IOException
synchronized void receive(byte b[], int off, int len) throws
IOException
synchronized void receivedLast()
public synchronized int read()  throws IOException
public synchronized int read(byte b[], int off, int len) throws
IOException
public void close() throws IOException
```

```
PipedOutputStream
    private PipedInputStream sink
    public PipedOutputStream(PipedInputStream snk) throws IOException
    public PipedOutputStream()
    public void connect(PipedInputStream snk) throws IOException
    public void write(int b)  throws IOException
    public void write(byte b[], int off, int len) throws IOException
    public void close()  throws IOException
```

```
PrintStream
    private boolean autoflush
    private boolean trouble
    public PrintStream(OutputStream out)
    public PrintStream(OutputStream out, boolean autoflush)
    public void write(int b)
    public void write(byte b[], int off, int len)
    public void flush()
    public void close()
    public boolean checkError()
    public void print(Object obj)
    synchronized public void print(String s)
    synchronized public void print(char s[])
    public void print(char c)
    public void print(int i)
    public void print(long l)
    public void print(float f)
    public void print(double d)
    public void print(boolean b)
    public void println()
    synchronized public void println(Object obj)
    synchronized public void println(String s)
    synchronized public void println(char s[])
    synchronized public void println(char c)
    synchronized public void println(int i)
    synchronized public void println(long l)
    synchronized public void println(float f)
    synchronized public void println(double d)
    synchronized public void println(boolean b)
```

PushbackInputStream
    protected int pushBack = -1
    public PushbackInputStream(InputStream in)
    public int read() throws IOException
    public int read(byte bytes[], int offset, int length) throws
    IOException
    public void unread(int ch) throws IOException
    public int available() throws IOException
    public boolean markSupported()

RandomAccessFile
    private FileDescriptor fd
    public RandomAccessFile(String name, String mode) throws
    IOException
    public RandomAccessFile(File file, String mode) throws IOException
    public final FileDescriptor getFD() throws IOException
    private native void open(String name, boolean writeable) throws
    IOException
    public native int read() throws IOException
    private native int readBytes(byte b[], int off, int len) throws
    IOException
    public int read(byte b[], int off, int len) throws IOException
    public int read(byte b[]) throws IOException
    public final void readFully(byte b[]) throws IOException
    public final void readFully(byte b[], int off, int len) throws
    IOException
    public int skipBytes(int n) throws IOException
    public native void write(int b) throws IOException
    private native void writeBytes(byte b[], int off, int len) throws
    IOException
    public void write(byte b[]) throws IOException
    public void write(byte b[], int off, int len) throws IOException
    public native long getFilePointer() throws IOException
    public native void seek(long pos) throws IOException
    public native long length() throws IOException
    public native void close() throws IOException
    public final boolean readBoolean() throws IOException
    public final byte readByte() throws IOException
    public final int readUnsignedByte() throws IOException
    public final short readShort() throws IOException
    public final int readUnsignedShort() throws IOException
    public final char readChar() throws IOException
    public final int readInt() throws IOException
    public final long readLong() throws IOException
    public final float readFloat() throws IOException
    public final double readDouble() throws IOException
    public final String readLine() throws IOException
    public final String readUTF() throws IOException
    public final void writeBoolean(boolean v) throws IOException
    public final void writeByte(int v) throws IOException
    public final void writeShort(int v) throws IOException
    public final void writeChar(int v) throws IOException
    public final void writeInt(int v) throws IOException
    public final void writeLong(long v) throws IOException

continued on next page

continued from previous page

```
            public final void writeFloat(float v) throws IOException
            public final void writeDouble(double v) throws IOException
            public final void writeBytes(String s) throws IOException
            public final void writeChars(String s) throws IOException
            public final void writeUTF(String str) throws IOException

    SequenceInputStream
        Enumeration e
        InputStream in
        public SequenceInputStream(Enumeration e)
        public SequenceInputStream(InputStream s1, InputStream s2)
        final void nextStream() throws IOException
        public int read() throws IOException
        public int read(byte buf[], int pos, int len) throws IOException
        public void close() throws IOException


    StreamTokenizer
        private InputStream input
        private char buf[]
        private int peekc = ' '
        private boolean pushedBack
        private boolean forceLower
        private int LINENO = 1
        private boolean eolIsSignificantP = false
        private boolean slashSlashCommentsP = false
        private boolean slashStarCommentsP = false
        private byte ctype[] = new byte[256]
        private static final byte CT_WHITESPACE = 1
        private static final byte CT_DIGIT = 2
        private static final byte CT_ALPHA = 4
        private static final byte CT_QUOTE = 8
        private static final byte CT_COMMENT = 16
        public int ttype
        public static final int TT_EOF = -1
        public static final int TT_EOL = '\n'
        public static final int TT_NUMBER = -2
        public static final int TT_WORD = -3
        public String sval
        public double nval
        public StreamTokenizer (InputStream I)
        public void resetSyntax()
        public void wordChars(int low, int hi)
        public void whitespaceChars(int low, int hi)
        public void ordinaryChars(int low, int hi)
        public void ordinaryChar(int ch)
        public void commentChar(int ch)
        public void quoteChar(int ch)
        public void parseNumbers()
        public void eolIsSignificant(boolean flag)
        public void slashStarComments(boolean flag)
        public void slashSlashComments(boolean flag)
        public void lowerCaseMode(boolean fl)
        public int nextToken() throws IOException
        public void pushBack()
```

```
    public int lineno()
    public String toString()

StringBufferedInputStream
    protected String buffer
    protected int pos
    protected int count
    public StringBufferInputStream(String s)
    public synchronized int read()
    public synchronized int read(byte b[], int off, int len)
    public synchronized long skip(long n)
    public synchronized int available()
    public synchronized void reset()


UTFDataFormatException
public UTFDataFormatException()
    public UTFDataFormatException(String s)
```

A.6 The java.lang Package

The java.lang package contains essential classes, including numerics, strings, objects, compiler, runtime, security, and threads. The java.lang package is automatically imported into every Java program.

```
java.lang

AbstractMethodError
    public AbstractMethodError()
    public AbstractMethodError(String s)

ArithmetricException
    public ArithmeticException()
    public ArithmeticException(String s)

ArrayIndexOutOfBoundsException
    public ArrayIndexOutOfBoundsException()
    public ArrayIndexOutOfBoundsException(int index)
    public ArrayIndexOutOfBoundsException(String s)

ArrayStoreException
    public ArrayStoreException()
    public ArrayStoreException(String s)

Boolean
    public static final Boolean TRUE = new Boolean(true)
    public static final Boolean FALSE = new Boolean(false)
    public static final char    MIN_VALUE = '\u0000'
    public static final char    MAX_VALUE = '\uffff'
    private boolean value
    public Boolean(boolean value)
    public Boolean(String s)
    public boolean booleanValue()
    public static Boolean valueOf(String s)
    public String toString()
```

continued on next page

continued from previous page

```
            public int hashCode()
            public boolean equals(Object obj)
            public static boolean getBoolean(String name)

    Character
            public static final int MIN_RADIX = 2
            public static final int MAX_RADIX = 36
            static char downCase[]
            static char upCase[]
            static
            public static boolean isLowerCase(char ch)
            public static boolean isUpperCase(char ch)
            public static boolean isDigit(char ch)
            public static boolean isSpace(char ch)
            public static char toLowerCase(char ch)
            public static char toUpperCase(char ch)
            public static int digit(char ch, int radix)
            public static char forDigit(int digit, int radix)
            private char value
            public Character(char value)
            public char charValue()
            public int hashCode()
            public boolean equals(Object obj)
            public String toString()

    Class
            private Class()
            public static native Class forName(String className) throws
            ClassNotFoundException
            public native Object newInstance() throws InstantiationException,
            IllegalAccessException
            public native String getName()
            public native Class getSuperclass()
            public native Class getInterfaces()[]
            public native ClassLoader getClassLoader()
            public native boolean isInterface()
            public String toString()

    ClassCastException
            public ClassCastException()
            public ClassCastException(String s)

    ClassCircularityError
            public ClassCircularityError()
            public ClassCircularityError(String s)

    ClassFormatError
            public ClassFormatError()
            public ClassFormatError(String s)

    ClassLoader
            protected ClassLoader()
            protected abstract Class loadClass(String name, boolean resolve)
            throws ClassNotFoundException
```

```
    protected native final Class defineClass(byte data[], int offset,
    int length)
    protected native final void resolveClass(Class c)
    protected native final Class findSystemClass(String name) throws
    ClassNotFoundException
    private native void init()

ClassNotFoundException
    public ClassNotFoundException()
    public ClassNotFoundException(String s)

CloneNotSupportedException
    public CloneNotSupportedException()
    public CloneNotSupportedException(String s)

Compiler
    private Compiler()
    private static native void initialize()
    static
    public static native boolean compileClass(Class clazz)
    public static native boolean compileClasses(String string)
    public static native Object command(Object any)
    public static native void enable()
    public static native void disable()

Double
    public static final double POSITIVE_INFINITY = 1.0 / 0.0
    public static final double NEGATIVE_INFINITY = -1.0 / 0.0
    public static final double NaN = 0.0d / 0.0
    public static final double MAX_VALUE = 1.79769313486231570e+308
    public static final double MIN_VALUE = 4.94065645841246544e-324
    public static native String toString(double d)
    public static native Double valueOf(String s) throws
    NumberFormatException
    static public boolean isNaN(double v)
    static public boolean isInfinite(double v)
    private double value
    public Double(double value)
    public Double(String s) throws NumberFormatException
    public boolean isNaN()
    public boolean isInfinite()
    public String toString()
    public int intValue()
    public long longValue()
    public float floatValue()
    public double doubleValue()
    public int hashCode()
    public boolean equals(Object obj)
    public static native long doubleToLongBits(double value)
    public static native double longBitsToDouble(long bits)

Error
    public Error()
    public Error(String s)
```

continued on next page

continued from previous page

```
Exception
    public Exception()
    public Exception(String s)

Float
    public static final float POSITIVE_INFINITY = 1.0f / 0.0f
    public static final float NEGATIVE_INFINITY = -1.0f / 0.0f
    public static final float NaN = 0.0f / 0.0f
    public static final float MAX_VALUE = 3.40282346638528860e+38f
    public static final float MIN_VALUE = 1.40129846432481707e-45f
    public static native String toString(float f)
    public static native Float valueOf(String s) throws
    NumberFormatException
    static public boolean isNaN(float v)
    static public boolean isInfinite(float v)
    private float value
    public Float(float value)
    public Float(double value)
    public Float(String s) throws NumberFormatException
    public boolean isNaN()
    public boolean isInfinite()
    public String toString()
    public int intValue()
    public long longValue()
    public float floatValue()
    public double doubleValue()
    public int hashCode()
    public boolean equals(Object obj)
    public static native int floatToIntBits(float value)
    public static native float intBitsToFloat(int bits)

IllegalAccessError
    public IllegalAccessError()
    public IllegalAccessError(String s)

IllegalAccessException
    public IllegalAccessException()
    public IllegalAccessException(String s)

IllegalArgumentException
    public IllegalArgumentException()
    public IllegalArgumentException(String s)

IllegalMonitorStateException
    public IllegalMonitorStateException()
    public IllegalMonitorStateException(String s)

IllegalThreadStateException
    public IllegalThreadStateException()
    public IllegalThreadStateException(String s)

IncompatibleClassChangeError
    public IncompatibleClassChangeError ()
```

```
        public IncompatibleClassChangeError(String s)

IndexOutOfBoundsException
        public IndexOutOfBoundsException()
        public IndexOutOfBoundsException(String s)

InstantiationError
        public InstantiationError()
        public InstantiationError(String s)

InstantiationException
        public InstantiationException()
        public InstantiationException(String s)

Integer
        public static final int    MIN_VALUE = 0x80000000
        public static final int    MAX_VALUE = 0x7fffffff
        public static String toString(int i, int radix)
        public static String toString(int i)
        public static int parseInt(String s, int radix) throws
        NumberFormatException
        public static int parseInt(String s) throws NumberFormatException
        public static Integer valueOf(String s, int radix) throws
        NumberFormatException
        public static Integer valueOf(String s) throws
        NumberFormatException
        private int value
        public Integer(int value)
        public Integer(String s) throws NumberFormatException
        public int intValue()
        public long longValue()
        public float floatValue()
        public double doubleValue()
        public String toString()
        public int hashCode()
        public boolean equals(Object obj)
        public static Integer getInteger(String nm)
        public static Integer getInteger(String nm, int val)
        public static Integer getInteger(String nm, Integer val)

InternalError
        public InternalError()
        public InternalError(String s)

InterruptedException
        public InterruptedException()
        public InterruptedException(String s)

LinkageError
        public LinkageError()
        public LinkageError(String s)

Long
        public static final long MIN_VALUE = 0x8000000000000000L
```

continued on next page

continued from previous page

```
    public static final long MAX_VALUE = 0x7fffffffffffffffL
    public static String toString(long i, int radix)
    public static String toString(long i)
    public static long parseLong(String s, int radix) throws
    NumberFormatException
    public static long parseLong(String s) throws NumberFormatException
    public static Long valueOf(String s, int radix) throws
    NumberFormatException
    public static Long valueOf(String s) throws NumberFormatException
    private long value
    public Long(long value)
    public Long(String s) throws NumberFormatException
    public int intValue()
    public long longValue()
    public float floatValue()
    public double doubleValue()
    public String toString()
    public int hashCode()
    public boolean equals(Object obj)
    public static Long getLong(String nm)
    public static Long getLong(String nm, long val)
    public static Long getLong(String nm, Long val)

Math
    private Math()
    public static final double E = 2.7182818284590452354
    public static final double PI = 3.14159265358979323846
    public static native double sin(double a)
    public static native double cos(double a)
    public static native double tan(double a)
    public static native double asin(double a)
    public static native double acos(double a)
    public static native double atan(double a)
    public static native double exp(double a)
    public static native double log(double a) throws
    ArithmeticException
    public static native double sqrt(double a) throws
    ArithmeticException
    public static native double IEEEremainder(double f1, double f2)
    public static native double ceil(double a)
    public static native double floor(double a)
    public static native double rint(double a)
    public static native double atan2(double a, double b)
    public static native double pow(double a, double b) throws
    ArithmeticException
    public static int round(float a)
    public static long round(double a)
    private static Random randomNumberGenerator
    public static synchronized double random()
    public static int abs(int a)
    public static long abs(long a)
    public static float abs(float a)
    public static double abs(double a)
    public static int max(int a, int b)
```

```
        public static long max(long a, long b)
        public static float max(float a, float b)
        public static double max(double a, double b)
        public static int min(int a, int b)
        public static long min(long a, long b)
        public static float min(float a, float b)
        public static double min(double a, double b)
        NegativeArraySizeException
        public NegativeArraySizeException()
        public NegativeArraySizeException(String s)

NoClassDefFoundError
        public NoClassDefFoundError()
        public NoClassDefFoundError(String s)

NoSuchFieldError
        public NoSuchFieldError()
        public NoSuchFieldError(String s)

NoSuchMethodError
        public NoSuchMethodError()
        public NoSuchMethodError(String s)

NoSuchMethodException
        public NoSuchMethodException()
        public NoSuchMethodException(String s)

NullPointerException
        public NullPointerException()
        public NullPointerException(String s)

Number
        public abstract int intValue()
        public abstract long longValue()
        public abstract float floatValue()
        public abstract double doubleValue()

NumberFormatException
        public NumberFormatException ()
        public NumberFormatException (String s)

Object
        public final native Class getClass()
        public native int hashCode()
        public boolean equals(Object obj)
        protected native Object clone() throws CloneNotSupportedException
        public String toString()
        public final native void notify()
        public final native void notifyAll()
        public final native void wait(long timeout) throws
        InterruptedException
        public final void wait(long timeout, int nanos) throws
        InterruptedException
```

continued on next page

continued from previous page

```
        public final void wait() throws InterruptedException
        protected void finalize() throws Throwable


OutOfMemoryError
        public OutOfMemoryError()
        public OutOfMemoryError(String s)


Process
        abstract public OutputStream getOutputStream()
        abstract public InputStream getInputStream()
        abstract public InputStream getErrorStream()
        abstract public int waitFor() throws InterruptedException
        abstract public int exitValue()
        abstract public void destroy()


Runnable
        public abstract void run()


Runtime
        private static Runtime currentRuntime = new Runtime()
        public static Runtime getRuntime()
        private Runtime()
        private native void exitInternal(int status)
        public void exit(int status)
        private native Process execInternal(String cmdarray[], String
        envp[]) throws IOException
        public Process exec(String command) throws IOException
        public Process exec(String command, String envp[]) throws
        IOException
        public Process exec(String cmdarray[]) throws IOException
        public Process exec(String cmdarray[], String envp[]) throws
        IOException
        public native long freeMemory()
        public native long totalMemory()
        public native void gc()
        public native void runFinalization()
        public native void traceInstructions(boolean on)
        public native void traceMethodCalls(boolean on)
        private synchronized native String initializeLinkerInternal()
        private native String buildLibName(String pathname, String file
        name)
        private native boolean loadFileInternal(String filename)
        private String paths[]
        private void initializeLinker()
        public synchronized void load(String filename)
        public synchronized void loadLibrary(String libname)
        public InputStream getLocalizedInputStream(InputStream in)
        public OutputStream getLocalizedOutputStream(OutputStream out)


RuntimeException
        public RuntimeException()
        public RuntimeException(String s)
```

```
SecurityException
    public SecurityException()
    public SecurityException(String s)

SecurityManager
    protected boolean inCheck
    public boolean getInCheck()
    protected SecurityManager()
    protected native Class[] getClassContext()
    protected native ClassLoader currentClassLoader()
    protected native int classDepth(String name)
    protected native int classLoaderDepth()
    protected boolean inClass(String name)
    protected boolean inClassLoader()
    public Object getSecurityContext()
    public void checkCreateClassLoader()
    public void checkAccess(Thread g)
    public void checkAccess(ThreadGroup g)
    public void checkExit(int status)
    public void checkExec(String cmd)
    public void checkLink(String lib)
    public void checkRead(FileDescriptor fd)
    public void checkRead(String file)
    public void checkRead(String file, Object context)
    public void checkWrite(FileDescriptor fd)
    public void checkWrite(String file)
    public void checkDelete(String file)
    public void checkConnect(String host, int port)
    public void checkConnect(String host, int port, Object context)
    public void checkListen(int port)
    public void checkAccept(String host, int port)
    public void checkPropertiesAccess()
    public void checkPropertyAccess(String key)
    public void checkPropertyAccess(String key, String def)
    public boolean checkTopLevelWindow(Object window)
    public void checkPackageAccess(String pkg)
    public void checkPackageDefinition(String pkg)
    public void checkSetFactory()

StackOverflowError
    public StackOverflowError()
    public StackOverflowError(String s)

String
    private char value[]
    private int offset
    private int count
    public String()
    public String(String value)
    public String(char value[])
    public String(char value[], int offset, int count)
    public String(byte ascii[], int hibyte, int offset, int count)
    public String(byte ascii[], int hibyte)
    public String (StringBuffer buffer)
    public int length()
```

continued on next page

continued from previous page

```
public char charAt(int index)
public void getChars(int srcBegin, int srcEnd, char dst[], int
dstBegin)
public void getBytes(int srcBegin, int srcEnd, byte dst[], int
dstBegin)
public boolean equals(Object anObject)
public boolean equalsIgnoreCase(String anotherString)
public int compareTo(String anotherString)
public boolean regionMatches(int toffset, String other, int
ooffset, int len)
public boolean regionMatches(boolean ignoreCase, int toffset,
String other, int ooffset, int len)
public boolean startsWith(String prefix, int toffset)
public boolean startsWith(String prefix)
public boolean endsWith(String suffix)
public int hashCode()
public int indexOf(int ch)
public int indexOf(int ch, int fromIndex)
public int lastIndexOf(int ch)
public int lastIndexOf(int ch, int fromIndex)
public int indexOf(String str)
public int indexOf(String str, int fromIndex)
public int lastIndexOf(String str)
public int lastIndexOf(String str, int fromIndex)
public String substring(int beginIndex)
public String substring(int beginIndex, int endIndex)
public String concat(String str)
public String replace(char oldChar, char newChar)
public String toLowerCase()
public String toUpperCase()
public String trim()
public String toString()
public char[] toCharArray()
public static String valueOf(Object obj)
public static String valueOf(char data[])
public static String valueOf(char data[], int offset, int count)
public static String copyValueOf(char data[], int offset, int
count)
public static String copyValueOf(char data[])
public static String valueOf(boolean b)
public static String valueOf(char c)
public static String valueOf(int i)
public static String valueOf(long l)
public static String valueOf(float f)
public static String valueOf(double d)
private static Hashtable InternSet
public String intern()
int utfLength()

StringBuffer
private char value[]
private int count
private boolean shared
public StringBuffer()
```

```
public StringBuffer(int length)
public StringBuffer(String str)
public int length()
public int capacity()
private void copyWhenShared()
public synchronized void ensureCapacity(int minimumCapacity)
public synchronized void setLength(int newLength)
public synchronized char charAt(int index)
public synchronized void getChars(int srcBegin, int srcEnd, char
dst[], int dstBegin)
public synchronized void setCharAt(int index, char ch)
public synchronized StringBuffer append(Object obj)
public synchronized StringBuffer append(String str)
public synchronized StringBuffer append(char str[])
public synchronized StringBuffer append(char str[], int offset, int
len)
public StringBuffer append(boolean b)
public synchronized StringBuffer append(char c)
public StringBuffer append(int i)
public StringBuffer append(long l)
public StringBuffer append(float f)
public StringBuffer append(double d)
public synchronized StringBuffer insert(int offset, Object obj)
public synchronized StringBuffer insert(int offset, String str)
public synchronized StringBuffer insert(int offset, char str[])
public StringBuffer insert(int offset, boolean b)
public synchronized StringBuffer insert(int offset, char c)
public StringBuffer insert(int offset, int i)
public StringBuffer insert(int offset, long l)
public StringBuffer insert(int offset, float f)
public StringBuffer insert(int offset, double d)
public String toString()
StringIndexOutOfBoundsException
public StringIndexOutOfBoundsException()
public StringIndexOutOfBoundsException(String s)
public StringIndexOutOfBoundsException(int index)

System
    private System()
    public static InputStream in
    public static PrintStream out
    public static PrintStream err
    static
    private static SecurityManager security
    public static void setSecurityManager(SecurityManager s)
    public static SecurityManager getSecurityManager()
    public static native long currentTimeMillis()
    public static native void arraycopy(Object src, int src_position,
    Object dst, int dst_position, int length)
    private static Properties props
    private static native Properties initProperties(Properties props)
    public static Properties getProperties()
    public static void setProperties(Properties props)
    public static String getProperty(String key)
```

continued on next page

continued from previous page

```
        public static String getProperty(String key, String def)
        public static String getenv(String name)
        public static void exit (int status)
        public static void gc()
        public static void runFinalization()
        public static void load(String filename)
        public static void loadLibrary(String libname)

Thread
        private char      name[]
        private int priority
        private Thread threadQ
        private int PrivateInfo
        private int eetop
        private boolean      single_step
        private boolean      daemon = false
        private boolean      stillborn = false
        private Runnable target
        private static Thread activeThreadQ
        private ThreadGroup group
        private static int threadInitNumber
        private static synchronized int nextThreadNum()
        public final static int MIN_PRIORITY = 1
        public final static int NORM_PRIORITY = 5
        public final static int MAX_PRIORITY = 10
        public static native Thread currentThread()
        public static native void yield()
        public static native void sleep(long millis) throws
        InterruptedException
        public static void sleep(long millis, int nanos) throws
        InterruptedException
        private void init(ThreadGroup g, Runnable target, String name)
        public Thread()
        public Thread(Runnable target)
        public Thread(ThreadGroup group, Runnable target)
        public Thread(String name)
        public Thread(ThreadGroup group, String name)
        public Thread(Runnable target, String name)
        public Thread(ThreadGroup group, Runnable target, String name)
        public synchronized native void start()
        public void run()
        private void exit()
        public final void stop()
        public final synchronized void stop(Throwable o)
        public void interrupt()
        public static boolean interrupted()
        public boolean isInterrupted()
        public void destroy()
        public final native boolean isAlive()
        public final void suspend()
        public final void resume()
        public final void setPriority(int newPriority)
        public final int getPriority()
        public final void setName(String name)
```

```
        public final String getName()
        public final ThreadGroup getThreadGroup()
        public static int activeCount()
        public static int enumerate(Thread tarray[])
        public native int countStackFrames()
        public final synchronized void join(long millis) throws
        InterruptedException
        public final synchronized void join(long millis, int nanos) throws
        InterruptedException
        public final void join() throws InterruptedException
        public static void dumpStack()
        public final void setDaemon(boolean on)
        public final boolean isDaemon()
        public void checkAccess()
        public String toString()
        private native void setPriority0(int newPriority)
        private native void stop0(Object o)
        private native void suspend0()
        private native void resume0()

    ThreadGroup
        ThreadGroup parent
        String name
        int maxPriority
        boolean destroyed
        boolean daemon
        int nthreads
        Thread threads[]
        int ngroups
        ThreadGroup groups[]
        private ThreadGroup()
        public ThreadGroup(String name)
        public ThreadGroup(ThreadGroup parent, String name)
        public final String getName()
        public final ThreadGroup getParent()
        public final int getMaxPriority()
        public final boolean isDaemon()
        public final void setDaemon(boolean daemon)
        public final synchronized void setMaxPriority(int pri)
        public final boolean parentOf(ThreadGroup g)
        public final void checkAccess()
        public synchronized int activeCount()
        public int enumerate(Thread list[])
        public int enumerate(Thread list[], boolean recurse)
        private synchronized int enumerate(Thread list[], int n, boolean
        recurse)
        public synchronized int activeGroupCount()
        public int enumerate(ThreadGroup list[])
        public int enumerate(ThreadGroup list[], boolean recurse)
        private synchronized int enumerate(ThreadGroup list[], int n,
        boolean recurse)
        public final synchronized void stop()
        public final synchronized void suspend()
        public final synchronized void resume()
```

continued on next page

continued from previous page

```
        public final synchronized void destroy()
        private final synchronized void add(ThreadGroup g)
        private synchronized void remove(ThreadGroup g)
        synchronized void add(Thread t)
        synchronized void remove(Thread t)
        public synchronized void list()
        void list(PrintStream out, int indent)
        public void uncaughtException(Thread t, Throwable e)
        public String toString()

    Throwable
        private Object backtrace
        private String detailMessage
        public Throwable()
        public Throwable(String message)
        public String getMessage()
        public String toString()
        public void printStackTrace()
        public void printStackTrace(java.io.PrintStream s)
        private native void printStackTrace0(java.io.PrintStream s)
        public native Throwable fillInStackTrace()

    UnknownError
        public UnknownError()
        public UnknownError(String s)

    UnsatisfiedLinkError
        public UnsatisfiedLinkError()
        public UnsatisfiedLinkError(String s)

    VerifyError
        public VerifyError()
        public VerifyError(String s)

    VirtualMachineError
        public VirtualMachineError()
        public VirtualMachineError(String s)
```

A.7 The java.net Package

The java.net package provides very powerful tools for network support. The support includes URLs, TCP sockets, UDP sockets, and IP addresses.

```
java.net

    ContentHandler
        abstract public Object getContent(URLConnection urlc) throws
IOException
    ContentHandlerFactory
        ContentHandler createContentHandler(String mimetype)

    DatagramPacket
        private byte[] buf
        private int length
```

```
        private InetAddress address
        private int port
        public DatagramPacket(byte ibuf[], int ilength)
        public DatagramPacket(byte ibuf[], int ilength, InetAddress iaddr,
        int iport)
        public InetAddress getAddress()
        public int getPort()
        public byte[] getData()
        public int getLength()

DatagramSocket
        private int localPort
        private FileDescriptor fd
        static
        public DatagramSocket() throws SocketException
        public DatagramSocket(int port) throws SocketException
        public void send(DatagramPacket p) throws IOException
        public synchronized void receive(DatagramPacket p) throws
        IOException
        public int getLocalPort()
        public synchronized void close()
        protected synchronized void finalize()
        private native void datagramSocketCreate()
        private native int  datagramSocketBind(int port)
        private native void datagramSocketSend(DatagramPacket p)
        private native int datagramSocketPeek(InetAddress i)
        private native void datagramSocketReceive(DatagramPacket p)
        private native void datagramSocketClose()

InetAddress
        private static boolean inCheck = false
        String hostName
        int address
        int family
        static
        InetAddress()
        InetAddress(String hostName, byte addr[])
        public String getHostName()
        public byte[] getAddress()
        public int hashCode()
        public boolean equals(Object obj)
        public String toString()
        static Hashtable addressCache = new Hashtable()
        static InetAddress unknownAddress
        static InetAddress anyLocalAddress
        static InetAddress localHost
        static
        public static synchronized InetAddress getByName(String host)
        throws UnknownHostException
        public static synchronized InetAddress getAllByName(String host)[]
        throws UnknownHostException
        public static InetAddress getLocalHost() throws
        UnknownHostException
        private static native String getLocalHostName() throws
        UnknownHostException
```

continued on next page

continued from previous page

```
        private static native void makeAnyLocalAddress(InetAddress addr)
        private static native byte[] lookupHostAddr(String hostname) throws
        UnknownHostException
        private static native byte[][] lookupAllHostAddr(String hostname)
        throws UnknownHostException
        private static native String getHostByAddr(int addr) throws
        UnknownHostException
        private static native int getInetFamily()

MalformedURLException
        public MalformedURLException()
        public MalformedURLException(String msg)

PlainSocketImpl
        static
        protected synchronized void create(boolean stream) throws
        IOException
        protected void connect(String host, int port) throws
        UnknownHostException, IOException
        protected void connect(InetAddress address, int port) throws
        IOException
        protected synchronized void bind(InetAddress address, int lport)
        throws IOException
        protected synchronized void listen(int count) throws IOException
        protected synchronized void accept(SocketImpl s) throws IOException
        protected synchronized InputStream getInputStream() throws
        IOException
        protected synchronized OutputStream getOutputStream() throws
        IOException
        protected synchronized int available() throws IOException
        protected synchronized void close() throws IOException
        protected synchronized void finalize() throws IOException
        private native void socketCreate(boolean stream) throws IOException
        private native void socketConnect(InetAddress address, int port)
        throws IOException
        private native void socketBind(InetAddress address, int port)
        throws IOException
        private native void socketListen(int count) throws IOException
        private native void socketAccept(SocketImpl s) throws IOException
        private native int socketAvailable() throws IOException
        private native void socketClose() throws IOException

ProtocolException
        public ProtocolException(String host)
        public ProtocolException()

ServerSocket
        SocketImpl impl
        ServerSocket() throws IOException
        public ServerSocket(int port) throws IOException
        public ServerSocket(int port, int count) throws IOException
        public InetAddress getInetAddress()
        public int getLocalPort()
        public Socket accept() throws IOException
```

```
    public void close() throws IOException
    public String toString()
    private static SocketImplFactory factory
    public static synchronized void setSocketFactory(SocketImplFactory
    fac) throws IOException

Socket
    SocketImpl impl
    Socket()
    public Socket(String host, int port) throws UnknownHostException,
    IOException
    public Socket(String host, int port, boolean stream) throws
    IOException
    public Socket(InetAddress address, int port) throws IOException
    public Socket(InetAddress address, int port, boolean stream) throws
    IOException
    public InetAddress getInetAddress()
    public int getPort()
    public int getLocalPort()
    public InputStream getInputStream() throws IOException
    public OutputStream getOutputStream() throws IOException
    public synchronized void close() throws IOException
    public String toString()
    private static SocketImplFactory factory
    public static synchronized void
    setSocketImplFactory(SocketImplFactory fac) throws IOException

SocketException
    public SocketException(String msg)
    public SocketException()

SocketImlp
    protected FileDescriptor fd
    protected InetAddress address
    protected int port
    protected int localport
    protected abstract void create(boolean stream) throws IOException
    protected abstract void connect(String host, int port) throws
    IOException
    protected abstract void connect(InetAddress address, int port)
    throws IOException
    protected abstract void bind(InetAddress host, int port) throws
    IOException
    protected abstract void listen(int count) throws IOException
    protected abstract void accept(SocketImpl s) throws IOException
    protected abstract InputStream getInputStream() throws IOException
    protected abstract OutputStream getOutputStream() throws
    IOException
    protected abstract int available() throws IOException
    protected abstract void close() throws IOException
    protected FileDescriptor getFileDescriptor()
    protected InetAddress getInetAddress()
    protected int getPort()
    protected int getLocalPort()
```

continued on next page

continued from previous page

```
        public String toString()

    SocketImplFactory
        SocketImpl createSocketImpl()

    SocketInputStream
        private boolean eof
        private SocketImpl impl
        private byte temp[] = new byte[1]
        SocketInputStream(SocketImpl impl) throws IOException
        private native int socketRead(byte b[], int off, int len) throws
        IOException
        public int read(byte b[]) throws IOException
        public int read(byte b[], int off, int length) throws IOException
        public int read() throws IOException
        public int skip(int numbytes) throws IOException
        public int available() throws IOException
        public void close() throws IOException
        protected void finalize()

    SocketOutputStream
        private SocketImpl impl
        private byte temp[] = new byte[1]
        SocketOutputStream(SocketImpl impl) throws IOException
        private native void socketWrite(byte b[], int off, int len) throws
        IOException
        public void write(int b) throws IOException
        public void write(byte b[]) throws IOException
        public void write(byte b[], int off, int len) throws IOException
        public void close() throws IOException
        protected void finalize()

    UnknownHostException
        public UnknownHostException(String host)
        public UnknownHostException()

    UnknownServiceException
        public UnknownServiceException()
        public UnknownServiceException(String msg)

    URL
        private String protocol
        private String host
        private int port = -1
        private String file
        private String ref
        URLStreamHandler handler
        public URL(String protocol, String host, int port, String file)
        throws MalformedURLException
        public URL(String protocol, String host, String file) throws
        MalformedURLException
        public URL(String spec) throws MalformedURLException
        public URL(URL context, String spec) throws MalformedURLException
        protected void set(String protocol, String host, int port, String
```

```
        file, String ref)
        public int getPort()
        public String getProtocol()
        public String getHost()
        public String getFile()
        public String getRef()
        public boolean equals(Object obj)
        public int hashCode()
        boolean hostsEqual(String h1, String h2)
        public boolean sameFile(URL other)
        public String toString()
        public String toExternalForm()
        public URLConnection openConnection() throws java.io.IOException
        public final InputStream openStream() throws java.io.IOException
        public final Object getContent() throws java.io.IOException
        static URLStreamHandlerFactory factory
        public static synchronized void setURLStreamHandlerFactory
        (URLStreamHandlerFactory fac)
        static Hashtable handlers = new Hashtable()
        static synchronized URLStreamHandler getURLStreamHandler(String
        protocol)

URLConnection
        protected URL url
        protected boolean doInput = true
        protected boolean doOutput = false
        private static boolean defaultAllowUserInteraction = false
        protected boolean allowUserInteraction =
        defaultAllowUserInteraction
        private static boolean defaultUseCaches = true
        protected boolean useCaches = defaultUseCaches
        protected long ifModifiedSince = 0
        protected boolean connected = false
        abstract public void connect() throws IOException
        protected URLConnection (URL url)
        public URL getURL()
        public int getContentLength()
        public String getContentType()
        public String getContentEncoding()
        public long getExpiration()
        public long getDate()
        public long getLastModified()
        public String getHeaderField(String name)
        public int getHeaderFieldInt(String name, int Default)
        public long getHeaderFieldDate(String name, long Default)
        public String getHeaderFieldKey(int n)
        public String getHeaderField(int n)
        public Object getContent() throws IOException
        public InputStream getInputStream() throws IOException
        public OutputStream getOutputStream() throws IOException
        public String toString()
        public void setDoInput(boolean doinput)
        public boolean getDoInput()
        public void setDoOutput(boolean dooutput)
```

continued on next page

continued from previous page

```
public boolean getDoOutput()
public void setAllowUserInteraction(boolean allowuserinteraction)
public boolean getAllowUserInteraction()
public static void setDefaultAllowUserInteraction(boolean default
allowuserinteraction)
public static boolean getDefaultAllowUserInteraction()
public void setUseCaches(boolean usecaches)
public boolean getUseCaches()
public void setIfModifiedSince(long ifmodifiedsince)
public long getIfModifiedSince()
public boolean getDefaultUseCaches()
public void setDefaultUseCaches(boolean defaultusecaches)
public void setRequestProperty(String key, String value)
public String getRequestProperty(String key)
public static void setDefaultRequestProperty(String key, String
value)
public static String getDefaultRequestProperty(String key)
static ContentHandlerFactory factory
public static synchronized void setContentHandlerFactory
(ContentHandlerFactory fac)
private static Hashtable handlers = new Hashtable()
private static ContentHandler UnknownContentHandlerP = new
UnknownContentHandler()
private static String content_class_prefix = "sun.net.www.content."
synchronized ContentHandler getContentHandler() throws
UnknownServiceException
protected static String guessContentTypeFromName(String fname)
static Hashtable extension_map = new Hashtable()
static
static private void setSuffix(String ext, String ct)
static protected String guessContentTypeFromStream(InputStream is)
throws IOException
```

URLEncoder
```
static BitSet dontNeedEncoding
static
private URLEncoder()
public static String encode(String s)
```

URLStreamHandler
```
abstract protected URLConnection openConnection(URL u) throws
IOException
protected void parseURL(URL u, String spec, int start, int limit)
protected String toExternalForm(URL u)
protected void setURL(URL u, String protocol, String host, int
port, String file, String ref)
```

URLStreamHandlerFactory
```
URLStreamHandler createURLStreamHandler(String protocol)
```

A.8 The java.util Package

This package defines a number of utility classes, but should not be thought of as a separate "utility" package. Java depends heavily on many of the classes in the package. The package includes generic data structures, settable bits class, time, date, string manipulation, and random number generator.

```
java.util

    BitSet
        final static int BITS = 6
        final static int MASK = (1<<BITS)-1
        long bits[]
        public BitSet()
        public BitSet(int nbits)
        private void grow(int nbits)
        public void set(int bit)
        public void clear(int bit)
        public boolean get(int bit)
        public void and(BitSet set)
        public void or(BitSet set)
        public void xor(BitSet set)
        public int hashCode()
        public int size()
        public boolean equals(Object obj)
        public Object clone()
        public String toString()

    Date
        private long value
        private boolean valueValid
        private boolean expanded
        private short tm_millis
        private byte tm_sec
        private byte tm_min
        private byte tm_hour
        private byte tm_mday
        private byte tm_mon
        private byte tm_wday
        private short tm_yday
        private int tm_year
        private int tm_isdst
        public Date ()
        public Date (long date)
        public Date (int year, int month, int date)
        public Date (int year, int month, int date, int hrs, int min)
        public Date (int year, int month, int date, int hrs, int min, int sec)
        public Date (String s)
        public static long UTC(int year, int month, int date, int hrs, int min, int sec)
        private static short monthOffset[] =
        public static long parse(String s)
        private final static String wtb[] =
        private final static int ttb[] =
        public int getYear()
        public void setYear(int year)
        public int getMonth()
```

continued on next page

continued from previous page

```
        public void setMonth(int month)
        public int getDate()
        public void setDate(int date)
        public int getDay()
        public int getHours()
        public void setHours(int hours)
        public int getMinutes()
        public void setMinutes(int minutes)
        public int getSeconds()
        public void setSeconds(int seconds)
        public long getTime()
        public void setTime(long time)
        public boolean before(Date when)
        public boolean after(Date when)
        public boolean equals(Object obj)
        public int hashCode()
        public native String toString()
        public native String toLocaleString()
        public native String toGMTString()
        public int getTimezoneOffset()
        private native void expand()
        private native void computeValue()

Dictionary
        abstract public int size()
        abstract public boolean isEmpty()
        abstract public Enumeration keys()
        abstract public Enumeration elements()
        abstract public Object get(Object key)
        abstract public Object put(Object key, Object value)
        abstract public Object remove(Object key)

EmptyStackException
        public EmptyStackException()

Enumeration
        boolean hasMoreElements()
        Object nextElement()

Hashtable
        int hash
        Object key
        Object value
        HashtableEntry next
        protected Object clone()

NoSuchElementException
        public NoSuchElementException()
        public NoSuchElementException(String s)

Observable
        public void notifyObservers(Observable who, Object arg)
```

```
Observer
    void update(Observable o, Object arg)

Properties
    protected Properties defaults
    public Properties()
    public Properties(Properties defaults)
    public synchronized void load(InputStream in) throws IOException
    public synchronized void save(OutputStream out, String header)
    public String getProperty(String key)
    public String getProperty(String key, String defaultValue)
    public Enumeration propertyNames()
    public void list(PrintStream out)
    private synchronized void enumerate(Hashtable h)

Random
    private long seed
    private final static long multiplier = 0x5DEECE66DL
    private final static long addend = 0xBL
    private final static long mask = (1L << 48) - 1
    public Random()
    public Random(long seed)
    synchronized public void setSeed(long seed)
    synchronized private int next(int bits)
    public int nextInt()
    public long nextLong()
    public float nextFloat()
    public double nextDouble()
    private double nextNextGaussian
    private boolean haveNextNextGaussian = false
    synchronized public double nextGaussian()

Stack
    public Object push(Object item)
    public Object pop()
    public Object peek()
    public boolean empty()
    public int search(Object o)

StringTokenizer
    private int currentPosition
    private int maxPosition
    private String str
    private String delimiters
    private boolean retTokens
    public StringTokenizer(String str, String delim, boolean
    returnTokens)
    public StringTokenizer(String str, String delim)
    public StringTokenizer(String str)
    private void skipDelimiters()
    public boolean hasMoreTokens()
    public String nextToken()
    public String nextToken(String delim)
    public boolean hasMoreElements()
```

continued on next page

continued from previous page

```
        public Object nextElement()
        public int countTokens()

Vector
        protected Object elementData[]
        protected int elementCount
        protected int capacityIncrement
        public Vector(int initialCapacity, int capacityIncrement)
        public Vector(int initialCapacity)
        public Vector()
        public final synchronized void copyInto(Object anArray[])
        public final synchronized void trimToSize()
        public final synchronized void ensureCapacity(int minCapacity)
        public final synchronized void setSize(int newSize)
        public final int capacity()
        public final int size()
        public final boolean isEmpty()
        public final synchronized Enumeration elements()
        public final boolean contains(Object elem)
        public final int indexOf(Object elem)
        public final synchronized int indexOf(Object elem, int index)
        public final int lastIndexOf(Object elem)
        public final synchronized int lastIndexOf(Object elem, int index)
        public final synchronized Object elementAt(int index)
        public final synchronized Object firstElement()
        public final synchronized Object lastElement()
        public final synchronized void setElementAt(Object obj, int index)
        public final synchronized void removeElementAt(int index)
        public final synchronized void insertElementAt(Object obj, int
        index)
        public final synchronized void addElement(Object obj)
        public final synchronized boolean removeElement(Object obj)
        public final synchronized void removeAllElements()
        public synchronized Object clone()
        public final synchronized String toString()
```

JAVA FREQUENTLY ASKED QUESTIONS (FAQ)

How do I play .WAV files in a Java applet?

At last report, this was not supported, and would not be in 1.0. The plan is to have translator classes for such things.

Can I unload a class from memory?

No. Everything but class objects is eventually reclaimed by the garbage collector. This is supposed to change eventually.

I thought Java was polymorphic. I defined several classes that support the m() method, but when I try to call m() using o.m() in my method m1(Object o), the compiler complains that there is no m() method defined for Object.

The compiler is correct: You told it that *o* can be an arbitrary Object, and indeed no method *m*() is defined for Object. You can do one of two things to fix this:

- Create a base class *b* which supports *m*(), make your classes be extensions of that base, and change the m1 declaration to m1(b o).

Or:

- Do the same, except with *b* as an interface

Why do I see garbage when I output *doubles* to a file using DataOutputStream?

DataOutputStream writes binary data, so it's good for recording data. If you want people to be able to read the output, you should use PrintStream instead.

Why do user events just seem to disappear when I override *handleEvent()*?

If you override *handleEvent()*, it is often wise to use *return(super.handleEvent(evt))* at the end of your *handleEvent()* method, to pass on the event.

Why do my animations still flicker, even though I use double buffering?

Make sure you override the *update()* method of the applet with a version that simply calls *paint()*.

Is Java big-endian or little-endian?

Neither Java nor the Java virtual machine inherently have any endian-ness built into them. The Java DataInputStream and DataOutputStream classes use XDR (External Data Representation) and XDR is big-endian. XDR has the advantage that you can do data exchange in a completely processor-independent manner, and therefore the underlying endian-ness of the processor is hidden from you.

I accidentally left out an & in and typed

```
if (p != null & p.boolmethod())
{ ... }
It produces a null pointer exception if p is null. Is this a compiler bug?
```

No, your code is correct Java, even if you didn't intend it to work that way. & is a Boolean operator as well as a bitwise operator. The difference between & and && is that the latter short-circuits the test and does not evaluate the right-hand side if the left-hand side is False.

How do I make a TextArea scroll?

Keep a counter of where you are, and then use

```
TextArea.select(counter,counter);
```

I wrote a class X with a properly declared *main* method (public static void *main(String arg[ ])*). I extend X in class Y, but the Java interpreter can't find the *main()* method when I try to run Y. What's wrong?

You're trying to inherit class methods, but only instance methods can be inherited. You'll have to define *main()* in Y properly. You can invoke *X.main(args)* from within *Y.main()*, but the definition has to be there.

How do I rotate text so I can draw it at an angle?

The API does not currently support rotating text, but Sun is working on a new 2D rendering API that will include the feature. Of course, you could draw your text in an off-line image, rotate it, and draw it, but the results leave something to be desired.

How do I turn off debugging statements in my program at compile time without removing the statements and without having them show up in the byte code? I can do this in C with #ifdef/#endif—how do I do it in Java?

The Java compiler optimizes out branches that it determines cannot be followed. If you have a final Boolean "variable" on which executing the debugging code depends, then you should be fine. Something like:

```
final boolean debug = true // or false;
if(debug) {
    // Debugging code
}
```

I can't play my own AU sound file in Java. What's wrong?

Your AU file needs to be saved with mu-law encoding, at 8,000 KHz, in 8-bit mono. People have successfully used SoundForge XP and Goldwave v.3.0.3 (but *not* v 3.0.2) to create audio files.

I get an error from *java.util.Runtime.exec()*—it can't seem to find the command.

Providing you're allowed to execute a system command (that is, you're running in an application or running trusted code), you're probably just forgetting to give the full path name of the command you want to run. It's not enough to give it "ls." You have to give it "/usr/bin/ls" (or whatever).

Is it possible to put an applet and all of its classes into a ZIP file?

Yes and no. Apparently it's possible if the code is local, but it won't work over the Net. Sun is apparently working on it.

Why does your code have to be synchronized in order to wait or notify?

It's part of the monitor concept. If you really just want semaphores, then you can simulate them with a monitor using synchronized methods.

What happens if a thread dies inside the monitor?

Currently, when a thread dies (through exiting *run()* or through an exception), the stack is unwound, so all monitors are exited. *Thread.destroy()* is another way the thread could die (not yet implemented), and it is defined as not releasing any monitors.

Which thread proceeds after a *notifyAll()* or do they all?

One will, and it's a race to see who gets it.

If you're already synchronized on object A and you try to synchronize again, what happens?

You merrily enter the new synchronized block without delay; the lock is held until you exit the original block or *wait()*.

Can I *wait()* and *notify()* if I'm in a synchronized block?

Sure. That's the only place you can do that, if the method is not declared synchronized.

How do I copy part of a bitmap from an off-screen bitmap to an on-screen location; that is, something similar to Mac's "copybits" or PC's "biblt"?

Use *drawImage()* with negative offset, and set a clip region so that you get only the bits you desire.

What encodings does Java understand?

Currently, GIF and JPEG.

Is it possible to print the display of an applet?

Support for printing is in development, and it will be included in a future version of Java.

How do I display an image from an application?

First, make a string that has the path to your image file.

```
String url = "file:////home/chrisk/PJ/Gifs/buzz.jpg";
```

Second, use this to load the image:

```
try {
image = Toolkit.getDefaultToolkit().getImage(new URL(url));
} catch (MalformedURLException e) {
System.out.println("MalformedURLException on: " + url);
}
```

You will also need to install a dummy SecurityManager, or the *getImage* will fail with applications. Here is one you can use:

```
import java.io.FileDescriptor;
public class EmptySecurityManager extends SecurityManager {
public void checkCreateClassLoader() {}
public void checkAccess(Thread g) {}
public void checkAccess(ThreadGroup g) {}
public void checkExit(int status) {}
```

```
public void checkExec(String cmd) {}
public void checkLink(String lib) {}
public void checkRead(FileDescriptor fd) {}
public void checkRead(String file) {}
public void checkRead(String file, Object context) {}
public void checkWrite(FileDescriptor fd) {}
public void checkWrite(String file) {}
public void checkConnect(String host, int port) {}
public void checkConnect(String host, int port, Object context) {}
public void checkListen(int port) {}
public void checkAccept(String host, int port) {}
public void checkPropertiesAccess() {}
public void checkPropertyAccess(String key) {}
public void checkPropertyAccess(String key, String def) {}
public boolean checkTopLevelWindow(Object window) { return true; }
public void checkPackageAccess(String pkg) {}
public void checkPackageDefinition(String pkg) {}
public void checkSetFactory() {}
}
```

This must be installed at app startup by using (putting it in *main()* works):

```
try {
System.setSecurityManager(new EmptySecurityManager());
} catch (SecurityException e) {
System.out.println("Caught SecurityException trying to set Security
manager");
}
```

How do you repaint just part of a window?

Use

```
repaint(x,y,w,h);
```

How do I get packages to work? My code compiles fine when I leave out the package statement, but I get lots of errors when I put it in.

You're probably either compiling from the wrong directory, or using the wrong name. When you create a package named Foo, you must put all the code in a directory named Foo (yes, case-sensitive, even on Win 95). Use a package Foo; statement in your source files, and (important!), compile the files from the parent directory. This seems to be the most reliable method.

How can I access environment variables?

You can use *getProperty()* to access any variables that were specified on the command line in an application (note: these are not parameters) using the -Dname convention; for example:

```
java -DFoobar=barfoo baz arg1 ...
```

defines the environment variable Foobar and invokes class baz with arguments arg1.

Why can't I access environment variables from an applet, and why is it so hard in an application?

Portability and security. Not all systems have environment variables, so having an access mechanism for them would make Java nonportable. Instead, the concept of a system property has been introduced—you have free access to these environment variable substitutes from both applets and applications. As for security, environment variables can include user names and other private information. For the sake of privacy, access to these variables is sealed off.

Why don't I see images right away (that is, as soon as they can be loaded in from the Net) when I execute getImage()?

Because the image download may not actually start until you use the image, via *drawImage()* or the like. (So you think you've got the image, but you don't.)

How do I change my mouse cursor?

Use

```
frame.setCursor(int);
```

where *int* is a one of frame.DEFAULT_CURSOR to frame.MOVE_CURSOR (and therein lies the key to switching back to the default cursor). To use this in an Applet, you need to get the Frame first—simply follow the parent links via *getParent(),* and you're done! Unfortunately, you can't use an arbitrary cursor.

Can source code be "stolen" from a Java applet if it is decompiled?

javap can be used to disassemble .class files into Java byte code, but it can't decompile back to Java source code.

How do I reload an applet in Netscape?

If you are modifying and viewing your own applets, "touch" (or resave) the HTML file containing the applet and reload the page. If you are browsing a remote applet, press <SHIFT> and click on Reload; it will work on some versions of Netscape.

Is there a way to create a persistent applet that allows a thread to be executed while the user views other pages?

Threads continue to execute unless the *stop()* method is used, so if you omit this method, the thread should continue to execute.

Do I need special server software to use applets?

No. Java applets may be served by any HTTP server. On the server side they are handled the same as any other file, such as a text, image, or sound file. All the special action happens when the applet class files are interpreted on the client side by a Java-enabled browser, such as HotJava or Netscape 2.0.

Where did the Java name come from? What does it stand for?

The name was chosen during one of several brainstorming sessions held by the Java team. They were aiming to come up with a name that evoked the essence of the technology—liveliness, animation, speed, interactivity, and more. "Java" was chosen from among many, many suggestions. The name is not an acronym, but rather a reminder of that hot, aromatic stuff that many programmers like to drink.

Will Java work with DOS file size limitations (8.3)?

No, they rely on many files with longer names than the old DOS limits. Even if your drive allows long file names, be careful not to unzip your release package with WinZip that does not support file names longer than 8.3, since this will truncate the file names to the old 8.3 DOS limits. Instead, extract the files from a DOS window and make sure that the resulting files have their full (long) names.

THE JAVA VIRTUAL MACHINE SPECIFICATION

The Java virtual machine is an abstract architecture that may be implemented on any physical machine. The machine is essentially a stack-based architecture that accepts and executes bytecodes. This approach enjoys a number of advantages: bytecode generation is straightforward, bytecode interpreters are small and simple, and translation to hardware machine code can be done by using well-known techniques available to the compiler designer.

Data Types

The virtual machine supports 1-, 2-, 4-, and 8-byte integers and 4- and 8-byte floating-point types. The integers are all two's complement, and the floating-point types conform to IEEE 754 standards for single- and double-precision floating-point. In addition, a 2-byte unsigned integer type is also supported for Unicode characters. Specific instructions exist for operating on each of the data types. For example, the iadd instruction adds two 4-byte integers, and the dadd instruction adds two 8-byte floating-point numbers.

Registers

The registers in effect during execution include the program counter (pc), the local variable space pointer (vars), operand stack pointer (optop), and the execution environment structure pointer (frame). Each of these registers is 32 bits wide.

The local variables are addressed as offsets from the vars register. 8-byte integers and 8-byte floating-point numbers occupy two local variable locations and are referenced by the index of the first location. These 64-bit values need not be aligned on 64-bit boundaries.

The operand stack is used for arithmetic operations as well as parameter-passing to methods. A binary arithmetic operation like integer add will remove the top two values from the operand stack, add them, and store the result on the top of the stack. This implementation reduces the difficulty of emulation on processors with few physical registers.

Heap Storage

Dynamic memory allocation for objects is performed in a heap storage area. Deallocation is performed by an automatic garbage collector. Memory cannot be explicitly deallocated by the programmer. No specific garbage collection algorithm is defined; various methods may be used depending on system requirements.

Realization

The first implementations of the virtual machine were bytecode interpreters. The performance of interpreted machines is approximately 10 to 15 times slower than compiled native code. Just-in-time compilation and precompilation to native machine code should yield performance close to compiled C code. There are instances where just-in-time compilation can outperform compiled C code. This can be accomplished by considering memory and cache limits on the target machine during native code translation. This type of dynamic optimization cannot be performed with statically compiled code. In this way, the Java virtual machine may become the de facto standard for machine code interchange across a variety of platforms.

JAVA HALL OF FAME
APPLET GALLERY

The following five third-party Java applets have achieved *Java How-To* "Hall of Fame" status, as they are all outstanding examples that often employ techniques discussed in this book. Each description that follows includes the Hall of Fame applet's name, author, URL, a discussion of the techniques demonstrated, and an illustration showing it in action. These applets are included on the CD-ROM accompanying this book. Check them out!

SearchApplet
Author: Danno Ferrin

URL: http://www.mines.edu/students/d/drferrin/ Cool_Beans/#SearchApplet

The SearchApplet, written by Danno Ferrin, is a Java interface to many of the popular Web search engines. The user may then select a search engine to use via a choice list. The search returns may be displayed in a new browser window by selecting the appropriate radio button.

Web search engines are invoked by calling *showDocument()* with the URL and search criteria as an argument. A separate target frame may be specified for flexibility. Figure D-1 shows an example of the SearchApplet.

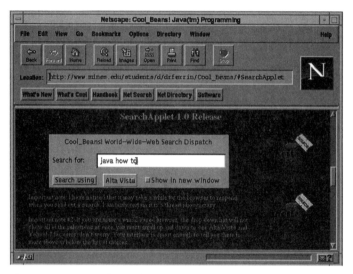

Figure D-1 SearchApplet in action

PositionLayout
Author: Danno Ferrin

URL: http://www.mines.edu/students/d/drferrin/Cool_Beans/#SearchApplet

The PositionLayout applet is an example of a custom layout manager. It allows the programmer to create components at absolute positions similar to those shown in How-To 6.9.

The *Vector* class is also used to allow for an arbitrary number of components. The PositionLayout Applet is displayed in Figure D-2.

Java File System (JFS)
Author: Jamie Cameron

URL: http://www.ncs.com.sg/java/jfs/

JFS is a network file system written entirely in Java. This is an excellent demonstration of the networking classes available to Java programmers. Java applets may not directly access the local hard disk for saving information. JFS allows a Java applet to create, write, and read files on a remote host running the JFS server.

Jamie Cameron provides several example applets demonstrating the use of JFS for a variety of applications. Figure D-3 shows a screenshot of the FileBrowser utility using JFS.

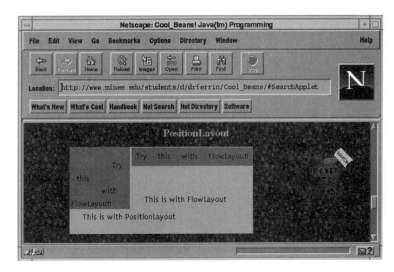

Figure D-2 The PositionLayout applet

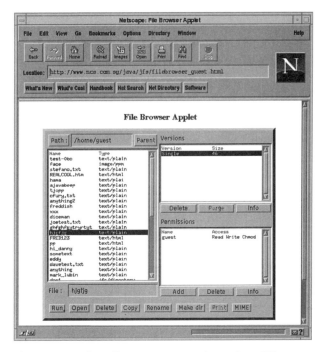

Figure D-3 The FileBrowser applet using JFS

ClickBoard

Author: Steve Fu

URL: http://users/aimnet.com/~foureyes/clickboard/Clickboard.html

The ClickBoard is a nice way to perform animation and interaction in a Web page without writing Java programs. This is useful for HTML authors and Web administrators who don't have the time to write unique Java applets for every application.

The author must supply a "click file," which contains all of the necessary parameters. The click file is located in the same directory (on the server) as the applet itself. When the applet is loaded and started, it will read the click file via http and continue operation. Steve Fu provides several examples illustrating different concepts. Figure D-4 shows Steve's angry fish example.

Figure D-4 The angry fish ClickBoard applet

DancingText

Author: Stanley Poon

URL: http://www.myna.com/~stan/java/dt/dancingtext.html

The dancing text applet is similar to the CrazyText applet in How-To 3.7. DancingText has many more features, such as variable pitch font, comprehensive color control, shadowing, and the ability to send the browser to an arbitrary URL.

Applet parameters are used to specify the font, color, dancing speed, and so on. When the user clicks on the applet, *showDocument()* is called to send the browser to the predefined URL. One interesting feature is that the HTML designer may specify a target frame in the browser. This gives the applet even greater flexibility. Figure D-5 shows the DancingText applet in action.

Figure D-5 The Dancing Text applet

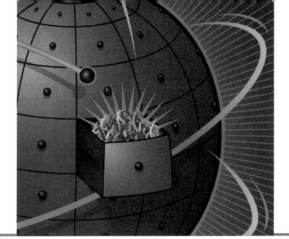

INDEX

NOTES

NOTES

NOTES

NOTES

D I G I T A L
C O N N E C T I O N™

About Digital Connection™

Digital Connection is a premier developer of information technologies. It has been integral in the development of major U.S. commercial online services and the Internet for more than a decade. Digital Connection is a leader in graphical user interfaces, networking, object-oriented development, and database technologies, and is recognized as a pioneer in Java development.

Its accomplishments range from multimedia games and complex financial transaction systems to interactive videodisc kiosks and million-plus user online services.

The Digital Connection team possesses a unique combination of expertise in technology, usability, and business strategy that translates into well-integrated, high-impact solutions for its corporate clients.

Digital Connection is proud to have been technical consultant on *Java How-To* for Waite Group Press™.

We can be reached at:
http://www.pangaea.net/digital/

Digital Connection
372 Central Park West
New York, NY 10025
212.866.7000 (voice)
212.662.9560 (fax)
digital@pangaea.net

Partial Client List:

Avis, CBS Technology, Chemical Bank, Children's Television Workshop, Citicorp, Continental Grain, IBM Corporation, Meca Software, Merck, Montage Picture Processor, NY Philharmonic, Philips Electronics, Prodigy Services Company, Simon & Schuster, Tishman Spear, US West, WGBH:Nova

Books have a substantial influence on the destruction of the forests of the Earth. For example, it takes 17 trees to produce one ton of paper. A first printing of 30,000 copies of a typical 480-page book consumes 108,000 pounds of paper, which will require 918 trees!

Waite Group Press™ is against the clear-cutting of forests and supports reforestation of the Pacific Northwest of the United States and Canada, where most of this paper comes from. As a publisher with several hundred thousand books sold each year, we feel an obligation to give back to the planet. We will therefore support organizations which seek to preserve the forests of planet Earth.

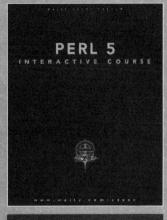

This is a legal agreement between you, the end user and purchaser, and The Waite Group®, Inc., and the authors of the programs contained in the disk. By opening the sealed disk package, you are agreeing to be bound by the terms of this Agreement. If you do not agree with the terms of this Agreement, promptly return the unopened disk package and the accompanying items (including the related book and other written material) to the place you obtained them for a refund.

SOFTWARE LICENSE

1. The Waite Group, Inc. grants you the right to use one copy of the enclosed software programs (the programs) on a single computer system (whether a single CPU, part of a licensed network, or a terminal connected to a single CPU). Each concurrent user of the program must have exclusive use of the related Waite Group, Inc. written materials.

2. The program, including the copyrights in each program, is owned by the respective author and the copyright in the entire work is owned by The Waite Group, Inc. and they are therefore protected under the copyright laws of the United States and other nations, under international treaties. You may make only one copy of the disk containing the programs exclusively for backup or archival purposes, or you may transfer the programs to one hard disk drive, using the original for backup or archival purposes. You may make no other copies of the programs, and you may make no copies of all or any part of the related Waite Group, Inc. written materials.

3. You may not rent or lease the programs, but you may transfer ownership of the programs and related written materials (including any and all updates and earlier versions) if you keep no copies of either, and if you make sure the transferee agrees to the terms of this license.

4. You may not decompile, reverse engineer, disassemble, copy, create a derivative work, or otherwise use the programs except as stated in this Agreement.

GOVERNING LAW

This Agreement is governed by the laws of the State of California.